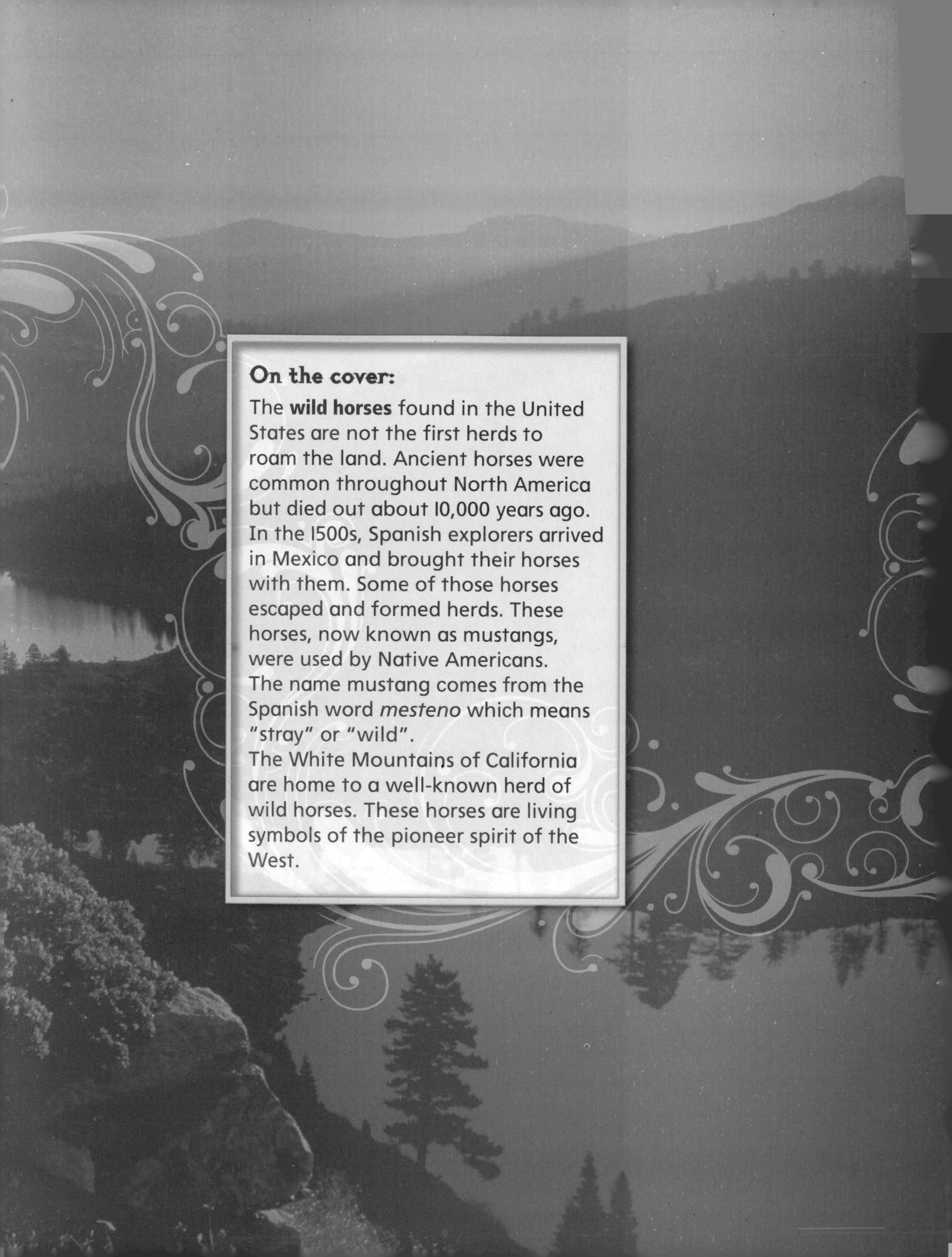

On the cover:

The **wild horses** found in the United States are not the first herds to roam the land. Ancient horses were common throughout North America but died out about 10,000 years ago. In the 1500s, Spanish explorers arrived in Mexico and brought their horses with them. Some of those horses escaped and formed herds. These horses, now known as mustangs, were used by Native Americans.

The name mustang comes from the Spanish word *mesteno* which means "stray" or "wild".

The White Mountains of California are home to a well-known herd of wild horses. These horses are living symbols of the pioneer spirit of the West.

California Treasures

A Reading/Language Arts Program

Program Authors

Diane August
Donald R. Bear
Janice A. Dole
Jana Echevarria
Douglas Fisher
David Francis
Vicki Gibson
Jan E. Hasbrouck
Scott G. Paris
Timothy Shanahan
Josefina V. Tinajero

Macmillan/McGraw-Hill

Contributors

Time Magazine, The Writers' Express, Accelerated Reader

Students with print disabilities may be eligible to obtain an accessible, audio version of the pupil edition of this textbook. Please call Recording for the Blind & Dyslexic at 1-800-221-4792 for complete information.

C

The McGraw·Hill Companies

 Macmillan/McGraw-Hill

Published by Macmillan/McGraw-Hill, of McGraw-Hill Education, a division of The McGraw-Hill Companies, Inc., Two Penn Plaza, New York, New York 10121.

Printed in the United States of America

ISBN: 978-0-02-199972-9/6

MHID: 0-02-199972-4/6

5 6 7 8 9 (RJE/LEH) 12 11

Welcome to
California *Treasures*

Imagine peering over the edge of an active volcano, learning what life was *really* like in ancient Greece, or reading about a dog that saved an entire town. Your **Student Book** contains these and other award-winning fiction and nonfiction selections.

Treasures Meets California Standards

The instruction provided with each reading selection in your **Student Book** will ensure that you meet all the **California Reading/Language Arts Standards** for your grade. Throughout the book, special symbols (such as) and codes (such as **R 1.1.2**) have been added to show where and how these standards are being met. They will help you know *what* you are learning and *why*.

What do these symbols mean?

CA = Tested Standards in California

 = Skill or Strategy that will appear on your test

R = Reading Standards

W = Writing Standards

LC = Language Conventions Standards

LAS = Listening and Speaking Standards

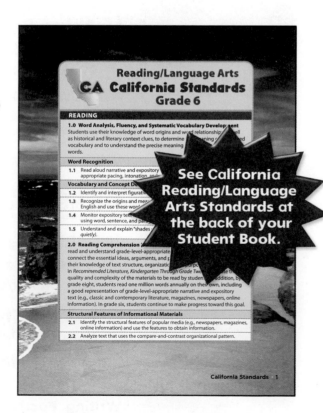

Reading/Language Arts
CA California Standards
Grade 6

READING

1.0 Word Analysis, Fluency, and Systematic Vocabulary Development
Students use their knowledge of word origins and word relationships, as well as historical and literary context clues, to determine the meaning of specialized vocabulary and to understand the precise meaning of grade-level-appropriate words.

Word Recognition
1.1 Read aloud narrative and expository text fluently and accurately and with appropriate pacing, intonation, and expression.

Vocabulary and Concept Development
1.2 Identify and interpret figurative language and words with multiple meanings.
1.3 Recognize the origins and meanings of frequently used foreign words in English and use these words accurately in speaking and writing.
1.4 Monitor expository text for unknown words or words with novel meanings by using word, sentence, and paragraph clues to determine meaning.
1.5 Understand and explain "shades of meaning" in related words (e.g., softly and quietly).

2.0 Reading Comprehension (Focus on Informational Materials) Students read and understand grade-level-appropriate material. They describe and connect the essential ideas, arguments, and perspectives of the text by using their knowledge of text structure, organization, and purpose. The selections in Recommended Literature, Kindergarten Through Grade Twelve illustrate the quality and complexity of the materials to be read by students. In addition, by grade eight, students read one million words annually on their own, including a good representation of grade-level-appropriate narrative and expository text (e.g., classic and contemporary literature, magazines, newspapers, online information). In grade six, students continue to make progress toward this goal.

Structural Features of Informational Materials
2.1 Identify the structural features of popular media (e.g., newspapers, magazines, online information) and use the features to obtain information.
2.2 Analyze text that uses the compare-and-contrast organizational pattern.

California Standards 1

See California Reading/Language Arts Standards at the back of your Student Book.

Mc Graw Hill Macmillan/McGraw-Hill

Unit 1

Personal Experiences
Our Stories

History/Social Science
Ancient Civilizations

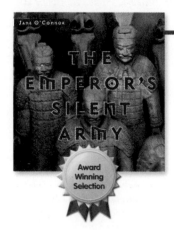

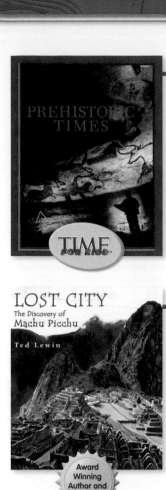

Unit 3

Creative Expression
A Question of Values

Unit 4

Teamwork
Achieving Dreams

THE BIG QUESTION

THEME: Determination Does It

THEME: Working to Win

Unit 5

Science

Our Incredible Earth

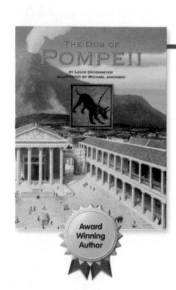

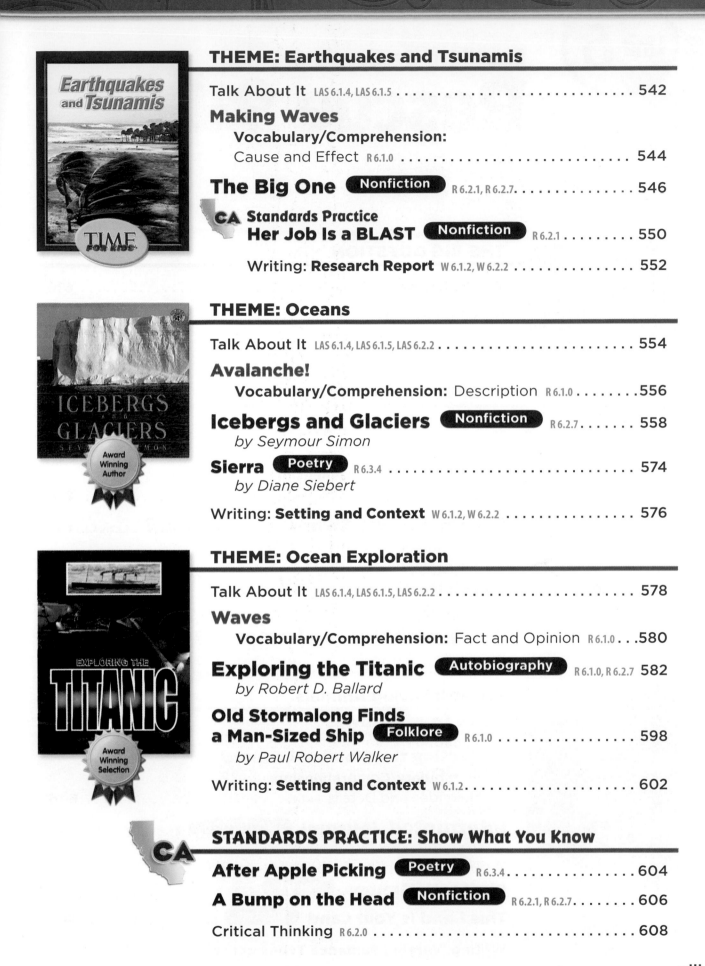

Unit 6

Spotlight on Grade 6
Rescue 9-1-1

Award Winning Selection

Award Winning Selection

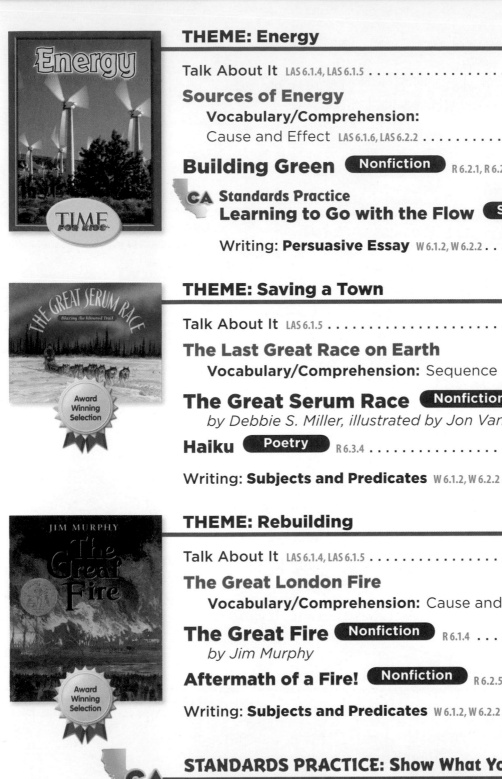

The Big Question

Why do people write?

Theme Launcher Video

 Find out more about local authors at **www.macmillanmh.com**.

The Big Question

Why do people write?

Historians cannot agree whether writing, and therefore history, began with the cave paintings of 31,000 years ago or the Mesopotamian clay tablets of 3100 B.C. that were used to keep track of treasures in a temple. Everyone agrees, however, that writing is a unique activity that only humans do. We write to keep records, to communicate experiences, to entertain each other, and to share thoughts and events.

Learning how people express themselves can teach us how to develop our own ideas and share our experiences.

Research Activities

Throughout the unit, you will be reading about the many ways people express themselves through their stories. As you read you will gather information about writers and their stories. Think of an author whose stories have inspired, informed, or entertained you. Use research strategies to find out more about the author's stories, life, and inspiration. You will create a theme project and also create a presentation of your project at the end of the unit.

Keep Track of Ideas

As you read, keep track of what you are learning about authors and why they write. Use the Layered Book to help organize your ideas. On the top section of the organizer write the unit theme, **Our Stories**. As you read the selections in the unit, write the information you learn each week in the other sections of your organizer. This will help you keep track of what you are learning and help you organize ideas for your research.

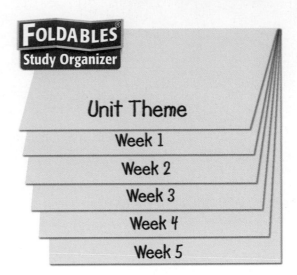

FOLDABLES®
Study Organizer

Unit Theme
Week 1
Week 2
Week 3
Week 4
Week 5

Research Toolkit

Conduct Your Unit 1 Research Online with:

Research Roadmap
Follow step-by-step guide to complete your research project.

Online Resources
- Topic Finder and other Research Tools
- Videos and Virtual Fieldtrips
- Photos and Drawings for Presentations
- Related Articles and Web Resources

California Web Site Links

 Go to **www.macmillanmh.com** to learn about her work.

California People

Pam Muñoz Ryan, Author
Pam Muñoz Ryan has written many popular books for children.

CA Talk About It

What do you think inspires people to record the events in their lives?

LOG ON ▶ Find out more about writing at **www.macmillanmh.com**.

TELLING OUR STORIES

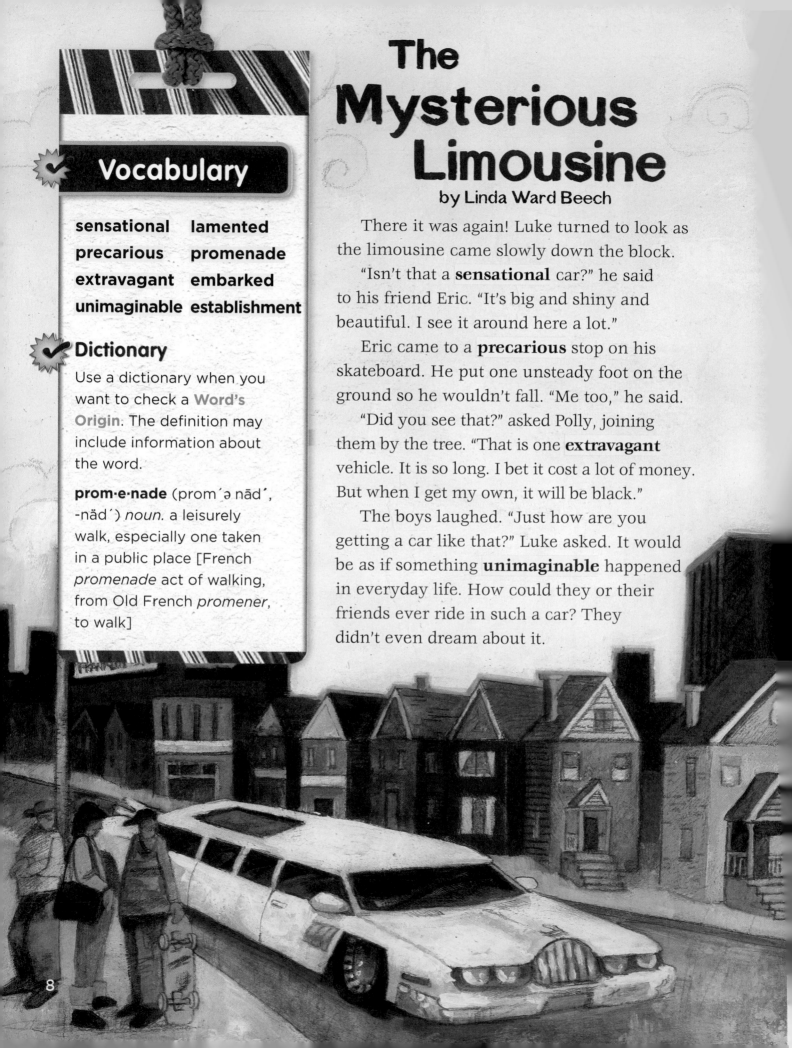

Vocabulary

sensational	lamented
precarious	promenade
extravagant	embarked
unimaginable	establishment

Dictionary

Use a dictionary when you want to check a **Word's Origin**. The definition may include information about the word.

prom·e·nade (prŏm´ə nād´, -näd´) *noun.* a leisurely walk, especially one taken in a public place [French *promenade* act of walking, from Old French *promener*, to walk]

The Mysterious Limousine

by Linda Ward Beech

There it was again! Luke turned to look as the limousine came slowly down the block.

"Isn't that a **sensational** car?" he said to his friend Eric. "It's big and shiny and beautiful. I see it around here a lot."

Eric came to a **precarious** stop on his skateboard. He put one unsteady foot on the ground so he wouldn't fall. "Me too," he said.

"Did you see that?" asked Polly, joining them by the tree. "That is one **extravagant** vehicle. It is so long. I bet it cost a lot of money. But when I get my own, it will be black."

The boys laughed. "Just how are you getting a car like that?" Luke asked. It would be as if something **unimaginable** happened in everyday life. How could they or their friends ever ride in such a car? They didn't even dream about it.

Polly asked, "Who do you think owns that one?"

Luke shrugged. "Who around here can afford it?" he **lamented**. He regretted he'd never have that kind of money.

"Well, someone must," said Polly, "or else it wouldn't be here so much. I think I'll take a quick **promenade** around the neighborhood to check things out. Maybe I can write a story for the block's newsletter. Want to walk with me?"

Eric looked at Luke. "Might as well." So they set off down Franklin Street on their boards.

A while later Luke stopped. "Let's go home. We're not going to find it. That car is gone."

But Polly had **embarked** on a mission. Once she started something, she liked to finish it. So she walked on as Luke and Eric turned back.

The next day Polly joined the boys again.

"So?" said Luke. "Did you learn anything?"

"I did. I talked to a lot of our neighbors," Polly said. "Do you remember Mr. Gomez? He used to be our school bus driver. His wife works in that fine **establishment** on Allen Street. She's a real chef."

"But what does Mr. Gomez have to do with the limo?" asked Luke.

Polly smiled. "You'll see," she said.

A few minutes later, the white limousine appeared down the street. Polly waved. Much to the boys' surprise, the car stopped in front of them. It was Mr. Gomez. He explained that he drove for a limousine company. Even better, Mr. Gomez said he had permission to give them and their parents a ride on his day off.

"Way to go, Polly!" said Eric.

Polly was already on the way to her computer. "This is such a great story," she said. "I know it will get published in the newsletter!"

Reread for Comprehension

Monitor Comprehension

Draw Conclusions

To draw conclusions you think about various pieces of information and what you already know to arrive at a new understanding about the characters or story events. This will help you monitor your comprehension as you read.

Use the Conclusions Chart as you reread "The Mysterious Limousine."

What I Know	Text Evidence	Conclusions

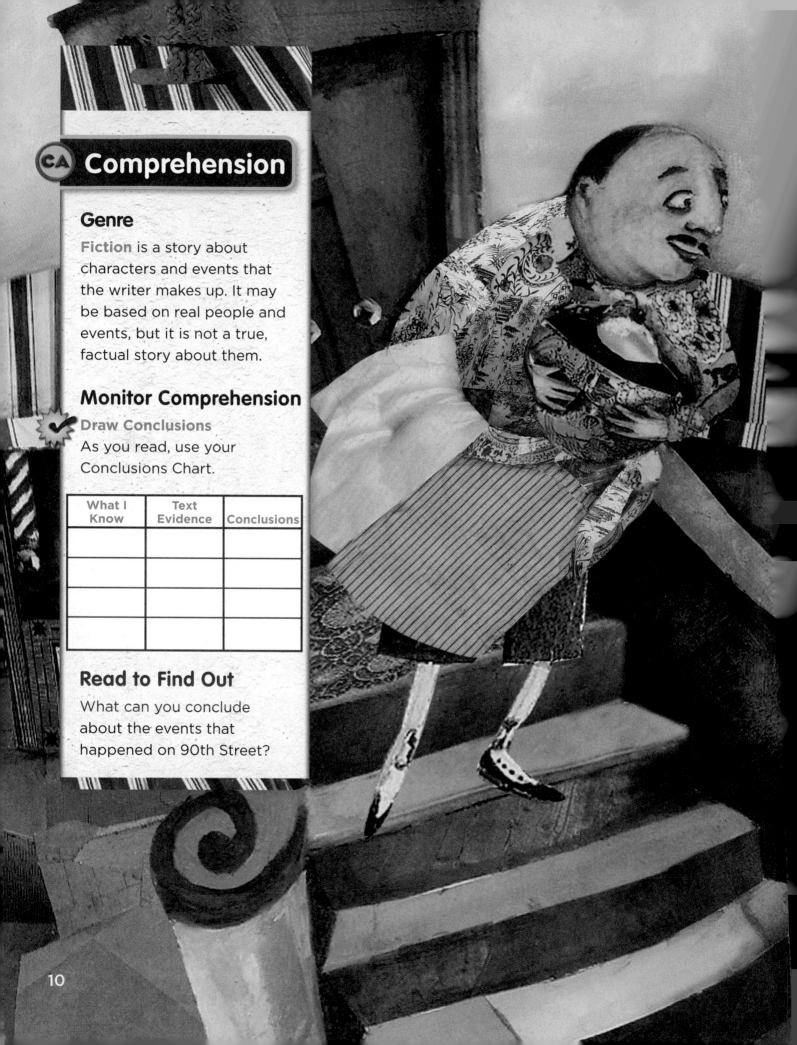

Comprehension

Genre
Fiction is a story about characters and events that the writer makes up. It may be based on real people and events, but it is not a true, factual story about them.

Monitor Comprehension

Draw Conclusions
As you read, use your Conclusions Chart.

What I Know	Text Evidence	Conclusions

Read to Find Out

What can you conclude about the events that happened on 90th Street?

NOTHING EVER HAPPENS ON 90TH STREET

BY RONI SCHOTTER

ILLUSTRATED BY KYRSTEN BROOKER

Award Winning Selection

FOR RENT

SEAFOOD

11

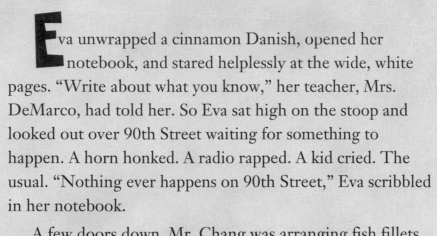

Eva unwrapped a cinnamon Danish, opened her notebook, and stared helplessly at the wide, white pages. "Write about what you know," her teacher, Mrs. DeMarco, had told her. So Eva sat high on the stoop and looked out over 90th Street waiting for something to happen. A horn honked. A radio rapped. A kid cried. The usual. "Nothing ever happens on 90th Street," Eva scribbled in her notebook.

A few doors down, Mr. Chang was arranging fish fillets in his newly opened Seafood Emporium. No one was buying, and his shop looked as empty and ignored as the tiny, boarded-up store next door to it. He nodded to a woman passing by and called hello to Eva.

Out the door of Eva's building came Mr. Sims, the actor, carrying his enormous cat, Olivier. Mr. Sims was "on hiatus again," which meant out of work, in between shows, and so, every day, dressed in his finest, he **embarked** on a daily **promenade** with Olivier under his arm. "Writing?" he asked.

"Trying to," Eva answered, "but nothing ever happens on 90th Street!"

"You are mistaken, my dear," Mr. Sims said. "The whole world's a stage—even 90th Street—and each of us plays a part. Watch the stage, observe the players carefully, and don't neglect the details," he said, stroking Olivier. "Follow an old actor's advice and you will find you have plenty to write about."

"Thanks," Eva said, and fast as she could, using as many details as she could recall, Eva described Mr. Sims in her notebook—his felt fedora hat, his curly gray hair, his shiny button shoes. When she looked up, he was halfway down the street and Mr. Morley, the mousse maker, was at his window.

Just as he did every day, Mr. Morley set his chocolate pot and coffee urn out on his ledge with a sign. Mr. Morley dreamed of having a catering business where the fanciest people demanded his dessert. But the trouble was . . . Mr. Morley's mousse was missing something. No matter how he tried, his mousse never had much taste, and Mr. Morley never had many customers.

"Writing?" he asked.

"Um. Hmmm," Eva answered, chewing on her pencil.

"Try to find the poetry in your pudding," Mr. Morley said softly. "There's always a new way with old words."

"You're right," Eva said, wishing Mr. Morley would one day find the poetry in *his* pudding. Taking his advice, she tried to think up a new way to describe the look of Mr. Morley's mousse. Smooth and dark as midnight. Or maybe more like mink! Yes, that was it! Eva thought, writing in her notebook.

The door to the building slammed and a gust of wind sent dead leaves soaring and dipping like crazy kites. Alexis Leora nodded to Eva and stepped gracefully down the steps to do her warm-up exercises. Alexis was a dancer. When she wanted to, she could hold an extremely long leg straight up against her ear like a one-legged woman with three arms. But she couldn't smile. Eva decided it was because Alexis Leora was lonely.

"Writing?" Alexis Leora asked Eva.

"Yes," Eva answered.

Alexis Leora did six deep knee bends and then sighed. "Stretch," she said sadly. "Use your imagination. If your story doesn't go the way you want it to, you can always stretch the truth. You can ask, 'What if?' and make up a better story."

"You're right," Eva said, thinking "What if?" What if Alexis Leora met someone? Would she smile then? What would that look like? Eva closed her eyes to try to picture it, but all she could picture was soup—Spanish soup—rich and brown and so spicy it seemed as if she could actually smell it.

She could! When Eva opened her eyes, Mrs. Martinez was standing beside her. She nodded to Alexis Leora as she handed Eva a bowl of soup. "Have some," she said. "Writers *need* soup. What's your story about?"

"Nothing much." Eva sighed. "Nothing ever happens on 90th Street."

"Add a little action," Mrs. Martinez said. "Like soup. A little this. A little that. And don't forget the spice. Mix it. Stir it. Make something happen. Surprise yourself!" She nodded again to Alexis Leora and went inside.

Eva put down her pencil and tasted Mrs. Martinez's wonderful, surprising soup. She thought about her story. It wasn't wonderful. It wasn't surprising. But what could she do? Nothing ever happened on 90th Street. How could she possibly "add a little action" and "make something happen"? Eva had no ideas. She was stuck!

Draw Conclusions
What conclusions can you draw about Eva's neighbors? Support your answer.

16

Then Mrs. Friedman from up the block came wheeling Baby Joshua in his stroller. He was holding a bright red ball in two tiny, fat hands. "Bird!" he called out to a pigeon hunting for something to eat. "Bird. Hungry!"

"Pigeon," Mrs. Friedman told him.

Eva sighed and looked down at her half-eaten Danish, then at her notebook. She looked at Baby Joshua, then at the pigeon. She remembered Alexis Leora's words of advice. "What if?" Eva thought. Suddenly she had an idea.

What if she stood up, broke her Danish into dozens of tiny pieces, and scattered them wide and wild into the street? What would happen? Eva laughed to think of it. . . .

From lampposts and ledges dozens of pigeons swooped down to dine on Danish. Eva eagerly picked up her pencil and began to write again. "Bird!" Baby Joshua called out, pointing. "More bird!" he cried, panting. The bright red ball dropped out of his tiny, fat hands and bounced onto the sidewalk. "Bye, bye, ball!" Baby Joshua screamed.

The ball rolled off the curb, into the street, and straight into the path of a pizza delivery man on his bicycle!

Everyone gasped in horror. Alexis Leora paused in mid-plié and leaped to the rescue. She got there just as the pizza delivery man landed, right side up, at her feet. Alexis Leora looked down at the pizza man and he looked up at her. And then something almost **unimaginable** happened: Alexis Leora smiled! "Are y-y-you all right?" she asked, shyly. Her smile was sweet and bright. Her teeth were straight and white. (It was the first time Eva or anyone on 90th Street had seen them!)

"Yes," said the pizza man, smiling up at her. It was love at first sight. Pepperoni and peppers rained down on the happy couple. The pizza man pulled a pepper out of his hair as horns began to honk.

Eva added this to her notebook and wondered what could possibly happen next. . . .

A long, white limousine was honking its horn loudest of all. The limo driver rolled down his window. "Whad'ya wanna block traffic for?" he called out. The back door of the limo opened and out stepped a woman in sunglasses, wearing a turban and a coat the color of a taxi.

"There seems to be a problem, Henry," she said in a fake English accent. "There's some sort of accident here. Perhaps—"

"It's *Sondra*!" someone suddenly screamed, interrupting her. "Sondra! Can I have your autograph?" Mrs. Martinez called out.

"Sondra Saunderson!" Mr. Morley blushed.

Was Eva dreaming? There, in the middle of 90th Street, larger than life, stood Sondra Saunderson, star of stage, screen, and the **sensational** soap opera "One World To Live In."

"Darlings, what's happening here? I'm sure I . . . *Lar*-ry!" she called out suddenly, and stretched her arms toward Mr. Sims, who had just returned from his promenade. "It's been an age since we saw each other!"

Mr. Sims' cat, about to be crushed in an **extravagant** embrace, leaped out of Mr. Sims' arms to chase after Baby Joshua's ball.

"Olivier!" Mr. Sims called out. "Come back!"

Everyone raced into the street after the ball, but it was the limo driver who, in the right place at the right time, leaned into the gutter and picked it up.

> **Draw Conclusions**
> How does the action so far prove that things do happen on 90th Street?

19

With a flick of the wrist, he tossed the ball to Mrs. Friedman, who presented it to a drooling but grateful Baby Joshua.

"How's that for a throw?" the limo driver proudly asked the crowd.

No one, not even Baby Joshua, had a chance to answer. Olivier, frightened by so many people, raced past Eva, scrambled onto Mr. Morley's ledge, where he knocked over his coffee urn, spilling all the coffee into his mousse pot.

"Ruined!" Mr. Morley cried, wringing his hands.

At that, Olivier bounded to the top of a ginkgo tree, where he swayed dangerously like a heavy, white balloon.

"Now he'll *never* come down!" Mr. Sims **lamented**. "He's terribly stubborn."

"There, there, Larry," Sondra Saunderson comforted him. "I'm sure someone on 90th Street will have a solution."

Eva tried to imagine who that could possibly be. . . .

"I have one!" she heard Mr. Chang call out. Generously, he offered trout, fresh from his store, to Olivier.

High up in the tree, Olivier barely blinked.

"Raw trout?" Mr. Sims sighed. "My regrets, Mr. Chang. He won't eat it. He's a *gourmet* cat. I'm afraid I've spoiled him. Whatever will I do?"

"What if?" Eva asked herself for the second time that day, and suddenly she had another idea. A truly great one! She whispered it to Mr. Morley, Mrs. Martinez, and Mr. Chang.

"Brilliant!" Mr. Morley exclaimed. And with that he, Mrs. Martinez, and Mr. Chang, still clutching his trout, vanished into the building.

Eva righted Mr. Morley's coffee urn and stuck her finger into his ruined mousse, then into her mouth to determine the degree of damage. "Mocha!" she called out in surprise. "Mr. Morley's mousse is mocha now and . . ." She paused, trying to find the perfect word. "*Magnificent*!" she announced to the assembled throng. And, giving the pot a stir, she dished out samples to all assembled.

"Delicious!" Alexis Leora said, spooning some into the pizza man's mouth.

"Poetry!" Sondra Saunderson pronounced.

Now on 90th Street, people who had never spoken to one another before were speaking at last. The pizza delivery man and the limo driver shook hands, and everyone tried to tempt Olivier down from his **precarious** perch.

And then . . . Mr. Morley appeared on the steps, followed by Mrs. Martinez and Mr. Chang. Mrs. Martinez carried a large pot of her surprising soup, while Mr. Morley carried a platter of Mr. Chang's trout, now surrounded by many tiny vegetables and cooked to perfection. With the addition of a cup of Mr. Morley's cat-created mocha mousse— it was a meal worthy of the finest culinary **establishment**.

"Do you smell that, Olivier?" Mr. Sims called, fanning the steam so it rose up the ginkgo tree.

Olivier took one deep sniff and bolted down the tree to dine!

Everyone on 90th Street sampled each course and everyone on 90th Street sighed with delight. "Superb!" "*Fantastico!*" "Yum!"

Eva smiled and glanced up from her notebook. For the third time that day she asked herself, "What if?"

"Mr. Chang," she began, "you and Mr. Morley and Mrs. Martinez are such great cooks. The boarded-up store next to your Seafood Emporium, what if all of you used it for a restaurant?"

"A restaurant?" The three chefs looked at one another. "What a wonderful idea," they said, shaking Eva's hand. "Everyone on 90th Street could be our customers. You too, Sondra."

"Everyone but me," Mr. Sims said regretfully. "Just now, I'm between jobs and a bit low on cash."

"No longer!" Sondra called out. "You'll be on my show! I'll arrange it."

Mr. Sims kissed Sondra's hand, and everyone cheered.

"What an amazing day!" Mrs. Martinez said. "Who would believe it? If only someone had written it all down."

"I did," Eva announced, and she opened her notebook and began to read her story (the same story you're reading now) about how *nothing* ever happened on 90th Street.

"What a story!" Sondra exclaimed. "Full of detail. Dialogue. Suspense. A bit of poetry. A hint of romance. Even a happy ending. Why, you'd almost think some of it was made up!"

Eva smiled mysteriously. "Thanks," she said proudly. "But just wait. It'll be even better . . . after I rewrite it."

WHAT'S HAPPENING WITH RONI

Roni Schotter writes because she loves words. Words are powerful. Words can start people thinking. Words give people courage to reach out to the world. Roni also wants to help people use their imaginations. Don't ever tell Roni that "nothing ever happens!" When Roni uses her imagination, anything can happen! She hopes her books will help her readers imagine their own stories, too.

Other books by Roni Schotter: *F Is for Freedom* and *Dreamland*

LOG ON ▶ Find out more about Roni Schotter at **www.macmillanmh.com**.

CA **Author's Purpose**
For what purpose does Roni Schotter use humor, dialect, and unexpected situations? Explain.

 **Critical Thinking**

Summarize

Use your Conclusions Chart to help you summarize *Nothing Ever Happens on 90th Street*. Tell about what the people on 90th Street were like at the beginning of the story and what they are like at the end.

What I Know	Text Evidence	Conclusions

Think and Compare

1. Use the **sensational** events in the story to **draw conclusions** about the way Eva has changed her feelings about her own writing abilities. **Monitor Comprehension: Draw Conclusions**

2. Why did Mr. Chang cook the trout? Support your answer with evidence from the story. **Analyze**

3. Eva engages in many dialogues throughout the story. In your opinion, what is the best piece of advice Eva gets? How is it helpful? Support your opinion. **Evaluate**

4. Eva is surrounded by different types of people who have different talents. Why do you think it is important for a writer to understand people with various jobs and abilities? **Evaluate**

5. Read "The Mysterious Limousine" on pages 8–9. How is what Polly and her friends find out similar to what Eva learns in *Nothing Ever Happens on 90th Street*? **Reading/Writing Across Texts**

Genre

Nonfiction: An interview is an account of questions asked by one person and answered by another.

✔ Text Features

Questions and Answers are set off by using a different typeface or by shortening the words to **Q** and **A**.

Content Vocabulary

preferences   aspiring

spontaneous

Student Interview with Author

Karen Odom

by Perry Faulkner

Question: When and how did you get into writing?

Answer: I've been writing for as long as I can remember, starting with letters and my diary, where I faithfully wrote down my feelings almost every day. But I really became hooked when I became a reporter for my school newspaper when I was in third grade. I also remember writing a play called *The Silver Locket* in sixth grade.

Question: What kind of unique training do you need to be a writer?

Answer: Many writers have been known to say the best training for a writer is living. I agree with that to a point. I think good writers also need discipline, creative talent, and a little bit of luck too. Writers are natural readers. Reading what others have written helps you not only appreciate good writing but also helps you understand different writing styles and how they affect you as a reader. If you're serious about being a writer, it's also important when you have the opportunity, whether it's in school or through special workshops, to take formal writing courses.

Question: What gives you ideas? What are your **preferences** when writing: people, places, things, or all of them?

Answer: You probably guessed it—I get ideas from all of them! I get ideas all the time, even when I'm not consciously thinking about it—when I'm driving to the store, in a meeting, watching TV, cooking, relaxing on the beach—you name it!

Question: What is your writing process? Do you write all at once or in fragments?

Answer: It all depends on what I'm writing. If I'm writing a nonfiction article that requires a lot of research and interviews, I do the research first, taking notes along the way. I organize my notes, but I also write a word or phrase by different sections of my notes so I can easily know what topic each section covers. Then I start writing. At this stage, I'm not concerned about sentence structure or how it reads or even how long the piece is running. Making sure it reads well, grabs the reader's attention, makes sense, and is the right length will come later when I begin editing and rewriting. And, believe me, there will be plenty of editing and rewriting!

Question: How do you organize your thoughts before writing? Do you create an outline? Or are you **spontaneous**?

Answer: I believe in outlines, but I'm also flexible. If the ideas are rushing in, I'll write down my thoughts (usually on my computer if I'm in my office) so I don't lose them, and then edit and rearrange them later. Otherwise I write out an outline.

Question: How have you changed the way you write over time?

Answer: Rewriting many times over has become second nature to me now. Luckily, it's a lesson I learned when I was very young. Some writers learn that in a much more painful way when they first begin writing professionally. There's ALWAYS a great deal of rewriting and editing that occurs before the final version that the reader sees. It's also much easier for me to let the material go now than it used to be. I'm less concerned about making the work "perfect."

Question: What is your favorite part of writing?

Answer: Actually I have two favorite things that I like about writing. The first is the excitement I feel when I'm brainstorming for a new project. The thoughts come almost faster than I can write them. My second favorite thing is finishing. There's something so satisfying about looking over the finished piece, liking the end result, and knowing that you've created it yourself.

Question: What are your plans for future writing? Are you going to write a book?

Answer: I plan to continue writing for both children and adults. There are many ways to earn a living as a writer. I've chosen writing for magazines, publishing companies, and business writing. It's interesting that you asked the question about writing a book. I have several books in mind, both fiction and nonfiction, but the first one—a children's picture book—is ready for publishing. I have been approaching different publishers to see if they are interested. I even entered it into a contest and was so excited when it won honorable mention in the *2003 Writer's Digest Annual Writing Competition*. I'll let you know what happens!

Question: What advice would you give a young, **aspiring** writer?

Answer: I have four main pieces of advice:

- Write, write, write, write, write, and write some more! Nothing beats just doing it.
- The life of a writer can be tough sometimes, and you have to be prepared for rejection along the way. You have to learn not to take it personally or dwell on it when something you've written is criticized or not accepted.
- Stick with it and never give up!
- And, remember, while you're writing the "Great American Novel," you may need to write some less exciting material to pay the bills!

Critical Thinking

1. Reread the questions in the interview. What kind of organizational plan do they show? Explain. **Reading an Interview**

2. How can Karen Odom's advice help you become a better writer? **Evaluate**

3. What writing advice do you think Karen Odom would give Eva in *Nothing Ever Happens on 90th Street*? **Reading/Writing Across Texts**

 History/Social Science Activity

Choose somebody to interview about his or her career. Ask at least five questions. Write your completed interview in a question-and-answer format.

LOG ON ▶ Find out more about interviews at **www.macmillanmh.com**.

Reading and Writing Connection

Writing

CA

✔ **Focus on Moment**

Writers provide details, such as precise action and sensory words, to describe a specific **moment** in time.

Read the passage below. Notice how author Roni Schotter focuses on a moment in her story.

An excerpt from
Nothing Ever Happens on 90th Street

The author focuses on the moment when Mrs. Friedman and her baby are walking by. She fills such a tiny moment with details, we feel like we are experiencing it along with Eva.

Then Mrs. Friedman from up the block came wheeling Baby Joshua in his stroller. He was holding a bright red ball in two tiny, fat hands. "Bird!" he called out to a pigeon hunting for something to eat. "Bird. Hungry."

"Pigeon," Mrs. Friedman told him.

Read and Find

Read Justine's writing below. How does she focus on one moment? Use the Writer's Checklist to help you.

Making Soup

by Justine Y.

I cut up the carrots. Mom had already put the butter and onions in the pan and it smelled so good, my stomach began to gurgle. The knife I was using sliced through the carrots easily even though I still had a tough time making them all the same size like my mom usually did.

"Those carrots look perfect," she said and I smiled at my work.

Read about an attempt at making soup.

Writer's Checklist

 Does the writer write a lot about one moment?

 Does the writer include specific details even though the writing piece is short?

 Can you imagine exactly what Justine experienced?

33

Becoming a Writer

CA **Talk About It**

Have you ever written about your own life? What is it that causes humans to write about themselves?

LOG ON ▶ Find out more about why people feel the need to write at **www.macmillanmh.com**.

Vocabulary

reputation
uttered
quickened
migrant
mistreated
wrath
illegally
ruptured

Word Parts

Word Families are groups of words that share the same base word.

il**legal**
il**legal**ly
legally
legalize

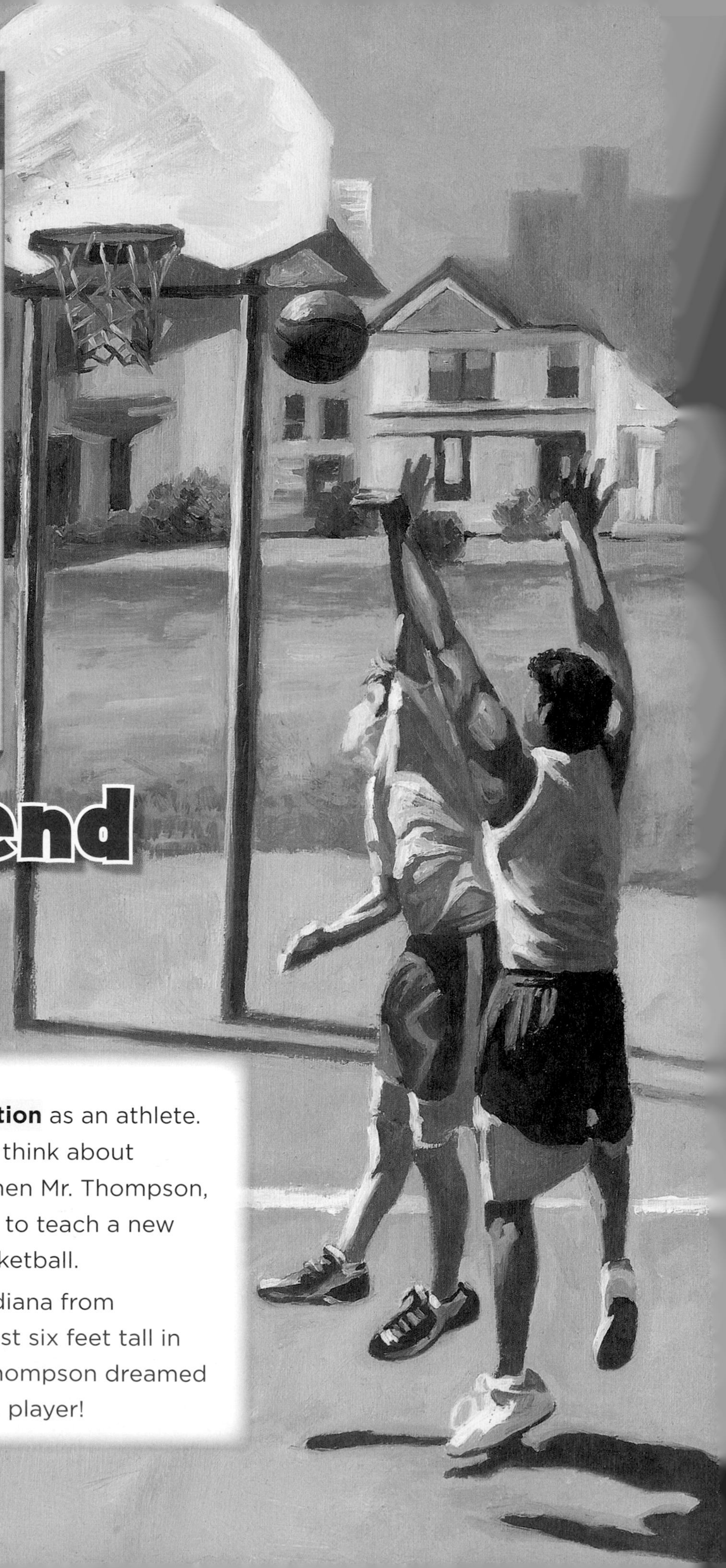

My Friend Mateo

by Kareem Williams

I have always had a **reputation** as an athlete. When people think of me, they think about sports. So it was no surprise when Mr. Thompson, my basketball coach, asked me to teach a new student the ins and outs of basketball.

Mateo had just moved to Indiana from California. He was already almost six feet tall in eighth grade! No wonder Mr. Thompson dreamed of making him into a basketball player!

Mateo was shy. The first time I met him at basketball practice he **uttered** the word "hello" to me, but he didn't move his eyes away from the floor. That shyness didn't last for long, however. Soon he had **quickened** his running and perfected his dribbling. Before long, I couldn't get him to stop talking!

The more I got to know Mateo, the more I liked him. He had lived a life that was different from mine, and I was very interested in the stories he told. He said that his parents were **migrant** farmworkers when they first moved to the United States. The family moved from town to town so his parents could find farmwork. He said that a few of the bosses were not kind to his parents and that some even **mistreated** them. Mateo said that sometimes his parents were treated unkindly when they made a mistake, but sometimes they suffered the boss's **wrath** just because the boss was in a bad mood. Often this anger would drive Mateo's family to move and find new work.

Mateo got to be pretty good at basketball. He was probably even better than I was! He could drive to the net without traveling **illegally**. But during our fourth game of the season, Mateo **ruptured** the tendon in his right knee. This means that the band of tissue holding his knee together had ripped or broken. All I know is that Mateo was done with basketball for a while. But I wasn't done with Mateo! We've been best friends ever since!

Reread for **Comprehension**

Evaluate

Author's Purpose

Understanding why an author wrote a selection will help you to better evaluate that piece. Authors write to inform, to persuade, or to entertain.

Use the Author's Purpose Chart to keep track of the clues that reveal the author's purpose as you reread "My Friend Mateo."

Clues	Author's Purpose

 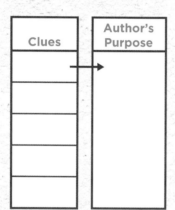
Genre

An **Autobiography** tells of a specific period of a person's life written and often embellished by that person.

Evaluate

Author's Purpose

As you read, use your Author's Purpose Chart.

Clues	Author's Purpose

Read to Find Out

How does Francisco's drive help him succeed?

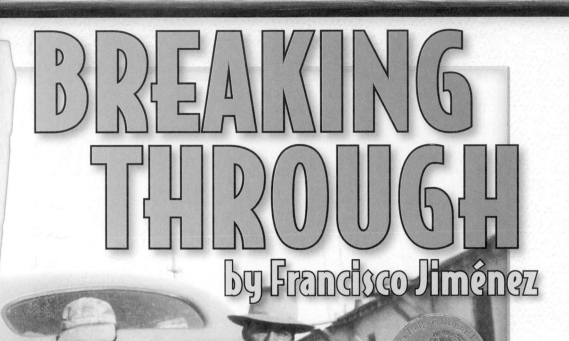

BREAKING THROUGH

by Francisco Jiménez

Francisco Jiménez has written several books about growing up in California after leaving Mexico. In this chapter, he writes about a special teacher and how she helped him to learn to enjoy reading, a discovery that changed his life.

At the end of my freshman year, I received good grades in all subjects except English, even though I had worked the hardest in it. Writing was difficult for me. My freshman English teacher told me that my writing was weak. She suggested that I read more, that reading would improve my writing. "At least read the newspaper every day," she told me. "Read for enjoyment." I had little time to read. I read only for information for my classes, and I could barely keep up. Besides, we had no reading material at home and we didn't get the newspaper. I never got more free time to read all during high school, but I did learn to read for enjoyment. It happened in my sophomore year, in English class.

Miss Audrey Bell, my teacher, had a **reputation** for being hard. When she walked into the class the first day and wrote her name on the board, I heard moans from classmates sitting next to me. "I am sunk!" one of them said. "Hello, F," another **uttered**. Now I was even more worried.

Miss Bell had a round face, a small turned-up nose, full lips, and lively blue eyes, and she wore wire-rimmed glasses. Her smile never left her, even when she was upset. When she wrote on the board, her upper arm shook like jelly, just like Mamá's arms. The back of her hands were covered with small brown spots the size of raisins, and her shiny nails looked like the wings of red beetles. She teased students and often made comments that made the class laugh. I laughed too, even though sometimes I did not understand her jokes.

No one laughed at her homework assignments, though. Every week she gave us vocabulary and spelling lists and a poem to memorize. I wrote the poems on notecards and attached them to the broom handle or placed them in my shirt pocket and memorized them as I cleaned the offices after school. I did the same thing with spelling and vocabulary words. I had a harder time with reading and writing. I was a slow reader and often had to read each assignment twice. At times my mind wandered off as I worried about Papá.

A typical school and
classroom from the 1950s

When we discussed the readings in class, I was surprised to find out that I had not really understood what I read.

Writing was even more difficult for me. Miss Bell asked us to write short compositions analyzing short stories we read for class. I was happy whenever I understood the plot and summarized it, but this was not good enough. "Don't tell me the story," she would say, smiling. "I know it. I want you to analyze it." I thought I knew what she meant, so in my next composition I wrote about the lesson I learned from reading the story. I hoped this was what she wanted. The stories I had heard from Papá and Mamá, Tío Mauricio, and other **migrant** workers all had a lesson in them about right and wrong, like "La Llorona," "The Boy and His Grandfather," or "The Three Brothers."

When Miss Bell returned our compositions, I fixed my eyes on the stack of papers as she walked around the aisles passing them out, trying to spot mine. The one with the most writing in red was sure to be mine. My papers always came back looking as though she had poured red ink on them. My heart pounded faster with each step she took toward me. She grinned as she handed me my paper. I quickly grabbed it. It had fewer corrections than my previous papers, but the grade was only a disappointing C. I stuck it in my binder, and for the rest of the class I had a hard time concentrating. During study hall, I took out the paper. She had written "Good progress" at the bottom of it. I felt better. I then went over the corrections carefully to make sure I understood them. I did not want to make the same mistakes in my next writing assignment, which Miss Bell announced the following day.

Author's Purpose
Why does the author focus on his writing skills?

"Our next unit is on autobiography, the history of a person's life written or told by that person," she explained. "So for your next composition, I want you to write about a personal experience, something that happened to you." I liked the assignment, but it was harder than I expected. I thought of writing about being deported, but I did not want my teacher to know that my family had crossed the border **illegally** and that I was born in Mexico.

An idea finally came to me late that evening. As I was sitting at the kitchen table trying to figure out what to write, Trampita entered the room, pulling up his white shorts. "What are you doing up?" I asked.

Francisco, José Francisco (Trampita),
and Roberto, Tent City, Santa Maria, California

Papá, Trampita, and neighbor Don Pancho at Bonetti Ranch,
Santa Maria, California

"I am getting a glass of water," he responded, half asleep.
His small body cast a thin shadow on the wall. We called him
"Trampita," "little tramp," because Mamá had dressed him in
baby clothes we found in the city dump. As he passed me on
his way back to bed, I noticed his bulging navel, the size of
an egg, that had **ruptured** when he was a few months old.

We had been living in a farm labor camp in Santa Rosa. It
was winter. Papá and Mamá worked at an apple cannery at
night and left Roberto to take care of Trampita and me while
they were gone. One evening, before leaving for work, Mamá
prepared the milk bottle for Trampita and laid him on a wide

mattress that was on the dirt floor. After my parents left, Roberto and I sat on the mattress and told ghost stories until we got sleepy. We said our prayers and went to bed next to Trampita. We kept our clothes on because it was freezing cold. At dawn, we woke up, frightened by our parents' screams. "Where's Trampita?" Mamá cried out. "Where is he?" Papá shouted. They had terror in their eyes when they saw Trampita was gone.

"I don't know, Mamá," Roberto stuttered, shivering from the cold. Papá noticed an opening at the foot of the tent near the mattress. He rushed out. Seconds later he returned with Trampita in his arms. My baby brother was stiff and purple.

(left) José Francisco (Trampita) and Roberto, picking plums in Orosi, California. (right) José Francisco

I decided to write about that experience. I wrote three drafts, making sure I did not make any mistakes. I turned it in feeling confident. When I got my paper back, I was disappointed to see the red marks again. I had made a few errors. I felt worse when I read Miss Bell's note at the bottom of the paper, asking me to see her after class. *She must be pretty upset with the mistakes I made,* I thought. I half listened to what she said during the rest of class. When class was over, I waited until everyone had left the room before I approached her, folding the paper in half to hide the red marks.

"Is what you wrote a true story?" Miss Bell asked.

"Yes," I answered, feeling anxious.

"I thought so," she said, smiling. "It's a very moving story. Did your brother die?"

"Oh, no!" I exclaimed. "He almost did, but God saved him. He rolled off the mattress, landed outside the tent, and cried so much that he hurt his navel."

"His hernia must have really hurt," she said thoughtfully. "I am sorry." She looked away and cleared her throat. "Now, let's look at your paper." I handed it to her, lowering my head. "You're making a lot of progress," she said. "Your writing shows promise. If you're able to overcome the difficulties like the one you described in your paper and you continue working as hard as you have, you're going to succeed." She gave me back the paper and added, "Here, take it home, make the corrections, and turn it in to me tomorrow after class."

"I will. Thank you, Miss Bell." I floated out of the room, thinking about how lucky I was to be in her class. She reminded me of Mr. Lema, my sixth-grade teacher, who had helped me with English during the lunch hour.

That evening when I got home I worked on the paper. I looked at the mistakes I had made and corrected them, following Miss Bell's suggestions. As I retyped it on the kitchen table, Mamá came over and sat next to me. "It's late, Panchito," she said softly. "Time for bed."

An old typewriter from the 1950s

"I am almost finished."

"What are you working on, *mijo*?"

"It's a paper I wrote for my English class on Trampita. My teacher liked it," I said proudly.

"On Trampita!" she exclaimed.

She got up and stood behind me. She placed her hands on my shoulders and asked me to read it. When I finished, I felt her tears on the back of my neck.

The next day after class I turned in my revised paper to Miss Bell. She glanced at it, placed it on a pile of papers on her desk, and picked up a book. "Have you read *The Grapes of* **Wrath**?" she asked. "It's a wonderful novel by John Steinbeck."

"No," I said, wondering what the word *wrath* meant.

"I'd like for you to read it." She handed it to me. "I think you'll enjoy it. You can read it for your book report."

When am I going to find time to read such a thick book? I thought, running my fingers along its spine. I was planning to read a smaller book for my report. Miss Bell must have noticed the pain in my face because she added, "And you'll get extra credit because it's a long book." I felt better.

"Thanks!" I said. "It'll give me a chance to improve my grade." Her gentle smile reminded me of Mamá and the blessing she gave every morning when I left the house.

After my last class, I picked up the books and binders I needed from my locker and walked to the public library to study before going to work at five o'clock. I double-checked to make sure I had the novel with me. On the way, I kept thinking about how I was going to get through such a long book. I felt its weight on my shoulders and the back of my neck. I **quickened** my pace, passing students left and right. The honking of car horns from students cruising by sounded far away. I rushed into the library and went straight to my table in the left back corner, away from the main desk. I piled my books and binders on the table.

I took a deep breath, picked up the novel, and placed it in front of me. I grabbed my worn-out pocket dictionary from the stack and set it next to it. I muttered the title, "*The Grapes of Wrath.*" The word *grapes* reminded me of working in the vineyards for Mr. Sullivan in Fresno. I looked up the word *wrath* and thought of the anger I felt when I lost my blue notepad, my *librito*, in a fire in Orosi. I began reading. It was difficult; I had to look up many words, but I kept on reading. I wanted to learn more about the Joad family, who had to leave their home in Oklahoma to look for work and a better life in California. I lost track of time. Before I knew it, five o'clock had passed. I was late for work.

When I got home that evening, I continued reading until one o'clock in the morning. That night I dreamed that my family was packing to move to Fresno to pick grapes. "We don't have to move anymore! I have to go to school!" I kept yelling, but Papá and Mamá could not hear me. I woke up exhausted.

Author's Purpose
What is the author's purpose in describing Francisco's fascination with the book?

Saturday night I skipped the school dance and stayed home to read more of the novel. I kept struggling with the reading, but I could not put it down. I finally understood what Miss Bell meant when she told me to read for enjoyment. I could relate to what I was reading. The Joad family was poor and traveled from place to place in an old jalopy, looking for work. They picked grapes and cotton and lived in labor camps similar to the ones we lived in, like Tent City in Santa Maria. Ma Joad

Francisco, freshman at Santa Maria High School

was like Mamá and Pa Joad was a lot like Papá. Even though they were not Mexican and spoke only English, they had many of the same experiences as my family. I felt for them. I got angry with the growers who **mistreated** them and was glad when Tom Joad protested and fought for their rights. He reminded me of my friend Don Gabriel, the *bracero* who stood up to Díaz, the labor contractor, who tried to force Don Gabriel to pull a plow like an ox.

After I finished reading the novel, I could not get it out of my mind. I thought about it for days, even after I had turned in the book report to Miss Bell. She must have liked what I wrote, because she gave me a good grade. My success made me happy, but, this time, the grade seemed less important than what I had learned from reading the book.

Meet the Author

Francisco Jiménez's family came to the United States from Mexico as migrant workers when he was four years old. Francisco worked in the fields, too. When he started school, he found it hard because he did not speak or understand English. He even failed first grade. But he soon realized that learning and knowledge were important. When he started writing, he wrote about how it felt to grow up in two cultures. Today he is a professor of modern languages at a university in California.

Francisco Jiménez

  Find out more about Francisco Jiménez at **www.macmillanmh.com**.

CA **Author's Purpose**
The author wants to persuade readers of the power of education, entertain readers with a story, and inform readers about migrant workers in the 1950s. Give an example from the story of each purpose.

 Critical Thinking

Summarize

Summarize what happens in *Breaking Through*. Miss Bell suggests that reading will help improve a person's writing skills. How does her suggestion shape the events in the story?

Think and Compare

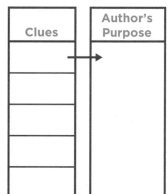

Clues	Author's Purpose

1. What is the **author's purpose** in telling about his time in Miss Bell's class? Use the Author's Purpose Chart to help you support your answer. **Evaluate: Author's Purpose**

2. The narrator has a **reputation** for performing inadequately on written assignments. What is he doing or not doing in his writing that causes Miss Bell to give him only fair grades? Use evidence from the text to support your answer. **Analyze**

3. The teacher asks Francisco to read *The Grapes of Wrath* for his book report. What book has had the greatest impact on how you think and act? How did it change your ideas? **Apply**

4. How can writing change how people view themselves, other people, and the world? **Evaluate**

5. Read "My Friend Mateo" on pages 36–37. How are Mateo's family and the narrator's family in *Breaking Through* similar? **Reading/Writing Across Texts**

51

Mentoring Matters

When members of a sixth-grade mentoring group realized they needed more mentors, they decided to invite other students. Mark, one of the mentors, offered to write a letter to **persuade** readers of the school newspaper to become mentors.

To the Editor:

I am writing on behalf of One-on-One, the sixth-grade mentoring group. Our group is two years old and our mission is to help students reach their goals through mentoring. You could consider this good classroom citizenship as it helps others in your school.

Our group consists of 14 students who **excel** in different subjects. Each member is assigned to a student who can use help in one of these subjects and has similar interests and schedules.

We hope the readers of this school newspaper will join our group. Many students would benefit from the **exceptional** skills of a mentor. Mentors can inspire other students who want to follow a similar path. This is my first year as a mentor, but I have already learned that everyone involved in mentoring gets something out of it. I was assigned to a mentor last year.

As it turns out, mentoring was one of the best things that happened to me. It helped me focus on certain math concepts that I just didn't get. I was able to turn the corner at an important point in my studies, going from nearly failing math, to not only passing, but to having math become one of my favorite subjects! It still amazes me that I completely changed from almost hating math to loving it! Would you believe I'm even thinking of studying math in college? Even if I don't, I have skills that I will use for the rest of my life.

My own experience convinced me to become a mentor this year and help other students like myself. Now that I am a mentor, I realize what a good feeling you get from helping someone else and knowing that you're making a difference in his or her life. In many cases, lasting friendships are made as well. My mentor and I hit it off right away, and we're still good friends today.

Becoming a mentor is a serious **commitment**. Mentors spend one hour every week with the student they are mentoring.

Considering your responsibilities, it may be difficult to add another commitment to your schedule. But I hope you will at least consider the possibility.

Please come to our next meeting on Wednesday at 1:00 P.M. (bring your lunch). You can meet the other mentors, learn more about what we do, and hear from a few students who will share their own personal stories.

Thank you for considering our invitation. We look forward to hearing from you.

Sincerely,

Mark Lopez

Time for Mentoring

Knowing your weekly schedule is just one of several factors you need to consider if you are thinking about becoming a mentor. By comparing your schedule with the schedule of the student you might be mentoring, you will be able to tell when you both are available. Meghann will have to compare her schedule with Christine's to see when it will be possible for them to meet.

Meghann's Schedule

	Monday	Tuesday	Wednesday	Thursday	Friday
8:15–8:30	Homeroom	Homeroom	Homeroom	Homeroom	Homeroom
8:30–10:00	Math	PE	Math	PE	Math/PE
10:00–11:30	Science	Spanish	Science	Spanish	Science/Spanish
11:30–1:00	Art/Chorus	Computer/Drama	Art/Chorus	Computer/Drama	Art/Chorus Computer/Drama
1:00–1:30	Lunch	Lunch	Lunch	Lunch	Lunch
1:30–3:00	Language Arts	Social Studies	Language Arts	Social Studies	Language Arts/Social Studies
3:00–5:00	Volleyball Practice		Volleyball Practice	Volleyball Practice	
5:00–7:00		Home Game			Away Game

Christine's Schedule					
	Monday	**Tuesday**	**Wednesday**	**Thursday**	**Friday**
8:15–8:30	Homeroom	Homeroom	Homeroom	Homeroom	Homeroom
8:30–10:00	Language Arts	PE	Language Arts	PE	Language Arts/ PE
10:00–11:30	Math	Spanish	Math	Spanish	Math/Spanish
11:30–1:00	Social Studies	Science	Social Studies	Science	Social Studies/ Science
1:00-1:30	Lunch	Lunch	Lunch	Lunch	Lunch
1:30–3:00	Art/Band	Computer/ Library	Art/Band	Computer/ Library	Art/Band/ Computer
3:00–5:00	Soccer Practice		Soccer Practice	Soccer Practice	
5:00–7:00					Soccer Game

Critical Thinking

1. Compare the two schedules. When can the girls meet? **Reading a Schedule**

2. How do you think Mark's experience last year will help him as a mentor this year? **Analyze**

3. Think about Mark and the student in *Breaking Through*. Explain why they both would be good mentors. **Reading/Writing Across Texts**

History/Social Science Activity

Research mentoring programs in your area. Write a letter to your school newspaper about the value of mentors.

 Find out more about mentors at **www.macmillanmh.com**.

Writing

CA

✓ Focus on Moment

Writers provide details, such as precise action and sensory words, to describe a specific **moment** in time.

Read the passage below. Notice how author Francisco Jimenez focuses on a moment in his story.

An excerpt from
Breaking Through

The author focuses on the one or two minutes right before he begins to read. He fills such a tiny moment with details so we feel like we are experiencing it along with Francisco.

I took a deep breath, picked up the novel, and placed it in front of me. I grabbed my worn-out pocket dictionary from the stack and set it next to it. I muttered the title, "The Grapes of Wrath." The word grapes reminded me of working in the vineyards for Mr. Sullivan in Fresno. I looked up the word wrath and thought of the anger I felt when I lost my blue notepad, my librito, in a fire in Orosi. I began reading.

BREAKING THROUGH

by Francisco Jiménez

Read and Find

Read Raymond's writing below. How does he focus on one moment in time? Use the Writer's Checklist to help you.

Baby Slobber

by Raymond M.

While feeding my little brother, I got slobbered. He drooled all over my shirt. The icky, sticky slobber all over me made my baby brother giggle. He kept laughing and decided to attack my fingers. More disgusting, slippery drool began to cover my hands. Finally, I picked him up and put him in his crib so that he would stop sliming me!

Read about feeding a baby brother.

Writer's Checklist

 Does the writer write a lot about one moment?

 Does he include specific details about the moment?

 Can you envision exactly what Raymond experienced?

Powerful Words

isolated
connection
immigrants
poverty
probably

Poetry Power!

Pick me! Everybody's a poet at Pelham Middle School.

When John Rybicki visits schools, he's like a music star or sports hero. For example, at Pelham Middle School in Detroit, Michigan, students hang on his every word and try to impress him. "Mr. Rybicki, pick me, pick me!" several boys shout. They all want to take up Rybicki's challenge to "get sassy and unleash out loud!"

Rybicki's star power comes from poetry. He is a professional writer, one of 14 hired to help kids at public schools across Detroit find their inner poet. The excitement isn't **isolated** to just one day. Students fine-tune their writing all year long.

Four times a month, Rybicki travels to Pelham to recite the works of famous poets. He also sprinkles in bits of his own work and life story. Rybicki likes to form a **connection** with students. He uses this bond to encourage them to "unleash out loud"—in other words, create their own verse.

The program is sponsored by InsideOut, a group that aims to get students writing and get their work published and heard. "Writers can be powerful role models," says InsideOut founder Terry Blackhawk, a poet and former writing teacher. "They bring emotion and passion into the classroom."

¡Vivan Los Libros!

"Our culture deserves clean, well-lit bookstores with the best service," says Rueben Martinez.

Books can do a lot for a person—just ask Rueben Martinez. His parents were **immigrants** from Mexico, and he lived in **poverty** as a child but taught himself to read. He opened a barbershop in 1976 and stocked it with books. After a while he started selling the books. "I started with two books. Then five. Then twenty-five. Then the big one hundred," he says. He now stocks 17,000 titles. His store, Libreria Martinez, has one of the largest collections of Spanish-language volumes in the nation. The writer Sandra Cisneros says, "He believes in the power of books to change lives."

LOG ON ▶ Find out more about libraries at www.macmillanmh.com.

Top 5 Largest Libraries in the U.S.

You **probably** think your school library has a lot of books, but check out how many titles these libraries hold.

The Library of Congress

Rank	Institution	Number of volumes held
1	Library of Congress	29 million
2	Harvard University	15 million
3	Boston Public Library	14.9 million
4	Yale University	11.1 million
5	Chicago Public Library	10.7 million

Source: American Library Assoc.

A Life in Words

Comprehension

Genre

A **Nonfiction Article** in a newspaper or magazine presents facts and information.

Summarize

Main Idea and Details

The main idea of an article is what the story is about. Details give more information about the main idea.

How does an author shape life experiences into stories?

"Write what you know" is the advice that many teachers give to young writers. Esmeralda Santiago is one author who has definitely taken that advice to heart. Her memoirs—books about her own life—have been huge successes around the world, and one has even been made into a movie.

An Author Is Born

The oldest of 11 children, Santiago was born in 1948 in Puerto Rico and raised by a single mother. She grew up in **poverty**, without much money or comforts. Santiago spent her first years in a tiny village and knew little about the developments of the outside world. In 1961, when she was 13, she moved to Brooklyn, New York, with her family.

Esmeralda (center) at age 4, with her sister and father in Puerto Rico

When Santiago applied to the Performing Arts High School, one of the top acting and singing schools in New York City, teachers asked her to pretend that she was decorating a Christmas tree. Santiago's family had never had a Christmas tree—but her acting was so good that the teachers admitted her.

Later, Santiago was accepted to Harvard University with a full scholarship. After she graduated in 1976, Santiago and her husband started a company that produces movies. She began writing movie scripts, then started to write essays and articles for newspapers and magazines.

Her Own Story

In the early 1990s, Santiago wrote and published her first book, *When I Was Puerto Rican.* It's the story of a 13-year-old girl who moves from rural Puerto Rico to New York City. The book is a memoir. It's a story she wrote about her own life.

In the book Santiago described her family's struggles. She learned that it can be difficult to write about something so personal. "I was worried that my family would be angry with me," Santiago says, "when I first began to write. As a family, we don't sit around talking about the old days."

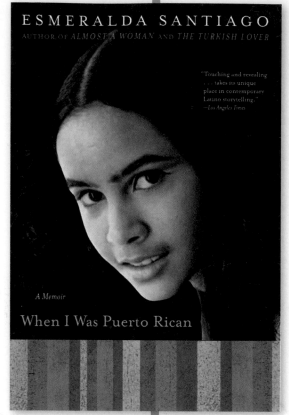

If she thought it would be difficult, why did she write the book? "I knew that it was important to tell our story because so many newcomers to this culture, myself included, have been **isolated**. . . ." Santiago says. "I trusted that if I told the truth as I saw it, my family would understand and support my right to speak."

Tackling Tough Issues

Santiago isn't afraid to point out problems in society. In her first book, she describes how she had a tough time as a newcomer to America. She learned early on that **immigrants** from Puerto Rico, Cuba, Mexico, and other Spanish-speaking countries are put in one category, Hispanic. Santiago is not sure if this label shows how different these people can be.

Santiago did well growing up in America and was accepted by people. However, she describes a loss when she moved away from Puerto Rico. She felt as if she had lost a **connection** with the culture there. She found this to be confusing—and it made her wonder where she really belonged in the world.

Books for Children

When I Was Puerto Rican is a great book for older readers. Younger kids will **probably** enjoy another of Esmeralda Santiago's books, *A Doll for Navidades.* In this book, she tells the tale of little Esmeralda, who wants to get a doll as a present more than anything else. But in the end, she receives a far more special gift. She discovers the power of her family's love for her.

Did you notice the first name of the main character in *A Doll for Navidades*? Once again, Santiago has used her own experiences to write a special book.

A Love of Reading

Santiago loves to read almost as much as she enjoys writing. She says, "I listen to audiobooks while I drive or during my daily walks. I read while waiting on hold or waiting on line. I read when I eat alone at home or in restaurants. I read before I fall asleep. I've always read like this, many things at once, in English or Spanish."

Books themselves are also important to her. "Books are the decoration of my life," she has said. "They are lined up on shelves in my office, in the dining room and hallways of my house, in drawers in the kitchen, on the coffee tables in the living room. And of course, the bedside tables are stacked with books waiting to be read . . . before drifting off to sleep."

Beyond Books

In addition to being a writer, Santiago volunteers her time in various causes. She has made speeches to support public libraries and created after-school programs for teens.

Santiago travels the country speaking at colleges and grade schools. She talks about the importance of finding your own voice in our society. She says it is important to encourage young people to write. Santiago is the perfect example of why that is true. As a young writer, she received criticism and encouragement from a teacher. This gave her the confidence to keep on writing. Santiago is glad she became inspired to write, and so are her many readers!

Esmeralda Santiago reads one of her books to children.

Critical Thinking

1. What type of book is *When I Was Puerto Rican*?

2. Why do you think the author of *A Doll for Navidades* chose the name Esmeralda for the main character?

3. If you were to write the story of your life up to now, what would you name it?

4. What do John Rybicki in "Poetry Power!" and Esmeralda Santiago both try to do for young writers?

A Father's Story

During World War II, a young Jewish girl, Anne Frank, and her family went into hiding to escape the Nazis, a German political group. At that time, the Nazis were rounding up and putting all Jewish people into concentration camps.

For 25 months the Franks lived in a secret part of a building in Amsterdam. After the family was captured, a diary kept by Anne was found. In 1947 *The Diary of a Young Girl* was published.

Now letters written by Anne's father, Otto Frank, have been discovered. They describe how he desperately tried to send his family to safety in the U.S. or Cuba. Nothing worked. Anne died in 1945, at age 15, in the Bergen-Belsen concentration camp.

Anne's story continues to inspire millions of people. Now her father's letters add to her moving account of life under the Nazis.

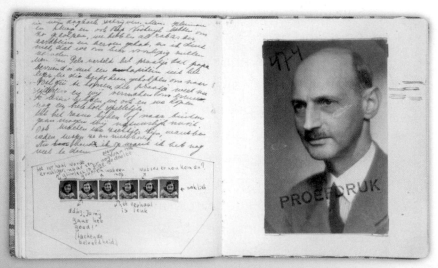

A page from Anne's diary shows a picture of her father, Otto Frank.

Go on ▶

Now answer questions 1 through 5. Base your answers on the article "A Father's Story."

1. **This article is _mostly_ about**

   A   the secret place in Amsterdam where the Franks hid.

   B   the discovery and content of Otto Frank's letters.

   C   Anne Frank's diary about her family's time in hiding.

   D   Otto Frank's efforts to get his family to safety.

> **Tip**
> You have to think about the entire passage to choose the best answer.

2. **Which statement would the author _most likely_ agree with?**

   A   It is a shame that Otto Frank's letters were found.

   B   Very few people will want to read Otto Frank's letters.

   C   Like Anne's diary, Otto Frank's letters can inspire people.

   D   Otto Frank's letters do not add anything to Anne's story.

3. **According to the author, his letters show that Otto Frank**

   A   did not object to the Nazis' plans for the Jewish people.

   B   was concerned about saving his business from the Nazis.

   C   believed his family would be safe in Amsterdam during the war.

   D   tried everything he could to get his family out of Amsterdam.

4. **How did Otto Frank try to save his family during World War II?**

5. **Why do you think Anne Frank's diary has been read by so many people? Do you think these people will read Otto Frank's letters? Why or why not?**

STOP   67

Write on Demand

 CA People help each other in many ways. <u>Write a story about a time</u> when you helped someone. Include details about what happened, what you did to help, and how you felt.

Narrative writing tells about a personal or fictional experience.

To figure out if a writing prompt asks for narrative writing, look for words such as <u>tell about a time</u> or <u>write a story about</u>.

Below see how one student begins a response to the prompt above.

> Two weeks ago, our class read about hunger in the world. I learned that millions of people really are starving.
>
> That night after dinner, I looked at the plates. We were actually throwing out food! Right then, I decided to do something. First, I talked to community leaders about how to help people in need. They suggested we raise money to buy food.
>
> Our teacher agreed to let us organize a Bike for Hunger day. Next, we signed up sponsors. They agreed to donate money for each mile.
>
> Yesterday, we had our ride. We rode 30 miles in all. Then my dad said, "You raised over a thousand dollars today." I could have jumped over the moon!

The writer used chronological order and finished with a strong ending.

Writing Prompt

Respond in writing to the prompt below. Write for
8 minutes. Write as much as you can as well as you can.
Review the hints before and after you write.

 People who do things for others deserve recognition.
Think about a person who did something special for
others. Now write a story that tells about that person.

Writing Hints for Prompts

- ☑ Carefully read the prompt.
- ☑ Organize your ideas to plan your writing.
- ☑ Support your writing by focusing on the theme.
- ☑ Use details to support your story.
- ☑ Choose words that help your readers understand your ideas.
- ☑ Review your writing and edit as needed.

Talk About It

Why do people enjoy reading stories about the future?

LOG ON ▶ Find out more about science fiction at **www.macmillanmh.com**.

STORIES IN TIME

Vocabulary

tinkering   destination
honorable   immigrated
concentrate   unsteady
formally   fidget

Thesaurus

Synonyms in a thesaurus are not always exactly the same. *Glumly* means "with low spirits because depressed." *Sullenly* means "in a bad mood because angry."

Sci-Fi Prep

by Gary Hillerman

Marge slumped into the apartment.

"Hi. What's the matter?" Her mother could always tell when Marge was upset.

"We have to read a science fiction story for homework tonight," Marge said glumly. "Why can't we read a sports story or a story about something that really happened?"

"Well," said her mother, "lots of people think science fiction is interesting. Did you know many ideas that appeared in this type of literature have actually come true at a later time?"

"Like what?" asked Marge. She was **tinkering** with the headset to her cell phone, adjusting the knobs.

"Robots, for example," said her mother. "When science fiction writers such as Isaac Asimov first wrote about robots, they really were imaginary. Today robots exist and are used in lots of ways."

"That's right," said Marge's brother, William, as he entered the kitchen. "In the 1940s, Asimov and another writer set up three rules to control the way robots act in science fiction. The first rule says that robots may not injure a person or allow a person to be harmed if robots can help."

"That's very **honorable**," said Marge. "I'll keep that good behavior in mind if I meet a robot."

She didn't wait to hear the other rules. She went to her room and tried to **concentrate** on her homework.

That night Marge had a dream. The door to her room opened and in came a robot. Despite her words to William, she was trembling.

"Good evening, Marjorie," said the robot, speaking very **formally**, not using her nickname. "I have come to escort you on a special journey."

"Where?" whispered Marge.

"Our **destination** is a lost world," answered the robot. "I left my home and **immigrated** here many years ago. Now it is time for me to return . . . and you must come with me."

"Why?" Marge's voice was **unsteady** and she stammered. Her fingers began to **fidget** with the cover on the bed, picking at loose threads. Too bad she hadn't stayed to hear the other rules for controlling robots.

"Ah, good question," said the robot. "Tomorrow you will be assigned to write a science fiction story for homework. It's time you learned more about the subject. Come!"

Slowly, Marge got out of bed and followed the robot into the world of science fiction.

Reread for Comprehension

Generate Questions

Sequence
Generating, or asking, questions as you read can help you to summarize a story. As you read, ask yourself what the most important events are. Then list in order what happened first, next, and last.

Use a Sequence Chart as you reread "Sci-Fi Prep."

Event
↓
↓
↓

Genre

Science Fiction is a story that tells of fictional events, usually set in the future, and is based on science or technology.

Generate Questions

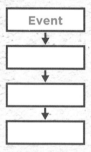

Sequence
As you read, use your Sequence Chart.

Event

↓

↓

↓

Read to Find Out

How does the use of a time machine in the story affect the sequence of events?

LAFFF

by Lensey Namioka
illustrated by Raúl Colón

Award Winning Author and Illustrator

In movies, geniuses have frizzy white hair, right? They wear thick glasses and have names like Dr. Zweistein.

Peter Lu didn't have frizzy white hair. He had straight hair, as black as licorice. He didn't wear thick glasses, either, since his vision was normal.

Peter's family, like ours, had **immigrated** from China, but they had settled here first. When we moved into a house just two doors down from the Lus, they gave us some good advice on how to get along in America.

75

I went to the same school as Peter, and we walked to the school bus together every morning. Like many Chinese parents, mine made sure that I worked very hard in school.

In spite of all I could do, my grades were nothing compared to Peter's. He was at the top in all his classes. We walked to the school bus without talking because I was a little scared of him. Besides, he was always deep in thought.

Peter didn't have any friends. Most of the kids thought he was a nerd because they saw his head always buried in books. I didn't think he even tried to join the rest of us or cared what the others thought of him.

Then on Halloween he surprised us all. As I went down the block trick-or-treating, dressed as a zucchini in my green sweats, I heard a strange, deep voice behind me say, "How do you do."

I yelped and turned around. Peter was wearing a long, black Chinese gown with slits in the sides. On his head he had a little round cap, and down each side of his mouth drooped a thin, long mustache.

"I am Dr. Lu Manchu, the mad scientist," he announced, putting his hands in his sleeves and bowing.

He smiled when he saw me staring at his costume. It was a scary smile, somehow.

Some of the other kids came up, and when they saw Peter, they were impressed. "Hey, neat!" said one boy.

I hadn't expected Peter to put on a costume and go trick-or-treating like a normal kid. So maybe he did want to join the others after all—at least some of the time. After that night he wasn't a nerd anymore. He was Dr. Lu Manchu. Even some of the teachers began to call him that.

When we became too old for trick-or-treating, Peter was still Dr. Lu Manchu. The rumor was that he was working on a fantastic machine in his parents' garage. But nobody had any idea what it was.

One evening, as I was coming home from a baby-sitting job, I cut across the Lus' backyard. Passing their garage, I saw through a little window that the light was on. My curiosity got the better of me, and I peeked in.

Sequence
What events happened to change the narrator's opinion of Peter?

I saw a booth that looked like a shower stall. A stool stood in the middle of the stall, and hanging over the stool was something that looked like a great big shower head.

Suddenly a deep voice behind me said, "Good evening, Angela." Peter bowed and smiled his scary smile. He didn't have his costume on and he didn't have the long, droopy mustache. But he was Dr. Lu Manchu.

"What are you doing?" I squeaked.

Still in his strange, deep voice, Peter said, "What are *you* doing? After all, this is my garage."

"I was just cutting across your yard to get home. Your parents never complained before."

"I thought you were spying on me," said Peter. "I thought you wanted to know about my machine." He hissed when he said the word *machine*.

Honestly, he was beginning to frighten me. "What machine?" I demanded. "You mean this shower-stall thing?"

He drew himself up and narrowed his eyes, making them into thin slits. "This is my time machine!"

I goggled at him. "You mean . . . you mean . . . this machine can send you forward and backward in time?"

"Well, actually, I can only send things forward in time," admitted Peter, speaking in his normal voice again. "That's why I'm calling the machine LAFFF. It stands for Lu's Artifact For Fast Forward."

Of course Peter always won first prize at the annual statewide science fair. But that's a long way from making a time machine. Minus his mustache and long Chinese gown, he was just Peter Lu.

"I don't believe it!" I said. "I bet LAFFF is only good for a laugh."

"Okay, Angela. I'll show you!" hissed Peter.

He sat down on the stool and twisted a dial. I heard some *bleeps, cheeps,* and *gurgles*. Peter disappeared.

He must have done it with mirrors. I looked around the garage. I peeked under the tool bench. There was no sign of him.

"Okay, I give up," I told him. "It's a good trick, Peter. You can come out now."

Bleep, cheep, and *gurgle* went the machine, and there was Peter, sitting on the stool. He held a rose in his hand. "What do you think of that?"

I blinked. "So you produced a flower. Maybe you had it under the stool."

"Roses bloom in June, right?" he demanded.

That was true. And this was December.

"I sent myself forward in time to June when the flowers were blooming," said Peter. "And I picked the rose from our yard. Convinced, Angela?"

It was too hard to swallow. "You said you couldn't send things back in time," I objected. "So how did you bring the rose back?"

But even as I spoke I saw that his hands were empty. The rose was gone.

"That's one of the problems with the machine," said Peter. "When I send myself forward, I can't seem to stay there for long. I snap back to my own time after only a minute. Anything I bring with me snaps back to its own time, too. So my rose has gone back to this June."

I was finally convinced, and I began to see possibilities. "Wow, just think: If I don't want to do the dishes, I can send myself forward to the time when the dishes are already done."

"That won't do you much good," said Peter. "You'd soon pop back to the time when the dishes were still dirty."

Too bad. "There must be something your machine is good for," I said. Then I had another idea. "Hey, you can bring me back a piece of fudge from the future, and I can eat it twice: once now, and again in the future."

"Yes, but the fudge wouldn't stay in your stomach," said Peter. "It would go back to the future."

"That's even better!" I said. "I can enjoy eating the fudge over and over again without getting fat!"

It was late, and I had to go home before my parents started to worry. Before I left, Peter said, "Look, Angela, there's still a lot of work to do on LAFFF. Please don't tell anybody about the machine until I've got it right."

A few days later I asked him how he was doing.

"I can stay in the future time a bit longer now," he said. "Once I got it up to four minutes."

"Is that enough time to bring me back some fudge from the future?" I asked.

"We don't keep many sweets around the house," he said. "But I'll see what I can do."

A few minutes later, he came back with a spring roll for me. "My mother was frying these in the kitchen, and I snatched one while she wasn't looking."

I bit into the hot, crunchy spring roll, but before I finished chewing, it disappeared. The taste of soy sauce, green onions, and bean sprouts stayed a little longer in my mouth, though.

It was fun to play around with LAFFF, but it wasn't really useful. I didn't know what a great help it would turn out to be.

Every year our school held a writing contest, and the winning story for each grade got printed in our school magazine. I wanted desperately to win. I worked awfully hard in school, but my parents still thought I could do better.

Winning the writing contest would show my parents that I was really good in something. I love writing stories, and I have lots of ideas. But when I actually write them down, my stories never turn out as good as I thought. I just can't seem to find the right words, because English isn't my first language.

I got an **honorable** mention last year, but it wasn't the same as winning and showing my parents my name, Angela Tang, printed in the school magazine.

The deadline for the contest was getting close, and I had a pile of stories written, but none of them looked like a winner.

Then, the day before the deadline, *boing,* a brilliant idea hit me.

I thought of Peter and his LAFFF machine.

I rushed over to the Lus' garage and, just as I had hoped, Peter was there, **tinkering** with his machine.

"I've got this great idea for winning the story contest," I told him breathlessly. "You see, to be certain of winning, I have to write the story that would be the winner."

"That's obvious," Peter said dryly. "In fact, you're going around in a circle."

"Wait, listen!" I said. "I want to use LAFFF and go forward to the time when the next issue of the school magazine is out. Then I can read the winning story."

After a moment Peter nodded. "I see. You plan to write down the winning story after you've read it and then send it in to the contest."

I nodded eagerly. "The story would *have* to win, because it's the winner!"

Peter began to look interested. "I've got LAFFF to the point where I can stay in the future for seven minutes now. Will that be long enough for you?"

"I'll just have to work quickly," I said.

Peter smiled. It wasn't his scary Lu Manchu smile, but a nice smile. He was getting as excited as I was. "Okay, Angela. Let's go for it."

He led me to the stool. "What's your **destination**?" he asked. "I mean, *when's* your destination?"

Suddenly I was nervous. I told myself that Peter had made many time trips, and he looked perfectly healthy.

Why not? What have I got to lose—except time?

I took a deep breath. "I want to go forward three weeks in time." By then I'd have a copy of the new school magazine in my room.

"Ready, Angela?" asked Peter.

"As ready as I'll ever be," I whispered.

Bleep, cheep, and *gurgle.* Suddenly Peter disappeared.

What went wrong? Did Peter get sent by mistake, instead of me?

Then I realized what had happened. Three weeks later in time Peter might be somewhere else. No wonder I couldn't see him.

There was no time to be lost. Rushing out of Peter's garage, I ran over to our house and entered through the back door.

Mother was in the kitchen. When she saw me, she stared. "Angela! I thought you were upstairs taking a shower!"

Sequence
Why is Angela's mother confused by her presence?

"Sorry!" I panted. "No time to talk!"

I dashed up to my room. Then I suddenly had a strange idea. What if I met *myself* in my room? Argh! It was a spooky thought.

There was nobody in my room. Where was I? I mean, where was the I of three weeks later?

Wait. Mother had just said she thought I was taking a shower. Down the hall, I could hear the water running in the bathroom. Okay. That meant I wouldn't run into me for a while.

I went to the shelf above my desk and frantically pawed through the junk piled there. I found it! I found the latest issue of the school magazine, the one with the winning stories printed in it.

How much time had passed? Better hurry.

The shower had stopped running. This meant the other me was out of the bathroom. Have to get out of here!

Too late. Just as I started down the stairs, I heard Mother talking again. "Angela! A minute ago you were all dressed! Now you're in your robe again and your hair's all wet! I don't understand."

I shivered. It was scary, listening to Mother talking to myself downstairs. I heard my other self answering something, then the sound of her—my—steps coming up the stairs. In a panic, I dodged into the spare room and closed the door.

I heard the steps—my steps—go past and into my room.

The minute I heard the door of my room close, I rushed out and down the stairs.

Mother was standing at the foot of the stairs. When she saw me, her mouth dropped. "But . . . but . . . just a minute ago you were in your robe and your hair was all wet!"

"See you later, Mother," I panted. And I ran.

Behind me I heard Mother muttering, "I'm going mad!"

I didn't stop and try to explain. I might go mad, too.

It would be great if I could just keep the magazine with me. But, like the spring roll, it would get carried back to its own time after a few minutes. So the next best thing was to read the magazine as fast as I could.

It was hard to run and flip through the magazine at the same time. But I made it back to Peter's garage and plopped down on the stool.

At last I found the story: the story that had won the contest in our grade. I started to read.

Suddenly I heard *bleep, cheep,* and *gurgle,* and Peter loomed up in front of me. I was back in my original time again.

But I still had the magazine! Now I had to read the story before the magazine popped back to the future. It was hard to concentrate with Peter jumping up and down impatiently, so different from his usual calm, collected self.

I read a few paragraphs, and I was beginning to see how the story would shape up. But before I got any further, the magazine disappeared from my hand.

So I didn't finish reading the story. I didn't reach the end, where the name of the winning writer was printed.

That night I stayed up very late to write down what I remembered of the story. It had a neat plot, and I could see why it was the winner.

I hadn't read the entire story, so I had to make up the ending myself. But that was okay, since I knew how it should come out.

The winners of the writing contest would be announced at the school assembly on Friday. After we had filed into the assembly hall and sat down, the principal gave a speech. I tried not to **fidget** while he explained about the contest.

Suddenly I was struck by a dreadful thought. Somebody in my class had written the winning story, the one I had copied. Wouldn't that person be declared the winner, instead of me?

The principal started announcing the winners. I chewed my knuckles in an agony of suspense, as I waited to see who would be announced as the winner in my class. Slowly, the principal began with the lowest grade. Each winner walked in slow motion to the stage, while the principal slowly explained why the story was good.

At last, at last, he came to our grade. "The winner is . . ." He stopped, slowly got out his handkerchief, and slowly blew his nose. Then he cleared his throat. "The winning story is 'Around and Around,' by Angela Tang."

I sat like a stone, unable to move. Peter nudged me. "Go on, Angela! They're waiting for you."

I got up and walked up to the stage in a daze. The principal's voice seemed to be coming from far, far away as he told the audience that I had written a science fiction story about time travel.

The winners each got a notebook bound in imitation leather for writing more stories. Inside the cover of the notebook was a ballpoint pen. But the best prize was having my story in the school magazine with my name printed at the end.

Then why didn't I feel good about winning?

After assembly, the kids in our class crowded around to congratulate me. Peter **formally** shook my hand. "Good work, Angela," he said, and winked at me.

That didn't make me feel any better. I hadn't won the contest fairly. Instead of writing the story myself, I had copied it from the school magazine.

That meant someone in our class—one of the kids here—had actually written the story. Who was it?

My heart was knocking against my ribs as I stood there and waited for someone to complain that I had stolen his story.

Nobody did.

As we were riding the school bus home, Peter looked at me. "You don't seem very happy about winning the contest, Angela."

"No, I'm not," I mumbled. "I feel just awful."

"Tell you what," suggested Peter. "Come over to my house and we'll discuss it."

"What is there to discuss?" I asked glumly. "I won the contest because I cheated."

"Come on over, anyway. My mother bought a fresh package of humbow in Chinatown."

I couldn't turn down that invitation. Humbow, a roll stuffed with barbecued pork, is my favorite snack.

Peter's mother came into the kitchen while we were munching, and he told her about the contest.

Mrs. Lu looked pleased. "I'm very glad, Angela. You have a terrific imagination, and you deserve to win."

"I like Angela's stories," said Peter. "They're original."

It was the first compliment he had ever paid me, and I felt my face turning red.

After Mrs. Lu left us, Peter and I each had another humbow. But I was still miserable. "I wish I had never started this. I feel like such a jerk."

Peter looked at me, and I swear he was enjoying himself. "If you stole another student's story, why didn't that person complain?"

"I don't know!" I wailed.

"Think!" said Peter. "You're smart, Angela. Come on, figure it out."

Me, smart? I was so overcome to hear myself called smart by a genius like Peter that I just stared at him.

He had to repeat himself. "Figure it out, Angela!"

I tried to **concentrate**. Why was Peter looking so amused?

The light finally dawned. "Got it," I said slowly. "*I'm* the one who wrote the story."

"The winning story is your own, Angela, because that's the one that won."

My head began to go around and around. "But where did the original idea for the story come from?"

"What made the plot so good?" asked Peter. His voice sounded **unsteady**.

"Well, in my story, my character used a time machine to go forward in time . . ."

"Okay, whose idea was it to use a time machine?"

"It was mine," I said slowly. I remembered the moment when the idea had hit me with a *boing*.

"So you s-stole f-from yourself!" sputtered Peter. He started to roar with laughter. I had never seen him break down like that. At this rate, he might wind up being human.

When he could talk again, he asked me to read my story to him.

I began. "'In movies, geniuses have frizzy white hair, right? They wear thick glasses and have names like Dr. Zweistein. . . .'"

Lensey Namioka was born in China. She is the only person in the world named Lensey because her father made it up just for her! She started learning to read Chinese at age two. In college Lensey studied mathematics but decided she liked being a writer better. Since then she has written more than 20 books.

Another book by Lensey Namioka: *Half and Half*

HALF and HALF

Lensey Namioka

Raúl Colón is an artist who has done work for the *New York Times* and *Time* magazine. He has also created theater posters and artwork for the advertising industry. But he is best known for the picture books he has illustrated. And now he has written one too: *Orson Blasts Off!*

LOG ON ▶ Find out more about Lensey Namioka and Raúl Colón at **www.macmillanmh.com**.

CA Author's Purpose

What makes science fiction different from other types of fiction? Do science fiction writers usually write for a different purpose than other fiction writers? Explain.

CA Critical Thinking

Summarize

Use your Sequence Chart to help you summarize *LAFFF*. Think about how the events of the story lead back to the beginning.

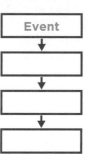

Think and Compare

1. How does Angela's opinion of Peter Lu change throughout the course of the story? What is the **sequence** of events that are responsible for this change? **Generate Questions: Sequence**

2. What events in the story would change if Angela had met herself in the future? **Analyze**

3. Suppose that, after scientists spend years **tinkering**, time travel becomes possible. To what time period would you like to travel? What are the potential drawbacks of time travel? **Synthesize**

4. What if Angela did steal another student's story? Do you think Angela and Peter were right or wrong to use the time machine to steal the winning story? Support your answer. **Evaluate**

5. Read "Sci-Fi Prep" on pages 72–73. How might Peter Lu's time machine help Marge write a science-fiction story? **Reading/Writing Across Texts**

Time Travel

Genre

Nonfiction: An Internet article gives verifiable information and facts about a topic.

✔ Text Features

A **Hyperlink** is an electronic connection within the text that provides direct access to more information. A **Keyword** is a specific word typed into the search box that helps you find information on the Internet.

Content Vocabulary

access	aeronautics
universally	mass
fleeting	

There are many different sources of information on the Internet. There are search engines, encyclopedias, newspapers, and other online reference sources. However, it is crucial to evaluate the sources you choose.

Evaluate your source. Decide if the online source of information is both reliable and appropriate. Historical records, encyclopedias, magazine articles, and newspaper articles usually contain reliable information.

Decide if you should check more than one source. Determine if you need to check more than one site to confirm your findings.

Use menus, toolbars, and links. Web sites are constructed to offer lots of choices while you are reading an article. Menus can help you decide what you want to read next. If you want to look for another topic, conduct a search simply by typing a key word in the search box and clicking "Go" or "Search." The computer will find it for you. Toolbars and links give you related information.

Choose your hyperlink. Click on one or more of the available hyperlinks within the text to get direct **access** to other information you need.

Science Online
Offering great articles on science topics

You Are a Time Traveler
by Louis Kamsky

Time travel has long fascinated people. Traveling to the past or future would allow you to live in exciting periods of history or to get a glimpse of what the world would be like in the future. You might even travel to the near future and see yourself as a grandparent! Think about it. If you were allowed to go back to the past, whom would you want to meet? Michelangelo? King Henry VIII? Eleanor Roosevelt? What historical event would you like to witness? The French Revolution? The Allied invasion of Normandy? You might set your sights more modestly with a visit to yourself as a baby.

Since these ideas are so **universally** tempting, it is natural that time travel would interest so many writers, filmmakers, and scientists. But you might be surprised to realize that in the smallest sense of the term, we are all time travelers. Even as you sit here reading this article, time is racing forward. The future becomes the past as soon as it happens. Think about it: The present is so **fleeting**! Everything you do quickly becomes part of the past, and so it is that we move through time. The famous scientist, Albert Einstein, assigned a mathematical formula to this idea, which is called the Theory of Relativity.

Black hole at the center of a galaxy

Albert Einstein

| Jules Verne | Time Machines in Movies | Time Machines in Fiction | Albert Einstein | Black Holes |

Science Online

Jules Verne

LINKS

Jules Verne (1828–1905)

Jules Verne was a French novelist and a pioneer writer of science fiction. After he tried to run away to become a sailor at age 11, he promised his family he would only travel in his imagination. He fulfilled this promise, writing at least 50 tales of extraordinary voyages.

Verne was very interested in geography and new discoveries in **aeronautics** and travel. His first famous work, *Five Weeks in a Balloon* (1863), gained him fame and wealth. Most of his books are adventure stories based on wide research. He is best known for his classic works of science fiction such as *From the Earth to the Moon* (1865) and 20,000 Leagues Under the Sea (1870), which show extraordinary cleverness in predicting submarines and space travel. In general, Verne influenced literature by giving credibility to scientific efforts.

Science Fiction Writers ▶

19th Century Science Predictions ▶

Black Holes

When stars that are more than four times the **mass** of the sun reach the end of their life and have used all their fuel, they collapse under the pressure of their own weight. The center of this collapse becomes a black hole. Black holes have such a strong force that even light cannot escape from them. They suck everything in and are shaped like an ice-cream cone, whose point is called a *singularity*.

Black Hole

Critical Thinking

1. In what ways would hyperlinks in this article be useful? **Using Hyperlinks**

2. Why might an online science article be a reliable source? **Analyze**

3. What facts discussed in "You Are a Time Traveler" complement the ideas in *LAFFF*? How does *LAFFF* qualify as science fiction? Explain. **Reading/Writing Across Texts**

Science Activity

Research and investigate the concept of time travel on the Internet. Then use your results to write your own evaluation of time travel.

LOG ON ▶ Find out more about science fiction at **www.macmillanmh.com**.

Reading and Writing Connection

✔ **Argument**

Writers often make an **argument**, or take a position, about something in their writing.

Read the passage below. Notice how author Lensey Namioka provides details to support her argument.

An excerpt from
LAFFF

The character Angela believes that Peter doesn't have any friends. This is her argument. She then gives details or examples to support what she believes to be true.

Peter didn't have any friends. Most of the kids thought he was a nerd because they saw his head always buried in books. I didn't think he even tried to join the rest of us or cared what the others thought of him.

Read and Find

Read Jalen's writing below. How did he use focus to try to convince you to agree with him? Use the Writer's Checklist to help you.

Lockers: A Necessity

by Jalen C.

I stay organized by using my locker. My desk overflows with folders and notebooks I use during class. I couldn't hand in my homework on time if I didn't have a locker. One time when I forgot my combination, I couldn't use my locker. By the end of the day, my desk looked like it had exploded.

Read about why one person thinks lockers are important.

Writer's Checklist

 Does the writer choose one argument and write a lot about it?

 Does the writer include convincing evidence because he goes into depth about his argument?

 Do you see an experience the writer had that influenced his opinion?

CA **Talk About It**

How does making new discoveries through research help you in your writing?

LOG ON ▶ Find out more about doing research at **www.macmillanmh.com**.

Write to Discover

The Unusual Robot

by *Wilson Jenkins*

"Wow!" said Dominic as he finished reading the script for the school play. "We've got a winner."

Angela nodded. "Don't you love that detective robot?" she asked. "She really is **charismatic**. What a winning personality!"

"How about the line where she says a detective's job is **sleuthing**?" chimed in Bonnie.

"My favorite part is where she **mimics** the parrot. I mean a robot copying what a parrot says? It's too funny," said Carl.

The students chatted on about the **array** of different and colorful characters in the play. All the roles sounded first-rate.

A Problem

Each year the students produce a play for the community. The money they raise helps pay for a sixth-grade trip to Washington, DC. It is an event of great pride and **significance** to the students.

"This play will be expensive to do," Ms. Tiroli warned the class. "We'll need special scenery, costumes, and even music. You'll have to figure out if you can do this play and have enough left for the trip."

The students began to list their expenses. Then they subtracted that amount from

what they would probably earn selling tickets to the play.

"It's not enough," said Carl. "Can we charge more for the tickets?"

Dominic said, "People won't come if we charge too much."

Ms. Tiroli suggested holding a meeting the next day.

Some Solutions

The students met and shared their ideas. One was to choose another play that didn't cost so much. "Oh!" said Angela **despondently**. "I'd be so sad if we didn't do *The Charismatic Robot*."

"I have an idea," piped up Paulo. "You know how some businesses in town are always **sponsoring** events for the high school sports teams? Maybe we can get them to sponsor our costumes."

"Great idea!" said Bonnie.

The students decided to talk to some business owners.

The Show Goes On

During the next few weeks, students were raising money, rehearsing the play, making posters, and selling tickets.

"We have enough to pay for all the materials," announced Paulo. "We'll list each sponsor in the program. None of them wants to be **anonymous**."

"Well, wait until they see the play," said Dominic. "They'll probably ask us to do one a month!"

"Actually," said Paulo, "they're all hoping to find a charismatic robot to work for them."

Reread for Comprehension

Monitor Comprehension

Draw Conclusions
A Conclusions Chart helps you to draw conclusions about information. When you draw a conclusion, look for facts or details about a character or event. Use these facts and logical reasoning to draw a conclusion.

Use the Conclusions Chart as you reread "The Unusual Robot."

Text Clues	Conclusion

97

◯ Comprehension

Genre

A **Drama** is a story that is intended to be performed and has features such as a prologue, stage directions, scene descriptions, and dialogue.

Monitor Comprehension

✔ **Draw Conclusions**
As you read, use your Conclusions Chart.

Text Clues	Conclusion

Read to Find Out

Who is the Phantom Poet?

The Case of the Phantom Poet

Award Winning Author

Time: The present

Setting: A small suburban town in the U.S.A.

Prologue: A local newspaper, *The Town Caller*, is **sponsoring** a writing competition for sixth-grade students. From a wide **array** of entries, a team of judges at the paper has narrowed the competition to two students: Delia Marcus and Latisha Walker. To decide the winning student, Mr. Tolliver, the school principal, has requested that both girls write a human interest story, featuring someone of special **significance** to the school. The race is on! It's Thursday and the deadline to submit the articles is Tuesday afternoon.

a play
by **Karen English**

illustrated by
Nicole Tadgell

Characters (in order of appearance):

Latisha Walker	A bright but shy young writer
Michael Johnson	Latisha's friend and star basketball player
Rhonda Watts	Latisha's friend since kindergarten
Carlos Hernandez	Michael's friend
Delia Marcus	Popular, overly confident winner of several writing competitions
Ms. Singh	School librarian
Miss Mackey	Woman who works in the cafeteria
Mr. Tolliver	School principal

SCENE 1

The school library; Latisha, Michael, Rhonda, and Carlos are huddled at a table, discussing the writing competition.

Michael: *(slowly, as if thinking aloud)* Someone of special significance to the school . . . someone dynamic, appealing, **charismatic**—*(pause)* Hey, why don't you just write about me!

(Everyone laughs, including Michael.)

Latisha: Let's get serious. I'm facing major competition here. Delia Marcus wins just about every writing contest around.

Rhonda: There was the Robert Frost Poetry Contest last year and the haiku competition at the recreation center.

Carlos: And the short story competition that WBAE sponsored last month.

> **Draw Conclusions**
> Why is everyone concerned about competing against Delia?

100

Michael: *(shaking his head)* Hey, remember me? *(with pride)* Michael Johnson, Most Valuable Player at the school regionals this year! Slam dunk!

*(Everyone **mimics** cheering and applauding.)*

Latisha: *(holding a phony microphone up)* Michael, tell us how you got your start.

Michael: *(humble)* Well, I owe it all to Coach Greer. He's a great guy and a great role model. *(Everyone looks at one another, then, in unison . . .)*

All: Coach Greer!

Latisha: *(slowly)* Someone of significance to the school! *(puts arm around Michael's shoulder)* Michael, old friend, do you think you can get me an interview with Coach Greer?

(Enter Delia Marcus.)

Delia: *(smug)* Too late, Latisha. I just arranged an interview with him for tomorrow morning. Coach Julius Greer, college all-star and pride of our town, as my mom always says. She went to school with him! *(turns to leave)* Good try, Latisha, but life is like sports, you've got to be quick on your feet. *(walks away, leaving the other kids dumbfounded)*

Fade out.

The next day, back in the library; Latisha, Carlos, Rhonda, and Michael sit morosely, with their chins in their palms.

Latisha: Oh, well, back to square one.

(Carlos drums the table with a folded piece of paper.)

Rhonda: Stop that. I can't think.

(Carlos absentmindedly gives the table another tap and then opens the paper and reads to himself but audibly.)

Carlos: *(recites)* Do not despair of desserts not won; Soon you will find your place in the sun. *(sighs)* Courtesy, the Phantom Poet.

Latisha: *(absently)* What's that one about?

Carlos: This one? I didn't place in the last track meet and I was feeling kind of bad.

Michael: Are you going to turn it in to Ms. Singh? She's been collecting those couplets.

(All turn to look at the librarian writing at her desk. A large glass jar filled with folded paper sits on the desk.)

Rhonda: *(pause, as if thinking)* That's it! That's the subject of your human interest story—the Phantom Poet!

Latisha: Nobody knows who the Phantom Poet is.

Michael: We'll just have to find out. How long has this Phantom Poet been dropping those couplets all over the place? A year? A zillion of us have gotten them. Always when something disappointing has happened or when we need a boost.

Rhonda: Remember when the Student Council overlooked Mr. Sauer, the custodian, on Recognition Day? The whole Student Council got one. What'd it say?

Latisha: Um . . . *(recites)* Forgetting to include Mr. Sauer; Is like baking a cake without flour.

Carlos: I've got an idea. *(leaves the table, huddles with Ms. Singh, then returns with the jar)* Let's get to work! Latisha, you're going to write about the Phantom Poet.

(Light fades, then comes up on group sitting at the same table, this time covered with small squares of paper. Latisha and Michael are frowning at notes in their hands.)

Michael: I'm stumped. What do we have so far?

Carlos: The poet's got to be an adult. Check the style—no one our age writes this way.

Latisha: I think Carlos is right. They're too literary for a kid.

Michael: Mmm . . . literary . . . *(studies Ms. Singh, others follow his gaze)*

> **Draw Conclusions**
> Who does Michael think is the Phantom Poet?

Rhonda: You think Ms. Singh might be the Phantom Poet?

Latisha: There's only one way to find out. (*leaves the table to confer with Ms. Singh*)

Ms. Singh: How can I help you, Latisha?

Latisha: Um . . . Can I get a list of contemporary women journalists? I'm interested in reading about them.

Ms. Singh: No problem. (*consults her computer, writes something on a piece of paper, and hands it to Latisha*)

Latisha: (*returning to the table, waving paper*) I've got a writing sample. Now we can compare Ms. Singh's handwriting with the writing on the couplets.

(*Heads bend over the writing sample.*)

Michael: (**despondently**) It's not her. The poet's *e*'s have this little flourish. Not one of these *e*'s has that.

Latisha: (*disappointed*) Let's call it a day. Think about any adult who fits the profile of the poet. Tomorrow's Saturday. We can all meet at my house at 10:00 A.M. We've got to find the Phantom Poet!

Fade out.

SCENE 3

The next morning, Latisha's living room; Michael tosses a basketball. Kids are seated on the floor.

Michael: I hope you know I'm going to be late for basketball practice. Let's get started.

Carlos: *(clears throat)* You're going to thank me for this. I must admit my **sleuthing** has been pretty brilliant.

Michael: Speed it up, please.

Carlos: The poet's Mr. Tolliver.

All: Mr. Tolliver!

Carlos: Think about it. He's always giving us pep talks and little lessons at every opportunity.

Rhonda: But poems? How are we going to find out for sure? Latisha's deadline is Tuesday morning.

Carlos: Didn't I say I was brilliant? *(pulls paper from his pocket)* I suspected Mr. Tolliver on my way home, so I stopped by his office and asked him if he could write me an excuse for first period when I have to help put away sports equipment. Note the word *equipment*. Note it has two *e*'s.

Michael: Let's have it.

Carlos: Did I hear, "Thank you"?

Michael: *(snatching the note)* Thank you! *(He studies the note.)* Did you look at this, Einstein? The *e*'s are different.

Carlos: All right, they're different but check out the *a*'s. They look pretty similar.

(Latisha also studies the note.)

Latisha: No way, Carlos! Not at all!

Rhonda: *(continues studying the notes while the others argue)* Hold the phone! Check this out. Every single couplet has something to do with food or flowers. *(recites)* A time sweet as mangoes will resume; Take heart, a new day will chase your gloom. *(pause)* That was mine last winter—stuffed in my locker when my parents temporarily separated and I was all depressed.

Latisha: Who'd you confide in?

Rhonda: Only Miss Mackey in the caf . . . e . . . te . . . ri . . . a.

Carlos: Yeah, she's really great. And she always smells like . . . *(pause, as the kids look at one another)*

All: . . . flowers!

Latisha: *(thoughtfully)* Miss Mackey . . . Miss Mackey . . . Food, flowers . . . Looks like I have to go see Miss Mackey first thing Monday morning.

Fade out.

SCENE 4

Monday morning, the school cafeteria; Miss Mackey, in a hairnet and apron, with a pen and clipboard, is doing inventory. Latisha stands for a moment looking at her. She notes Miss Mackey's sweater with a flower in the lapel.

Latisha: It's you, isn't it?

Miss Mackey: Pardon me?

Latisha: You're the Phantom Poet. It all fits. *(points at the flower, waves her hand over the room)* Flowers . . . food . . . it's you.

Miss Mackey: *(sitting down, heavily)* Smart girl. Yes, it's me. I'm the poet. In fact, I've had a few of my poems published in *The Town Caller.*

Latisha: But without your name.

Miss Mackey: I never wanted a fuss. My reward comes from all of you. Giving you the right words when you need it.

Latisha: *(softly)* Miss Mackey, I want to write about you. I know it's for a selfish reason. Delia Marcus and I are finalists for the newspaper competition. We've got to write competing human interest stories to decide the winner. I want to be the winner, Miss Mackey, and your story will give me a good shot.

Miss Mackey: I can tell you my story, Latisha, but you can't give away my identity.

Latisha: I won't reveal your name.

Miss Mackey: Let's just say someone helped me with the right words when I needed it. I'm simply passing along the favor my way.

Latisha: Tell me more, Miss Mackey.

Both sit down to talk, quietly. Fade out.

Mr. Tolliver's office; he's sitting behind his desk while Delia and Latisha stand holding their stories.

Mr. Tolliver: I look forward to your stories. And I'm curious about whom you chose to write about.

Delia: *(stepping forward, confidently)* I did my piece on Coach Greer, three time Most Valuable Player on his college basketball team, and the driving force behind our championship for the last two years.

Latisha: I chose the Phantom Poet.

Delia: *(shocked)* What?

Latisha: I found out who the poet is and interviewed *(pause)* the poet. The poet chooses to remain **anonymous** for personal reasons but I still got a great story. My article is about the rewards of writing words of inspiration to kids who need it.

Delia: How do we know you're not just making it up?

Mr. Tolliver: I'll know—since I, too, know the identity of the Phantom Poet. *(smiles at Latisha)* You'll have my decision by Friday. Good luck, girls.

Latisha: *(extending a hand to Delia; Delia takes it)* May the better story win.

Fade out.

Starring Karen and Nicole

Karen English has four children and has taught school for many years. She knows the joys and the problems of growing up. She used this reservoir of memory, and perhaps the psychology she studied in college, to write this play. It was clever the way she didn't quite tell us the ending. She knew it was a better story letting the reader guess who might win—Delia or Latisha. Whom do you want to win?

Nicole Tadgell was born in Highland Park, Michigan, and now makes her home in Spencer, Massachusetts, with her husband, Mark, and two border terriers. She has illustrated numerous books and is the winner of the Children's Africana Book Award for illustrating *Fatuma's New Cloth*.

LOG ON ▶ Find out more about Karen English and Nicole Tadgell at **www.macmillanmh.com**.

CA Author's Purpose

A play is meant to be performed as entertainment. What text features tell you that this piece is a play and may be performed?

 Critical Thinking

Summarize

Use your Conclusions Chart to help you summarize *The Case of the Phantom Poet*. What is the most important information in each scene?

Text Clues	Conclusion

Think and Compare

1. Use information from the text to **draw conclusions** about the ways Miss Mackey was a person of "special significance" to the school. **Monitor Comprehension: Draw Conclusions**

2. Miss Mackey mentions that someone once helped her with the right words. If that person were another character in the play, who do you think that person might be? **Evaluate**

3. The Phantom Poet chooses to remain **anonymous**. If you were the Phantom Poet, why would you choose to keep your identity a secret? **Synthesize**

4. Do you think small acts of kindness can make a difference in people's lives? Why or why not? **Evaluate**

5. Read "The Unusual Robot" on pages 96–97. How do the students in this story accomplish their goal? How are their methods similar to those of Latisha and her friends? **Reading/ Writing Across Texts**

Genre

Nonfiction Some nonfiction articles give facts and information about a topic.

✔ Text Feature

Tables present information visually using rows (across) and columns (down).

Content Vocabulary

estimate

random sample

representative sample

biased sample

Students Who Would Attend *Annie*

Method of Selecting Sample	Percent
Frank asked 50 of his friends.	30%
Sue put the names of all sixth-grade students in a hat and selected 50 names from the hat.	80%
Ellen put the names of all the students in a hat and selected 50 names from the hat.	60%

This table shows the data from the surveys.

How to Conduct a Survey

Frank, Sue, and Ellen conducted surveys to **estimate** how many students in their school would attend a student production of *Annie*. What is the best prediction (or guess) for the percentage of students in the whole school that would attend *Annie*?

In a **random sample**, a group of subjects (a sample) is selected from a total group of people (a population). Each subject is chosen completely by chance and each member of the total group (the population) has an equal chance of being included in the sample. When you pick names out of a bag without looking, you are selecting a random sample of the names in the bag.

Ellen took a random sample of all the students in the school. Each student had an equal chance of being chosen. Frank and Sue did not take random samples.

In their samples, each student in the school did not have an equal chance of being selected.

A sample that gives you a good idea of what a total group (whole population) is like is called a **representative sample**.

A sample that does not represent the total group is called a **biased** **sample**. For example, Frank asked only his friends, and Sue asked only sixth-grade students.

Ellen's method is most likely to represent the total school. It is the best one to use for predicting (or guessing) the percentage of students in the school who would attend *Annie*. The best prediction is 60%.

 ## Critical Thinking

1. Look at the table on page 114. What percentage of sixth-grade students would be likely to attend *Annie*? **Reading a Table**

2. Which method would you use to conduct a survey? Why? **Evaluate**

3. How should the students in *The Case of the Phantom Poet* plan and conduct a survey to find out who everyone thinks the mystery poet is? **Reading/Writing Across Texts**

 ## Math Activity

Conduct a survey of your own. Include a random sample and a biased sample. Present your findings using a table.

 Find out more about surveys at **www.macmillanmh.com**.

Writing

CA

Argument

Writers sometimes find focus to make an **argument** about an issue in their writing.

Read the passage below. Notice how Karen English's characters don't say much about the Phantom Poet's identity.

An excerpt from
The Case of the Phantom Poet

The characters in the play briefly state their theories, but they don't focus on them enough to help us see why they believe those theories. We aren't convinced that Carlos is right because he hasn't shown us any details that prove he's right.

Carlos: The poet's Mr. Tolliver.

All: Mr. Tolliver!

Carlos: Think about it. He's always giving us pep talks and little lessons at every opportunity.

Rhonda: But poems? How are we going to find out for sure?

The Case of the Phantom Poet
a play by Karen English
illustrated by Nicole Tadgell

Read and Find

Read Tiffany's writing below. How did she find a focus to try to convince you to agree with her? Use the Writer's Checklist to help you.

My Secret Energy Source

by Tiffany W.

Junk food and sugary stuff are not helpful when I'm low on energy. I try to have a healthful snack, such as fruit or protein, in the afternoon, especially before a sports activity. This is the kind of boost I need for the long-lasting endurance to get me through a game. Sugary stuff gives me quick energy and then lets me down quickly, too.

Read about how to get quick energy.

Writer's Checklist

 Does the writer write a lot about one argument?

 Does the writer include convincing evidence because she goes into depth about her argument?

 Can you imagine an experience the writer had that influenced her opinion?

✔ Review

Author's Purpose
Main Idea and Details
Sequence
Synonyms
Charts

DON'T TELL MY MUMMY
A DETECTIVE STORY

I got the call at midnight. My name is Eddie Grimes, and I solve crimes.

At the crime scene, the museum, I saw Sergeant Tommy Drake of the Police Department.

Drake said, "The Isis Ruby has been stolen. It's a rare gem from a London museum. This place was locked with guards on every door. Nobody could get in or out."

"You're wrong, Tommy," I said. "Nobody was **supposed** to get in or out, but someone did. Hey, this coffin looks interesting." Suddenly, I heard footsteps.

"Hey! That's a priceless ancient artifact. I'm Dr. Donald Bloom, Head of the City Museum," said the guy who had just entered.

Drake said, "This is Eddie Grimes, a private investigator."

"Sorry, no one opens that sarcophagus except to clean it. The paintings inside must not be exposed to the light. Their green pigment is already flaking."

"So this coffin is part of the same collection as the ruby?" I asked.

"Yes. We just got it back from the restoration department, and I haven't even seen the inside of it yet."

"Who does the restoring?" I asked.

"Dr. Peterson. Her office is across the street."

At the restoration department, I called out, "Hello, anybody home?"

"Back here," Dr. Peterson shouted.

"My name is Eddie Grimes, private investigator. What do you know about the disappearance of the Isis Ruby?" I inquired.

"I know that its value is beyond measure. But I don't know how the thief did it," she said.

I strolled around the place. There were books on mummies, and jewels, and magic tricks. Magic tricks?

A pair of old boots with flecks of green paint sat under the desk. That was strange. But even stranger—they were men's boots. Then, in the middle of a work bench, I spotted the largest ruby I had ever seen.

"The Isis Ruby!" Drake exclaimed.

"No, just a copy," said Dr. Peterson. "I'm going to replace the real ruby until it's found. If you'll excuse me, I really have a lot to do before the exhibit opens."

I replied, "Don't let me keep you."

I went back to my office. I thought about what Dr. Bloom had said when I was messing with his creaky old coffin. Then it hit me. . . !

I called Drake and told him to round up the doctors and meet me at the museum.

"What's the meaning of this?" grumbled Dr. Bloom. "I was sleeping soundly."

"You'll have plenty of time to sleep in prison, Dr. Bloom," I snapped. "You stole the Isis Ruby."

"This is outrageous. Where's your proof?" he snarled.

"Here's my proof," I said. "This Egyptian sarcophagus has a false back wall."

"That's a lie," yelled Dr. Peterson.

"I knew she did it!" blustered Dr. Bloom.

"Not so fast, Dr. Bloom! You said you hadn't seen the inside of the sarcophagus yet, but you told me that the paintings were flaking. How would you know unless you had seen inside? You snuck the ruby out of the museum inside this coffin when it went for restoration. Those size thirteen boots under her desk aren't Dr. Peterson's. They're yours!"

"Drake, stop Dr. Peterson!" I warned. "That ruby isn't glass—it's the real thing!"

It was just another night in the big city. I'm Eddie Grimes, and I solve crimes.

The Pulitzer Prize

Among the many well-known writing contests and competitions, one of the most prestigious awards is the Pulitzer Prize. Awarded every year, the prize is given to writers who show exceptional skill in their field, from journalism to music, drama, and literature.

The Pulitzer is named after Joseph Pulitzer, who was born in Hungary in 1847 and immigrated to the United States in 1864, during the American Civil War. After his service in the army, he made his way to St. Louis. His entrance into the field of journalism came by chance, when he was observing a chess game in St. Louis's Mercantile Library. As the story goes, he made a comment on one of the player's moves and the player, impressed by his observation, started up a conversation. It turned out that the players were editors for a daily newspaper. They offered Joseph a position at the newspaper, and so began his lifetime career in journalism.

After many years as a journalist, Joseph Pulitzer went on to become a publisher of the *St. Louis Post-Dispatch* and the *New York World*, which was known for its popular appeal. Joseph believed that the press should be of service to the public, and set himself as a journalist for the common man. He pledged to "expose all fraud and sham, fight all public evils and abuses" and to "battle for the people with earnest sincerity." In pursuit of this, he wanted to encourage and improve the education and training of journalists.

Joseph Pulitzer

Joseph died in 1911. In his will, he endowed $2 million toward prizes and scholarships for journalists, writing, "I am deeply interested in the progress and elevation of journalism, having spent my life in that profession, regarding it as a noble profession and one of unequaled importance for its influence upon the minds and morals of the people."

One year after his death, Columbia University established the School of Journalism in his honor. In 1917, the first Pulitzer Prizes were awarded in the categories of reporting, editorial writing, history, and biography. Today there are over 20 categories of awards, including prizes in journalism in the public service, reporting, and cartooning, as well as fiction and nonfiction writing, poetry, and music.

The award process is intensive. Each year, thousands of entries for the award are submitted to a team of judges for review. The judges make three nominations for each category. These nominations are reviewed by a board of members, which oversees the final awards. For each category, the board takes a vote, and the nomination that receives the majority of the vote is awarded the prize.

It is an honor and distinction to receive a Pulitzer Prize. The award continues Joseph Pulitzer's legacy of the promotion and recognition of outstanding works in journalism and literature.

Some Recipients of the Pulitzer Prize

Year	Recipient	Work
1931	Robert Frost	Collected Poems
1944	Richard Rodgers and Oscar Hammerstein II	Oklahoma
1950	Gwendolyn Brooks	Annie Allen
1951	Carl Sandburg	Complete Poems
1953	Ernest Hemingway	The Old Man and the Sea
1957	John F. Kennedy	Profiles in Courage
1961	Harper Lee	To Kill a Mockingbird
1978	E.B. White	Full Body of Work
1983	Alice Walker	The Color Purple

CA Critical Thinking

Now answer numbers 1 through 4. Base your answers on the passage "Don't Tell My Mummy."

1. **Read this sentence from the passage.**

> "Sorry, no one opens that <u>sarcophagus</u> except to clean it.'

A synonym for *sarcophagus* in the passage is:

A restoration

B investigator

C coffin

D pigment

2. **How was the Isis Ruby smuggled out of the museum?**

A in Dr. Peterson's pocket

B in Dr. Bloom's boots

C in a false compartment at the back of the sarcophagus

D in Dr. Peterson's workbench

3. **To whom do the boots in Dr. Peterson's office belong?**

A Dr. Peterson

B Dr. Bloom

C Eddie Grimes

D Isis

4. **In what sequence did Eddie Grimes recognize the clues that helped him find the culprits in the crime?**

Use details from the story and sequence words to support your answer.

Now answer numbers 1 through 4. Base your answers on the article "The Pulitzer Prize."

1. **The author probably wrote this passage because he wanted to**

    A   entertain people.

    B   give information about the Pulitzer Prize and its founder.

    C   tell people how to apply for the Pulitzer Prize.

    D   persuade people to vote for the Pulitzer Prize.

2. **Who decides the final recipient of the Pulitzer Prize?**

    A   a board of members

    B   Joseph Pulitzer

    C   popular vote

    D   publishers

3. **This article is *mainly* about**

    A   the American Civil War.

    B   a journalist and publisher who established a famous prize.

    C   growing up in Hungary.

    D   winning a prize.

4. **There was a period of 20 years between the awarding of the Pulitzer Prize to two poets.**

    Use the information on the chart to help answer this question.

    Who were the two poets?

    A   Gwendolyn Brooks and Carl Sandburg

    B   Robert Frost and Harper Lee

    C   Carl Sandburg and Harper Lee

    D   Robert Frost and Carl Sandburg

Write on Demand

PROMPT Think of what it would be like to be starting out as a journalist. Write a paragraph about who would be your first subject to interview and why you chose that person. Write 10 questions you would ask that person. Write for 8 minutes. Write as much as you can as well as you can.

The Big Question

How did people live long ago?

Theme Launcher Video

LOG ON ▶ Find out more about how people lived in the past at **www.macmillanmh.com**.

125

The Big Question

How did people live long ago?

Ancient civilizations fascinate us because the ways people lived a long time ago help us to understand our lives today. We ask ourselves such questions as: What happened to these people? How did they live? Why did they disappear? Studying artifacts and objects from older civilizations illuminates our own lives because of the similarities and differences between people then and people now.

Because of this ongoing interest historians and archaeologists continue to make discoveries that give us a greater understanding of the past.

Research Activities

Throughout the unit, you will be gathering information about different cultures of the past. Choose one culture to focus your research on and write a booklet about how people in that culture lived long ago.

Keep Track of Ideas

As you read, keep track of all you are learning about cultures of the past. Use the Accordion Book organizer to do this. On the top section, write the unit theme: Ancient Civilizations. On each layer, write facts you learn each week that will help you in your research and your understanding of the unit theme.

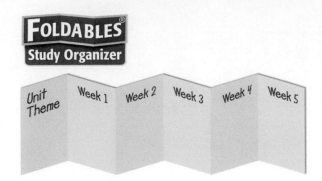

FOLDABLES®
Study Organizer

Unit Theme | Week 1 | Week 2 | Week 3 | Week 4 | Week 5

Research Toolkit

Conduct Your Unit 2 Research Online with:

Research Roadmap
Follow step-by-step guide to complete your research project.

Online Resources
• Topic Finder and other Research Tools
• Videos and Virtual Fieldtrips
• Photos and Drawings for Presentations
• Related Articles and Web Resources

California Web Site Links

 Go to **www.macmillanmh.com** for more information.

California People

Mark Hylkema, California State Parks Archaeologist

Mark Hylkema studies, teaches, and writes about the history of Native American settlements along the coast of California.

127

DISCOVERY IN CHINA

CA **Talk About It**

Why do you think this Great
Wall of China was built?

LOG
ON ▶ Find out more about
China at
www.macmillanmh.com.

by Sam Ames

An archaeologist is a kind of science detective. By studying objects from the past, an archaeologist can find clues about what life was like long ago.

An archaeologist can learn about the food people ate and the **utensils** they used to eat with. An archaeologist can learn from the weapons, art, and tools a people left behind. These objects help archaeologists figure out what a group's customs and beliefs were and if they were **superstitious**, holding unreasonable fears. They can help an archaeologist determine the **civilized**, or advanced group, versus the primitive.

Gathering Information

Archaeologists **excavate** in places where long-ago people once lived. Digging to uncover these places is exacting work. First, the scientists take surveys and make maps of the site. They dig long trenches around tombs or buildings. They try not to disturb any evidence buried in the earth.

Archaeologists work carefully and **steadfastly** for long hours to recover small objects. With patient determination, they often use paintbrushes to clean dirt off pieces of pottery or other delicate things. As an item

An archaeologist dusts off his discovery.

PAST TO THE PRESENT

is uncovered, the archaeologists photograph it and describe it. Sometimes objects can be **restored** to their original beauty.

Understanding the Findings

Archaeologists follow several steps to learn from what they find. First, they sort the items and look for patterns. Then they determine how old something is, a process known as dating. Scientists also want to know how old something is in relation to other things. Did a certain object **precede** others that were found, or did it come after?

Finally, archaeologists try to answer these questions: How did this culture develop? When and why did it change?

A Big Job

Work at a dig takes many years. One reason is that most archaeologists have jobs in museums or as teachers. Bad weather can also **prolong** the time it takes to excavate. Then, too, some archaeological sites are underwater or beneath existing cities.

Archaeologists have a big job in bringing the past to the present!

Reread for **Comprehension**

Monitor Comprehension

Summarize

One way to monitor your understanding of a selection is to summarize events in a selection. As you summarize, look for major points and for the details that support them. Always use your own words.

Use the Summary Chart as you reread "Bringing the Past to the Present."

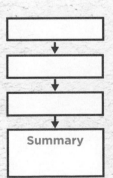

Summary

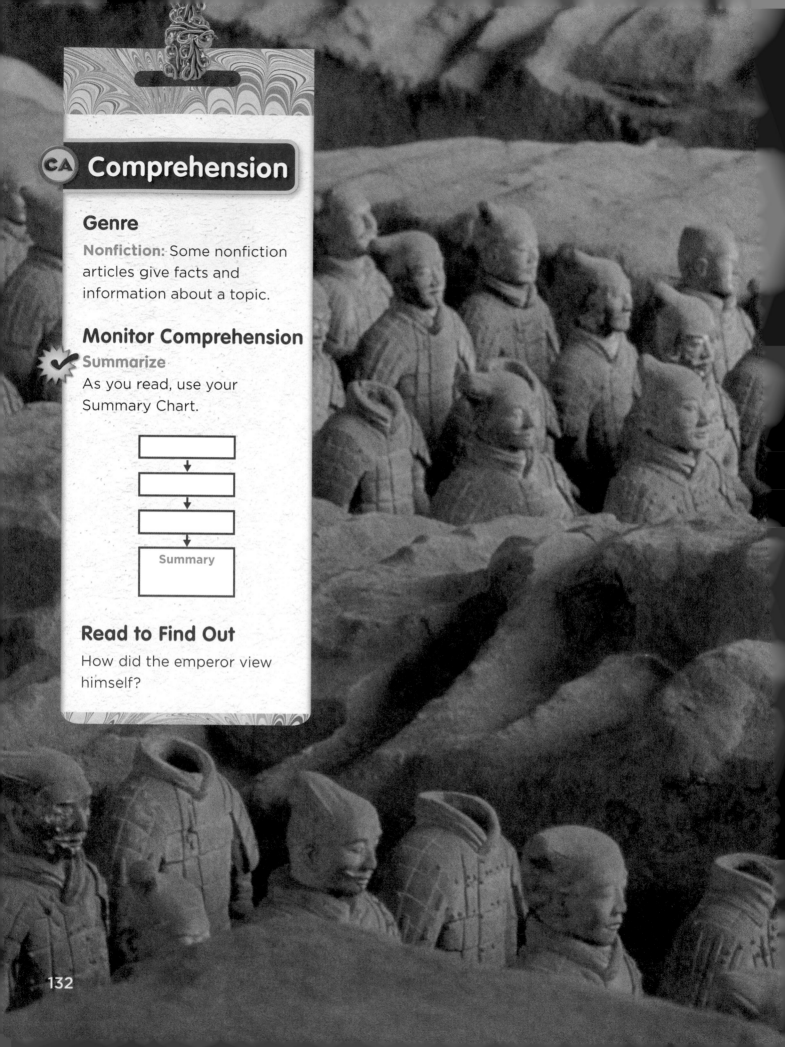

CA Comprehension

Genre

Nonfiction: Some nonfiction articles give facts and information about a topic.

Monitor Comprehension

Summarize

As you read, use your Summary Chart.

Summary

Read to Find Out

How did the emperor view himself?

THE EMPEROR'S SILENT ARMY

TERRACOTTA WARRIORS *of* ANCIENT CHINA

BY JANE O'CONNOR

A Strange Discovery

Lintong County, People's Republic of China, March 1974

It's just an ordinary day in early spring, or so three farmers think as they trudge across a field in northern China. They are looking for a good place to dig a well. There has been a drought, and they must find water or risk losing their crops later in the year.

The farmers choose a spot near a grove of persimmon trees. Down they dig, five feet, ten feet. Still no water. They decide to keep on digging a little deeper. All of a sudden, one of the farmers feels his shovel strike against something hard. Is it a rock? It's difficult to see at the bottom of the dark hole, so the farmer kneels down for a closer look. No, it isn't a rock. It seems to be clay, and not raw clay but clay that has been baked and made into something. But what?

The terracotta army was discovered when well-diggers found the head of a "pottery man" like this one. No photographs were taken that day.

A buried army of terracotta soldiers was found in the countryside of northern China.

Now, more carefully, the men dig around the something. Perhaps it is a pot or a vase. However, what slowly reveals itself is the pottery head of a man who stares back at them, open-eyed and amazingly real looking. The farmers have never seen anything like it before. But they do remember stories that some of the old people in their village have told, stories of a "pottery man" found many years ago not far from where they are now. The villagers had been scared that the pottery man would bring bad luck so they broke it to bits, which were then reburied and forgotten.

The three well-diggers are not so **superstitious**. They report their discovery to a local official. Soon a group of archeologists arrives to search the area more closely. Maybe they will find pieces of a clay body to go with the clay head.

In fact, they find much more.

These soldiers' hands are clenched as if still holding their bronze weapons.

During the weeks and months that follow, the archeologists dig out more pottery men, which now are called by a more dignified term—terracotta figurines. The figurines are soldiers. That much is clear. But they come from a time long ago, when Chinese warriors wore knee-length robes, armor made from small iron "fish scales," and elaborate topknot hairdos. All of the soldiers are life-size or a little bigger and weigh as much as four hundred pounds. They stand at attention as if waiting for the command to charge into battle. The only thing missing is their weapons. And those are found too—hundreds of real bronze swords, daggers, and battle-axes as well as thousands of scattered arrowheads—all so perfectly made that, after cleaning, their ancient tips are still sharp enough to split a hair!

Summarize
What three important details would you include in a summary of this paragraph?

Today, after years of work, terracotta soldiers are still being uncovered and **restored**. What the well-diggers stumbled upon, purely by accident, has turned out to be among the largest and most incredible archeological discoveries of modern times. Along with the Great Pyramids in Egypt, the buried army is now considered one of the true wonders of the ancient world. Spread out over several acres near the city of Xian, the soldiers number not in tens or hundreds but in the thousands! Probably 7,500 total. Until 1974, nobody knew that right below the people of northern China an enormous underground army has been standing guard, silently and watchfully, for more than 2,200 years. Who put them there?

One man.

Known as the fierce tiger of Qin, the divine Son of Heaven, he was the first emperor of China.

The Quest for Immortality

Before the time of Qin Shihuang (pronounced chin shir-hwong), who lived from 259 to 210 B.C., there was no China. Instead, there were seven separate kingdoms, each with its own language, currency, and ruler. For hundreds of years they had been fighting one another. The kingdom of Qin was the fiercest; soldiers received their pay only after they had presented their generals with the cut-off heads of enemy warriors. By 221 B.C. the ruler of the Qin kingdom had "eaten up his neighbors like a silkworm devouring a leaf," according to an ancient historian. The name China comes from Qin.

The map shows the Qin kingdom in brown and the Qin empire in stripes. The dot indicates where the terracotta army was found.

The king of Qin now ruled over an immense empire—around one million square miles that stretched north and west to the Gobi desert, south to present-day Vietnam, and east to the Yellow Sea. To the people of the time, this was the entire **civilized** world. Not for another hundred years would the Chinese know that empires existed beyond their boundaries. To the ruler of Qin, being called king was no longer grand enough. He wanted a title that no one else had ever had before. What he chose was Qin Shihuang. This means "first emperor, God in Heaven, and Almighty of the Universe" all rolled into one.

But no title, however superhuman it sounded, could protect him from what he feared most—dying. More than anything, the emperor wanted to live forever. According to legend, a magic elixir had granted eternal life to the people of the mythical Eastern Islands. Over the years, the emperor sent expeditions out to sea in search of the islands and the magic potion. But each time they came back empty-handed.

This painting from the seventeenth century shows the first emperor carried on a covered litter called a palanquin.

If he couldn't live forever, then Qin Shihuang was determined to live as long as possible. He ate powdered jade and drank mercury in the belief that they would **prolong** his life. In fact, these "medicines" were poison and may have caused the emperor to fall sick and die while on a tour of the easternmost outposts of his empire. He was forty-nine years old.

Summarize
Summarize what you know about Qin Shihuang so far. What details did you include?

For thousands of years, the Chinese have made silk fabric. This detail of a silk robe shows an embroidered dragon, the symbol of Chinese emperors.

If word of Qin Shihuang's death got out while he was away from the capital there might be a revolt. So his ministers kept the news a secret. With the emperor's body inside his chariot, the entire party traveled back to the capital city. Meals were brought into the emperor's chariot; daily reports on affairs of state were delivered as usual—all to keep up the appearance that the emperor was alive and well. However, it was summer, and a terrible smell began to come from the chariot. But the clever ministers found a way to account for the stench. A cart was loaded with smelly salted fish and made to **precede** the chariot, overpowering and masking any foul odors coming from the dead emperor. And so Qin Shihuang returned to the capital for burial.

The tomb of Qin Shihuang had been under construction for more than thirty years. It was begun when he was a young boy of thirteen and was still not finished when he died. Even incomplete, the emperor's tomb was enormous, larger than his largest palace. According to legend, it had a domed ceiling inlaid with clusters of pearls to represent the sun, moon, and stars. Below was a gigantic relief map of the world, made from bronze. Bronze hills and mountains rose up from the floor, with rivers of mercury flowing into a mercury sea. Along the banks of the rivers were models of the emperor's palaces and cities, all exact replicas of the real ones.

In ancient times, the Chinese believed that life after death was not so very different from life on earth. The soul of a dead person could continue to enjoy all the pleasures of everyday life. So people who were rich enough constructed elaborate underground tombs filled with silk robes, jewelry with precious stones, furniture, games, boats, chariots—everything the dead person could possibly need or want.

Qin Shihuang knew that grave robbers would try their best to loot the treasures in his tomb. So he had machines put inside the tomb that produced the rumble of thunder to scare off intruders, and mechanical crossbows at the entrance were set to fire arrows automatically should anyone dare trespass. The emperor also made certain that the workers who carried his coffin in to its final resting place never revealed its exact whereabouts. As the men worked their way back through the tunnels to the tomb's entrance, a stone door came crashing down, and they were left to die, sealed inside the tomb along with the body of the emperor.

Even all these measures, however, were not enough to satisfy the emperor. And so, less than a mile from the tomb, in underground trenches, the terracotta warriors were stationed. Just as flesh-and-blood troops had protected him during his lifetime, the terracotta troops were there to protect their ruler against any enemy for all eternity.

Beautiful silk robes, like this one from the nineteenth century, would be placed in the tomb of an important person to be worn in the afterlife.

Inside the Emperor's Tomb

What exactly is the terracotta army guarding so **steadfastly**? What, besides the body of the dead emperor, is inside the tomb? The answer is that nobody knows. And the government of China has no plans at present to **excavate** and find out.

In ancient China it was the custom to build a natural-looking hill on top of a person's tomb. The more important a person was, the bigger the hill. Thousands of years of harsh weather have worn down the emperor's mound; originally it was four hundred feet high, almost as high as the biggest of the three Great Pyramids in Egypt.

Like the ancient Egyptians, the ancient Chinese believed that the body of a dead person should be preserved as a "home" for the soul. However, the Chinese did not make a person's body into a mummy. They believed that jade had magic powers, among them the ability to keep a dead body from decaying. In Chinese tombs from the first century B.C., bodies of noblemen and princesses have been found wearing entire suits of jade. It is believed that Qin Shihuang is buried

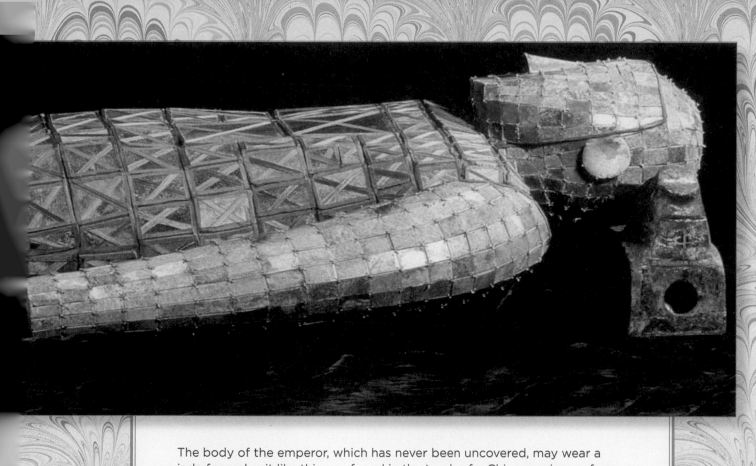

The body of the emperor, which has never been uncovered, may wear a jade funeral suit like this one found in the tomb of a Chinese princess from the late second century.

in just such a suit, the thousands of small tiles all beautifully carved and sewn together with gold thread. And over this jade burial outfit, his body is supposedly covered in a blanket of pearls.

As for all the things placed with the emperor, certainly they must be grand beyond imagining—silk robes embroidered with dragons, gem-encrusted crowns and jewelry, musical instruments, hand-carved furniture, lamps, beautiful dishes, cooking pots, and golden **utensils**. Like the pharaohs of ancient Egypt, the first emperor would have made certain that he had everything he might possibly want in the afterlife. But unless his tomb is excavated, what these treasures look like will remain a mystery.

MEET THE AUTHOR

Jane O'Connor knows a lot about books. She's worked as an editor and a publisher, and has written more than thirty books. Sometimes she writes her books with her husband, her older son, or another author. Jane had lots of research to do for this book. She included many of the amazing details that she found in this story. She also had to help find just the right photographs to make the terracotta warriors come alive in our imaginations.

CA Author's Purpose

How can you tell Jane O'Connor probably admires archaeologists? How may that have affected her purpose for writing? How well did she achieve her purpose?

LOG ON ▶ Find out more about Jane O'Connor at **www.macmillanmh.com**.

CA Critical Thinking

Summarize

Use your Summary Chart to summarize *The Emperor's Silent Army.* What purpose did the silent army serve?

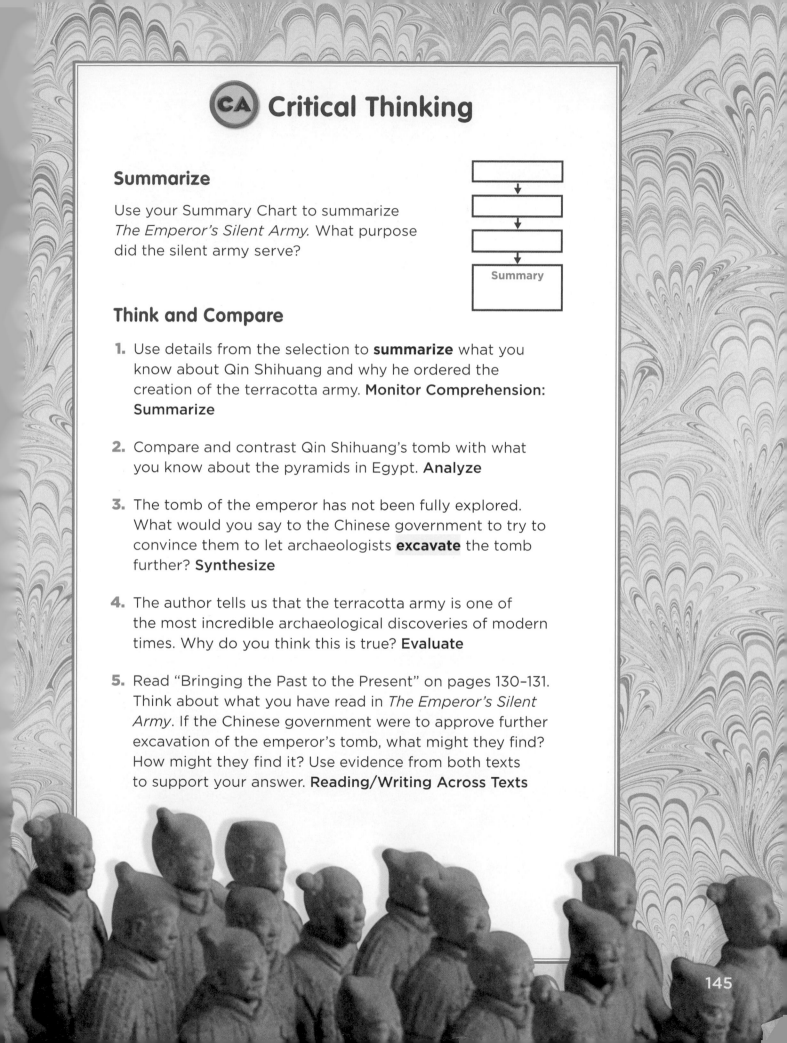

Summary

Think and Compare

1. Use details from the selection to **summarize** what you know about Qin Shihuang and why he ordered the creation of the terracotta army. **Monitor Comprehension: Summarize**

2. Compare and contrast Qin Shihuang's tomb with what you know about the pyramids in Egypt. **Analyze**

3. The tomb of the emperor has not been fully explored. What would you say to the Chinese government to try to convince them to let archaeologists **excavate** the tomb further? **Synthesize**

4. The author tells us that the terracotta army is one of the most incredible archaeological discoveries of modern times. Why do you think this is true? **Evaluate**

5. Read "Bringing the Past to the Present" on pages 130–131. Think about what you have read in *The Emperor's Silent Army*. If the Chinese government were to approve further excavation of the emperor's tomb, what might they find? How might they find it? Use evidence from both texts to support your answer. **Reading/Writing Across Texts**

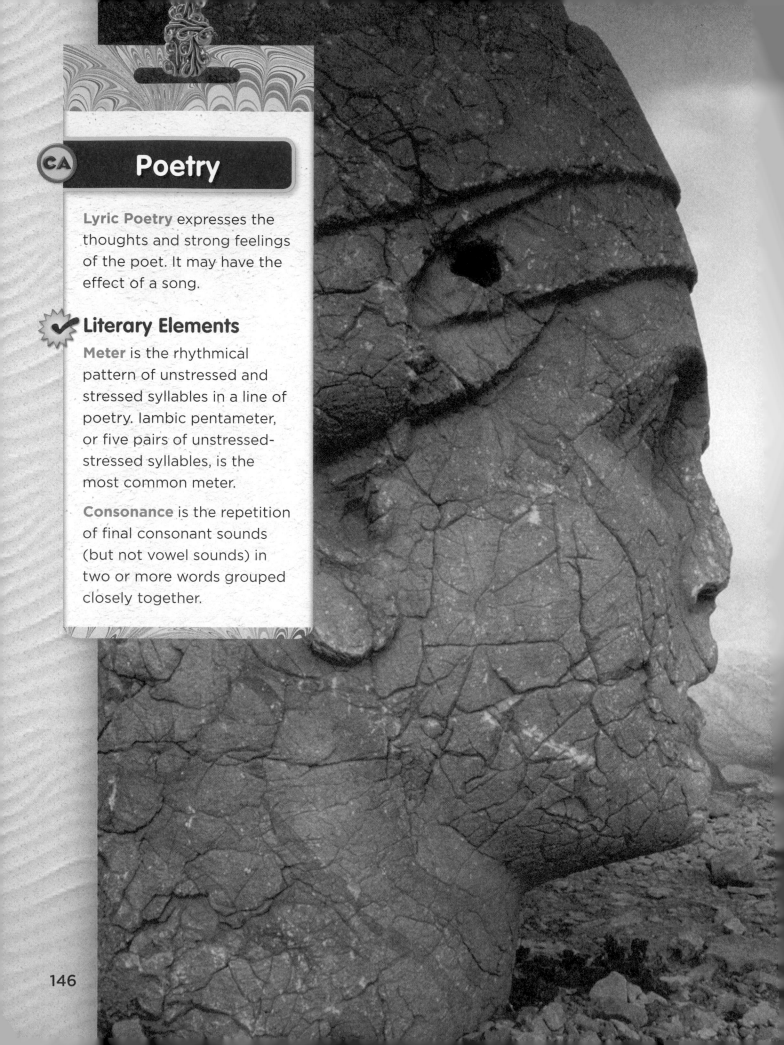

Poetry

Lyric Poetry expresses the thoughts and strong feelings of the poet. It may have the effect of a song.

Literary Elements

Meter is the rhythmical pattern of unstressed and stressed syllables in a line of poetry. Iambic pentameter, or five pairs of unstressed-stressed syllables, is the most common meter.

Consonance is the repetition of final consonant sounds (but not vowel sounds) in two or more words grouped closely together.

OZYMANDIAS

by Percy Bysshe Shelley

I met a traveler from an antique land
Who said: Two vast and trunkless legs of stone
Stand in the desert. . . . Near them, on the sand,
Half sunk, a shattered visage lies, whose frown,
And wrinkled lip, and sneer of cold command,
Tell that its sculptor well those passions read
Which yet survive, stamped on these lifeless things,
The hand that mocked them, and the heart that fed:
And on the pedestal these words appear:
"My name is Ozymandias, king of kings:
Look on my works, ye Mighty, and despair!"
Nothing beside remains. Round the decay
Of that colossal wreck, boundless and bare
The lone and level sands stretch far away.

> **The meter is iambic pentameter.**

> **The words "cold command" end in *d*, an example of consonance.**

CA Critical Thinking

1. What strong feelings can be found in the poem? How does the meter of the poem support the poem's meaning? **Meter**

2. Was King Ozymandias a just, kind ruler or a harsh tyrant? Use words and phrases from the poem to support your opinion. **Analyze**

3. Think about *The Emperor's Silent Army* and "Ozymandias." How are the emperor and King Ozymandias similar? **Reading/Writing Across Texts**

 Find out more about poetry at **www.macmillanmh.com**.

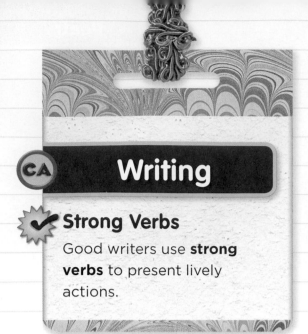
Reading and Writing Connection

Read the passage below. Notice how author Jane O'Connor uses strong verbs in her article.

An excerpt from
The Emperor's Silent Army

The author helps us "see" the action in certain parts of her article. Wherever she uses a strong verb, we are able to picture that moment a little more clearly.

So he had machines put inside the tomb that produced the rumble of thunder to scare off intruders, and mechanical crossbows at the entrance were set to fire arrows automatically should anyone dare trespass. The emperor also made certain that the workers who carried his coffin to its final resting place never revealed its exact whereabouts. As the men worked their way back through the tunnels to the tomb's entrance, a stone door came crashing down, and they were left to die, sealed inside the tomb along with the body of the emperor.

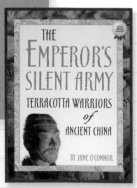

THE EMPEROR'S SILENT ARMY
TERRACOTTA WARRIORS of ANCIENT CHINA
BY JANE O'CONNOR

Read and Find

Read Trevor's writing below. What kind of verbs did he use to help you imagine the moment? Use the Writer's Checklist to help you.

Read about how Trevor launched hot air balloons.

Hot Air Balloons

by Trevor B.

After a week of preparation, we were ready to launch our hot air balloons! While Jocelyn steadied the stovepipe in her gloved hands, I positioned the mouth of the balloon over the jet of hot air. The crinkly balloon quickly bulged out and silently strained to be released. I let go and it floated up into the sky. The brightly colored tissue paper seemed to glow in the sunlight.

Writer's Checklist

 Does the writer choose verbs that describe specific actions?

 Are there verbs you can "feel" as well as "see"?

 Is there a verb that is used in an interesting or unusual way?

Ancient Greece

CA Talk About It

What do you think it was like to live in ancient Greece?

LOG ON ▶ Find out more about ancient Greece at www.macmillanmh.com.

151

★ **Vocabulary**

foundation	promoted
reliable	restricted
maintain	regions
feature	principal

✓ **Homophones**

Homophones are words that sound alike but have different spellings and meanings. *Principal* and *principle* are homophones.

Plato and Aristotle

The word *philosophy* comes from the Greek word *philosophia*, which means "love of wisdom." Greek thinkers who believed humans could understand everything about the world and our place in it were called philosophers. Among the greatest of the ancient Greek philosophers were two men named Plato and Aristotle. These two men laid the **foundation**, or the beginnings, for the way Europeans and Americans would one day think about government.

Plato's work *The Republic* explains his ideas about government. He decided that democracy was not a good system of government, based on his life in Athens. Plato did not think rule by the people was **reliable** or trustworthy. He felt it did not produce sensible or fair policies. In his ideal government, Plato divided people into three basic groups. At the top were philosopher-kings, who ruled using wisdom. Warriors made up the second group, and were meant to **maintain** the state against enemies. The third group included the rest of the people, who produced the state's food, clothing, and shelter.

Plato believed that men and women should have an opportunity to get the same education. This was one **feature**, or part, of his idea that was revolutionary for the time. Although Plato worked for and **promoted** the suggestion that education should be required, schooling was expensive. Not every family could afford it. Plato also felt that women should not be **restricted** to getting married and making a home. Men and women should be free to pursue, or seek, the same jobs.

Plato opened a school in Athens called the Academy around 388 B.C. One of his best students was a young man named Aristotle. Like Plato, Aristotle also wrote about government. He studied many different kinds of governments in **regions** of Egypt, Mesopotamia, and in the Greek city-states. Aristotle noticed that governments run by a few people were usually run by the rich. Democracies were often run by the poor. Aristotle thought that the best government should involve both the rich and the poor. This important, **principal** idea of Aristotle's was an inspiration to the founders of the United States and the writers of its Constitution.

Reread for Comprehension

Evaluate

Main Idea and Details

The main idea is the most important point of a paragraph or section. Details give information that supports the main idea. Understanding the main idea and the details that support the main idea will help you to better evaluate what you read. A Main Idea and Details Chart can help you evaluate what you've read. Reread the selection to find the main idea and supporting details.

Main Idea _____

Detail 1 _____

Detail 2 _____

Summary _____

DAILY LIFE IN ANCIENT GREECE

by Stewart Ross

illustrated by Adam Hook

154

INTRODUCTION: WHO WERE THE ANCIENT GREEKS?

THE ANCIENT GREEKS WERE A remarkable people who helped lay the **foundation** of our civilization. They lived in what is now Greece, on the surrounding Mediterranean islands, and on the neighboring coast of Asia Minor.

Ancient Greek civilization began on the island of Crete in about 2000 B.C. Spreading to the mainland, it reached its height during the Classical Period (480–330 B.C.). It lost political independence in about 150 B.C. to the Roman empire but played a major role in shaping Roman life.

The ancient Greeks lived in small, independent city-states. Each one consisted of a city and its surrounding farmland. The most powerful city-states were Attica (Athens) and Laconia (Sparta), a tough soldier-state. The Athenians were rich traders whose influence extended across the Mediterranean Sea. Their city was also a center for the arts and learning. It was home to some of the finest thinkers, writers, and artists the world has ever seen. The Athenians wrote and performed the first plays and developed the idea of democratic government. It is largely because of them that we remember the ancient Greeks today.

At Home

Greek homes ranged from small, poorly built homes to neat town houses and elegant villas. Beds, couches, chairs, and a range of storage chests were common furniture. Only the bigger houses had kitchens. Most Greeks did their cooking outside.

In Athens, the walls of ordinary houses were so thin that robbers broke in by digging through them. Most city homes were one story, made of mud bricks, and had three rooms: a bedroom, a living room, and a storeroom. Bigger homes had a second story, approached by a wooden staircase from the outside. The flat roofs served as outdoor bedrooms during the hot summer months. Fancier homes had more rooms, including a kitchen and bathroom, and were sometimes built around a courtyard with a pool and gardens.

> The whole town should not be laid out in straight lines, but only certain quarters or regions; thus security will be combined with beauty.
>
> **—ARISTOTLE, POLITICS**

The columns that remain of a fine house on the island of Delos marked the edge of an inner courtyard.

Lysias's remark touches on an interesting **feature** of traditional Athenian society: the separation of men and women. In the wealthier homes, women lived upstairs, in the *gynaikeia*, and the men lived downstairs. Women ran the household and did indoor activities such as weaving. They were not expected to take jobs and had to be accompanied by **reliable** male slaves or members of the family if they went out.

Historians believe women in other city-states were not as **restricted** as the Athenians. Spartan women had much greater freedom, and in the countryside, wives and daughters helped men around the farm.

> I must tell you, sirs . . . my dwelling is on two floors, the upper being equal in space to the lower, with the women's quarters above and the men's below.
> —**Lysias, On the Murder of Eratosthenes**

Athenian women spent much of their time on indoor activities such as weaving cloth.

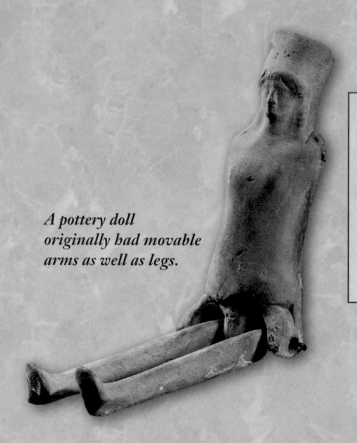

A pottery doll originally had movable arms as well as legs.

[W]e are not speaking of education in this narrower sense, but other education in virtue from youth upwards, which makes a man eagerly pursue the ideal perfection of citizenship, and teaches him how rightly to rule and how to obey.

—**PLATO, LAWS**

Fun and Games

The Greeks certainly knew how to enjoy themselves. Children, especially boys, had all kinds of toys. These ranged from hoops and marbles to wheeled carts. Dolls were made of wood, clay, or cloth. Children also played with knucklebones that were thrown into the air and caught in a game of chance, like jacks.

Serious-minded Greeks, such as the philosopher Plato, did not think that playing for amusement was good enough. He wanted all games to teach children something. Music, for example, taught harmony and balance, and sports developed a boy's body so that as an adult he would make a good hunter or soldier.

Main Idea and Details
What is the main idea of the second paragraph on this page? Is the idea stated or unstated?

When they grew up, Greeks continued to enjoy sports. Indeed, one of their greatest accomplishments was the idea of an international sports meeting. The most famous, held every four years from 776 B.C., is the Olympic Games. After a gap of more than 1,500 years, they were restarted in 1896 and are still held today.

Oionos' sprinting made him a hero, which is why the poet Pindar remembered him. Running was by no means the only event at a sports meeting. These meetings also included, among other activities, horse and chariot racing, wrestling, boxing, long-distance running, the long jump, and discus and javelin throwing. Separate games were held for women.

> In the foot-race the best was Oionos, Likymnios's son, who ran a straight stretch on his feet.
>
> —**PINDAR, ODES, OLYMPIAN X**

The Greeks did not organize games just for enjoyment. Sports kept them fit, but more importantly, they were also a way of honoring a deity. The games were therefore a religious festival as well as a sporting festival. The Olympic Games, for instance, were held in honor of Zeus, the king of the gods.

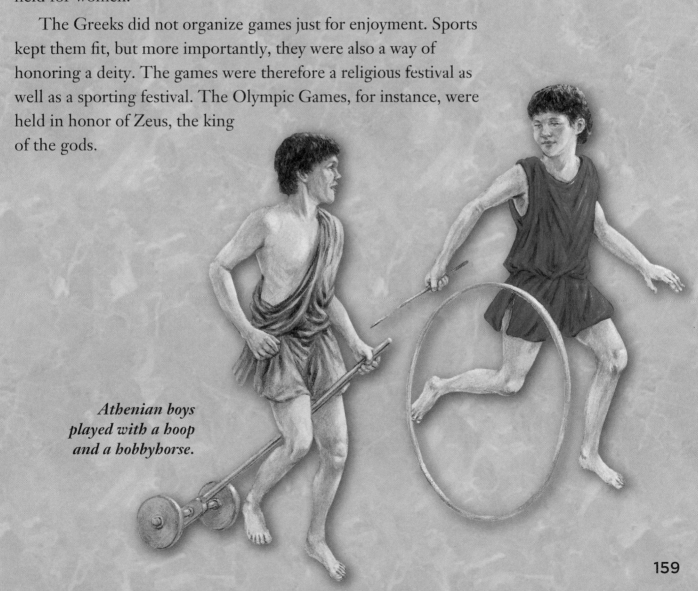

Athenian boys played with a hoop and a hobbyhorse.

Education and Training

Education was mostly for male citizens. There were exceptions, though. Some slaves learned enough to become doctors, and a few Athenian women were able to hold their own in intellectual discussions. Furthermore, there was a vast difference between the education system of Athens and that of its rival Sparta.

Plato **promoted** the idea that education was valuable and should be required. In Athens, however, there was no guarantee that a citizen would be well-educated. All depended on the parents, who had to pay for schooling.

The philosopher Plato helped lay the foundations of Western thought.

[S]ee whether you think that any man who has knowledge ever would wish to have the choice of saying or doing more than another man who has knowledge.

—PLATO, THE REPUBLIC

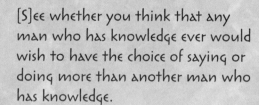

Boys started school at about age 7, going off each day to the house of their schoolmaster, where the lessons were given. The main subjects were reading, writing, and music. Memorization was an important part of lessons, and pupils were whipped for doing poorly. Games took place after school. Getting out onto the sports field at the end of the day must have been quite a relief.

Spartan education was much different from the education of other city-states. Its purpose was to **maintain** a powerful citizen army. Boys, taken from their families at the age of 7, were raised by the government. They had their heads shaved, slept in dormitories, and had only one item of clothing.

> Reading and writing they gave them [Spartan boys], just enough to see their turn; their chief care was to . . . teach them to endure pain and conquer in battle.
>
> —PLUTARCH, LIFE OF LYCURGUS

An Athenian student, seated in class, wrote on a wax and wooden tablet.

Farmers, Traders, and Craftsmen

The Greeks believed that everyone had a particular place in society. At the top were the citizens, descended from the families that had set up the city-states. Then came non-Greek resident traders and merchants, known as *metics*. The lowest-ranking group were the slaves. In some states, particularly Sparta, there was a fourth group, known as *helots*. These were native farmers whom the Greeks looked down on and often mistreated.

> Whoever said that farming is the mother and nurse of all the other arts spoke finely indeed . . . when farming goes well, all the other arts also flourish.
>
> **—Xenophon, Oeconomica**

The Greeks were famous for their cities, but the cities could not have existed without the surrounding farms. The life of the citizen-farmer was a simple and regular round of plowing, sowing, harvesting crops, and tending flocks of sheep and goats. The most important crops were grain for bread, and olives, which were beaten off the trees with sticks when ripe.

Main Idea and Details

What is the main idea of the first paragraph on this page? Is it stated or unstated? What details support it?

A farmer prepares the soil with a wooden plow, pulled by a team of oxen.

Classical Athens was the business heart of the Mediterranean area. The harbors of its port, Piraeus, teemed with ships from far and wide. They came with grain, wood, and rare luxuries such as Oriental silk and African ivory and left with wine, oil, and the city's famous manufactured goods. Much of the trade was with the colonies that the Greeks had established around the Mediterranean.

Athens' crowded streets hummed to the sound of people making things. Carpenters, blacksmiths, armorers, carvers, wheelwrights (wheel makers), coopers (barrel makers), potters, and dozens of other craftsmen worked from dawn to dusk to earn their daily bread.

> [I]f the poor, the common people, and the lower classes do well and increase in number, they will increase the power of the democracy.
>
> **—PSEUDO-XENOPHON, THE CONSTITUTION OF ATHENS**

This fifth-century B.C. vase shows a shoemaker cutting leather for a pair of sandals.

Religion

The Greeks believed in many gods and goddesses. These were not particularly sacred, but more like super-powerful, immortal human beings. The **principal** deities, led by Zeus, king of the gods, were said to live on top of Mount Olympus.

Because the deities were said to have human emotions, dealing with them was tricky. They had to be kept happy with prayers and sacrifices and by holding festivals in their honor. For example, the god Apollo was honored by the Pythian Games, held at Delphi every four years.

Chryses reminded Apollo, a god linked to music, prophesy, and archery, of all the things he has done to please him. The best way to win a god's favor was to make sacrifices. This meant offering the god something valuable.

> Hear me, Silverbow! . . . If I have ever built a temple to thy pleasure, if I have ever burnt for thee fat slices of bulls or of goats, bestow on me this boon.
>
> **—CHRYSES PRAYING TO APOLLO IN HOMER'S ILIAD**

A Greek temple at Segesta, Sicily, was built in the fifth century B.C. It was probably never finished.

Simple sacrifices might be fruit, vegetables, or wine. Sacrificing a living animal, like a sheep, goat, or ox, was thought even more effective. The beast was slaughtered on an altar, usually during a festival, and its flesh roasted. Sacrificers ate some of the meat, leaving the rest for the god.

An oracle was a person through whom a deity foretold the future. The most important oracle was at Delphi, where a priestess answered questions with messages that supposedly came from Apollo. These prophesies were normally worded to have more than one meaning.

A priestess called for a sign from Apollo in the famous oracle at Delphi.

After sending these presents to the Delphians, Croesus a third time consulted the oracle, for having once proved its truthfulness, he wished to make constant use of it.

—HERODOTUS, HISTORIES

EXPLORE HISTORY WITH STEWART ROSS AND ADAM HOOK

Stewart Ross taught at many places in Britain, the United States, the Middle East, and Sri Lanka before he became a full-time writer more than 15 years ago. He has published over 175 titles and is one of the most popular authors in Britain. He lives near Canterbury, England, with his wife and four children. He works in a large hut in his garden and says that his children are excellent critics of his work.

Another book illustrated by Adam Hook: *Roman Auxiliary Cavalryman*

Another book written by Stewart Ross: *Greece in Spectacular Cross Section*

Adam Hook specializes in minutely detailed historical scenes. He studied graphic design and began working as an illustrator in 1983. His work has been featured in publications and exhibitions all over the world.

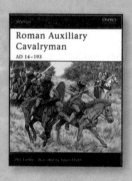

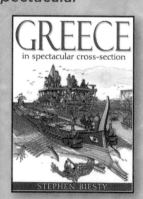

 Author's Purpose

Books about history usually are meant to inform readers. Explain how *Daily Life in Ancient Greece* also entertains its audience.

 Find out more about Stewart Ross and Adam Hook at **www.macmillanmh.com**.

CA Critical Thinking

Summarize

Use your Main Idea and Details Chart to summarize *Daily Life in Ancient Greece*. State the main ideas and the details that support those main ideas.

Main Idea _____
_____
Detail 1 _____
_____
Detail 2 _____
_____

↓

Summary _____
_____
_____
_____

Think and Compare

1. What is the **main idea** of this selection? Use some of the **details** in the text to explain how the author supports the main idea. **Evaluate: Main Idea and Details**

2. How did the ancient Greeks help lay the **foundation** for American and European civilization? Use evidence from the text to support your answer. **Analyze**

3. If you had been born in ancient Greece do you think you would have liked it? Why or why not? Use examples from the selection to reinforce your position. **Synthesize**

4. Describe the importance of sports in Greek life. What did Plato, for instance, believe that games should teach children? **Evaluate**

5. Reread "Plato and Aristotle" on pages 152–153. What important ideas about government were first developed in the Greek city-states, and how did they contribute to the founding of the United States and the writing of its Constitution? **Reading/Writing Across Texts**

THE ODYSSEY OF HOMER

The ancient Greek poet Homer created a long poem about the Trojan War. The war lasted ten years. Then the Greek hero, Odysseus, tried to return to his home, but he had earned the anger of the sea god. Another ten years passed before Odysseus would see his wife and son again. In the excerpt below, he has been released from an island prison after seven years. His raft is caught in a storm sent by the sea god.

He was washed from the raft and deep he sank into the roaring mouth of the storm-tossed sea. His elegant robes were soaked and heavy, dragging him down like clawing fists. With a mighty effort, he forced himself upward and his head emerged from the sea. Spitting water from his throat, he clutched at his raft, brave man. Again and again he tried until he clambered on to it and lay, panting from his efforts.

> Imagery often appeals to the senses. In this case, we can almost feel the heavy robes pulling him down.

The storm continued, tossing his raft like a leaf until a sea goddess saw him. Her heart wept for him. She took the shape of a gull and settled onto his raft, saying, "Unhappy Odysseus! Why does the sea god punish you like this? Take off your heavy robes. See that island yonder? When you reach its shores, you will be safe from the sea god's wrath!"

Then she swept away on her gull-soft wings. But Odysseus did not know what to think. "This could be a trap," he thought. "The sea god would like to drown me as I swim." And while he wondered what to do, wave after towering wave swept over his raft.

At last the raft broke up and Odysseus was forced to cling to one floating beam. He stripped off his storm-soaked robes and pushed off into the raging sea.

The sea god roared with laughter! "Swim away, little man, for I will cause you greater troubles before you reach your home."

Now, Odysseus was always a favorite of the goddess Athena. She saw his difficulties and she raised one reed-slim hand. The winds and waves dropped away at once, and the sea became calm. Odysseus swam

> Figurative language compares two unlike things.

for two days and two nights until at last he sighted land. But then his heart sank. For as he looked, he could see that there was no place for him to land. Stone cliffs rose straight out of the sea and the waves dashed hard against them.

At last he came to a river. Odysseus could taste the fresh water of the river and he prayed to the river god for help. "Save me, oh river king, for I am flying from the sea god's anger."

And the river god heard him and welcomed him. He made the river smooth and so, Odysseus was able at last to set his foot upon the land.

CA Critical Thinking

1. Find an example of imagery. How does the use of imagery add dramatic impact to the story? **Imagery**

2. Odysseus is considered a heroic or legendary figure. What qualities does Odysseus possess that make him both heroic and at the same time human? **Analyze**

3. After reading *Daily Life in Ancient Greece*, why do you think the citizens of Greece might want to hear about the heroic exploits of Odysseus? **Reading/Writing Across Texts**

CA
Writing

✓ **Strong Verbs**

Writers use **strong verbs** to demonstrate action and give readers a picture of events.

Reading and Writing Connection

Read the passage below. Notice how author Stewart Ross uses strong verbs in his article about daily life in ancient Greece.

An excerpt from
Daily Life in Ancient Greece

The author helps us "see" the action at the port, streets, and sacrifice by choosing verbs that put specific pictures in our heads. Some of the verbs might even call forth sounds when you read them.

The harbors of its port, Piraeus, teemed with ships from far and wide . . . . Athens' crowded streets hummed to the sound of people making things. . . . The beast was slaughtered on an altar, usually during a festival, and its flesh roasted.

DAILY LIFE IN ANCIENT GREECE
by Stewart Ross

Read and Find

Read Anthony's writing below. What did he do to help you envision the moment? Use the Writer's Checklist to help you.

Observing the Seed
by Anthony H.

When I first buried my bean seed in its little cup of dirt, I didn't think I'd be interested in it again until it gave me something to eat. But after a few days, my sprout started pushing out of the dirt. Every day it strained upward, shoving aside the dirt around it. I found myself rooting for the tiny sprout as it shouldered its way out of the soil.

Read about how a seed sprouts.

Writer's Checklist

✓ Does the writer choose verbs that show specific actions?

✓ Does the writer use different verbs instead of the same verb over and over?

☑ Find a verb that is used in an unusual way.

Talk About It

Why do you think it has always been important for people to figure out ways to communicate with each other?

Find out more about communication at **www.macmillanmh.com**.

PREHISTORIC TIMES

172

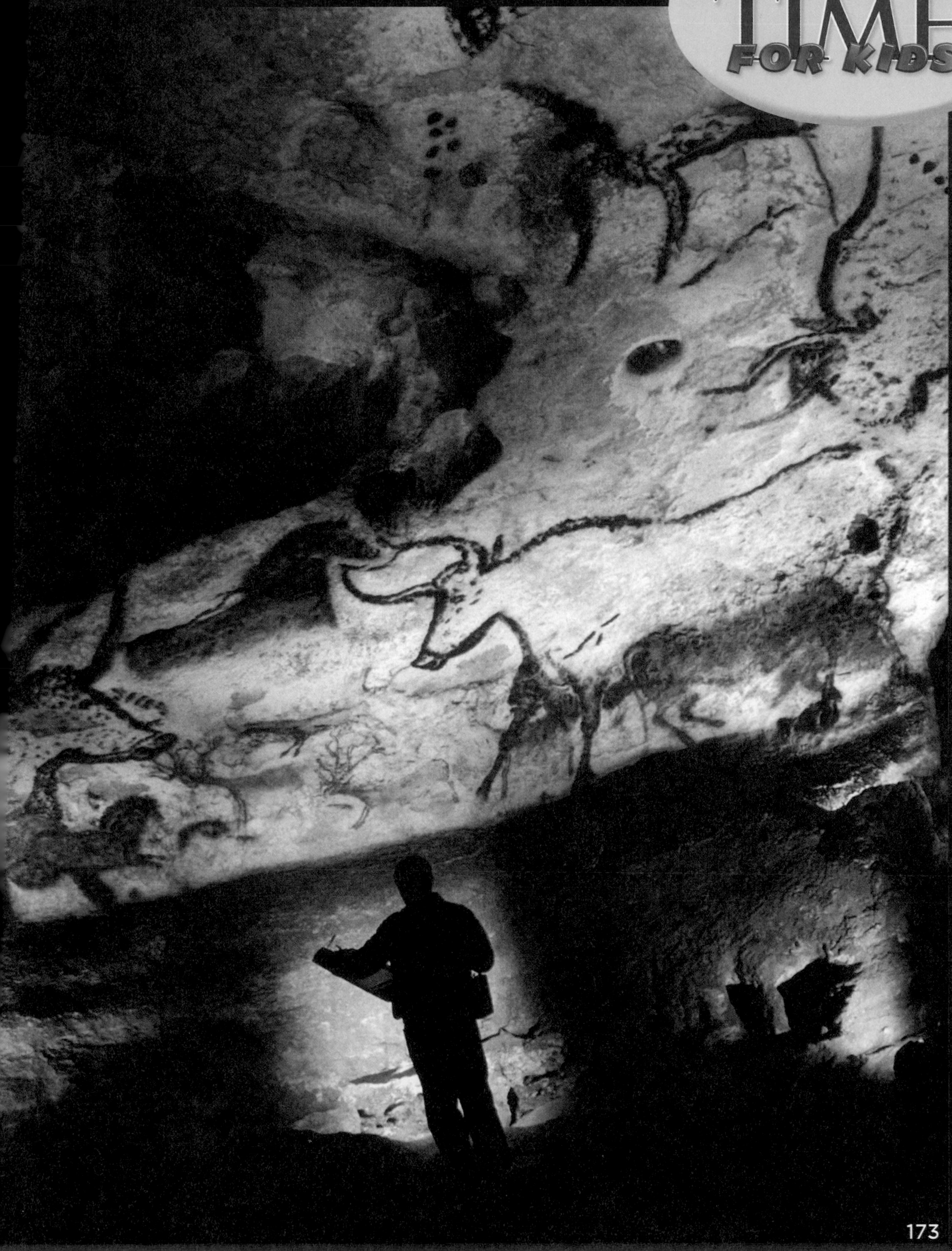

This 2,600-year-old stone cylinder was found in La Venta, Mexico.

AMERICA'S OLDEST WRITTEN WORDS

Scientists made a discovery in southern Mexico. The group's project leader, Mary E. D. Pohl, made the announcement: a 2,600-year-old stone cylinder, carved with symbols that seem to represent words, had been found. Pohl believes the cylinder shows the earliest known system of writing in the Americas. Although some experts doubt this claim, Pohl's report could change history as we know it!

Pohl and her team made the discovery near the city of La Venta. The Olmec lived there from 1300 B.C. to 400 B.C. The Olmec are best known for creating large stone sculptures. They also built massive pyramids and cities and created a formal government long before the Maya.

Anthropologists are scientists who study human beings and their cultures. Before this discovery, they believed that ancient civilizations in what is now Mexico didn't have a writing system until about 300 B.C. That's when the Olmec's neighbors, the Zapotec, began writing. Pohl's findings suggest that the Olmec wrote 300 years earlier.

Olmec traditions were later adopted by other cultures and, **presumably**, they adopted Olmec writing, too. "It makes sense that they would be the first to use a system of writing," says Pohl, who will look for more proof.

UNITED STATES OF AMERICA

MEXICO

Gulf of Mexico

La Venta

PACIFIC OCEAN

Mexico City

Oaxaca

0   500 Miles

SAY IT IN QUECHUA

Quechua (KETCH•wah) is the ancient language of the Inca—the native people of Peru, in South America. About 5 million people in Peru still speak it. You may already know a little Quechua. *Cocoa, lima* (bean), *condor,* and *llama* are Quechua words. Try saying these words and phrases. (See if you can say, "Hello, friend.")

Napaykullayki

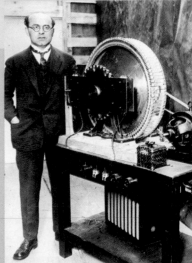

ENGLISH	QUECHUA	HOW YOU SAY IT
Hello	Napaykullayki	(nah•pie•coo•YAH•key)
Friend	Kuchuqmasi	(coo•chew•MAH•see)
Father	Tayta	(TIE•ta)
Mother	Mama	(MAH•mah)
Please	Allichu	(ah•YEE•chew)
Yes	Ari	(ah•REE)
No	Mana	(MAH•nah)
My name is ____.	Noqa kani _____.	(Nee•OH•ha CHA•nee _____)

 Find out more about the Inca at www.macmillanmh.com.

Communication Time Line

In the past two hundred years, we have made **immense** strides in the ways we communicate with each other.

- **1829** Braille, which allows blind people to read, is created.
- **1837** Invention of the telegraph.
- **1876** Invention of the telephone.
- **1893** Thomas Edison opens the first motion-picture studio.
- **1906** The first radio program is broadcast.
- **1928** Television is invented.
- **1972** Electronic mail (later called e-mail) is introduced.

- **1973** First call on a **portable** cell phone is made.
- **1989** The first provider of dial-up Internet access for consumers debuts.
- **2003** Spam, unsolicited e-mail, becomes a server-clogging **nuisance**—and accounts for about half of all e-mails.

An early TV and its inventor, August Karolus, in 1928

175

THESE WALLS CAN TALK

How did the earliest human beings express themselves through art?

If you're looking for archaeological finds that really rock, you can travel to Europe, Africa, and Australia to find some of the earliest examples of the human creative spirit.

EXPLORING EUROPE'S CAVES

In 1994, three people exploring a cliff in southeastern France felt a breeze wafting from a pile of rock and debris. "That was a sign that there was a cave beneath it," recalls Jean-Marie Chauvet. With his companions, Chauvet cleared away an opening, then wriggled through a tunnel into a complex of large caves.

Then, in the pale glow of their headlamps, the explorers noticed two red lines on a cavern wall. Chauvet recognized the markings as "characteristic of the Stone Age." They had discovered an **immense** archaeological trove and, **presumably**, a clear window on prehistoric life.

Six days later they returned with **portable** lighting and plastic sheets that they spread about to avoid disturbing artifacts on the cavern floors. Probing deeper into the cavern system, they began coming upon exquisite, intricately detailed wall paintings and engravings of animals, as well as numerous images

A colleague of Jean-Marie Chauvet inspects the Stone Age cave paintings found in France.

of human hands, some in red, others in black pigment. "I thought I was dreaming," says Chauvet.

The art was in pristine condition, apparently undisturbed for up to 20,000 years. The walls show images of lions, bison, deer, bears, horses, and some 50 woolly rhinos.

For now, tourists are not allowed in this amazing cave. The French Culture Ministry has put the Chauvet cave off-limits to all but a handful of **anthropologists** and other experts. The French learned a lesson from a cave at Altamira in Spain, another site where amazing rock art has been discovered. Early unrestricted access to this Spanish cave obliterated archaeological clues and led to the rapid deterioration of artwork. At another well-known site of cave art in France—the Lascaux caves—the caves have also been sealed. Visitors tour a carefully created replica instead.

SAVING THE ROCK ART OF AFRICA

Equally beautiful works can be found in great abundance on rock shelters, walls, and overhangs throughout the African continent. Unfortunately, these ancient masterpieces are deteriorating at an alarming rate, and they may disappear entirely unless something is done to save them.

In an effort to record Africa's vanishing trove of rock art, David Coulson, a Nairobi-based photographer, and Alexander Campbell, former director of Botswana's National Museum and Art Gallery, began crisscrossing the continent. They visited known sites and stumbled across new ones, photographing as much of the art as they could. Campbell is convinced that if examples of Africa's rock art were counted, they would total many hundreds of thousands of individual images.

Everywhere Coulson and Campbell went, they found images dulled by sunlight, wind, and water, and damaged by chemical seepage from mining operations, tourism, and outright vandalism. An unthinking tourist, unaware of the art's significance and value, can be much more than just a **nuisance**. Amateur photographers have been known to throw water and cola drinks on the art to enhance its contrast and make the colors more vivid.

HOW OLD IS THE ROCK ART OF AUSTRALIA?

The Australian continent abounds in Aboriginal rock art, both paintings and engravings. Much of it lies in a 1,500-mile-long, boomerang-shaped area along the country's north coast.

Archaeologist Darrell Lewis of the Australian National University estimates that there are at least 10,000 rock-art sites on the Arnhem Land plateau alone, in the Northern Territory. "Each of these sites," he says, "can have several hundred paintings." But unlike early inhabitants of Europe, who often decorated caves over a short period and then abandoned them, the Australian Aborigines would return

Ancient carvings show a herd of giraffes on a stone in Africa.

Scientists date these ancient drawings by Australian Aborigines to 23,000 B.C.

over and over to the same sites. This is a practice that still goes on today. Unraveling the history of a single site can thus be extremely complicated.

How old is Australia's art? It is clear that artists were at work in Australia at roughly the same time as their European cousins. Anthropologist Alan Thorne of the Australian National University claims that a small piece of red ochre (a kind of clay), dated to 50,000 years ago, was worn down on one side—like a piece of chalk—by humans. "Whether it was ground to paint a shelter or a person or part of a wall, I don't think anyone would disagree that it is evidence of art," says Thorne.

These ancient masterpieces found around the world offer windows into the rich lives of our prehistoric ancestors. But if nothing is done to save and preserve the rock art, some of these windows could close forever.

 CA **Critical Thinking**

1. What problem is discussed in this selection, and what solutions are described?

2. What difference between European and Australian cave art is described?

3. If you were given the task of preserving for the future a single work of art from the present, what would it be? Explain your choice.

4. Summarize the common thread in all the selections you've read in this section.

179

Show What You Know

Think and Search

Read on to find the answer. Look for information in more than one place.

LeRoy Sealy helps his niece Patricia learn Choctaw.

Languages at Risk

When you hear the word *endangered* or *extinct*, you may think of rhinos, tigers, and other wildlife. But languages can also become endangered or extinct. Linguists, people who study languages, say about half of the world's 6,500 languages are in trouble. Some have fewer than five living speakers, and nearly 3,000 may disappear in the next 100 years.

Concerned linguists are working to save endangered languages. They are publishing books and making recordings of languages that are at risk.

The most common reason for a language to become endangered is that a small group of people speaking one language comes into contact with a larger community speaking another language. Over time, the smaller group begins speaking the dominant language. Technology and travel have also contributed to the problem by helping the rapid spread of common languages such as English and Spanish.

Says one linguist, "Every language has its way of expressing ideas about the world. When a language dies, we lose that insight."

Go on ▶

Now answer questions 1 through 5. Base your answers on the article "Languages at Risk."

1. **What problem is described in this selection?**

A   Certain languages are being banned in some places.

B   Because of technology and travel, the world needs a single, common language.

C   Thousands of the world's languages are in trouble and may become extinct.

D   People who speak one language have trouble learning to speak a new language.

> **Tip**
> Look for information in more than one place.

2. **Concerned linguists are working on this problem by**

A   teaching common languages such as Spanish and English in schools.

B   publishing books and recordings to preserve languages that could disappear.

C   introducing new languages in communities where only one language is spoken.

D   simplifying the spelling of words in endangered languages.

3. **A linguist is a person who**

A   teaches foreign languages to high school students.

B   studies and preserves languages.

C   publishes books about technology and travel.

D   works with endangered animals.

4. **Explain the most common cause of a language becoming endangered or extinct.**

5. **Do you believe that it is important to preserve every language currently being spoken in the world? Explain your ideas. Use details from the article in your response.**

Write on Demand

Libraries can be fun and useful resources of information. Think about how you use your library. Now write to <u>tell how</u> people can make the most of their public library.

Expository writing explains, defines, or tells how to do something.

To figure out if a writing prompt asks for expository writing, look for clue words such as <u>explain what</u> or <u>tell how</u>.

The writer uses details that support the response to the prompt.

I want to tell you about a place I go to all the time. I can borrow a book or just read one. I can borrow CDs and DVDs. I can learn to use a computer or log on to the Internet. I can do research for a paper or it can be a quiet place to do homework.

It's my local library and I love it. The library has special activities such as book talks, poetry readings, story hours, and classes for all ages.

I often go to the library after school, but the best time is Saturday. I take my brother and drop him off in the children's room. He loves to listen to the stories being read. I go to the main reading area, where I can look through magazines and books before I pick what I want to read for the week.

I recommend a visit to your local library. Try it. You'll like it, too.

Writing Prompt

Respond in writing to the prompt below. Write for 10 minutes. Write as much as you can as well as you can. Review the hints before and after you write.

Think about a place you like to go.

Think about what you like to do when you get to that place.

Now write to explain what your special place is and what you do when you are there.

Writing Hints for Prompts

☑ Read the prompt carefully.

☑ Organize your ideas to plan your writing.

☑ Support your ideas by giving reasons or using more details.

☑ Combine sentences to add variety and show emotion.

☑ Choose words that help readers understand your ideas.

☑ Review your writing and edit it as needed.

UNCOVERING THE INCA

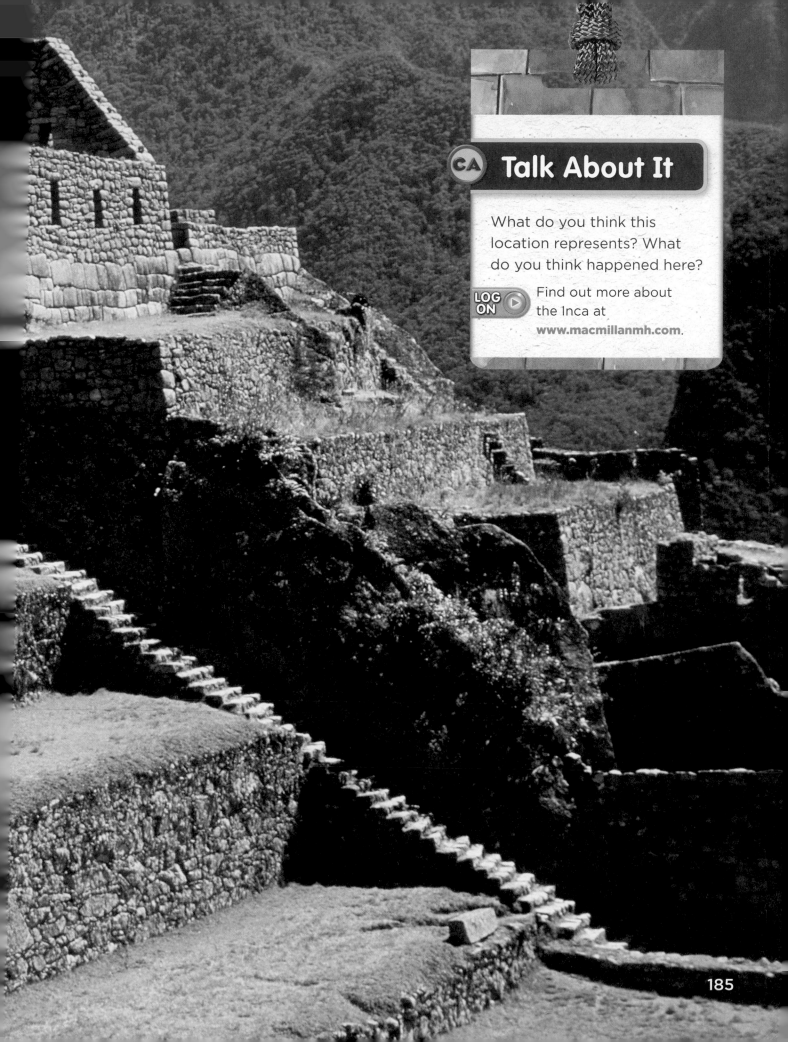

CA Talk About It

What do you think this location represents? What do you think happened here?

LOG ON ▶ Find out more about the Inca at www.macmillanmh.com.

185

AN INCA CITY

by Miguel Rojas

Dear Li,

I'm sorry I didn't write sooner. I was away for the last month. I **accompanied** my mom and dad to Peru. My mom's company sent her there on business. It was great! We flew into Cusco. One weekend we took a train to visit Machu Picchu.

"What is Machu Picchu?" you ask. Well, it is a **remote**—and I mean secluded—Inca city. Actually, it is the remains of that city. Machu Picchu is on top of a mountain peak that overlooks the Urubamba River. It is more than 7,000 feet above sea level!

Greetings from Machu Picchu

How did we get up that high? We could have hiked the Inca Trail for four days. Instead we decided to ride the train. It runs right along the river. It takes only a few hours. Our **escort** was a man from the area who is descended from the Inca. Not only did he provide information about the area, he also worked as our **interpreter**. Some of the people of Peru speak Quechua, which of course we don't understand.

As we rode the train, our escort pointed out unfamiliar **vegetation** that grows in the rain forest. The undergrowth, the plants that grow near the floor of the rain forest, was so thick I could hardly imagine trying to get through it back in 1911. That was when Hiram Bingham, the man who searched for the ruins, started his expedition. We also learned about the animals that inhabit the region. There are some **venomous** snakes that live there.

One bite can kill a person. It must have been quite a journey that Bingham took!

His trip was well worth it, in my opinion. Machu Picchu was so big and beautiful! The stones have **withstood** the test of time. They have been there since the 1400s. There were terraces cut into the sides of the mountain, and green was everywhere. To top it all off, we were in the clouds!

We saw where the people lived, where they worshipped, and where they farmed. The history is fascinating!

The travel brochure **foretold** we would have an amazing adventure, and it certainly didn't lie!

Yours truly,
Maria

Reread for **Comprehension**

Story Structure

Character, Setting, Plot
By analyzing the structure of a story readers can see how the characters, setting, and events are depicted and how they develop.

Use a Character, Setting, Plot Chart to help you note particular people, places, and events as you reread "An Inca City."

Character	Setting	Plot

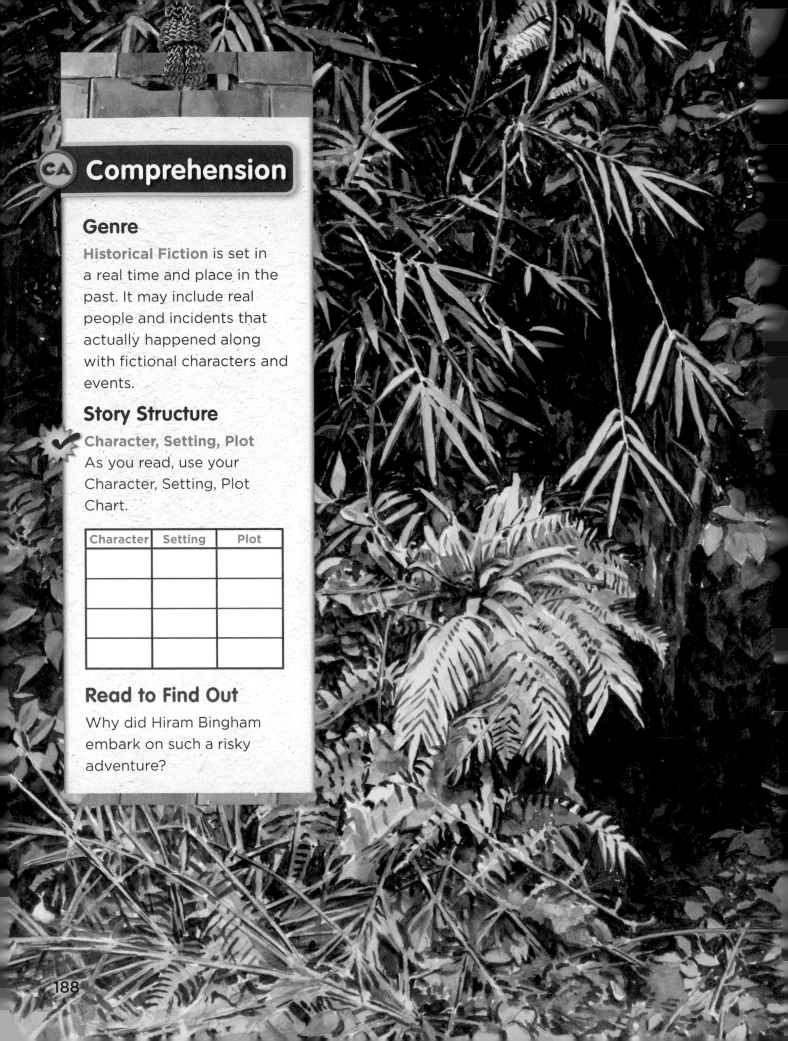

Genre

Historical Fiction is set in a real time and place in the past. It may include real people and incidents that actually happened along with fictional characters and events.

Story Structure

Character, Setting, Plot
As you read, use your Character, Setting, Plot Chart.

Character	Setting	Plot

Read to Find Out

Why did Hiram Bingham embark on such a risky adventure?

Lost City

The Discovery of
Machu Picchu

written and illustrated
by Ted Lewin

In his first journey to South America, Yale professor Hiram Bingham longed to explore the hidden lands that lay beyond the snowcapped peaks of the Andes. Legend had it that the lost city of the Inca, Vilcapampa, lay there. Bingham was determined to discover it. So in 1910 the Yale Peruvian Expedition was organized. Finally, in July 1911, Bingham and his fellow adventurers arrived in Cusco, the first capital city of the Inca. What lay ahead for them was far from what they had expected. And more amazing. Our story begins high in the mountains of Peru . . . .

The boy looked out at the cloud-covered peaks all around him. Already his papa was working in the terraced fields. But last night he had dreamed of a tall stranger carrying a small black box. He could not get the dream out of his mind.

Suddenly, the clouds burned off and the mountains were bathed in glorious light. The dream **foretold** of something wonderful, he was sure.

Sixty miles south, in Cusco, Hiram Bingham gazed thoughtfully at the old Incan stone wall. He had come to Peru in search of Vilcapampa, the lost city of the Inca. But right here was the most beautiful stonework he had ever seen—huge stones cut so perfectly that not even a razor blade could be slipped between them.

The Inca had no iron tools to carve them, no wheel or draft animals to move them. The wall had **withstood** time and earthquakes. How had the Inca built them!

It was a mystery.

He walked through the cobbled streets of the old capital. The Spanish had come to this city, conquered the Inca, taken their gold, and built churches over their temples. Suddenly, he stopped. Before him was the famous Temple of the Sun. He placed his hands on the sun-warmed stones so beautifully carved, as if they had grown together.

191

Hidden in the mountains, the lost city would be built of stones like these. Would it hold gold and fabulous riches like the Spanish had found in Cusco?

More than ever he was determined to find that city.

The next day Bingham began his search. He would look for ruins—that might be the key.

He and his party, **accompanied** by military **escort** Sergeant Carrasco, left by mule train for the sacred valley of the Urubamba River.

They came to the sleepy old village of Ollantaytambo, long ago an important city. Its ancient stone terraces stepped up into the clouds.

"Are there any ruins nearby?" Bingham asked. He went door to door. He sat for hours in the cantina. "Are there any ruins near here?" he asked anyone who came in. "Do you know of the lost city of Vilcapampa?" No one knew of it.

Traveling north, the adventurers came upon a **remote** and wild canyon. Granite cliffs rose thousands of feet above the roaring rapids of the Urubamba River. In the distance were snowcapped mountains over three miles high. Bingham's determination to find the lost city grew with each turn of the increasingly wild trail.

Meanwhile, high on one of these granite ridges, the boy tried to help his papa on the terraces. But he couldn't shake the dream from his mind. Who was this stranger with the black box? When would he come? What was in the black box? Anxiously, he searched the mountains for a sign.

Far below in the valley, Bingham's party camped on a sandy beach alongside the thundering rapids of the Urubamba. Days had gone by. He was tired and discouraged. No one knew of any ruins.

But now the travelers aroused the curiosity of a local farmer named Arteaga.

"Are there ruins nearby?" Bingham asked when Arteaga ventured into camp.

This time, through the **interpreter**, the farmer said, "Yes. There are very good ruins on top of the mountain called Machu Picchu."

The farmer pointed straight up.

"Can you take us there?" Bingham asked.

"No," said Arteaga. "It is a very hard climb and there are many snakes." Bingham offered him coins. Arteaga nodded—he would show them the way.

Arteaga led them down the river trail. Suddenly, he plunged into the jungle. Bingham and the sergeant followed Arteaga through dense undergrowth down to the very edge of the river to a flimsy bridge made of slim logs. What was he getting himself into!

Sergeant Carrasco and Arteaga took off their shoes and crossed easily, gripping with their bare feet. Bingham was terrified—he crept across the bridge on hands and knees. One slip and he would be dashed to pieces in the roaring torrent below.

> **Setting and Plot**
> How does the dangerous setting contribute to the story's suspense?

They climbed the bank into dense jungle. Now the slopes were slippery and the heat terrible. Arteaga had warned them of the fer-de-lance, a very **venomous** snake. Bingham's eyes searched the jungle.

Up and up they climbed. The wide river was now but a silver thread, far below. Arteaga could think of nothing but the fer-de-lance; Sergeant Carrasco thought about his good, sturdy shoes; Bingham thought of nothing but the lost city. They cut their way through tangled thickets. Up and up they climbed.

Had an hour passed? Two? Three? Now they crept on all fours. They slipped and slid. In some places, they held on by their fingertips.

Finally, thirsty and exhausted, they broke through the jungle into sunlight. Above them stood a little Quechua boy beside a stone hut. What could he be doing at the top of this mountain?

"*Ama llulla, ama quella, ama su'a*" (Don't lie, don't be lazy, don't steal), the boy called out in the traditional Quechua greeting.

It was the tall stranger from his dream. Carrying the black box!

The boy's whole family crowded around to greet the exhausted travelers, then brought gourds of cool water and boiled sweet potatoes.

Bingham, still gasping for breath, asked, "Where are the ruins?"

The boy said, "*Amuy, amuy!*" (Come, come!)

Bingham and the sergeant left Arteaga behind and followed at the boy's urging. "*Amuy, amuy!*" he kept saying.

At first they saw only stone terraces like the ones they had seen at Ollantaytambo. They looked as if they had been recently cleared of jungle and the **vegetation** burned off in order to plant crops.

But there were no ruins. Just more jungle beyond. Bingham had climbed this mountain and found—no lost city.

"*Amuy, amuy!*" Still, the boy beckoned him into the jungle beyond. Weary and discouraged, Bingham followed. At first all he saw were bamboo thickets and more tangled vines. Then he looked closer. Through the vines, he saw—stones. Inca stones. Then walls, beautiful stone walls! They were covered with mosses. And trees.

"*Jaway, jaway!*" (See, see!) the boy whispered, pointing ahead to a curved stone wall. Bingham pushed his way to it and placed his hands on the fine granite stones. A sun temple. More beautiful even than the one in Cusco.

They came to a grand stone staircase. Where could this lead? What else was here?

"*Jaway, jaway,*" the boy called.

At the top of the staircase was a clearing. A small vegetable garden, and then . . . a temple built of enormous stones. Grander than any Bingham had ever seen. It stole his breath away.

Something was going on here, he could sense it. Something just beyond his eyes. What was it?

He followed the boy to another temple. As magnificent. This one had three windows. But now he looked across the countryside. He looked past the thickets, past the vines. He began to see the outlines of stone streets and stone cottages. He began to see the outlines of a city!

"Here, boy," he said as he opened the black box that he had been carrying, extended the bellows and focused his camera.

Character and Plot
Why does Bingham decide to stop and take the picture?

199

The first picture would be of the boy. The boy who had led him to Vilcapampa, lost city of the Incas.

But about this Bingham was wrong. When the vines were removed and the tales told, he had discovered not Vilcapampa, but a place even more amazing.

He had stumbled on Machu Picchu, a city lost in time, a city lost in the clouds.

Traveling with Ted Lewin

Ted Lewin grew up with a lion, an iguana, a chimpanzee . . . oh, and a mom, a dad, a sister, and two brothers. He always wanted to be an illustrator and paid for art school by being a professional wrestler. Today he and his wife, Betsy, also an artist, travel the world finding stories. In Machu Picchu, Ted took thousands of pictures, which he used to sketch his illustrations. After that, the painting went very fast. Ted says it was more fun than anything he has ever done before.

Other books illustrated by Ted Lewin:
Peppe the Lamplighter and *Elephant Quest*

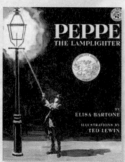

CA Author's Purpose

Ted Lewin's account of the discovery of Machu Picchu is both entertaining and informative. Describe three things that you enjoyed learning from this selection.

  Find out more about Ted Lewin at **www.macmillanmh.com**.

CA Critical Thinking

Summarize

Use your Character, Setting, Plot Chart to help you summarize *Lost City: The Discovery of Machu Picchu*. How does Professor Bingham find the lost city?

Character	Setting	Plot

Think and Compare

1. Before he realizes what he has really discovered, what is Professor Bingham searching for? Use evidence from the text to support your answer. **Story Structure: Character, Setting, Plot**

2. Professor Bingham's **character** contributes a great deal to his discovery. Describe his character and tell why it is so important to the **plot**. **Analyze**

3. Think about a time when you discovered something that surprised you. What was it? Describe the **setting**. Why was it important to you? **Synthesize**

4. Why do you think it would be important to uncover something like these **remote** ruins? Explain your answer. **Evaluate**

5. Read Maria's letter to Li on pages 186–187. Pretend that Maria has written you a similar letter detailing her trip to Machu Picchu. Write her back and tell her about *Lost City*. Talk about a character or an event that she might find interesting. **Reading/Writing Across Texts**

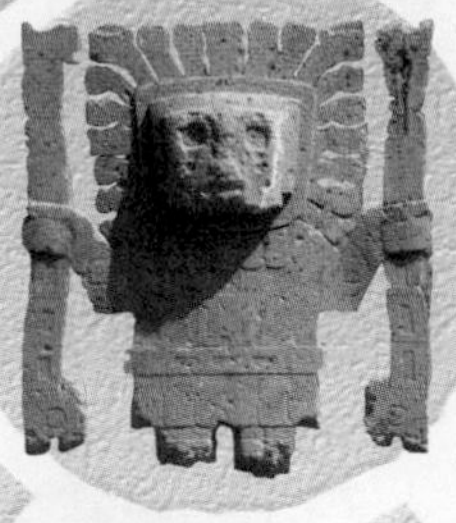

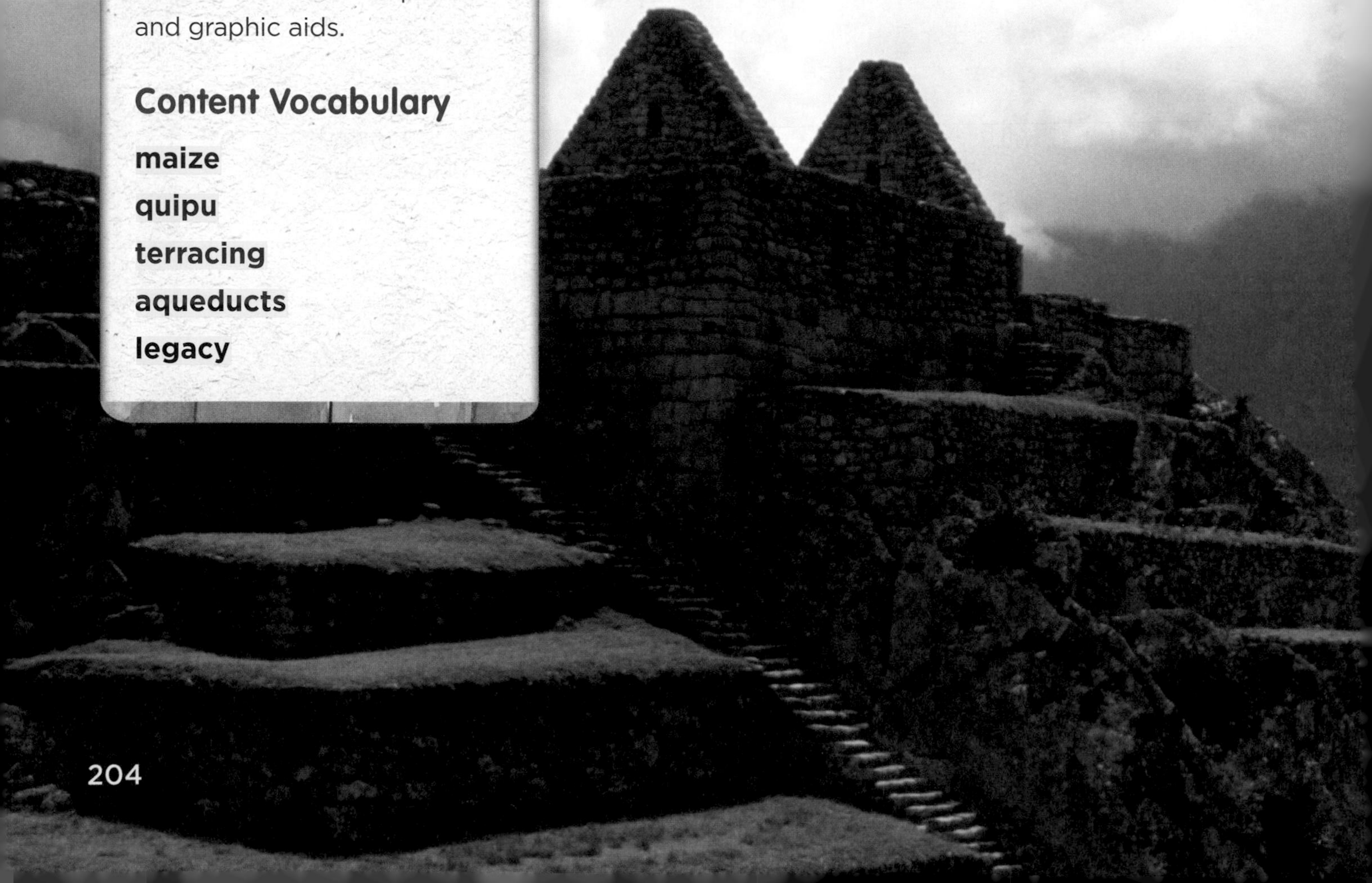

EMPIRE IN THE ANDES

Once a great empire grew in the Andes mountains of South America. This civilization took its name from its ruler, the Inca. The empire stretched from what is today Ecuador to central Chile.

Like the Aztec, the Inca worshiped the sun, depended on **maize**, and organized a strong army.

History/ Social Science

Genre

Nonfiction: Textbooks present facts and ideas about nonfiction topics.

Text Features

Textbook segments often feature changes in print, such as key words in color and boldface or italicized type. Headings and subheadings help to organize information. Captions and labels provide more information for photos and graphic aids.

Content Vocabulary

maize
quipu
terracing
aqueducts
legacy

FROM VILLAGE TO EMPIRE

The Inca Empire began around 1200 in Cusco (KOOS koh), a small village in a fertile mountain valley in what is today Peru. A drought reduced their farmland, so the Inca took over their neighbors' land. During the 1300s, the Inca ruled most of the valley.

In 1438, a ruler called Pachakuti (pah chah KOO tee) Inca extended the Inca borders west to the Pacific Ocean and south to Lake Titicaca high in the central Andes.

SWEAT OF THE SUN

The Inca worked rich gold mines. They called the metal "sweat of the sun" and used it to decorate temples to their sun god. The sun god's temple in Cusco had a huge sculpture of him decorated with precious stones. There was even a golden "garden" with flowers and birds made of gold.

THE INCA CAPITAL

Cusco served as the center of government, religion, and trade. The temples and government buildings at the center of Cusco were constructed of stone blocks. These blocks still fit together so well that it is impossible to put a knife between them. They can also withstand earthquakes.

Beyond the main plaza were the palaces of the emperor and wealthy nobles. The nobles wore special headbands and earrings. One of the Spanish soldiers who visited the city was impressed by Inca wealth and skill. He wrote the following description in the 1500s:

> *The interior of the temple [of the sun] was . . . a mine of gold. On the western wall was . . . [the sun god] . . . engraved on a massive plate of gold of enormous [size], thickly powdered with emeralds and special stones. . . . The morning sun fell directly upon it at its rising, lighting up the whole apartment.*

The ruins of Machu Picchu, an ancient city of the Inca Empire, high in the Andes

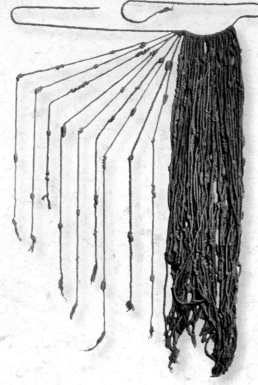

Peruvian quipu for counting and recording facts and events; of Inca workmanship

TECHNOLOGY: SPEAKING WITH THREAD

The Inca used a special cord called a **quipu** (KEE poo). A quipu was about two feet long and had many threads of different colors hanging from it. For example, white threads stood for silver, yellow stood for gold, and red stood for war. By tying knots in the strings in a particular order, the Inca could send messages and keep records of battles, items traded, and births and deaths in a village.

PUTTING IT TOGETHER

Inca farmers began **terracing** and using fertilizer to increase the crops their land produced. In addition to many roads, Inca engineers built large **aqueducts**.

The Inca Empire controlled much of western South America until it was conquered by the Spanish in 1532. However, the Inca **legacy** remains. Millions of people still speak the Inca language, and many of the songs and poems of the Inca are still recited today.

A LOST CITY

The Inca built a vast network of highways over 19,000 miles in length. One road climbed into the Andes and ended at the city called Machu Picchu (MAHCH oo PEEK choo). This town was forgotten until an American explorer named Hiram Bingham came across it in 1911.

No one is sure why Machu Picchu was built or why it was abandoned. Machu Picchu is just one of many Inca mysteries. Although Spanish conquerors destroyed many Inca treasures in the 1500s, those remaining can give us a sense of the brilliant culture created by the "Children of the Sun."

The Inca built terraces on hillsides to hold rainwater for crops.

A stone wall (right) from Machu Picchu

CA Critical Thinking

1. How do the subheadings, photos, and captions help you understand the text better? **Reading Text Features**

2. How do we know the Inca were brilliant engineers? **Analyze**

3. Compare "Empire in the Andes" with *Lost City*. Give examples of two details in *Lost City* that are explained further here. **Reading/Writing Across Texts**

 History/Social Science Activity

If you were with Hiram Bingham in Machu Picchu in 1911, what would you include in a journal entry? Include some facts you have read about Machu Picchu.

 Find out more about Machu Picchu at **www.macmillanmh.com**.

Writing

CA

✔ Sensory Details

Writers use **sensory details** to help the reader recreate a moment.

Read the passage below. Notice how author Ted Lewin uses sensory details in his story.

An excerpt from
Lost City: The Discovery of Machu Picchu

The author scatters sensory details throughout his story to help us feel and taste the characters' experience. Each time we encounter a sensory detail, we are in the shoes of the character, not just watching him or her.

He placed his hands on the sun-warmed stones so beautifully carved, as if they had grown together. . . . They climbed the bank into dense jungle. Now the slopes were slippery and the heat terrible. . . . Finally, thirsty and exhausted, they broke through the jungle into sunlight. . . . The boy's whole family crowded around to greet the exhausted travelers, then brought gourds of cool water and boiled sweet potatoes.

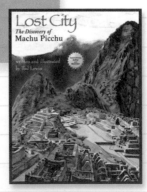

Read and Find

Read Julie's writing below. How did she use sensory details to help you picture the moment? Use the Writer's Checklist to help you.

At the Beach

by Julie S.

I felt the hot sun beating down on my back. My wet hair hung heavy on the back of my neck. Suddenly, I heard barking coming closer. A pair of excited labs raced past!

Yuck! Their flying paws flung sand right into my eyes! My eyes watered as I tried to blink out the gritty bits. When my eyes finally felt clear again, I muttered, "No dogs allowed at the beach!"

Read about how it feels to lie on a beach.

Writer's Checklist

 ✓ Does the writer use words related to sight, hearing, smell, taste, or touch?

✓ Does the writer help you experience the moment?

 ☑ Can you imagine the way Julie experienced this moment?

AFRICAN STORYTELLING

CA **Talk About It**

What can we learn from stories passed down through the centuries?

LOG ON ▶ Find out more about storytelling at www.macmillanmh.com.

211

Vocabulary

rummaged	pathetic
undetected	famine
chameleon	scrounging
generosity	pursuing

Context Clues

Context Clues provide hints to help readers figure out the meaning of an unfamiliar word. Restatement is a kind of context clue that gives a definition of the unfamiliar word.

"Her great-grandmother left her village because of a famine, a time of extreme scarcity of food."

Keira's Magical Moment

by Leonora Halvi

As Keira climbed into bed, she thought about tomorrow's field trip. Her class was going to a presentation by a West African traditional storyteller. Keira was excited because she was of West African descent. Her great-grandmother had come to the United States from Senegal. Until now, Keira hadn't thought much about her roots.

When her alarm went off, Keira **rummaged** through her closet. She was looking for something that showed her West African roots. She dug through every drawer, but she couldn't find anything that really stood out. Finally, she put on a white shirt and jeans. Despite her plain clothes, she hoped that her interest in her heritage would not go **undetected**.

At the community center, Keira was lucky enough to get a front-row seat. The first speaker talked about African writers and how they often use traditional stories with traditional characters, such as the Tortoise and the Spider. The speaker mentioned writers her mother and grandmother liked! Also, Tortoise was a favorite character in Keira's bedtime stories. Finally, the speaker mentioned Doudou N'Diaye Rose. He was Keira's favorite drummer. He was from Senegal. She began to realize just how much her West African heritage influenced her American life.

Finally, the griot, or storyteller, took the stage. He told a story that explained how the **chameleon**, a small lizard, changed its colors. Then he introduced the tricksters Spider and Tortoise. They were known to fake **generosity** while actually looking for a handout. Some of the stories made these characters seem **pathetic** as they fought for every last scrap. However, they were simply naughty. They certainly did learn their lessons!

Keira couldn't keep her mind from ricocheting through all the different stories her mother had told. Her memory was bouncing around like a ball! She knew about everything the griot said.

After the presentation, the class talked to the griot. Keira told about how her great-grandmother had moved to the United States from Senegal. Her great-grandmother left her village because of a **famine**, a time of extreme scarcity of food. She had explained to Keira's grandmother that the villagers spent days **scrounging** for food. Her great-grandmother, **pursuing** a better life, came to the United States. Keira told the griot about the familiar bedtime stories.

When Keira was finished, the griot pointed out that she had just taken on his job. She had described her family and the stories they told. Keira could hardly wait to tell her mother and grandmother the news!

Reread for Comprehension

Make Inferences and Analyze

Cause and Effect

In a story, the actions of the characters often cause a series of events to unfold. Making inferences about a character's actions can help you identify cause-and-effect relationships between events in the story.

Use your Cause and Effect Chart to record important causes of events as you reread "Keira's Magical Moment."

Cause	→	Effect
	→	
	→	
	→	
	→	

CA Comprehension

Genre

A **Folktale** is a story based on the traditions of a people or region which is handed down from one generation to the next and becomes legendary.

Make Inferences and Analyze

Cause and Effect
As you read, use your Cause and Effect Chart.

Cause → Effect
→
→
→
→

Read to Find Out

What is the cause of Chameleon's generosity?

214

The Magic Gourd

by Baba Wagué Diakité

Award Winning Author and Illustrator

It all began

when the sun refused to allow the
clouds to gather, and there was
no rain. First came drought. Then
came **famine**. Everyone was hungry.
And it was then that Brother Rabbit
wandered around the parched
countryside searching for wild roots
to feed his starving family. As he
walked, he sang . . .

Feeyeh ku, feeyeh ku.
Waara sa kun tay.
Luck will come. Life will be good.

216

Suddenly, Rabbit was interrupted by a sweet little voice that called out, "Dogo Zan! Dogo Zan! Rescue me from this thorny bush! My arms are being poked and scratched! Help me, and I will pay you well."

Rabbit was busy, but still he stopped. "I will help simply to avoid seeing my brother suffer," said Rabbit. Gently he lowered his hand between the thorny branches and saved the green **chameleon**. As Rabbit turned to leave, Chameleon called out to him once again.

"Dogo Zan! Don't go yet! Would you mind getting my gourd from the bush, too?"

"A gourd?" cried Brother Rabbit. "You want me to scratch myself again for a little gourd?"

"Please, Dogo Zan," begged Chameleon. "I will reward you well."

Again, Rabbit's kind nature got the best of him, and he bent into the thorny bush and **rummaged** around.

Rabbit brought out a beautifully decorated gourd and handed it to Chameleon. But Chameleon just said, "Keep it. It's your reward."

"It's just an empty gourd," Rabbit cried.

"It's not *just* an empty gourd," Chameleon replied. "It's MAGIC!"

"*Ee ko dee!*" cried Rabbit. "A magic gourd?"

"Oh, yes!" said Chameleon. "Watch this: Magic Gourd, fill yourself up with insects!"

Brother Rabbit watched in amazement as Chameleon licked up a bowl full of insects.

"Why are you giving me such a valuable gift?" Rabbit asked.

"You were kind to me, Brother Rabbit," Chameleon said. "Besides, I have my own secret for catching insects," and he quickly unrolled his lo-o-o-o-ong tongue for Rabbit to admire.

Rabbit thanked Brother Chameleon and rushed home with his gourd.

Cause and Effect
What happened as a result of Rabbit's kindness?

As soon as he arrived home, his entire family eagerly gathered around.

"An empty gourd?" they all gasped in disbelief.

"It's not *just* an empty gourd," said Brother Rabbit. "It's a magic gourd! Watch this: Magic Gourd!" he said. "Fill yourself up with carrots!"

To their astonishment, the gourd magically filled with carrots. Happily, they ate them all.

"Magic Gourd! Fill yourself up with couscous!" he said.

Again they ate until they were satisfied.

"Magic Gourd! Fill yourself up with water!" he said, and they drank deeply.

219

From that day on, Brother Rabbit's family drank and ate well.

But as much as they wanted to keep the magic gourd a family secret, they also could not sit and watch friends and neighbors suffer. So they invited them to share their meals every day.

And this is how word floated around from one to the other until it came to the house of Mansa Jugu, the greedy king.

One day, the greedy king and his soldiers broke into Rabbit's compound and forced the little gourd away from him. Now, with the magic gourd in his possession, Mansa Jugu sat day and night commanding the little gourd to fill and refill with more and more gold.

Meanwhile, unable to get the magic gourd back, Rabbit returned once again to his poor life, **scrounging** for wild roots to feed his hungry family. Despite the hardships of the moment, he still had courage to sing . . .

> *Feeyeh ku, feeyeh ku. Waara sa kun tay.*
> *Luck will come. Life will be good.*

Cause and Effect
What happened when Rabbit decided to share the gourd with his neighbors?

One day, while hunting for roots, Rabbit heard his name being called again.

"Dogo Zan, Dogo Zan!"

Recognizing the sweet little voice, he turned and looked in all directions. Slowly the chameleon came into view right next to him on a sparkling green rock.

"Dogo Zan! What has happened to you?" cried Chameleon. "You look skinny and **pathetic**!"

Rabbit told him all about the greedy king who stole the gourd. Again, Brother Chameleon offered a gift to Brother Rabbit. This time, it was the beautiful crystal rock he had been standing on.

"What is this, Brother Chameleon?" asked Rabbit.

"This is just a *fara*, a little rock!" As soon as the words came out of his mouth, the rock leaped into the air and bounced off his head.

"*Eee-heeeee! Fara!*" cried Rabbit. "Stop! Stop!"

Again, the rock knocked his head.

"Excuse me, Dogo Zan," said the chameleon. "You must call him by his name, *Fara-Ba*!" With that, the rock dropped silently to the ground. Rabbit thanked Chameleon for this unusual gift and returned home.

The next day, Brother Rabbit rolled the rock in a fresh *sheeyo* leaf and walked to the king's palace. "I have brought you a mysterious gift, your Majesty," said Brother Rabbit.

"*Aaa ha! Moondon!* What is it?" asked the king anxiously. Rabbit slowly unrolled the rock from the *sheeyo* leaf and showed it to Mansa Jugu.

"*Eeeeeeh! Fara doron?*" exclaimed the king. "A simple rock?"

And with that, the little rock began ricocheting off the head of the king.

"*A toh! A toh!* Stop this rock!" cried the king, but no one could capture it. All day and all night the little rock played music on the heads of the king and his soldiers. The annoyance continued and the king became troubled. Mansa Jugu was finally forced to call on Rabbit for help.

Cleverly, Brother Rabbit demanded his little gourd back first.

"You may take all the gold, but leave me the gourd," said the greedy king.

222

"But the gourd was a gift to me," replied Rabbit.

"Then take all my food from my royal storage bins, but leave me the gourd," cried the annoyed king.

"*Ee dusu dah*. Let us bargain," countered Rabbit. "My little gourd is my prize."

The king angrily shouted, "*U-TAH*, *U-TAH*—TAKE IT ALL! Take the gold, the food, and the little gourd!"

Rabbit took the gourd, but left the gold and the food behind. And before he turned to flee, he shouted, "*Fara-Ba!*"

Calmly, the little rock dropped into Rabbit's hand.

Fearing revenge from the king, Rabbit's family escaped to the country to join their faithful friend Chameleon. From Chameleon's great lessons in disguises, Brother Rabbit learned the skill of hiding in the bush. Today Dogo Zan and his family are masters at going **undetected**. One could be hiding in your backyard right now.

Mansa Jugu, the greedy king, and his soldiers felt embarrassed by their defeat at the hand of a rabbit and a small rock. The king could not believe that in his moment of weakness, he had given away the wealth of his kingdom. Exhausted and hungry, the king sat down to eat before **pursuing** Brother Rabbit for revenge. Upon opening his storage bins, he was surprised to discover that all of his wealth and food remained.

"Come eat!" he called to his soldiers and servants. "Let us appreciate what we have been given."

From this final kind act of Rabbit, the greedy king, Mansa Jugu, began to learn the importance of **generosity** and friendship.

As for Rabbit and Chameleon, they have always understood that loyal friendships are the true treasures that make one rich.

And for their many good deeds, all sang a song of praise to Rabbit and Chameleon.

Glossary

Here are some words from the story that are in Bambara, the national language of Mali.

Dogo Zan (DOE-go ZAHN) – Brother Rabbit

Mansa Jugu (MAHN-sah JOO-goo) – greedy king (mansa means ruler; jugu means greedy)

* **Ee dusu dah** (ee du-SU dah) – Let us bargain; calm down

* **Ee ko dee** (EE ko DEE) – exclamation of surprise when a person doesn't believe what they have just heard (What did you say?)

Fara (FAH-rah) – rock

* **Fara-ba** (FAH-rah BAH) – Mr. Rock (title of respect)

Fara doron (FAH-rah DOH-ron) – a simple rock

Moondon (MOON-don) – What is it?

Sheeyo (SHEE-yoh) – a bush with large leaves found in Mali

A toh! (ah TOH) – Stop!

U-tah (OO-tah) – Take it all!

* **Feeyeh ku, feeyeh ku.** (FEE-yeh koo) **Waara sa kun tay.** (WA-rah sah KOON-teh) – This is a chant of encouragement to give hope for survival in difficult times.

(Note: Bambara is a metaphorical language, so the English translation is not always literal.)

* Not a literal translation

Meet the Storyteller

Baba Wagué Diakité with his daughters, Penda and Amina

Baba Wagué Diakité grew up in Mali, West Africa. During the evening meal, his whole family told stories, often about the rabbit Zozani [Zoh-Zah-NEE]. Zozani was clever and could always find a way to solve a problem. In the end, Zozani sings a song of praise, something storytellers in Mali have been doing for centuries.

In addition to ceramic art, Baba Wagué Diakité used mud cloth designs to illustrate this story. These are traditional designs painted with dark mud on cotton cloth. Each design means something special. For example, a flower means family happiness.

Other books by Baba Wagué Diakité: *The Hatseller and the Monkeys* and *The Hunterman and the Crocodile*

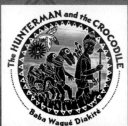

LOG ON ▶ Find out more about Baba Wagué Diakité at **www.macmillanmh.com**.

Author's Purpose

The main purpose of this tale is to entertain. It also teaches that kindness pays and gives a fictional origin for rabbits' ability to hide. Why do rabbits need to hide in the real world?

CA Critical Thinking

Summarize

Use your Cause and Effect Chart to help you summarize *The Magic Gourd*. What causes Brother Chameleon to give Brother Rabbit the gourd? What effect does the gourd have on Brother Rabbit and the King?

Cause → Effect
→
→
→
→

Think and Compare

1. Something unexpected takes place at the end of *The Magic Gourd.* What is the **cause and effect** of this event? How does this event help you understand the moral of the story? **Make Inferences and Analyze: Cause and Effect**

2. How does the weather affect the characters in the story? Use examples from the text to support your answers. **Synthesize**

3. Think of a time when you did a good deed for someone. What happened? How did your **generosity** help? How did it make you feel? **Evaluate**

4. Who gets the bigger reward from the gourd: the King or Brother Rabbit? Explain why. **Analyze**

5. In "Keira's Magical Moment" on pages 212–213, Keira says her great-grandmother left Senegal because of a famine. What do you think the role of a folktale such as *The Magic Gourd* would have in Keira's great-grandmother's native culture? **Reading/Writing Across Texts**

By the 700s, the empire of Ghana was already a major power in Africa. It grew rich and powerful as a source of gold for the Mediterranean world.

THE ORIGIN OF GHANA

by Patricia and Fredrick McKissack

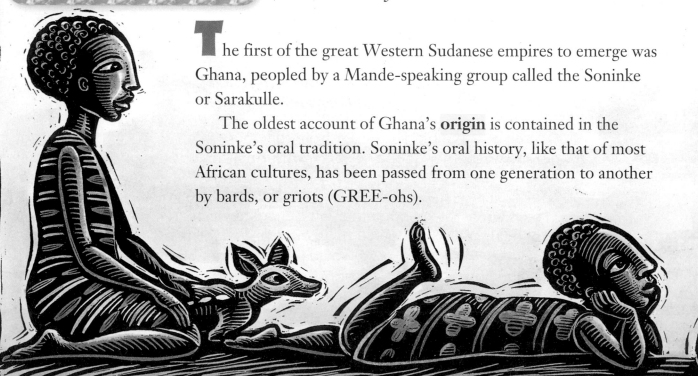

The first of the great Western Sudanese empires to emerge was Ghana, peopled by a Mande-speaking group called the Soninke or Sarakulle.

The oldest account of Ghana's **origin** is contained in the Soninke's oral tradition. Soninke's oral history, like that of most African cultures, has been passed from one generation to another by bards, or griots (GREE-ohs).

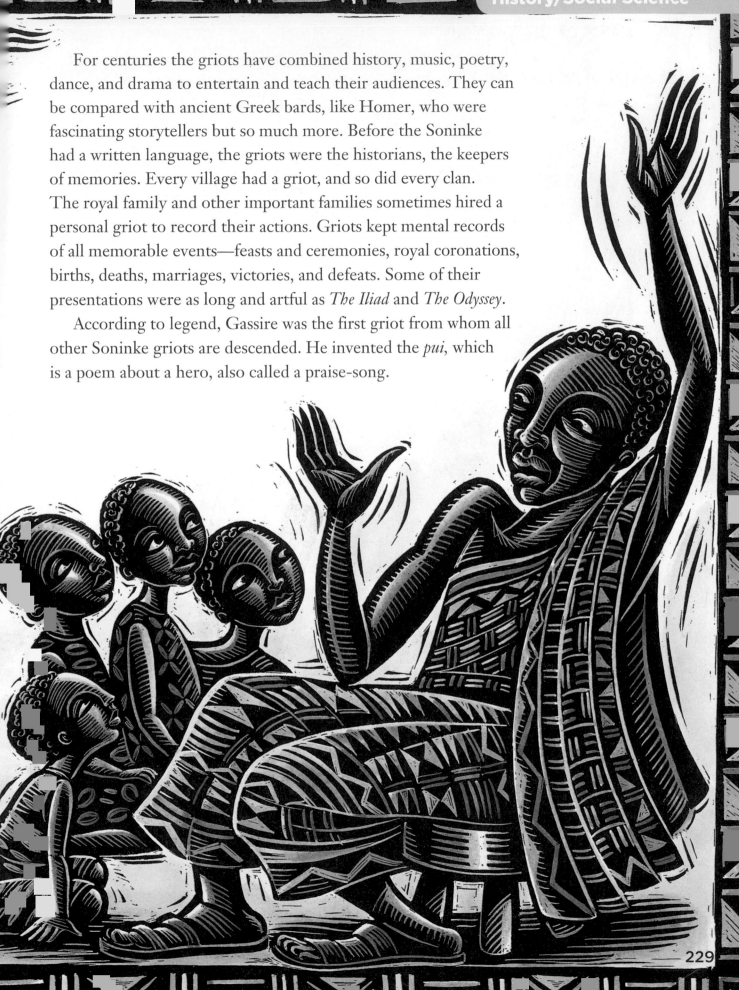

For centuries the griots have combined history, music, poetry, dance, and drama to entertain and teach their audiences. They can be compared with ancient Greek bards, like Homer, who were fascinating storytellers but so much more. Before the Soninke had a written language, the griots were the historians, the keepers of memories. Every village had a griot, and so did every clan. The royal family and other important families sometimes hired a personal griot to record their actions. Griots kept mental records of all memorable events—feasts and ceremonies, royal coronations, births, deaths, marriages, victories, and defeats. Some of their presentations were as long and artful as *The Iliad* and *The Odyssey*.

According to legend, Gassire was the first griot from whom all other Soninke griots are descended. He invented the *pui*, which is a poem about a hero, also called a praise-song.

One of the first stories a Soninke griot learns is the pui of Gassire. The story tells of a guinea hen who laid several large and beautiful eggs. While she was away, a fat snake came and ate her eggs. The hen was so angry, she declared war on the snake. To **bolster** her courage, she sang a song about what she was going to do. The hen defeated the snake, then flew to a tree to sing about her deeds. People say that Gassire heard the hen's victory song and learned it.

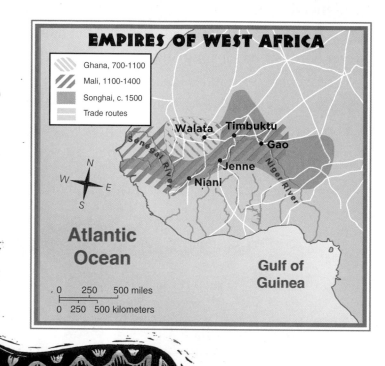

READING A TIME LINE

A time line is a diagram showing the order in which events took place. This time line shows dates important to the early history of Ghana, Mali, and Songhai.

1000	1100	1200	1300	1400	1500	1600

1067
Al-Bakri, a Muslim writer, was writing of Ghana's great wealth

1235
Battle of Kirina was important in the rise of the Mali Empire

1312
Mansa Musa, great ruler of Mali, came to power

1464
Sunni Ali, powerful ruler of Songhai, began reign

1591
Songhai army defeated by an army from Morocco

Historians believe this pui is a **mythological** retelling of Ghana's origin. The hen represents the early Soninke people who overthrew an enemy who was more powerful.

By the middle of the 1000s, Ghana had attracted many rivals who sought to share in the wealth of the gold trade. The new empire Mali (MAH lee) had great influence by about 1250. After 1337 the rulers of Mali grew weaker. They were unable to control the empire and its gold trade. Mali was replaced by an even stronger empire, the Songhai (SOHNG hī). By the late 1490s, Songhai included Mali and parts of present-day Benin, Niger, and Nigeria.

This West African brass weight was used with a scale to measure the weight of gold.

 Critical Thinking

1. Use the time line to find the year the Songhai army lost power. **Reading a Time Line**

2. Why do you think that the griots are still important today? **Analyze**

3. Why did the pui of Gassire and the narrator in *The Magic Gourd* use animal characters? **Reading/Writing Across Texts**

 History/Social Science Activity

Research one of the early West African kingdoms. Write and illustrate a fact card using the interesting facts you discovered during your research.

LOG ON ▶ Find out more about griots at **www.macmillanmh.com**.

Writing

Sensory Details

Writers use **sensory details** to help the reader imagine a moment.

Reading and Writing Connection

Read the passage below. Notice how author Baba Wagué Diakité uses sensory details in his story.

An excerpt from
The Magic Gourd

Even though folktales don't usually include lots of sensory details, the author uses them well here. Details about what Rabbit sees, hears, and feels help us recreate the scene in our minds.

Suddenly, Rabbit was interrupted by a sweet little voice that called out, "Dogo Zan! Dogo Zan! Rescue me from this thorny bush! My arms are being poked and scratched! Help me, and I will pay you well."

Rabbit was busy, but still he stopped. "I will help simply to avoid seeing my brother suffer," said Rabbit. Gently he lowered his hand between the thorny branches and saved the green chameleon.

Read and Find

Read Willow's writing below. How did she use sensory details to help you understand the moment? Use the Writer's Checklist to help you.

Kneading Bread

by Willow E.

Mom scooped the big lump of dough out of the bowl and dropped it on the table. Thump! Little swirls of flour puffed up as it landed. Gingerly, I sank my hands into the chilly, sticky mass and began to push and pull. My arm muscles ached after only a few minutes. The dough smelled great!

Read about how it feels to knead dough.

Writer's Checklist

 Does the writer use words related to sight, hearing, smell, taste, or touch?

 Does the writer help you imagine the moment?

 Can you feel the way Willow experienced this moment?

MONTEZUMA'S MANTLE

A clasp, or fastening, made out of jade that might have been used for a cloak

Dr. Frederick wiped the sweat from his brow. The noonday heat of Mexico City was unbearable. He bent his head closer to the ground, gently sweeping away the hot sand from a square slab of wood. The material and the outline made it look like a box. He didn't want to jump to conclusions too quickly, but he had a feeling that the piece he had been searching for must be near here. This could be it!

He looked up. Everyone else on the site had deserted for a break from the heat of midday. Anticipation alone made him press forward.

He had been searching for the ancient Aztec city of Tenochtitlán for years. Though he had uncovered many important Aztec artifacts, none of his excavations had revealed the one he had hoped to find: the mantle of Montezuma. The clasp of the cloak alone, made of precious jade, was one of the most sought-after gems in history.

"Dr. Frederick!"

He was jarred from his careful work by a student running toward him.

"Yes, what is it?" the doctor queried.

"It's the mantle. They think they've found it!"

Dr. Frederick, covering his work and tools with canvas, immediately followed the student back to the base camp. "Could this be?" he thought, "Will I finally set eyes on it?"

The students were huddled around a man clutching a box tightly under his arm, eagerly awaiting the arrival of Dr. Frederick.

"May I see it?" Dr. Frederick asked the man. The man set the box down and slowly opened the lid. Dust rose from the open box. Dr. Frederick's eyes got big. A glow of jade green lit his face.

Dr. Frederick reached for his lens. He touched the worn cloth of the mantle. He inspected the clasp carefully. "Hmmm . . . yes . . ." He held up the gem and examined it in the light. He stopped. "Hmm . . ." The students looked at each other, trying to read the doctor's reaction.

He put his lens down and turned to the man. "This, my friend, is quite extraordinary." A murmur went through the students. "However, I am afraid it is a fake." He turned to the man.

"This stone is too dull to be the real gemstone. But whoever made this has done their research. Wherever did you find it?"

The man suddenly became anxious. "Sorry to have bothered you with it. I'll be on my way then." He stood quickly and turned to go, leaving the mantle behind. Dr. Frederick looked at him strangely. "Please, wait!" Dr. Frederick called to him, "I'd like to ask you some questions!"

Out of the corner of his eye, he caught sight of billowing canvas in the distance. One of the sites had come uncovered. He turned back to see the man scurrying down the hill away from the excavation. He stood to go after him, and again looked at the canvas. Wait! That was his site!

Leaving the students behind, he ran to the site. There, amidst his tools, was an empty open box, still stuck in the earth.

"Catch that man!" he ordered. He scanned the area for the accomplice. A flash of green struck his eyes on the next hill. He headed in its direction.

235

GWENDOLYN BROOKS A Voice

Gwendolyn Brooks

Gwendolyn Brooks's poetry acted as a clear voice to help guide future generations through years of trouble and moments of triumph.

The Voice of a Child

Gwendolyn grew up in Chicago, IL. Her father worked as a janitor, though he had wanted to become a doctor. Early on, Gwendolyn knew that he was one kind of person she wanted to tell the world about. She would write about extraordinary people—the working man, the caring mother, the forgotten soldier, and the lonely child.

She wrote her first poem when she was only seven. When her parents saw how she took to writing, they gave her a desk of her own. At the age of 13, Gwendolyn published a poem called "Eventide" in American Childhood magazine. By 16, she had a portfolio of work that included more than 75 published poems.

The Voice of a Teenager

Gwendolyn took a job at a newspaper that focused on Chicago's African American community. Newspaper work taught Gwendolyn to observe and record the world. She saw life as a poem, a song that took place every day for everyone. In particular, she felt the need to write about African American Chicagoans, who were often overlooked.

Gwendolyn graduated from Wilson Junior College and attended poetry workshops in Chicago. Working with other talented young writers, she learned all of the techniques and tools of classic and modern poetry.

The Voice of the Silent

Gwendolyn noticed that people in her community expressed themselves differently from the poets she had studied. She believed how they spoke was just as musical, passionate, and important as any classic poem.

Gwendolyn Brooks's first collection of poetry, *A Street in Bronzeville*, was published in 1945. It overflowed with real life, rarely the subject of traditional poetry. Her voice appealed to everyone. *A Street in Bronzeville* was a huge hit with both critics and audiences, but her next book, *Annie Allen*, received even more attention. This story of an African American woman's growth was the first book by an African American writer to win the prestigious Pulitzer Prize.

The Voice of Equality

Gwendolyn examined and wrote about the changing experiences of African Americans all over the country. In 1967, she attended a writer's conference with young writers who had their own stories, poetry, and opinions. At that time, civil rights was a key issue in American politics. Listening to all those writers, Gwendolyn felt a part of the struggle for freedom. The conference inspired her to rediscover her writing and herself.

A Voice for All Time

Gwendolyn Brooks spent her later years using poetry to advance the rights of African Americans in the United States. She knew that people were listening. It was her gift.

When she died, her voice fell quiet, but her words live on.

The Life of Gwendolyn Brooks

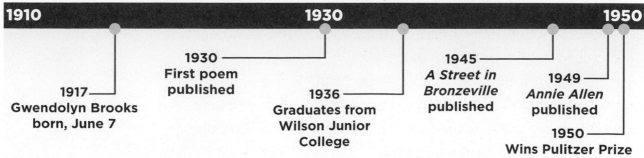

1910

1930

1950

1917
Gwendolyn Brooks
born, June 7

1930
First poem
published

1936
Graduates from
Wilson Junior
College

1945
*A Street in
Bronzeville*
published

1949
Annie Allen
published

1950
Wins Pulitzer Prize

CA Critical Thinking

Now answer numbers 1 through 4. Base your answers on the passage "Montezuma's Mantle."

1. **The best way to describe Dr. Frederick's character is:**

   A casual and indifferent

   B unobservant and lethargic

   C focused and determined

   D lazy and disinterested

2. **Dr. Frederick hopes to discover**

   A a box.

   B the ancient Aztec city of Tenochtitlán.

   C a fireplace.

   D Mexico City.

3. **Read this sentence from the passage.**

> Out of the corner of his eye, he caught <u>sight</u> of billowing canvas in the distance.

What is a homophone for the underlined word in the sentence?

   A site

   B sighed

   C sign

   D sit

4. **Write a brief summary of what happens in the story of "Montezuma's Mantle." Use details from the passage to support your answer.**

Now answer numbers 1 through 4. Base your answers on the article "Gwendolyn Brooks: A Voice."

1. **How did Gwendolyn Brooks solve the problem of the unheard voices of African American Chicagoans?**

   A She tried to change the people in her community.
   B She learned all the techniques and tools of poetry.
   C She used the community's language in her poetry.
   D She graduated from Wilson Junior College.

2. **What was the special thing Gwendolyn Brooks did that helped her rediscover her own writing and herself?**

   A She won the Pulitzer Prize for her book, *Annie Allen*.
   B She went to a writer's conference with young people.
   C She worked for a newspaper.
   D She published her first poem when she was 13 years old.

3. **Which word best describes Gwendolyn Brooks's character?**

   A independent
   B ambivalent
   C worried
   D angry

4. **Use the time line to tell how old Gwendolyn Brooks was when she won the Pulitzer Prize.**

   A She was 13 years old.
   B She had just graduated college.
   C She was 33 years old.
   D The information is not given.

Write on Demand

PROMPT Why do you think the poetry of Gwendolyn Brooks is so popular? Why can ordinary people understand it so easily? Use details from the article to support your answer. Write for 10 minutes. Write as much as you can as well as you can.

The Big Question

What values are important to your culture?

Theme Launcher Video

LOG ON ▶ Find out more about people's values at www.macmillanmh.com.

241

Values are core beliefs that are commonly held by members of the same culture or group of people. They are assumptions about behavior that guide the way people live. Values include people's ideas about what is right or wrong, helpful or harmful, lawful or unlawful. For example, one culture might value individual success or wealth while another might think that group cooperation and equality are more important values.

Values represent people's beliefs regarding what they consider to be most important in life. They are transmitted through traditions, rituals, and customs.

Research Activities

Throughout the unit, you will be learning about people who were true to their values. Choose a person from your culture to focus your research on and explain how you learned about values from this person.

Keep Track of Ideas

As you read, keep track of all you are learning about people's values. Use the Study Book to keep a record of information. On the top section, write the unit theme: A Question of Values. On each layer, write ideas you learn each week that will help you in your research and understanding of the unit theme.

FOLDABLES®
Study Organizer

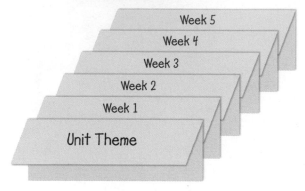

Week 5
Week 4
Week 3
Week 2
Week 1
Unit Theme

Research Toolkit

Conduct Your Unit 3 Research Online with:

Research Roadmap
Follow step-by-step guide to complete your research project.

Online Resources
- Topic Finder and other Research Tools
- Videos and Virtual Fieldtrips
- Photos and Drawings for Presentations
- Related Articles and Web Resources

California Web Site Links

Go to **www.macmillanmh.com** for more information.

California People

Dolores Huerta, Labor Leader
Dolores Huerta has been an activist for farm workers' rights for many years.

243

Honesty

CA **Talk About It**

What did this boy find?
What do you think he should
do with it?

LOG
ON ▶ Find out more about
honesty at
www.macmillanmh.com.

245

Anasazi bowl

A Win-Win Week

by Victor Sanchez

A Challenge

Maria's family had just arrived in Greensboro, North Carolina. Her father was going to take over as **foreman** in charge of a big building project. As an **employee** who worked for a large construction company, Maria's dad was sent to many places. This time his family had moved, too. Maria could not **deny** that she missed her life and friends back home.

Maria sighed and gritted her teeth. She bit down so hard it hurt. Then she entered the classroom. The first day of school was not easy for someone who was shy.

A Team Player

Mr. Hall, the teacher, greeted the students with an announcement. They would research how different parts of the nation had changed over time. The group with the best report would win a prize.

Maria felt hopeful when she got her assignment. Her group was to learn about the Old Southwest. Maria and her family were from New Mexico. Perhaps she would be able to **fulfill** her role and be a real member of this team.

Maria's team met and made a list of the groups who had lived in the Old Southwest. The list included Native Americans, Spanish, Mexicans, and settlers from other parts of the United States and the world. The team also made notes about resources to use. "This is useful," said Keith. "We also need some interesting information about the customs and the influence of these different groups."

Maria spoke up. "My grandfather still lives in New Mexico," she said. "He has collected many stories and examples of folk art of the region. We could e-mail him with questions."

"Way to go, Maria!" **gloated** Sara with a big grin. "Now we have a real chance of winning."

A Wonderful Week

A week later, Maria's team was ready. The result was a winning presentation about the Old Southwest. They showed slides of the old ranches, of the fiestas held there, and of Native American artifacts. Since the area was always known for abundant crops, they showed pictures of the ones that still **flourish** today. They even had a tape recording of a Mexican folktale. The class applauded **vigorously** as the team finished the presentation. They clapped loudly and cheered.

For Maria it was fun to be in touch with her grandfather, and she was proud of their presentation.

"We couldn't have done it without you," Sara and Keith told Maria.

Maria smiled **gleefully**. She was very happy. "I enjoyed working with you, too."

Reread for Comprehension

Story Structure

Character, Setting, Plot
A Character, Setting, and Plot Chart helps you understand the structure of a story. Recording key events in a story will help you recall what you have read. Take note of the narrator, the characters, the setting, and the events of the story.

Use the chart as you reread "A Win-Win Week."

Character	Setting	Plot

CA Comprehension

Genre

A **Folktale** is a story based on the traditions of a people or region which is handed down from one generation to the next and becomes legendary.

Story Structure

Character, Setting, Plot As you read, use your Character, Setting, and Plot Chart.

Character	Setting	Plot

Read to Find Out

How does Juan prove to be honest?

Juan Verdades
The Man Who Couldn't Tell a Lie

Award Winning Author

retold by Joe Hayes
illustrated by Joseph Daniel Fiedler

ONE LATE SUMMER DAY a group of wealthy rancheros was gathered on the village plaza, joking and laughing and discussing events on their ranches.

One of the men, whose name was don Ignacio, had a fine apple tree on his land. The rancher called the apple tree *el manzano real*—the royal apple tree—and was extremely proud of it. It had been planted by his great-grandfather, and there was something about the soil it grew in and the way the afternoon sun struck it that made the apple tree **flourish**. It gave sweeter and more flavorful fruit than any other tree in the country round about.

Every rancher for miles around knew about *el manzano real*, and each year they all hoped don Ignacio would give them a small basket of its sweet fruit. And so each of the ranchers asked don Ignacio how the fruit of the apple tree was doing. To each one don Ignacio replied, "It's doing beautifully, amigo, beautifully. My **foreman** takes perfect care of the tree, and every evening he reports how the fruit is ripening."

When don Ignacio said this to his friend don Arturo, the other man replied, "Do you mean to say, don Ignacio, that you don't tend your magnificent tree yourself? How can you have such faith in your **employee**? Maybe he's not doing all he says he is. Maybe he's not telling you the truth."

Don Ignacio wagged a finger at his friend. "*Mi capataz* has never failed me in any way," he insisted. "He has never told me a lie."

"Are you sure, *compadre*?" said don Arturo. "Are you sure that he has never lied to you?"

"Absolutely certain, *compadre*, absolutely certain. The young man doesn't know how to tell a lie. His name is Juan Valdez, but everyone calls him Juan Verdades because he is so truthful."

"I don't believe it. There never was an employee who didn't lie to his boss. I'm sure I can make him tell you a lie."

"Never," replied the proud employer.

The two friends went on arguing good-naturedly, but little by little they began to raise their voices and attract the attention of the other men on the plaza.

Finally don Arturo declared loudly, "I'll bet you whatever you want that within two weeks at the most I'll make this Juan Verdades tell you a lie."

"All right," replied don Ignacio. "It's a deal. I'll bet my ranch against yours that you can't make my foreman lie to me."

The other ranchers laughed when they heard that. "Ho-ho, don Arturo," they said, "now we'll see just how sure you are that you're right."

"As sure as I am of my own name," said don Arturo. "I accept the bet, don Ignacio. But you must allow me the freedom to try anything I wish." The two friends shook hands, and the other men in the group agreed to serve as witnesses to the bet.

The gathering broke up, and don Arturo and don Ignacio rode confidently away toward their ranches. But as don Arturo rode along thinking of what he had just done, he no longer felt so sure of himself. When he arrived home and told his wife and daughter about the bet, his wife began to cry. "What will we do when we lose our ranch?" she sobbed. And don Arturo began to think he had made a terrible mistake.

But his daughter, whose name was Araceli and who was a very bright and lively young woman, just laughed and said, "Don't worry, *Mamá*. We're not going to lose our ranch."

Araceli suggested to her father that he make up some excuse for them all to spend the next two weeks at don Ignacio's house. "If we're staying on don Ignacio's ranch," she said, "we'll surely discover a way to come out the winners."

> **Plot**
> What is the challenge facing don Arturo and his family?

252

The next day don Arturo rode to don Ignacio's ranch and told his friend, "My men are mending the walls of my house and giving them a fresh coat of whitewash. It would be more convenient for my family to be away. Could my wife and daughter and I stay at your house for a while?"

"Of course, my friend," don Ignacio answered. "Feel perfectly free."

That afternoon don Arturo and his family moved into don Ignacio's house, and the next morning Araceli rose at dawn, as she always did at home, and went to the ranch kitchen to prepare coffee. The foreman, Juan Verdades, was already there, drinking a cup of coffee he had made for himself and eating a breakfast of leftover tortillas. She smiled at him, and he greeted her politely: *"Buenos días, señorita."* And then he finished his simple breakfast and went off to begin his day's work.

That night don Arturo and his daughter made up a plan. Araceli rose before dawn the next day and went to the kitchen to prepare coffee and fresh tortillas for the foreman. She smiled sweetly as she offered them to Juan. He returned her smile and thanked her very kindly. Each morning she did the same thing, and Juan Verdades began to fall in love with Araceli, which was just what the girl and her father expected.

What Araceli hadn't expected was that she began to fall in love with Juan Verdades too and looked forward to getting up early every morning just to be alone with him. She even began to wish she might end up marrying the handsome young foreman. Araceli continued to work on the plan she and her father had made—but she now had a plan of her own as well.

Of course, Juan knew that he was just a worker and Araceli was the daughter of a wealthy ranchero, so he didn't even dream of asking her to marry him. Still, he couldn't help trying to please her in every way. So one morning when they were talking, Juan said to Araceli, "You're very kind to have fresh coffee and warm food ready for me every morning and to honor me with the pleasure of your company. Ask me for whatever you want from this ranch. I'll speak to don Ignacio and see that it's given to you."

This is exactly what the girl and her father thought would happen. And she replied just as they had planned. It was the last thing Juan expected to hear.

"There's only one thing on this ranch I want," she said. "I'd like to have all the apples from *el manzano real*."

The young man was very surprised, and very distressed as well, because he knew he couldn't **fulfill** her wish.

"I could never give you that," Juan said. "You know how don Ignacio treasures the fruit of that tree. He might agree to give you a basket of apples, but no more. I would have to take the fruit without permission, and then what would I say to don Ignacio? I can give you anything else from the ranch, but not what you're asking for."

With that the conversation ended and they separated for the day. In the evening Juan reported to don Ignacio, and they exchanged the exact words they said every evening:

"Good evening, *mi capataz*," the rancher said.

"Good evening, *mi patrón*," replied the foreman.

"How goes it with my cattle and land?"

"Your cattle are healthy, your pastures are green."

"And the fruit of *el manzano real*?"

"The fruit is fat and ripening well."

The next morning Juan and Araceli met again. As they sipped their coffee together, Juan said, "I truly would like to repay you for the kindness you've shown me. There must be something on this ranch you would like. Tell me what it is. I'll see that it's given to you."

But again Araceli replied, "There's only one thing on this ranch I want: the apples from *el manzano real*."

Each day they repeated the conversation. Araceli asked for the same thing, and Juan said he couldn't give it to her. But each day Juan was falling more hopelessly in love with Araceli. Finally, just the day before the two weeks of the bet would have ended, the foreman gave in. He said he would go pick the apples right then and bring them to the girl.

Juan hitched up a wagon and drove to the apple tree. He picked every single apple and delivered the wagonload of fruit to Araceli. She thanked him very warmly, and his spirits rose for a moment. But as he mounted his horse to leave, they sank once again. Juan rode away alone, lost in his thoughts, and Araceli hurried off to tell her father the news and then to wait for a chance to talk to don Ignacio too.

Juan rode until he came to a place where there were several dead trees. He dismounted and walked up to one of them. Then he took off his hat and jacket and put them on the dead tree and pretended it was don Ignacio. He started talking to it to see if he could tell it a lie.

"Good evening, *mi capataz*," he pretended he heard the tree say.

"Good evening, *mi patrón*."

"How goes it with my cattle and land?"

"Your cattle are healthy, your pastures are green."

"And the fruit of *el manzano real*?"

"The . . . the crows have carried the fruit away. . . ."

But the words were hardly out of his mouth when he heard himself say, "No, that's not true, *mi patrón*, I picked the fruit. . . ." And then he stopped himself.

He took a deep breath and started over again with, "Good evening, *mi capataz*."

And when he reached the end, he sputtered, "The . . . the wind shook the apples to the ground, and the cows came and ate them. . . . No, they didn't, *mi patrón*. I . . ."

He tried over and over, until he realized there was no way he could tell a lie. But he knew he could never come right out and say what he had done either. He had to think of another way to tell don Ignacio. He took his hat and coat from the stump and sadly set out for the ranch.

All day long Juan worried about what he would say to don Ignacio. And all day long don Ignacio wondered what he would hear from his foreman, because as soon as Araceli had shown the apples to her father he had run **gleefully** to tell don Ignacio what had happened.

"Now you'll see, *compadre*," don Arturo **gloated**. "You're about to hear a lie from Juan Verdades."

Don Ignacio was heartsick to think that all his apples had been picked, but he had agreed that don Arturo could try whatever he wanted. He sighed and said, "Very well, *compadre*, we'll see what happens this evening."

Don Arturo rode off to gather the other ranchers who were witnesses to the bet, leaving don Ignacio to pace nervously up and down in his house. And then, after don Ignacio received a visit from Araceli and she made a request that he couldn't **deny**, he paced even more nervously.

All the while, Juan went about his work, thinking of what he would say to his don Ignacio. That evening the foreman went as usual to make his report to his employer, but he walked slowly and his head hung down. The other ranchers were behind the bushes listening, and Araceli and her mother were watching anxiously from a window of the house.

> **Character**
> How do you think Juan will account for the missing apples? Support your answer.

The conversation began as it always did:

"Good evening, *mi capataz*."

"Good evening, *mi patrón*."

"How goes it with my cattle and land?"

"Your cattle are healthy, your pastures are green."

"And the fruit of *el manzano real*?"

Juan took a deep breath and replied:

"Oh, *patrón*, something terrible happened today.

Some fool picked your apples and gave them away."

Don Ignacio pretended to be shocked and confused. "Some fool picked them?" he said. "Who would do such a thing?"

Juan turned his face aside. He couldn't look at don Ignacio. The rancher asked again, "Who would do such a thing? Do I know this person?"

Finally the foreman answered:

"The father of the fool is my father's father's son.

The fool has no sister and no brother.

His child would call my father 'grandfather.'

He's ashamed that he did what was done."

Don Ignacio paused for a moment to think about Juan's answer. And then, to Juan's surprise, don Ignacio grabbed his hand and started shaking it excitedly.

The other ranchers ran laughing from their hiding places. "Don Arturo," they all said, "you lose the bet. You must sign your ranch over to don Ignacio."

"No," said don Ignacio, still **vigorously** shaking Juan's hand. He glanced toward the window where Araceli was watching and went on: "Sign it over to don Juan Verdades. He has proved that he truly deserves that name, and he deserves to be the owner of his own ranch as well."

Everyone cheered and began to congratulate Juan. Don Arturo's face turned white, but he gritted his teeth and forced a smile. He shook Juan's hand and then turned to walk away from the group, his shoulders drooping and his head bowed down.

But Araceli came running from the house and put her arm through her father's. *"Papá,"* she said, "what if Juan Verdades were to marry a relative of yours? Then the ranch would stay in the family, wouldn't it?"

Everyone heard her and turned to look at the girl and her father. And then Juan spoke up confidently, *"Señorita* Araceli, I am the owner of a ranch and many cattle. Will you marry me?"

Of course she said she would, and don Arturo heaved a great sigh. "Don Juan Verdades," he said, "I'll be proud to have such an honest man for a son-in-law." He beckoned his wife to come from the house, and they both hugged Juan and Araceli.

The other ranchers hurried off to fetch their families, and a big celebration began. It lasted all through the night, with music and dancing and many toasts to Juan and Araceli. And in the morning everyone went home with a big basket of delicious apples from *el manzano real*.

Storytelling with Joe and Joseph

Joe Hayes loves stories. When he is not writing, Joe is a professional storyteller. He recreates traditional stories, such as this one, and then crisscrosses the country, telling them to kids in schools and at festivals. How did he get started? By telling stories to his own children!

Joseph Daniel Fiedler lives in Talpa, a small village in the Hispanic Highlands of New Mexico. He is an award-winning artist of children's books and his paintings hang in art shows and galleries, too. He's a busy artist, but he has help—two cats named Iko and Obeah.

Other books by Joe Hayes: *¡El Cucuy!* and *Watch Out for Clever Women!*

 Find out more about Joe Hayes and Joseph Daniel Fiedler at **www.macmillanmh.com**.

CA **Author's Purpose**

Joe Hayes entertains the reader with this traditional folktale. What makes *Juan Verdades* informative, too?

Critical Thinking

Summarize

Use your Character, Setting, and Plot Chart to summarize *Juan Verdades*. How do plot events lead to a satisfactory conclusion?

Character	Setting	Plot

Think and Compare

1. What **plot** developments ruin don Arturo's plan to get don Ignacio's loyal **employee** to tell a lie? **Story Structure: Character, Setting, Plot**

2. If the entire story were told from the point of view of Araceli's **character**, what would be different? What would be the same? **Analyze**

3. If you lived in this **setting** where tradition and family are so important, and your father asked you to help trap Juan Verdades in a lie, what would you do? **Evaluate**

4. If Juan Verdades did lie about the apples, how would that affect the entire community? **Synthesize**

5. Read "A Win-Win Week" on pages 246–247. Pretend you are in Maria's group and have to complete the presentation on the Old Southwest. Think of *Juan Verdades* as a folktale that Maria's grandfather has e-mailed. What information from the story would you include in the presentation? **Reading/ Writing Across Texts**

IN THE DAYS OF THE VAQUEROS:

America's First True Cowboys

by Russell Freedman

Introduction: In the early days of the American Southwest, private landowners found many Native American vaqueros, or herders, to help in the rounding up of animals on the **ranchos**. *Author Russell Freedman describes what went into the work of the vaqueros.*

Tools of the Trade

Over the centuries, ranching changed very little in New Spain. The most important tools for working cattle on the open range continued to be the vaquero's horse and his lariat.

He looked upon his lariat as his good right arm, and it was seldom out of reach of his nimble fingers. With it, he was ready for almost any task that came along.

He made his lariat himself, cutting long strips of untanned cowhide, which he soaked and stretched until they were pliable. Then he braided the leather strips into a rope, which he stretched again, oiled, and softened, working it over with loving care until he was satisfied that it was ready to use.

A typical lariat was about 60 feet long and as thick around as a man's little finger. There were longer ropes, *reatas largas*, which ran to 110 feet or more. Children had their own pint-size lariats. It seemed that everyone was always roping for practice, and that every target was fair game. Dogs, pigs, and chickens became as expert at dodging the rope as the vaqueros were at throwing it.

Coyotes were considered the toughest wild animals to rope, and a man who managed to snare one was greatly admired. While he took pride in his **feat**, he would say with modesty, "*Ese fue un supo,*" "That was a lucky throw."

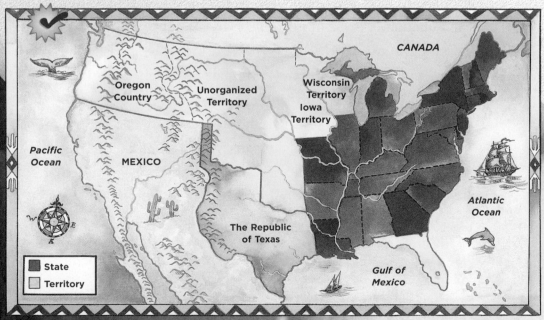

This map shows the Southwest in 1840.

267

A Vaquero by Frederic Remington
circa 1881–1909

Vaqueros also made fine horsehair ropes, *mecates*, which were used for reins and halters. Different colors of hair were blended together, forming ropes that were not only strong but beautiful.

In the early days, vaqueros made their own saddles as well. They took as a model the old Spanish war saddle on which the **conquistadores** had ridden into Mexico, and they gradually transformed it to meet the special needs of cowhands working in cattle country.

They added a large round-topped saddle horn as a sturdy anchor to which their lariats could be secured when they roped a steer. They made the saddle's stirrup straps longer, allowing the rider to get a better knee grip. The stirrups themselves were carved out of wood. They were big enough to let a man stand upright while riding down a steep slope or trotting along the trail.

Saddles became stronger and more compact. At first, vaqueros placed a blanket, a piece of leather, or an animal skin over the seat of the saddle to provide a little comfort. Later they devised the *mochila*, a removable leather covering that fit snugly over the entire saddle and often had built-in saddlebags.

Vaqueros working in brush country covered their stirrups with leather casings called *tapaderas*, or taps, which shielded the rider's feet from cactus thorns. In the deserts of northwestern Mexico, saddles were rigged with *armas*, huge slabs of cowhide that hung down from the saddle on either side, covering and protecting the rider's thighs and lower legs.

Later, vaqueros attached smaller, lightweight *armitas* directly to their legs. These in turn developed into seatless leather leggings called *chaparreras*, or chaps, for protection while riding through mesquite and chaparral thickets. Chaps also protected a rider against rope burns, abrasions from trees and corral posts, and horse bites. They were made of smooth buckskin, or of goat, sheep, wolf, bear, or lion pelts with the wool or fur left on the outside of the chaps.

Since the vaquero often spent his days from sunrise to sunset in the saddle, no single piece of equipment was more important. A well-made saddle, lovingly maintained, was important to his horse, too. A rider with a gentle hand and a good rig could travel for hours and still have a healthy horse, but a poorly made saddle could make a horse sore in no time at all.

 Critical Thinking

1. Study the map on page 267. What are some of the differences between this map and the United States today? **Reading a Map**

2. What would happen to a vaquero if his saddle was lost or damaged? **Analyze**

3. Think about this selection and *Juan Verdades.* How is Juan's life the same as and different from that of a vaquero? **Reading/ Writing Across Texts**

 History/Social Science Activity

Research information about vaqueros. Then imagine that you are a vaquero living on a California rancho. Write a journal entry that describes your day. Include information that you learned from your research.

LOG ON ▶ Go to **www.macmillanmh.com** for more activities.

Writing

✓ **Logical Structure: Sequence**

Writers use a **logical structure** that usually relies on a clear **sequence** to tell a story.

Reading and Writing Connection

Read the passage below. Notice how the author Joe Hayes uses logical structure in his story.

An excerpt from
Juan Verdades

The author makes sure to include some information about Araceli's and don Arturo's plan. If the author hadn't made sure to write that part first, we wouldn't have understood why a wealthy rancher would go and live with his friend.

"If we're staying at don Ignacio's house," she said, "we'll surely discover a way to come out the winners."

The next day don Arturo rode to don Ignacio's ranch and told his friend, "My men are mending the walls of my house and giving them a fresh coat of whitewash. It would be more convenient for my family to be away. Could my wife and daughter and I stay at your house a while?"

Juan Verdades
The Man Who Couldn't Tell a Lie

retold by Joe Hayes
illustrated by Joseph Daniel Fiedler

Read and Find

Read Maggie's writing below. What did she do to help make sure the reader got information in a useful order? Use the Writer's Checklist to help you.

Apple Crazy
by Maggie G.

Every fall, my town has a big apple festival to celebrate the harvest. There's an apple-eating contest, we have an Apple Queen and anything you could think of making out of apples—somebody is making and selling.

This year the barber came rolling down the street looking like a giant apple on roller skates. Imagine what a visitor to our town would think seeing this coming down Main Street!

Read about a town's apple festival and some of the events that take place there.

Writer's Checklist

 Does the writer include details that help you understand the big picture?

 Is the information in an order that makes sense?

☐ Do you feel as if you understand why the first part is important to the second part?

Hope

CA **Talk About It**

Hope is a belief in a positive outcome. What action are these people taking to bring hope to others?

LOG ON ▶ Find out more about hope at **www.macmillanmh.com**.

273

From Daughter to Daughter

by Ramón Pérez

It was a tradition. Every Delgado mother taught her daughter how to make "the famous Delgado empanadas." Empanada is a Spanish word that means "pie" or "meat pie." But the Delgados were not famous for meat pies. They were famous for their dessert empanadas.

Today Lucy Delgado would learn the recipe. She wanted to ask about her family's past, but she was feeling shy. She looked **sheepishly** at her grandmother. "Abuelita, how did we become famous for our empanadas? How did you start a bakery?" she asked.

Abuelita said, "I was making empanadas the way my mother did and the way her mother did. Then I started trying new things. I put rice pudding or chocolate inside an empanada. Some of my friends thought they tasted so good that they asked me to make the sweet pies for them. I wanted to start my own business but I did not have the money."

"So how did you get the money?" Lucy asked.

"By a series of strange **coincidences**. A businessman at a friend's party tasted my empanadas. He thought the **sumptuous** pies were wonderful. My friend had a space for rent so the businessman offered to help me start my bakery. To **sweeten** the pot, he said that he would give me a year's contract to supply his company's cafeteria with empanadas."

"Abuelita had the money and the space, but we still had **phase** three of our problems to face," Lucy's mom said.

"There was so little heat in the space we rented that our fingers were too numb to work," laughed Abuelita. "Sometimes it was so cold in the building that we had to wear gloves on our hands and mufflers around our necks while we made the dough! But we were **devoted** to our idea."

"I worked so hard some days that I **hobbled** home at night because my legs were so tired," Abuelita continued. "But soon the business **prospered**. We were making enough money to hire workers. And that's how the bakery still runs today."

Lucy smiled at Abuelita with pride. After hearing that story, the empanadas seemed to taste sweeter than before.

Reread for **Comprehension**

Summarize

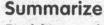

Problem and Solution

A Problem and Solution Chart can help you summarize the events of a story. Identify a story's problem and solution to help you capture its most important details in your summary.

Use a Problem and Solution Chart to help you identify the important parts of the story as you reread "From Daughter to Daughter."

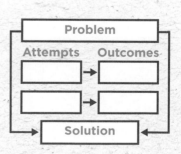

Genre

A **Fairy Tale** features imaginary characters and takes place long ago. It has a plot with a conflict between good and evil. A parody is a humorous imitation of another recognizable work.

Summarize

Problem and Solution
As you read, use your Problem and Solution Chart.

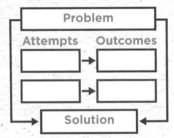

Read to Find Out

How does Rumpelstiltskin's daughter use the king's greed to solve her problem?

Rumpelstiltskin's Daughter

written & illustrated by Diane Stanley

Once there was a miller's daughter who got into a heap of trouble. It was all because her father liked to make up stories and pass them off as truth. Unfortunately, the story he told was that his daughter could spin straw into gold, which, of course, she could not. Even more unfortunately, he told this whopper in the hearing of a palace servant who rushed right off to tell the king. Since the king loved nothing in this world more than gold, he had the miller's daughter hauled up to the palace immediately and made her an offer she couldn't refuse. He put her in a room full of straw and ordered her to spin it into gold by morning, or die.

277

By one of those unlikely **coincidences** so common in fairy tales, no sooner had the king closed and bolted the door than a very small gentleman showed up and revealed that he really *could* spin straw into gold. Furthermore, he offered to do it in exchange for her necklace, which was made of gold-tone metal and wasn't worth ten cents. Naturally, she agreed.

The next morning, the king was so overjoyed with his room full of gold that he rewarded the miller's daughter by doubling the amount of straw and repeating his threat. Once again, Rumpelstiltskin (for that was his name) arrived to help her out. This time she gave him her paper-band pinkie ring.

After this second success, the king was practically apoplectic with greed. He proceeded to empty every barn in the neighborhood of straw and to fill the room with it. This time, he added a little sugar to **sweeten** the pot: If she turned it all into gold, he would make her his queen. You can just imagine how the miller's daughter was feeling when Rumpelstiltskin popped in for the third time.

"That's quite a pile," he said. "I suppose you want me to spin it into gold."

"Well, the situation has changed just a bit," said the miller's daughter (who also had a name—it was Meredith). "If you *don't*, I will die. If you *do*, I marry the king."

Now *that*, thought Rumpelstiltskin, has possibilities. After all, getting to be the queen was a big step up for a miller's daughter. She would surely pay him anything. And there was only one thing in the world he really wanted—a little child to love and care for.

"Okay, here's the deal," he said. "I will spin the straw into gold, just like before. In return, once you become queen, you must let me adopt your firstborn child. I promise I'll be an excellent father. I know all the lullabies. I'll read to the child every day. I'll even coach Little League."

"You've got to be kidding," Meredith said. "I'd rather marry *you* than that jerk!"

"Really?" said Rumpelstiltskin, and he blushed all the way from the top of his head to the tip of his toes (which admittedly wasn't very far, because he was so short).

"Sure," she said. "I like your ideas on parenting, you'd make a good provider, and I have a weakness for short men."

So Rumpelstiltskin spun a golden ladder, and they escaped out the window. They were married the very next day and lived happily together far, far away from the palace.

Meredith and Rumpelstiltskin lived a quiet country life, raising chickens and growing vegetables. Every now and then, when they needed something they couldn't make or grow, Rumpelstiltskin would spin up a little gold to buy it with.

Now, they had a daughter, and she was just as sunny and clever as you would expect her to be, having such **devoted** parents. When she was sixteen, they decided she ought to see more of the world, so every now and then they allowed her to take the gold into town to exchange it for coins and to do a little shopping.

The goldsmith grew curious about the pretty country girl who came in with those odd coils of gold. He mentioned it to his friend the baker, who mentioned it to the blacksmith, who mentioned it to the tax collector, who hurried to the palace and told the king.

It may not surprise you to learn that the king hadn't changed a bit. If anything, he was greedier than before. As he listened, his eyes glittered. "I once knew a miller's daughter who could make gold like that," he said. "Unfortunately, she got away. Let's make sure *this* one doesn't."

So the next time Rumpelstiltskin's daughter went to see the goldsmith, two of the king's guards were waiting for her. In a red-hot minute, she was in a carriage and speeding toward the palace. And what she saw on the way broke her heart. Everywhere the fields lay barren. Sickly children stood begging beside the road. Nobody in the kingdom had anything anymore, because the king had it all.

Finally they reached the palace. There were high walls around it and a moat full of crocodiles. Armed guards were everywhere, gnashing their teeth, clutching their swords, and peering about with shifty eyes. As the carriage went over the bridge and under the portcullis, the hungry people shook their fists at them. It was not a pretty sight.

Rumpelstiltskin's daughter was taken at once to the grand chamber where the king sat on his golden throne. He didn't waste time on idle pleasantries.

"Where did you get *this*?" he asked, showing her the gold.

"Uh . . . ," said Rumpelstiltskin's daughter.

"I thought so," said the king. "Guards, take her to the tower and see what she can do with all that straw."

Rumpelstiltskin's daughter looked around. She saw a pile of straw the size of a bus. She saw a locked door and high windows. She gave a big sigh and began to think. She knew her father could get her out of this pickle. But she had heard stories about the king all her life. One room full of gold would never satisfy him. Her father would be stuck here, spinning, until there was not an iota of straw left in the kingdom.

After a while she climbed the pile of straw and thought some more. She thought about the poor farmers and about the hungry children with their thin faces and sad eyes. She put the two thoughts together and cooked up a plan. Then Rumpelstiltskin's daughter curled up and went to sleep.

> **Problem and Solution**
> Identify the main problem Rumpelstiltskin's daughter faces. Look for actions she takes to solve the problem.

The next day, the king was very disappointed.

"Where's my gold?" he wanted to know.

"I'm sure you have rooms full of it upstairs," said Rumpelstiltskin's daughter. And she was right. He did.

"But I want *more!*" he said. "And I want *you* to make it for me."

"Alas," she said, "I never made gold in my life. But"—and here she paused for effect—"I saw my grandfather make it." When the king's face brightened, she added, "He died years ago."

"Surely you remember how he did it," cried the king. "Think! Think!"

"Well," she said slowly, "there is one thing I'm sure of. He didn't spin it, he *grew* it."

The next morning the king and Rumpelstiltskin's daughter got into his glittering coach, with two guards up front and two guards behind and a huge bag of gold inside. They drove under the portcullis, over the bridge, and out into the countryside. At the first farm they came to, they stopped and sent for the farmer. He was thin and ragged and barefoot. So were his wife and children.

"Now tell the farmer he must plant this gold coin in his field, and you will come back in the fall to collect everything it has grown. Tell him you will give him another gold coin for his pains," she whispered.

"Do I *have* to?" the king whined.

"Well, I don't know," she said. "That's how my grandfather always did it."

"Okay," said the king. "But this better work." He gave the farmer two gold coins, and they hurried on to the next farm. By the end of the week they had covered the entire kingdom.

All through the summer the king was restless. "Is it time yet?" he would ask. "Is the gold ripe?"

"Wait," said Rumpelstiltskin's daughter.

Finally August came and went.

"Now," she said. "Now you can go and see what has grown in the fields."

So once again they piled into the glittering coach (with two guards up front and two guards behind) and brought along wagons to carry the gold and a lot more guards to protect it.

As they neared the first farm, the king gasped with joy. The field shone golden in the morning sun.

"Gold!" he cried.

"No," said Rumpelstiltskin's daughter, "something better than gold."

"How can anything be better than gold?" said the king.

"It's wheat," she said. "You can eat it. You can't eat gold."

Before the king could start turning purple, the farmer and his family came running toward the carriage. In their arms they carried baskets of wheat and barley and apples and green beans and pumpkins and corn and I don't know what all. They piled it into the wagon and kissed the king's hand, grinning ear to ear. I can promise you that nothing like that had ever happened to the king before.

"Well," he said **sheepishly**, "maybe there will be gold at the next place."

But everywhere it was the same. The land **prospered**, the children looked healthy, and the king was a hero. At the end of the week they returned to the palace with all the food the wagons could carry.

The cook was so overjoyed, he put on a **sumptuous** feast
to celebrate. Unfortunately, there was no one to invite except
Rumpelstiltskin's daughter and the guards, who spent the whole meal
gnashing their teeth, clutching their swords, and peering about with
shifty eyes.

"I wish they'd quit that," said Rumpelstiltskin's daughter.

After dinner, the king spoke. "That was all very nice, my dear,"
he said, "but you must have been mistaken. That was how your
grandfather grew *food*, not how he made gold."

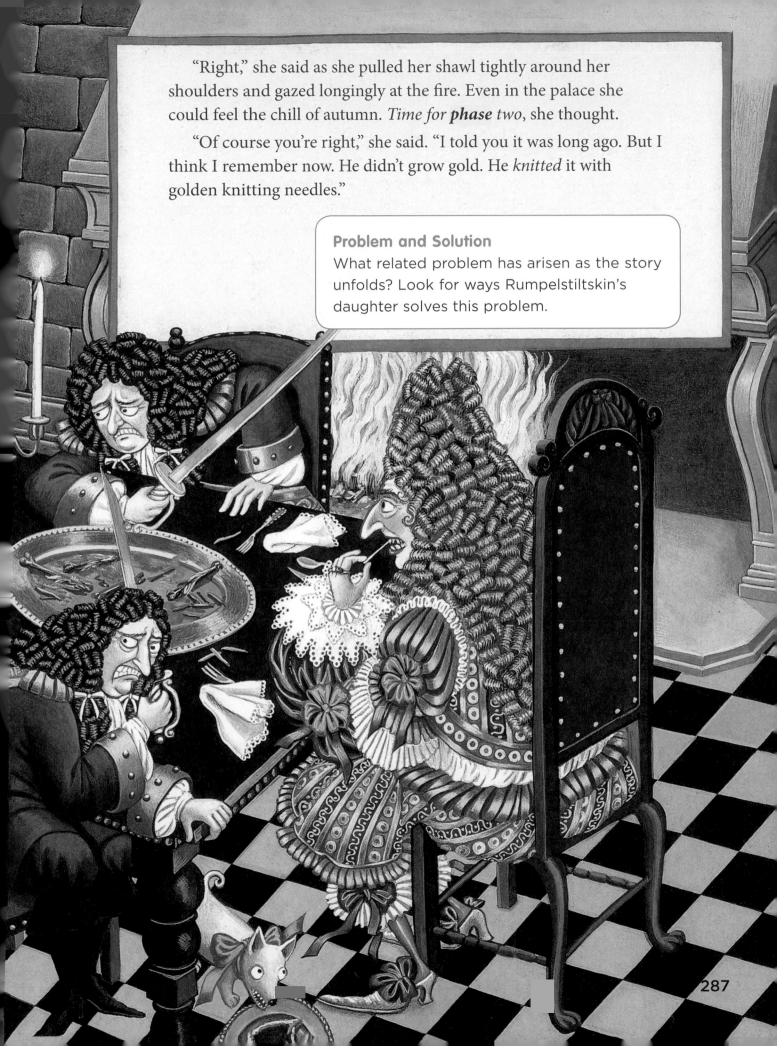

"Right," she said as she pulled her shawl tightly around her shoulders and gazed longingly at the fire. Even in the palace she could feel the chill of autumn. *Time for* **phase** *two*, she thought.

"Of course you're right," she said. "I told you it was long ago. But I think I remember now. He didn't grow gold. He *knitted* it with golden knitting needles."

Problem and Solution
What related problem has arisen as the story unfolds? Look for ways Rumpelstiltskin's daughter solves this problem.

So the next day they loaded the coach with knitting needles, a bag of gold, and lots and lots of yellow wool. Then they headed off under the portcullis, over the bridge (with two guards up front and two guards behind), and out into the countryside.

At the first cottage they came to, they asked to see the granny. She **hobbled** to the door in her rags and curtsied to the king.

"Now," whispered Rumpelstiltskin's daughter, "give her a bag of wool and a pair of needles. Tell her to knit it all up and you will come back in a month to collect your riches. Give her a gold coin for her pains."

"Do I *have* to?" the king whined.

"My grandfather always did," she said. "I would, if I were you."

And so they went all over the kingdom, hiring every granny they could find.

At the end of the month, the king ordered his coach and wagons, rounded up his guards, and went to see the grannies. As he neared the first cottage, he heard the sound of singing. Looking out the window, the king saw crowds of happy villagers waiting there to greet him, cheering wildly as he passed. And every one of them was warm as toast in yellow woolly clothes.

"Gold!" cried the king.

"Something better than gold," said Rumpelstiltskin's daughter. "Your people will be warm all winter."

Everyone brought presents for the king. By the time he got back to his palace, he had seventeen sweaters, forty-two mufflers, eight vests, one pair of knickers, one hundred and thirty-five pairs of socks, twelve nightcaps, and a tam-o'-shanter. All the color of gold.

"Do they suit me?" asked the king as he tried them on.

"Absolutely," said Rumpelstiltskin's daughter.

The guards just stood there, gnashing their teeth, clutching their swords, and peering about with shifty eyes.

"Don't you think it's time you got rid of them?" she suggested. "And the walls and the moat and the crocodiles, too. You don't need them anymore—your people love you now."

She was right, as
always, so the king set the
guards to work tearing down the
walls. And with the stones, they built a zoo
for the crocodiles and houses for the poor.

"Are you sure you don't remember how your
grandfather made gold?" asked the king one day.

"I'm afraid not," she said.

"It's a terrible pity," he sighed. "But you did try.
And as a reward, I have decided to make you
my queen."

"Why don't you make me prime minister
instead," suggested Rumpelstiltskin's daughter.

And so the king did just that. He built her a
nice house near the palace, and once a month she
took time off to visit her parents. The people of the
kingdom never went cold or hungry again. And whenever
the king started worrying about gold, she sent him on a
goodwill tour throughout the countryside, which cheered
him right up.

Oh, and I forgot to tell you—Rumpelstiltskin's
daughter had a name, too. It was Hope.

Once Upon a Time with Diane Stanley

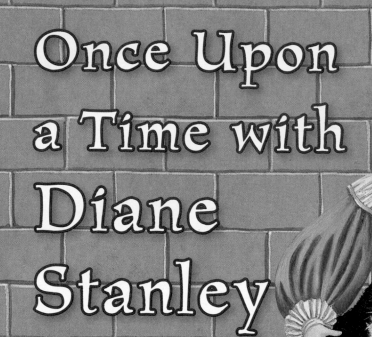

Diane Stanley researches everything about her topic before she starts writing and illustrating a book. For this story, she even investigated different types of food from the days when the characters might have lived. Maybe she pays such close attention to detail because she used to illustrate medical books. She always chooses a subject she loves—someone she considers the most interesting person or character in the world—and then reads everything she can on her subject. This helps her create the right setting, which is on top of Diane's how-to-write list.

 LOG ON ▶ Find out more about Diane Stanley at **www.macmillanmh.com**.

Another book by Diane Stanley:
Leonardo da Vinci

 Author's Purpose

Diane Stanley's main purpose is to entertain, but she is also informing by teaching that kindness is more valuable than gold. What makes this story entertaining?

CA Critical Thinking

Summarize

Use your Problem and Solution Chart to help you summarize *Rumpelstiltskin's Daughter*. What is the main problem that Rumpelstiltskin's daughter encounters? How does she solve it?

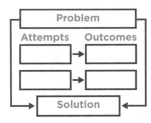

Think and Compare

1. What is the **problem** that Rumpelstiltskin's daughter faces and how does she find a **solution** to it? **Summarize: Problem and Solution**

2. What kind of a person is Rumpelstiltskin's daughter? Do you think she **prospered** in the end? Support your answer with story details. **Analyze**

3. The king's guards are always "gnashing their teeth, clutching their swords, and peering about with shifty eyes." If you were Hope, what might you do to change how the guards act? **Synthesize**

4. Rumpelstiltskin's daughter is named Hope. Why do you think the writer chose to end the story with that fact? Why is hope so important to so many people? **Evaluate**

5. Read "From Daughter to Daughter" on pages 274–275. What are the similarities between the way Lucy's grandmother makes special empanadas and the way Hope solves her problems in *Rumpelstiltskin's Daughter*? **Reading/Writing Across Texts**

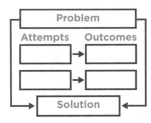

Genre

A **Myth/Legend** is a story that often explains occurrences in nature through the intervention of gods and goddesses.

✔ Literary Elements

A **Moral** is a practical lesson contained in the narrative.

Hyperbole is the deliberate use of exaggeration for emphasis. Myths often use hyperbole to describe human weaknesses.

The Golden Touch

retold by Mary Pope Osborne

Bacchus, the merry god, raised his goblet. "To you, King Midas," he said, "and because you have been so hospitable to me—ask for anything you wish, and I will grant it to you."

"What an idea!" said Midas. "Anything I wish?"

"Indeed, anything," said Bacchus.

"Anything?"

"Yes! Yes!"

"Ah, well," said the king, chuckling. "Of course, there's only one thing: I wish that everything I touch would turn to gold!" Midas looked sideways at Bacchus, for he couldn't believe such a gift could really be his.

"My friend, you already have all the gold you could possibly want," said Bacchus, looking disappointed.

"Oh, no! I don't!" said Midas. "One never has enough gold!"

"Well, if that's what you wish for, I suppose I will have to grant it," said Bacchus.

Bacchus soon took his leave. As Midas waved good-bye to him, his hand brushed an oak twig hanging from a tree—and the twig turned to gold!

The king screamed with joy, then shouted after Bacchus, "My wish has come true! Thank you! Thank you!"

The god turned and waved, then disappeared down the road.

Midas looked around excitedly. He leaned over and picked a stone up from the ground—and the stone turned into a golden nugget! He kicked the sand—and the sand turned to golden grains!

King Midas threw back his head and shouted, "I'm the richest man in the world!" Then he rushed about his grounds, touching everything. And everything, *everything* turned to gold: ears of corn in his fields! Apples plucked from trees! The pillars of his mansion!

When the king's servants heard him shouting, they rushed to see what was happening. They found their king dancing wildly on his lawn, turning the grass to glittering blades of gold. Everyone laughed and clapped as Midas washed his hands in his fountain and turned the water to a gleaming spray!

Finally, exhausted but overjoyed, King Midas called for his dinner. His servants placed a huge banquet meal before him on his lawn. "Oh, I'm so hungry!" he said as he speared a piece of meat and brought it to his mouth.

Midas's weakness is greed, which is treated as hyperbole.

But suddenly King Midas realized his wish may not have been as wonderful as he thought—for the moment he bit down on the meat, it, too, turned to gold.

Midas laughed uneasily, then reached for a piece of bread. But as soon as his hands touched the bread, it also became a hard, golden nugget! Weak with dread, Midas reached for his goblet of water. But alas! His lips touched only hard, cold metal. The water had also turned to gold.

Covering his head and moaning, King Midas realized his great wish was going to kill him. He would starve to death or die of thirst!

"Bacchus!" he cried, throwing his hands toward heaven. "I've been a greedy fool! Take away your gift! Free me from my golden touch! Help me, Bacchus!"

The sobbing king fell off his chair to his knees. He beat his fists against the ground, turning even the little anthills to gold. His servants grieved for him, but

none dared go near him, for they feared he might accidentally turn them to gold, too!

As everyone wailed with sorrow, Bacchus suddenly appeared on the palace lawn. The merry god stood before the sobbing king for a moment, then said, "Rise, Midas."

Stumbling to his feet, King Midas begged Bacchus to forgive him and to take away the curse of the golden touch.

"You were greedy and foolish, my friend," said Bacchus. "But I will forgive you. Now go and wash yourself in the Pactolus River that runs by Sardis, and you'll be cleansed of this desire to have more gold than anyone else!"

King Midas did as Bacchus said. He washed in the Pactolus, leaving behind streams of gold in the river's sands. Then he returned home and happily ate his dinner.

And that is why the sands of the Pactolus River were golden.

The moral is not to wish for more than you need.

MODERN WORDS WITH GREEK ORIGINS

arachnid term for spider groups; from Arachne, the girl whom Athena turned into a spider

iridescent like the colors in a rainbow; from Iris, the rainbow goddess

mnemonic a way to remember something; from Mnemosyne, goddess of memory

---

 Critical Thinking

1. What lessons does the myth teach? **Moral**

2. Think of another unwise wish that Midas might have made. What would be the unfortunate results of that wish? **Synthesize**

3. Compare the king in *Rumpelstiltskin's Daughter* with Midas at the beginning of the selections and at the end. **Reading/Writing Across Texts**

 Find out more about myths at **www.macmillanmh.com**.

Writing

CA

✔ **Logical Structure: Sequence**

Writers use a **logical structure** that depends on a clear **sequence** to tell a story.

Read the passage below. Notice how the author Diane Stanley uses logical structure in her story.

An excerpt from
Rumpelstiltskin's Daughter

The author makes sure to include some information about Rumpelstiltskin and Meredith, even though the story is mostly about their daughter. If the author hadn't made sure to write that part first, we would have been confused about why the king kidnapped Hope.

So Rumpelstiltskin spun a golden ladder, and they escaped out the window. . . . Meredith and Rumpelstiltskin lived a quiet country life, raising chickens and growing vegetables. . . . Now, they had a daughter, and she was just as sunny and clever as you would expect her to be, having such devoted parents. . . .

Read and Find

Read Arthur's writing below. What did he do to help make sure the reader got information in a useful order? Use the Writer's Checklist to help you.

Saving the Spring Fair
by Arthur U.

Everyone in my school does something to help out at the Spring Fair. Kids build booths and organize field games for the little kids. Teachers sit in the dunk tank or get hit with pies.

No one could understand why the superintendent cancelled the Spring Fair! Everyone was asking the same question: How can we get the Spring Fair back?

> Read how Arthur sets up a logical sequence about saving the school fair.

Writer's Checklist

 Does the writer include details that help you understand the overall situation?

 Is the information in an order that makes sense?

 Do you understand why the first part is important to the second part?

Talk About It

Helping others is often a choice that people make. What motivates people to help others?

LOG ON ▶ Find out more about ways to help others at **www.macmillanmh.com**.

Helping Others

Claude Shirts combines facial expressions with signs to convey his message.

Talking with His Hands

"Go, greased lightning. Go. Go. Go. Go. Go. Go. Go."

Those lyrics are fun when you hear them with a rollicking beat in the musical *Grease!* But they would be **bewildering** if you couldn't hear the music. And even if you weren't confused, you would probably be just plain bored.

Being able to capture the spirit of that song and project it to the audience without sound was a challenge for Claude Shirts. He uses sign language to interpret plays for deaf audiences. "I try to tell the story that the music is telling," he says. Rather than repeating the sign for "go" over and over, he imitated the motions of driving. "I showed the character sitting in a car with his hair going straight back in the wind."

Shirts, 37, works with Hands On!, a group that interprets theater shows for deaf people. *Grease!* was tough enough to interpret. But that was a **moderate** challenge compared with interpreting the plays of Shakespeare. Shirts says Shakespeare's plays are really tricky because they are written in old-fashioned language. "At first, I had not a clue what the characters were saying," he admits. "I had to do so much preparation."

At Hands On! performances, Shirts positions himself so that he doesn't **hamper** deaf audience members' view of the on-stage action. If he does his job well, the crowd does not cheer and applaud. Instead, they reward Shirts with the unique applause given by deaf audiences: the sight of outstretched arms and waving palms moving in silent circles.

A TRADITION OF GIVING

Daniel Cayce started helping needy people in his Arkansas community when he was just three years old. That was when he first volunteered at the food bank his family runs. Cayce's Charity provided more than 1,000 families with food each Thanksgiving. As an Eagle Scout, Daniel decided he wanted to do more. He started a new project that included collecting blankets and pots and pans for the holiday giveaway. His goal one year was to gather more than 1,000 blankets. "I like helping people," he said. It's as simple as that.

Daniel Cayce

Able to Work

In 1990, a landmark law was passed in the United States. The Americans with Disabilities Act (ADA) gave an estimated 30 million Americans with disabilities "a fighting chance in the work force," according to former California Congressman Tony Coelho. Coelho himself was once denied the chance to have the career he wanted because he is epileptic.

Ted Henter is blind. He runs a firm that makes software for others who are blind.

The ADA was designed to **prohibit** discrimination in the workplace against those with disabilities. In large ways and small, the law has brought about changes for the disabled as well as for their employers. It requires businesses to make offices and other workplaces **accessible** to people with disabilities. And it's working. According to Coelho, "There is still job discrimination out there, but the tide is turning."

Tony Coelho

LOG ON Go to **www.macmillanmh.com** for more activities.

Comprehension

Comprehension

Genre

Nonfiction: An article in a newspaper or magazine presents facts and information.

✔ Make Inferences and Analyze

Compare and Contrast When you look for similarities, you compare things. When you look for differences, you contrast them.

Oseola McCarty (third from the right) and her family in 1922

SAVING GRACE

How could a woman who spent her life doing laundry for others give $150,000 for university scholarships?

For most of her life, Oseola McCarty of Hattiesburg, Mississippi, did laundry for other people. It seems reasonable to assume that the modest income of a washerwoman would **prohibit** her from becoming a philanthropist. What people in Hattiesburg could not have guessed was that McCarty would wind up donating a small fortune to the local university. Large donations usually come from wealthy alumni. However, the University of Southern Mississippi announced that Oseola McCarty, then 87 years old, was giving the university $150,000 to finance scholarships for African American students. "I want them to have an education," said McCarty, who never married and had no children of her own. "I had to work hard all my life. They can have the chance that I didn't have."

HARD WORK

When McCarty was in the sixth grade, her aunt became unable to walk. McCarty left school to care for her. She also helped her mother and grandmother with their backyard laundry business. "Even when I was little," says McCarty, "I was always getting into the wash." By the time her aunt got back on her feet a year later, McCarty thought she was too far behind to return to school. "I was too big," she says. "So I kept on working."

McCarty's business was similar to running a laundromat. However, unlike the owner of a laundromat, she did not use washing machines and dryers. McCarty did all of the washing by hand. She had tried a washer and dryer, but found them inadequate. Instead, she boiled the clothes in a big black pot and hung them on the line to dry. Her place of business was the backyard of the wood-frame house she grew up in.

"She had a bench in the backyard with three tubs on it," says Helen Tyre, 89, who hired McCarty back in 1943. "She and her mother and grandmother carried the water from a hydrant."

McCarty in 1997

Tyre remembers a time when McCarty charged just 50 cents a bundle (a week's worth of laundry for a family of four). Eventually her fee climbed to $10 a bundle, still a very **moderate** price.

SO OTHERS CAN LEARN

McCarty thought for years about the scholarship project. But it was only after arthritis forced her to stop taking in wash—at the age of 87—that she reached out to the university. Many people in McCarty's shoes would have kept the money. "Frankly, I didn't believe it at first," said Bill Pace, executive director of the University of Southern

President Bill Clinton awarded the Presidential Medal of Honor to McCarty in 1996.

Mississippi Foundation. The foundation manages gifts to the university. "I was amazed that someone who made their money that way could save that much and then would give it away."

The scholarship fund was established in 1995. The scholarships were not supposed to go into effect until after McCarty's death. But Pace and other university officials didn't want to **hamper** McCarty's chance to see at least one of her beneficiaries graduate. So less than a year after the gift was made they awarded the first Oseola McCarty Scholarship of $1,000 to Stephanie Bullock, 18.

Stephanie's mother taught school in Hattiesburg and her father supervised a water-treatment plant. Stephanie has a twin brother, Stephen, and the Bullocks were worried about paying college tuition for two kids at the same time. The help from the McCarty scholarship fund would make college **accessible** to both twins.

McCarty and Stephanie Bullock, the first student to receive the Oseola McCarty Scholarship

306

McCarty in 1995, at age 87

CA Critical Thinking

1. What did Oseola McCarty do for a living?

2. What benefit did Oseola McCarty receive from giving $150,000 to the University of Southern Mississippi?

3. If you had a large sum of money to use to help others, what would you do with it?

4. Compare and contrast the ways of helping others that are described in "Saving Grace" and the three stories on pages 302–303.

THE GIFT OF A LIFETIME

Word of McCarty's gift and her life story caused others to open their pocketbooks. Local businesspeople pledged to match McCarty's $150,000 contribution, and in addition, checks arrived at the university from all over. McCarty, meanwhile, found all the fuss a bit **bewildering**. She continued to project an air of genuine puzzlement by the question she heard over and over: Why didn't you spend the money on yourself? "I am spending it on myself," she answered with a smile.

Oseola McCarty died in 1999 at the age of 91.

Show What You Know

Author and Me

The answer is not directly stated. Think about what you already know and link it to the text.

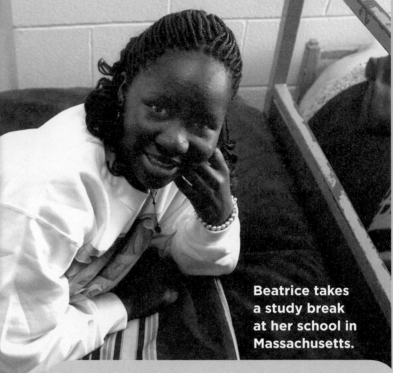

Beatrice takes a study break at her school in Massachusetts.

A GIFT OF HOPE

Beatrice Biira grew up in Kisinga, a small African village in Uganda. Beatrice had always dreamed of going to school. But her family could not afford to buy the uniforms, shoes, and books required for school. Most villagers could not, because they had nothing to sell for money.

In 1993, a charity called Heifer International gave Beatrice's family a goat named Mugisa. That name means "luck." And that is when the Biiras' luck began to change.

The goat provided milk for the family to drink and offspring to sell. The money from selling the goat kids was enough to enable Beatrice and her six siblings to go to school.

For 60 years, Heifer International has been helping families become self-sufficient. The organization provides them with livestock such as geese and goats. Each family must pass on the first female offspring to another family in need. Since it began in 1944, Heifer International has helped 5 million families in more than 125 countries.

Says Beatrice, "I want to get a good education so that I can give back to others the gift that was given to me."

Go on

Now answer questions 1 through 5. Base your answers on the article "A Gift of Hope."

1. What does it mean to be "self-sufficient"?

   A   You prefer to live alone.
   B   You can provide for your own needs.
   C   You are selfish and uncaring.
   D   You depend on the government to help you.

2. What is the *main* purpose of a charity?

   A   to organize fundraisers
   B   to bring people luck
   C   to sell toys and candy
   D   to improve people's lives

3. Why was Mugisa a good name for Beatrice's goat?

   A   The goat helped change the family's luck.
   B   The name means happiness.
   C   It was the name of the local school.
   D   The goat lived a lucky life.

4. How were Beatrice and her family helped by Heifer International?

5. Beatrice wants to repay the gift that she received. What was her gift? How did she use this gift? Use details from the article to support your response.

Tip
Connect the clues and ideas from the passage to choose the best answer.

STOP 309

Write on Demand

 CA Not everyone thinks the wall-size mural in your school is worth saving. Think about good reasons to save the mural. Write to <u>convince readers</u> to save the mural.

Persuasive writing tries to convince readers to accept the author's point of view.

To figure out if a writing prompt asks for persuasive writing, look for clue words like <u>write your opinion</u> or <u>convince readers</u>.

The writer clearly expresses point of view.

I've never paid much attention to it myself, but maybe that's because it is so faded. Still, I believe strongly that we should save the Garden Valley School mural.

Styles of art and tastes change all the time. But we don't go around burning paintings from the past because they are old and no one paints like that anymore. Think about what we'd lose if that happened.

That mural was there when our grandparents were born. The first students who ever walked through these halls made it. They were expressing their pride in their school. They were thinking about the students who would follow them; they were thinking about us.

The mural is part of school. It's part of us. If we don't save it, we'll be saying we don't care about the past, and we don't care about the future, either.

Writing Prompt

Respond in writing to the prompt below. Write for 10 minutes. Write as much as you can, as well as you can. Review the hints below before and after you write.

 Suppose a cave with ancient images is discovered during a construction project. You think the construction should be stopped to preserve the cave. Write to convince readers to save the cave.

Writing Hints for Prompts

- ☑ Carefully read the prompt.
- ☑ Organize your ideas to plan your writing.
- ☑ Support your ideas by giving reasons or using more details.
- ☑ Use a variety of sentence structures and consistent verb tenses.
- ☑ Choose precise words that help readers understand your ideas.
- ☑ Review your writing and edit as needed.

CELEBRATIONS

CA **Talk About It**

Why do people celebrate? What kinds of celebrations do you enjoy?

LOG ON ▶ Find out more about celebrations at **www.macmillanmh.com**.

313

Vocabulary

participate   grimaced
ordeals   dejectedly
nourishing   anticipated
encounter   victorious

Word Parts

Many English words have **Latin Roots**. Prefixes and/or suffixes are added to the roots to form words.

The root *ject* means *throw.*

The prefix *de* means *down.*

Dejectedly means in a downcast manner.

Rites of Passage

by Luis Rivera

Carlos sat in his friend Aaron's room listening to him describe the preparations for his bar mitzvah. This is a "rite of passage" that marks a Jewish boy's entry into manhood. Most people **participate** in rites of passage, but Carlos didn't act as if he were very interested in the topic.

In social science they had read about Native Americans, whose young people went through **ordeals**, or challenges, which tested their bravery. Some of the tests required young

Ana's quinceañera

people to spend time alone in the wilderness. They had to find **nourishing** food to stay healthy. They might have had to face a dangerous animal, which would have been a scary **encounter**. Carlos **grimaced** at the thought.

"Do you do anything as a rite of passage when you turn thirteen?" Aaron asked his friend.

"No," Carlos said **dejectedly**. "My sister, Ana, had a quinceañera. That means fifteenth year." Carlos thought of how Ana had **anticipated** the event all year. The family had a lot of fun, singing and dancing to traditional Mexican music.

Aaron said, "Yeah, my sister, Rachael, had a bat mitzvah, which means she's a young woman. Rachael felt **victorious** after she read aloud the Hebrew verse from the Torah in front of family and friends."

"When I stop to think about it," Carlos said, "These rites of passage are really important. They remind us of our culture—who we are and where we came from!"

"You're right," said Aaron, "and after my bar mitzvah, I'll be looking forward to my next rite of passage."

"What's that?" asked Carlos.

Aaron grinned. "Getting my driver's license when I'm sixteen!"

Rachael's bat mitzvah

Reread for Comprehension

Monitor Comprehension

✔ **Theme**

The theme of a selection is the overall idea or message an author wants to communicate. A Theme Chart helps you monitor your comprehension so you can determine the author's message.

Use your Theme Chart as you reread "Rites of Passage."

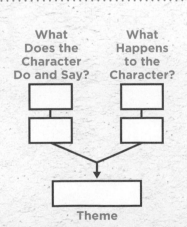

315

CA Comprehension

Genre

Fiction: Realistic fiction tells an invented story that could have happened in real life.

Monitor Comprehension

Theme

Look for the overall idea or message that is repeated throughout the story. As you read, use your Theme Chart.

What Does the Character Do and Say?	What Happens to the Character?

Theme

Read to Find Out

What is the theme of "Ta-Na-E-Ka"?

Ta-Na-E-Ka

by
Mary Whitebird

illustrated by
Shonto Begay

Award
Winning
Illustrator

As my birthday drew closer, I had awful nightmares about it. I was reaching the age at which all Kaw Indians had to **participate** in Ta-Na-E-Ka. Well, not all Kaws. Many of the younger families on the reservation were beginning to give up the old customs. But my grandfather, Amos Deer Leg, was devoted to tradition. He still wore handmade beaded moccasins instead of shoes, and kept his iron-gray hair in tight braids. He could speak English, but he spoke it only with white men. With his family he used a Sioux dialect.

Grandfather was one of the last living Indians (he died in 1953 when he was 81) who actually fought against the U.S. Cavalry. Not only did he fight, he was wounded in a skirmish at Rose Creek—a famous **encounter** in which the celebrated Kaw chief Flat Nose lost his life. At the time, my grandfather was only eleven years old.

Eleven was a magic word among the Kaws. It was the time of Ta-Na-E-Ka, the "flowering of adulthood." It was the age, my grandfather informed us hundreds of times, "when a boy could prove himself to be a warrior and a girl took the steps to womanhood."

"I don't want to be a warrior," my cousin, Roger Deer Leg, confided to me. "I'm going to become an accountant."

"None of the other tribes make girls go through the endurance ritual," I complained to my mother.

"It won't be as bad as you think, Mary," my mother said, ignoring my protests. "Once you've gone through it, you'll certainly never forget it. You'll be proud."

I even complained to my teacher, Mrs. Richardson, feeling that, as a white woman, she would side with me.

She didn't. "All of us have rituals of one kind or another," Mrs. Richardson said. "And look at it this way: How many girls have the opportunity to compete on equal terms with boys? Don't look down on your heritage."

Heritage, indeed! I had no intention of living on a reservation for the rest of my life. I was a good student. I loved school. My fantasies were about knights in armor and fair ladies in flowing gowns, being saved from dragons. It never once occurred to me that being an Indian was exciting.

But I've always thought that the Kaw were the originators of the women's liberation movement. No other Indian tribe—and I've spent half a lifetime researching the subject—treated women more "equally" than the Kaw. Unlike most of the sub-tribes of the Sioux Nation, the Kaw allowed men and women to eat together. And hundreds of years before we were "acculturated," a Kaw woman had the right to refuse a prospective husband even if her father arranged the match.

The wisest women (generally wisdom was equated with age) often sat in tribal councils. Furthermore, most Kaw legends revolve around "Good Woman," a kind of super-squaw, a Joan of Arc of the high plains. Good Woman led Kaw warriors into battle after battle from which they always seemed to emerge **victorious**.

And girls as well as boys were required to undergo Ta-Na-E-Ka.

The actual ceremony varied from tribe to tribe, but since the Indians' life on the plains was dedicated to survival, Ta-Na-E-Ka was a test of survival.

"Endurance is the loftiest virtue of the Indian," my grandfather explained.

"To survive, we must endure. When I was a boy, Ta-Na-E-Ka was more than the mere symbol it is now. We were painted white with the juice of a sacred herb and sent naked into the wilderness without so much as a knife. We couldn't return until the white had worn off. It wouldn't wash off. It took almost eighteen days, and during that time we had to stay alive, trapping food, eating insects and roots and berries, and watching out for enemies. And we did have enemies—both the white soldiers and the Omaha warriors, who were always trying to capture Kaw boys and girls undergoing their endurance test. It was an exciting time."

Theme
What message does the author want to get across in the grandfather's explanation of Ta-Na-E-Ka?

"What happened if you couldn't make it?" Roger asked. He was born only three days after I was, and we were being trained for Ta-Na-E-Ka together. I was happy to know he was frightened, too.

"Many didn't return," Grandfather said. "Only the strongest and shrewdest. Mothers were not allowed to weep over those who didn't return. If a Kaw couldn't survive, he or she wasn't worth weeping over. It was our way."

"What a lot of hooey," Roger whispered. "I'd give anything to get out of it."

"I don't see how we have any choice," I replied.

Roger gave my arm a little squeeze. "Well, it's only five days."

Five days! Maybe it was better than being painted white and sent out naked for eighteen days. But not much better.

We were to be sent, barefoot and in bathing suits, into the woods.

Even our very traditional parents put their foot down when Grandfather suggested we go naked. For five days we'd have to live off the land, keeping warm as best we could, getting food where we could. It was May, but on the northernmost reaches of the Missouri River the days were still chilly and the nights were fiercely cold.

Grandfather was in charge of the month's training for Ta-Na-E-Ka. One day he caught a grasshopper and demonstrated how to pull its legs and wings off in one flick of the fingers and how to swallow it.

I felt sick, and Roger turned green. "It's a darn good thing it's 1947," I told Roger teasingly. "You'd make a terrible warrior." Roger just **grimaced**.

I knew one thing. This particular Kaw Indian girl wasn't going to swallow a grasshopper no matter how hungry she got. And then I had an idea. Why hadn't I thought of it before? It would have saved nights of bad dreams about squooshy grasshoppers.

I headed straight for my teacher's house. "Mrs. Richardson," I said, "would you lend me five dollars?"

"Five dollars!" she exclaimed. "What for?"

"You remember the ceremony I talked about?"

"Ta-Na-E-Ka. Of course. Your parents have written me and asked me to excuse you from school so you can participate in it."

"Well, I need some things for the ceremony," I replied, in a half-truth. "I don't want to ask my parents for the money."

"It's not a crime to borrow money, Mary. But how can you pay it back?"

"I'll babysit for you ten times."

"That's more than fair," she said, going to her purse and handing me a crisp, new, five-dollar bill. I'd never had that much money at once.

"I'm happy to know the money's going to be put to a good use," Mrs. Richardson said.

A few days later, the ritual began with a long speech from my grandfather about how we had reached the age of decision, how we now had to fend for ourselves and prove that we could survive the most horrendous of **ordeals**. All the friends and relatives who had gathered at our house for dinner made jokes about their own Ta-Na-E-Ka experiences. They all advised us to fill up now, since for the next five days we'd be gorging ourselves on crickets. Neither Roger nor I was very hungry. "I'll probably laugh about this when I'm an accountant," Roger said, trembling.

"Are you trembling?" I asked.

"What do you think?"

"I'm happy to know boys tremble, too," I said.

At six the next morning, we kissed our parents and went off to the woods. "Which side do you want?" Roger asked. According to the rules, Roger and I would stake out "territories" in separate areas of the woods and we weren't to communicate during the entire ordeal.

"I'll go toward the river, if it's OK with you," I said.

"Sure," Roger answered. "What difference does it make?"

To me, it made a lot of difference. There was a marina a few miles up the river and there were boats moored there. At least, I hoped so. I figured that a boat was a better place to sleep than under a pile of leaves.

"Why do you keep holding your head?" Roger asked.

"Oh, nothing. Just nervous," I told him. Actually, I was afraid I'd lose the five-dollar bill, which I had tucked into my hair with a bobby pin. As we came to a fork in the trail, Roger shook my hand. "Good luck, Mary."

"N'ko-n'ta," I said. It was the Kaw word for *courage*.

The sun was shining and it was warm, but my bare feet began to hurt immediately. I spied one of the berry bushes Grandfather had told us about. "You're lucky," he had said. "The berries are ripe in the spring, and they are delicious and **nourishing**." They were orange and fat and I popped one into my mouth.

Argh! I spat it out. It was awful and bitter, and even grasshoppers were probably better tasting, although I never intended to find out.

I sat down to rest my feet. A rabbit hopped out from under the berry bush. He nuzzled the berry I'd spat out and ate it. He picked another one and ate that, too. He liked them. He looked at me, twitching his nose. I watched a red-headed woodpecker bore into an elm tree, and I caught a glimpse of a civet cat waddling through some twigs. All of a sudden I realized I was no longer frightened. Ta-Na-E-Ka might be more fun than I'd **anticipated**. I got up and headed toward the marina.

"Not one boat," I said to myself **dejectedly**. But the restaurant on the open shore, "Ernie's Riverside," was open. I walked in, feeling silly in my bathing suit. The man at the counter was big and tough-looking. He wore a sweatshirt with the words "Fort Sheridan, 1944," and he had only three fingers on one of his hands. He asked me what I wanted.

"A hamburger and a milk shake," I said, holding the five-dollar bill in my hand so he'd know I had money.

"That's a pretty heavy breakfast, honey," he murmured.

"That's what I always have for breakfast," I lied.

"Forty-five cents," he said, bringing me the food. (Back in 1947, hamburgers were twenty-five cents and milk shakes were twenty cents.)

"Delicious," I thought. "Better 'n grasshoppers—and Grandfather never once mentioned that I couldn't eat hamburgers."

While I was eating, I had a grand idea. Why not sleep in the restaurant? I went to the ladies' room and made sure the window was unlocked. Then I went back outside and played along the riverbank, watching the water birds and trying to identify each one. I planned to look for a beaver dam the next day.

The restaurant closed at sunset, and I watched the three-fingered man drive away. Then I climbed in the unlocked window. There was a night-light on, so I didn't turn on any lights. But there was a radio on the counter. I turned it on to a music program. It was warm in the restaurant, and I was hungry. I helped myself to a glass of milk and a piece of pie, intending to keep a list of what I'd eaten so I could leave money. I also planned to get up early, sneak out through the window, and head for the woods before the three-fingered man returned. I turned off the radio, wrapped myself in the man's apron, and in spite of the hardness of the floor, fell asleep.

"What the heck are you doing here, kid?"

It was the man's voice.

It was the morning. I'd overslept. I was scared.

"Hold it, kid. I just wanna know what you're doing here. You lost?

You must be from the reservation. Your folks must be worried sick about you. Do they have a phone?"

"Yes, yes," I answered. "But don't call them."

I was shivering. The man, who told me his name was Ernie, made me a cup of hot chocolate while I explained about Ta-Na-E-Ka.

"Darnedest thing I ever heard," he said, when I was through. "Lived next to the reservation all my life and this is the first I've heard of Ta-Na whatever-you-call-it." He looked at me, all goosebumps in my bathing suit. "Pretty silly thing to do to a kid," he muttered.

> **Theme**
> What are some of the unusual ways Mary is following her tribe's traditions?

That was just what I'd been thinking for months, but when Ernie said it, I became angry. "No, it isn't silly. It's a custom of the Kaw. We've been doing this for hundreds of years. My mother and my grandfather and everybody in my family went through this ceremony. It's why the Kaw are great warriors."

"Okay, great warrior," Ernie chuckled, "suit yourself. And, if you want to stick around, it's okay with me." Ernie went to the broom closet and tossed me a bundle. "That's the lost-and-found closet," he said. "Stuff people left on boats. Maybe there's something to keep you warm."

The sweater fitted loosely, but it felt good. I felt good. And I'd found a new friend. Most important, I was surviving Ta-Na-E-Ka.

My grandfather had said the experience would be filled with adventure, and I was having my fill. And Grandfather had never said we couldn't accept hospitality.

I stayed at Ernie's Riverside for the entire period. In the mornings I went into the woods and watched the animals and picked flowers for each of the tables in Ernie's. I had never felt better. I was up early enough to watch the sun rise on the Missouri, and I went to bed after it set. I ate everything I wanted—insisting that Ernie take all my money for the food. "I'll keep this in trust for you, Mary," Ernie promised, "in case you are ever desperate for five dollars." (He did, too, but that's another story.)

I was sorry when the five days were over. I'd enjoyed every minute with Ernie. He taught me how to make western omelets and to make Chili Ernie Style (still one of my favorite dishes). And I told Ernie all about the legends of the Kaw. I hadn't realized I knew so much about my people.

But Ta-Na-E-Ka was over, and as I approached my house, at about nine-thirty in the evening, I became nervous all over again. What if Grandfather asked me about the berries and the grasshoppers? And my feet were hardly cut. I hadn't lost a pound and my hair was combed.

"They'll be so happy to see me," I told myself hopefully, "that they won't ask too many questions."

I opened the door. My grandfather was in the front room. He was wearing the ceremonial beaded deerskin shirt which had belonged to his grandfather. "N'g'da'ma," he said. "Welcome back."

I embraced my parents warmly, letting go only when I saw my cousin Roger sprawled on the couch. His eyes were red and swollen. He'd lost weight. His feet were an unsightly mass of blood and blisters, and he was moaning: "I made it, see. I made it. I'm a warrior. A warrior."

My grandfather looked at me strangely. I was clean, obviously well-fed, and radiantly healthy. My parents got the message. My uncle and aunt gazed at me with hostility.

Finally my grandfather asked, "What did you eat to keep you so well?"

I sucked in my breath and blurted out the truth: "Hamburgers and milk shakes."

"Hamburgers!" my grandfather growled.

"Milk shakes!" Roger moaned.

"You didn't say we had to eat grasshoppers," I said sheepishly.

"Tell us about your Ta-Na-E-Ka," my grandfather commanded.

I told them everything, from borrowing the five dollars, to Ernie's kindness, to observing the beaver.

"That's not what I trained you for," my grandfather said sadly.

I stood up. "Grandfather, I learned that Ta-Na-E-Ka is important. I didn't think so during training. I was scared stiff of it. I handled it my way. And I learned I had nothing to be afraid of. There's no reason in 1947 to eat grasshoppers when you can eat a hamburger."

I was inwardly shocked at my own audacity. But I liked it. "Grandfather, I'll bet you never ate one of those rotten berries yourself."

Grandfather laughed! He laughed aloud! My mother and father and aunt and uncle were all dumbfounded. Grandfather never laughed. Never.

"Those berries—they are terrible," Grandfather admitted. "I could never swallow them. I found a dead deer on the first day of my Ta-Na-E-Ka—shot by a soldier, probably—and he kept my belly full for the entire period of the test!"

Grandfather stopped laughing. "We should send you out again," he said.

I looked at Roger. "You're pretty smart, Mary," Roger groaned. "I'd never have thought of what you did."

"Accountants just have to be good at arithmetic," I said comfortingly. "I'm terrible at arithmetic."

Roger tried to smile but couldn't. My grandfather called me to him. "You should have done what your cousin did. But I think you are more alert to what is happening to our people today than we are. I think you would have passed the test under any circumstances, in any time. Somehow, you know how to exist in a world that wasn't made for Indians. I don't think you're going to have any trouble surviving."

Grandfather wasn't entirely right. But I'll tell about that another time.

On a Journey with
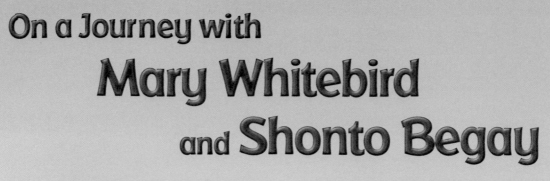
Mary Whitebird
and Shonto Begay

Mary Whitebird is a Native American. She first wrote this story for a young people's magazine. Although the story reflects the heritage of her culture, it is also about the challenges any young person might face in any culture. That makes it a classic coming-of-age story.

Shonto Begay was born on the Navajo Reservation in Arizona. His first canvas was the ground and his first brush a stick. He challenges all young people to find a space where they can think and dream. He calls this place a person's "story rock," where things are created from the heart and from the earth.

 LOG ON ▶ Find out more about Mary Whitebird and Shonto Begay at **www.macmillanmh.com**.

 CA **Author's Purpose**
What was the author's purpose in writing "Ta-Na-E-Ka"? Do you think the author succeeded?

332

# CA Critical Thinking

Summarize

Use your Theme Chart to help you summarize "Ta-Na-E-Ka." What did Mary realize about her own understanding of her culture after she began to talk to Ernie?

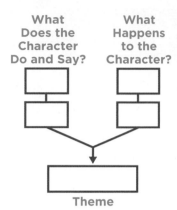

What Does the Character Do and Say?

What Happens to the Character?

Theme

Think and Compare

1. Describe the **theme** of this story in one or two sentences. Identify how the author conveys, or communicates, the theme through the characters and their actions. **Monitor Comprehension: Theme**

2. Compare and contrast traditional Ta-Na-E-Ka **ordeals**, such as Grandfather's or Roger's, with Mary's experience. How do you think the world of 1947 affected the traditions of the Kaw people? **Compare and Contrast**

3. Think of how you celebrate special occasions. What unique traditions do you have? How have those traditions changed over time? **Synthesize**

4. Mary's experience with Ta-Na-E-Ka represents a problem faced by many cultures: the desire to hold on to ancient traditions and the impulse to join with modern society. How do you think it is possible to strike a balance between them? **Evaluate**

5. Read "Rites of Passage" on pages 314–315. Which experiences mentioned are the ones that Mary dreaded having to face? Which traditions are different from the Kaw tradition of Ta-Na-E-Ka? **Reading/Writing Across Texts**

Language Arts

Genre

A **Fable** is a brief story that teaches a moral, often through the actions of animals that act like people.

✔ Literary Elements

A **Moral** is a lesson taught by a fable or story. It is usually stated outright at the end of the fable.

Personification is a literary device where human characteristics are given to animals or things.

Introduction

The real Aesop was born a slave about the year 620 B.C. in the ancient republic of Greece, where he was later granted freedom as a reward for his learning and wit. Though he died about 565 B.C., for years his clever wisdom was passed down orally from generation to generation. Somewhere around 300 B.C., about 200 stories were gathered into a collection called *Assemblies of Aesopic Tales*. No one knows how many of the narratives attributed to Aesop were actually composed by him. Interestingly, motifs from many of them occur in the storytelling traditions of a variety of cultures—proof of the universality of the themes and lessons of these tales.

The Crow and the Pitcher

For weeks and weeks there had been no rain. The streams and pools had dried to dust, and all of the animals were thirsty. Two crows, flying together in search of water, spotted a pitcher that had been left on a garden wall. They flew to it and saw that it was half full of water. But neither one could reach far enough inside the pitcher's narrow neck to get a drink.

"There must be a way to get that water," said the first crow. "If we think it through, we'll find an answer."

The second crow tried to push the pitcher over, straining with all of his might. But it was too heavy to budge. "It's hopeless!" he croaked, and flew away to look for water elsewhere.

But the first crow stayed by the pitcher and thought, and after a time he had an idea. Picking up some small pebbles in his beak, he dropped them one by one into the pitcher until at last the water rose to the brim. Then the clever bird happily quenched his thirst.

Wisdom and patience succeed where force fails.

CA Critical Thinking

1. Why does personification work especially well in fables? What would fables be like if they only featured humans? **Personification**

2. Why do you think an author who wanted to teach a lesson would choose to write a fable? **Analyze**

3. Compare "The Crow and the Pitcher" to "Ta-Na-E-Ka." How do the main characters in both stories use their brains to solve a problem in an unusual way? **Reading/Writing Across Texts**

LOG ON ▷ Find out more about fables at **www.macmillanmh.com**.

Logical Structure: Transitions

Writers use a **logical structure** that includes **transition** words to make their work easy to follow.

Read the passage below. Notice how the author Mary Whitebird uses transitions in her story.

An excerpt from *Ta-Na-E-Ka*

The author uses the last sentence of the first paragraph to move smoothly from the topic of the grandfather to the topic of Ta-Na-E-Ka. This transition sentence links the two topics and helps us move logically from one to the other.

Not only did he fight, he was wounded in a skirmish at Rose Creek—a famous encounter in which the celebrated Kaw Chief Flat Nose lost his life. At the time, my grandfather was only eleven years old.

Eleven was a magic word among the Kaws. It was the time of Ta-Na-E-Ka, "the flowering of adulthood." It was the age, my grandfather informed us hundreds of times, "when a boy could prove himself to be a warrior and a girl took the steps to womanhood."

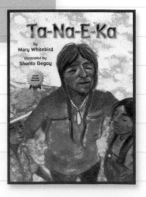

Ta-Na-E-Ka
by
Mary Whitebird
Illustrated by
Shonto Begay

Read and Find

Read Ounia's writing below. How did she use transition words to go from one topic to the next? Use the Writer's Checklist to help you.

Skateboarding Rules
by Ounia R.

I roll down our street on my board. The best part is when the Smiths' yappy poodle, Boopsy, barks when she hears me coming. As soon as I get close, she jumps back in terror as I laugh.

Right now, my town is trying to ban skateboarders. I wish the town would just leave me and all the other kids alone. They're probably just afraid of trying something new.

Read how Ounia uses transition words to go from one topic to another.

Writer's Checklist

 Does the writer move smoothly between topics?

 Does the writer help you to see a connection between the two topics?

 Do you feel as if you understand why the writer thought the topics belonged near each other?

What Would You Do?

CA **Talk About It**

What do you think the person responsible for this situation should do?

LOG ON ▶ To find out more about values, go to **www.macmillanmh.com**.

Vocabulary

instinctively	dilapidated
decrease	auction
swiveled	decades
shakily	rafters

Thesaurus

An **Antonym** is a word that means the opposite or nearly the opposite of another word. *Decrease* and *increase* are antonyms. You can find antonyms in a thesaurus.

GRANDPA and ME

by Susan Reilly

For six weeks in the summer of 1986, I went to live with my grandfather. When my mom first told me about the plans, without thinking, I **instinctively** groaned. Somewhere inside me a voice told me that I would be miserable. This meant no afternoon baseball games with my neighborhood friends. Plus, I just knew my popularity would **decrease**, or lessen, if I wasn't around all summer.

The first week with Grandpa was fine. We went out to dinner and watched TV together. One day, Grandpa was sitting at the table reading the newspaper. I sat on the couch and flipped through my baseball card collection. I had all my cards in a binder with plastic sleeve protectors. "Wish I had a Hank Aaron card," I muttered to myself.

When Grandpa heard me, he **swiveled** around on his chair so fast that the wheels almost flew off! He said, "I didn't know you liked baseball, Susan."

340

I explained that it was my favorite sport and that I usually play it all summer with my friends. Grandpa stood up **shakily**, balancing himself with his hand on the wall, and walked to the door. "Let's go," he said, smiling. "I want to show you something."

We drove for quite a while, and when Grandpa finally stopped the car, we were in front of some **dilapidated** old houses. They were abandoned and falling apart. A sign on each house said "Land will be sold to highest bidder. City Hall **auction**. Call for details." I started to say something, but I noticed that Grandpa had a faraway look in his eyes. "I haven't been here for **decades**," he whispered, "probably twenty or thirty years."

We walked onto one of the old porches. Grandpa pointed down the street and said, "That's the field where I used to play baseball every summer." Then I realized where we were: This was the house Grandpa grew up in! We peeked inside a window to see a big mess. The ceiling was falling down so that you could see the wooden **rafters**, or beams, hidden behind it. No one had lived here for a long time.

On the ride home, Grandpa was very quiet. I thought about how he must miss his old home and the friends he grew up with. Then I realized that six weeks away from home was not too bad, especially with Grandpa around.

Reread for Comprehension

Evaluate

Make Judgments
Good readers usually make judgments while they are reading. Evaluating the actions of the characters helps readers make judgments about the characters.

You can use a Judgments Chart to help you evaluate the characters in a story. Use the chart as you reread "Grandpa and Me."

Action	Judgment

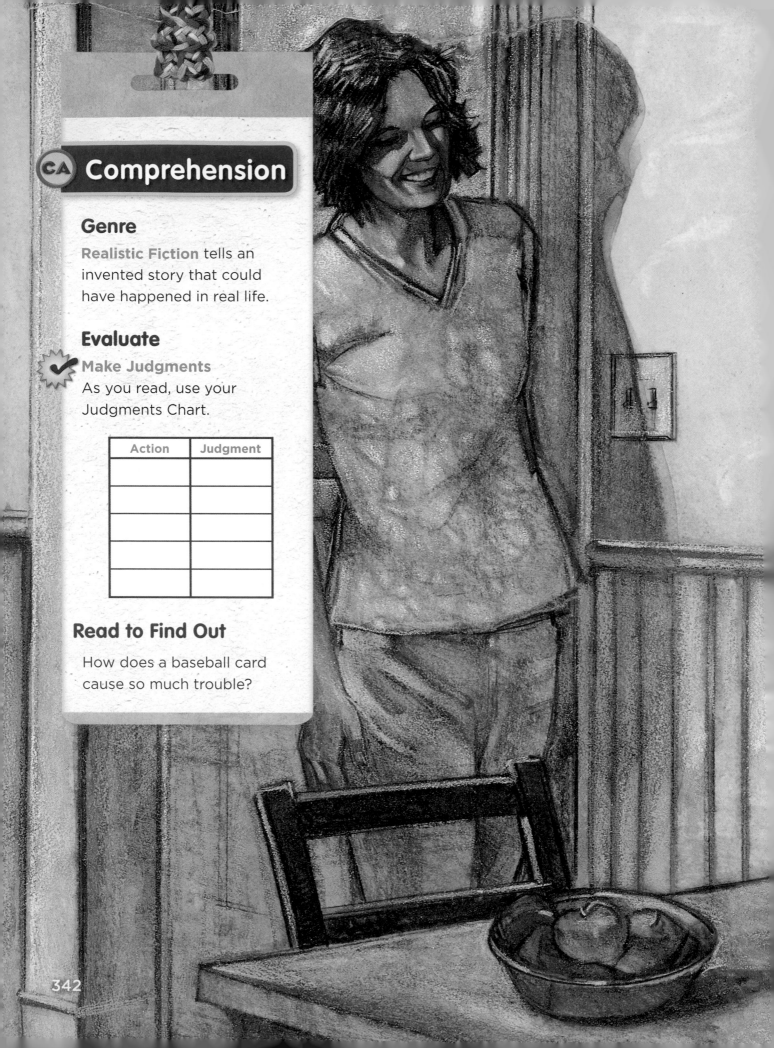

Genre

Realistic Fiction tells an invented story that could have happened in real life.

Evaluate

✓ **Make Judgments**
As you read, use your Judgments Chart.

Action	Judgment

Read to Find Out

How does a baseball card cause so much trouble?

HONUS and ME

by Dan Gutman
illustrated by Ron Mazellan

"JOEY, I'M HOME!" MOM SHOUTED AS THE SCREEN door slammed behind her. "How was the game?"

"Lousy," I reported honestly. "I fanned three times and let a grounder go between my legs to let the winning run score."

Mom threw her arms around me and ran her fingers through my hair.

"You'll get 'em next time, slugger."

She flopped down in a chair. I could tell she was exhausted. Mom is on her feet most of the day. She works as a nurse in Hazelwood Hospital here in Louisville.

"So what did you make for dinner?" she asked with a smile, "I'm beat."

"Oh, Mom, let's go out to eat tonight."

"Negative," she replied. "When you sign your big league contract, you'll take me out on the town. Till then, we're on a tight budget."

"Fast food?" I suggested hopefully.

"Ugh!" she replied, holding her nose. "I'd rather starve."

I wouldn't say we were *poor*, but I sure wouldn't say we were rich either. We never had a lot of money, but things got really tough after my parents split up two years ago. My dad lived in Louisville too, in an apartment. He came over to visit from time to time.

Money was always a problem. When I was a little kid my folks used to argue a lot about it. Dad always seemed to have a tough time landing a job. When he found one, he never seemed to be able to hold on to it very long.

I've always thought that if only my parents had had more money, they wouldn't have split up. Mom said that was ridiculous. Money had nothing to do with it, she told me. Besides, she said, money doesn't make you happy.

But how would she know? She never had any.

I always wished I had a million dollars. At least I could see if she was right or not. Even a half a million would have been nice.

Until we win the lottery, I'd try to make a few dollars here and there doing odd jobs. Yard work. Raking leaves and stuff. The winter before, Kentucky got a lot more snow than usual, and I made a bunch of money shoveling people's sidewalks and driveways. I gave some of the money to my mom. The rest of it I spent on baseball cards.

Dad gave me his baseball-card collection and got me started collecting cards when I was seven.

I may not have been a great hitter, but I knew more about cards than any kid around. I put together a complete set of guys who played shortstop. That was always my position.

Mom says buying baseball cards is like throwing money into a garbage can. But I figure a kid should be allowed to have one harmless vice.

And besides, my baseball cards actually *saved* us money. When I got holes in my sneakers, I would slip a card inside so I didn't need to buy a new pair right away. I always used lousy cards, of course. I wouldn't think of stepping on a card that was worth anything.

"I got you some work today, Joe," Mom said as we chowed down on leftovers.

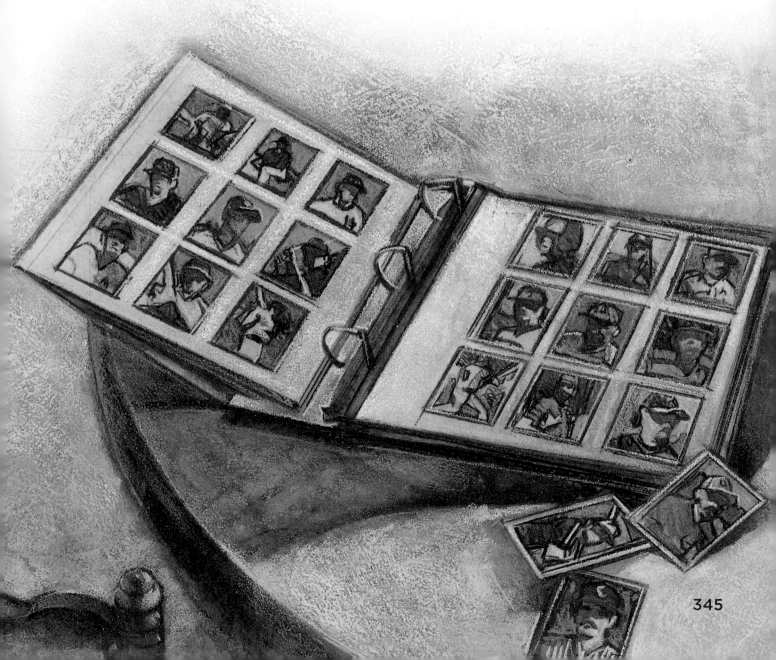

345

"Oh, yeah? What?"

"Miss Young needs her attic cleaned out. She'll pay you five dollars. I told her you'd take it."

"Oh, *man!*"

Amanda Young is this really old lady who lives next door. I know she's way over one hundred, because my mom showed me an article from the paper that talked about Louisville's Century Club. She's pretty peppy for an old lady. Her skin is really wrinkly, though.

Miss Young never had any kids, and she was never married. I don't even think she has any relatives who are still alive. She's been living by herself in that **dilapidated** old house for as long as anybody can remember. She never comes outside. Her groceries are brought in.

My mom stops over to Miss Young's now and then to see if she's okay. I guess that's how I got this job.

It's not like I don't appreciate the work or anything. It's just that Amanda Young is kinda weird. I've run a few errands for her, and she starts talking to me about nothing and she goes on and on. I can't understand what she's saying half the time. I nod my head yes to be polite.

Sometimes, I must admit, I pretend my mom is calling so I can go home. Miss Young doesn't hear very well, so she can't tell I'm lying.

I've never seen Miss Young smile. She seems really sad, as if somebody did something terrible to her a long time ago and she never got over it.

I've heard kids say that Amanda Young is a witch. Kids always make up stories like that. I think she's just a lonely old lady. I feel a little sorry for her.

Cleaning out Miss Young's attic isn't my idea of a fun afternoon, but five bucks is five bucks. There is a new set of baseball cards coming out next month, and I can use the money to buy a few packs.

> **Make Judgments**
> Was it appropriate for Joey's mother to accept a job offer without talking to Joey about it first? Explain.

I'm sure I would have felt differently about the job if I'd known what Miss Young had up in her attic.

We only had a half day of school the next day, so I thought it would be a good time to go over to Amanda Young's house. The shutters were hanging off the windows at an angle, and the place hadn't had a coat of paint in **decades**. You could tell home maintenance was not very important to the old lady.

Miss Young was in worse financial shape than we were. My mom said she could barely live off her Social Security checks.

After I rang the doorbell, I didn't hear a sound inside for a minute or two. I was afraid that maybe Miss Young was hurt or something, but then I heard her shuffling feet coming toward the door. She was really small, so when she opened the door a crack I could barely see her.

"Come in," she creaked. "Why Joseph Stoshack, you're getting to be *so* big!"

Inside, the house was like one of those historical houses some famous guy lived in and has been preserved just the way he left it when he died. It was filled with antiques, though I don't know if stuff is still called antique if somebody never stopped using it. The walls were covered with hats and dried flowers.

"Pirates, eh?" she said, peering at my baseball cap. "Are you a Pittsburgh rooter?"

"No, I just like this baseball cap, Miss Young."

"I used to root for the Pirates when I was a girl," she said. "Well, one Pirate anyway." She stopped for a moment and let out a sigh before changing the subject. "We didn't have television back then, or even radio. But we used to *pore* over the newspaper. Did you know that the manager of the Pirates invented those flip-up sunglasses outfielders wear?"

"Really?"

Miss Young had never brought up baseball the other times we'd spoken. For the first time, she had my interest.

"That's right," she continued. "His name was Fred Clarke. He's a Hall of Famer, you know."

I had heard of Clarke, but I didn't know too much about him.

"And the baseball bat was invented right here in Louisville, Joseph. There was this fella named Pete Browning. He broke his bat one day, and a little boy took him home and carved Pete a new one on his daddy's lathe. His dad was a woodworker you see, who made wooden butter churns. Do you know what a butter churn is, Joseph? Oh, of course not. You're too young. Well, anyway, Pete took his new bat and got three hits the next day. Naturally, his teammates *all* wanted new bats. The woodworker stopped making butter churns and went into the bat business. And that's how the Louisville Slugger was born. Of course, that was before my time."

I couldn't imagine *anything* being before her time.

"I want to show you something, Joseph."

She put on a pair of old-lady glasses and opened a drawer in the bureau in her front hallway. After sifting through the junk in there for a minute, she pulled out a photo and held it under a lamp. It was an old-time baseball player. The image was fuzzy, but I could make out the word "Louisville" across the chest of his uniform.

The photo looked like it had originally been larger, but it was ripped in half. There was a white border at the top, bottom, and left side, but the right side had no border and the edge was jagged.

The picture had been taken in a garden. The ballplayer was facing the camera and his left arm was extending out to the jagged edge, like he was holding hands with someone. It was impossible to tell who the other person was, because that half had been ripped off.

I looked up and saw there were tears in Miss Young's eyes.

"I was supposed to hold onto this half of the picture until we saw each other again," she said softly. "I waited and waited. But he never came back."

She handed me the picture abruptly. "Throw it away with the rest of the junk upstairs. It's worthless."

I'm a collector. I never throw *anything* away. Who knows? A ripped picture of an old-time ballplayer might be

worth something to somebody. It certainly meant something to Miss Young a long time ago. As I stuffed the picture in my backpack, I wondered why it had made her so upset.

Miss Young led me upstairs and told me she wanted me to take everything out of the attic and put it on the street for the garbage men to take away. I figured she knew she wasn't going to live forever, and she wanted to clean up her affairs while she was still around.

As soon as I stepped up into the attic, I knew it had been a mistake to take the job. It was dark, filthy, and it looked like a junkyard. This was no five-dollar job, I thought to myself.

But a deal is a deal. I started picking through the trash and hauling it out to the street. The whole time I was thinking I should have gotten a paper route or some other real job.

Being a collector and all, I couldn't resist peeking into a few of Miss Young's old boxes to see what kind of stuff she had decided to hang on to all these years. But it was exactly what she said it was—worthless junk. Broken candlesticks. Old clothes. A set of encyclopedias. I chucked it all out.

After a couple of hours I had cleared the entire attic except for a few boxes. I was dog tired, and I picked up the next box without holding it from the bottom. The box had deteriorated with age, and the bottom ripped open in my arms. The contents spilled all over the floor. I was angry at myself for not being more careful.

I decided to take a short break before cleaning up the mess, so I lay down on the dusty wooden slats and stared at the **rafters**. In a few minutes I felt rested and rolled over on my side to look at the junk strewn across the floor.

It was papers, mostly. Nothing too interesting. Bank statements and tax returns from a long time ago. I started picking them up and putting them into a pile. When I picked up the stack, a single piece of cardboard fell out and fluttered to the floor.

It didn't register at first. But when I picked up the card, I felt a strange tingling sensation.

I turned over the card and looked at the other side. I couldn't believe my eyes.

It was a picture of a man's face. I gasped. **Instinctively**, I looked around to see if anybody was watching. Of course nobody was there.

The man in the picture was a young man, with short brown hair parted in the middle. He had a solemn expression on his face, with his head **swiveled** slightly so he was looking off to the left. His shirt collar was navy blue, and the shirt was muddy gray. It had four white buttons.

On the right side of his chest were the letters "PITTS" and on the left were the letters "BURG." There was no H.

The background of the card was burnt-orange. There was a thin white border on all four sides. Across the bottom border, centered in the middle, were these magic words . . .

WAGNER, PITTSBURG

My breath came in short bursts. I suddenly felt warm. My heart was racing. My *brain* was racing. The tingling sensation was all over me, and stronger than I had ever experienced it.

No doubt about it. I had just stumbled upon a T-206 Honus Wagner card—*the most valuable baseball card in the world.*

Every serious collector knows the legend behind the Wagner card. These early baseball cards were printed by tobacco companies and were included with their products. All the players agreed to be on the cards except for Honus Wagner, the star shortstop of the Pittsburgh Pirates.

Wagner was against cigarette smoking, and he didn't want his name or picture used to sell tobacco. He forced the American Tobacco Company to withdraw his card—but they had already started printing them. A small number of the cards reached the public before the card was discontinued.

That's why the Honus Wagner card is so valuable. Only about forty of them are known to exist in the whole world, most of them in bad condition.

I just found No. 41, and it was *mint.* Nobody had *touched* it in over eighty years.

I knew the piece of cardboard in my hand was worth thousands of dollars, but I didn't know exactly how *many* thousands. I remembered that a few years ago some famous athlete had bought one at an **auction**, but I couldn't recall who he was or how much he paid for it. It was a huge amount of money, that was for sure.

All my problems, I suddenly realized, were solved. Or so I thought.

I slipped the card in my backpack, being careful not to bend any of the corners or damage it in any way. A tiny nick in a card this rare might **decrease** its value by thousands of dollars.

Quickly, I gathered up the rest of the junk in the attic and hauled it out to the curb.

I had almost forgotten about Miss Young, but she called me over just as I was about to run home.

"Aren't you forgetting something, Joseph?"

She held out a five-dollar bill and **shakily** placed it in my palm. She grabbed my other hand and looked me in the eye.

"Thank you for helping out an old lady," she said seriously. "And because you did such a fine job, I want you to have *ten* dollars. I bet that's a lot of money to a boy your age."

Ten bucks? In my head I was thinking that I had a fortune in my backpack.

"Yeah, I could use ten dollars," I sputtered. "Thanks Miss Young."

"Buy something nice for yourself," she called out as I dashed away. "Money won't do *me* any good."

"I will," I called out as I left. "Believe me, I *will*."

Mom wouldn't be home from work for an hour or so. I grabbed my bike, hopped on, and started pedaling east on Chestnut Street past Sheppard Park and Founders Square.

As I cruised down the streets I was filled with an overwhelming feeling of joy. Happiness washed over my body. Nobody could touch me. Nobody could hurt me. Nobody could tell me what to do. It was a feeling I had never experienced before.

I didn't know if I should tell the whole world about my good fortune, or if maybe I shouldn't tell *anybody* in the world.

As I whizzed down the street, I felt like everyone was looking at me. I felt like everyone must somehow know what had happened to me. They knew what I had in my backpack. It was as if the news had instantly been picked up and broadcast around the globe.

Those feelings lasted about a minute, when a different feeling came over me. A bad feeling. The baseball card wasn't mine to take, really. It was Miss Young's card. If anybody deserved to get rich from it, it was *her*. She had been nice enough to pay me *double* for cleaning out her attic, and I had stolen her fortune.

Almost as quickly, my brain came up with reasons I shouldn't feel badly. Miss Young herself said that money wouldn't do her any good, so why *shouldn't* I keep the card? After all, *she* told me to throw the stuff away. If I hadn't found the card, *she* wouldn't have found it. It would have ended up buried in a landfill someplace, worth nothing to anyone.

Finder's keepers, right?

And besides, I thought, Miss Young isn't going to live much longer.

I felt bad, again, thinking that last thought.

I was feeling very mixed up. Deep inside I knew the right thing would be to give Miss Young back her baseball card.

But that didn't necessarily mean I was going to *do* the right thing.

Make Judgments
Was Joey's action appropriate, or should he return the baseball card to Miss Young? Explain.

355

At Bat with DAN GUTMAN

DAN GUTMAN has a section on his Web site called "Read My Rejection Letters." *Honus and Me* was rejected seven times before a publisher accepted the manuscript. Dan said that during the three years he tried to get "Honus" published, he learned that persistence pays off! In the end, *Honus and Me* was nominated for 11 state book awards and won a California Young Reader's Award.

 Find out more about Dan Gutman at **www.macmillanmh.com**.

 Author's Purpose

Dan Gutman worked very hard to get *Honus and Me* published. What do you think was his main purpose for writing? Explain.

CA Critical Thinking

Summarize

Use your Judgments Chart to help you summarize *Honus and Me*. Consider how money has an impact on the events of the story.

Action	Judgment

Think and Compare

1. If Joey offered to split with Miss Young what the baseball card would bring in an **auction**, would this be an appropriate solution to his problem? Use facts from the text to support your answer. **Evaluate: Make Judgments**

2. Why do you think Joey is so excited to find the baseball card? How can it change his life? **Analyze**

3. This selection ends before we know what Joey decides to do about the baseball card. How would you end the story? Why? **Synthesize**

4. Joey could use the wealth from the Wagner card to help his family. Is it all right to take unfair advantage of a situation, as long as you help someone in the end? Explain. **Evaluate**

5. Read "Grandpa and Me" on pages 340–341. How do Susan and Joey in *Honus and Me* make false judgments about the older characters in the stories? **Reading/Writing Across Texts**

Genre

Nonfiction: Newspaper articles tell about current events and ask *who, what, when, where, how,* and *why.*

✔ Text Feature

Applications are special forms with blank spaces that need to be filled in when applying for something, such as a library or membership card.

Content Vocabulary

acquisition   inducted

memorabilia

1909 Honus Wagner Baseball Card

WAGNER, PITTSBURG

Card Sells for $2.35 Million

BY ESTHER CHEN — After paying a record-breaking 2.35 million dollars for a 1909 Honus Wagner baseball card, David Kohler felt as if he had just won the jackpot. Kohler and a California businessman bought the rare card from Brian Siegel who had paid 1.265 million dollars for the card in 2000.

Kohler's **acquisition** of the Wagner card crowns a 28-year career of collecting baseball cards. The rare card is one of only 60 known to be in existence. Kohler buys and sells sports **memorabilia**. "That's why we go to work every day," Kohler said. "You never know what's in somebody's attic."

Wagner played shortstop for the Pittsburgh Pirates and was one of the first five players to be **inducted** into the Baseball Hall of Fame. His nickname was the "Flying Dutchman" and he finished his career with a lifetime .329 average.

MOUNTAIN LION
BASEBALL LEAGUE

Player Registration Form

Player Name	Date of Birth
	Age
Address	Gender M F
City/State/Zip	Home Phone
E-mail	

CA Critical Thinking

1. What other information might be useful to have on the application for the Mountain Lion Baseball League? **Reading an Application**

2. Why do you think a collector might pay 2.35 million dollars for a baseball card? **Evaluate**

3. What do you think Joey from *Honus and Me* and David Kohler might discuss if they were to meet each other? **Reading/Writing Across Texts.**

RESEARCH INQUIRY History/Social Science Activity

Research the history of baseball. Then create an application for a baseball history club. Think about what kind of questions and information you would include on the application.

 Go to **www.macmillanmh.com** for more activities.

Writing

✔ Logical Structure: Transitions

Good writers use a **logical structure**, including **transition** words that make their work easy to follow and understand.

Reading and Writing Connection

Read the passage below. Notice how the author Dan Gutman uses transitions in his story.

An excerpt from *Honus and Me*

The author uses the last sentence of the first paragraph to move smoothly from the topic of money to the topic of baseball cards. This transition sentence links the two topics and helps the reader move logically from one to the other.

The winter before, Kentucky got a lot more snow than usual, and I made a bunch of money shoveling people's sidewalks and driveways. I gave some of the money to my mom. The rest I spent on baseball cards.

Dad gave me his baseball-card collection and got me started collecting cards when I was seven. I may not have been a great hitter, but I knew more about cards than any kid around. I put together a complete set of guys who played shortstop. That was always my position.

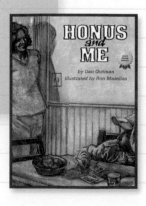

Read and Find

Read Ana's writing below. How did she transition from one topic to the next? Use the Writer's Checklist to help you.

Reality Television
by Ana V.

It's silly to watch reality television where people pretend to live on a desert island when they're surrounded by video crews. There are no desert islands in *my* reality. My life is about two things: my family and dancing.

Reality shows about dancing are the only shows that can get me interested. When I see people working hard and using moves that I know, then I'm fascinated by the whirling, jumping figures.

Read one writer's views about reality television shows and why she is not interested in them.

Writer's Checklist

 Does the writing flow smoothly between topics?

 Does the writer help you to see a connection between the two topics?

 Do you feel as if you understand why the writer thought the topics belonged near each other?

Review

Make Judgments
Theme
Problem and Solution
Base Words
Photos and Captions

A HELPING HAND

It was the last day of school and the students were anxious for vacation. Robert and Mario were telling each other their plans for the summer.

"I'm going to play basketball every day," Robert declared.

"Basketball, huh? I'm playing baseball. I've got to practice if I want to make the school team next year," Mario replied.

Ms. Blackwell interrupted them. "Okay class," she said.

The chatter of the class died down as all eyes moved to the front of the room. She raised a piece of blank, lined paper.

"As some of you may know, the school is in need of some repair. We are planning to paint the school this summer, but we are asking for student volunteers to help us. Before you leave today, I'd like to ask if any of you would like to participate. I'm going to leave this sign-up sheet at the front of the classroom. If any of you are interested, please sign up as you leave."

Robert and Mario gathered their backpacks and headed for the door. Mario stopped at the sign-up sheet. Robert kept walking. He turned back to Mario.

"I thought you were planning on playing baseball this summer, not painting! Do you want to spend your summer at school?"

Mario shrugged it off. "I can do both. Besides, the school needs it."

Robert laughed, "Okay, Picasso. Well, good luck with baseball practice. Maybe I will see you around this summer."

The next week, Robert headed down to the basketball courts. Passing the school, he looked up. Several students and teachers were gathered at the front of the building. Paint buckets were scattered at their feet. Robert spotted Mario, paintbrush in hand, painting as high as he could reach. He was laughing and talking with another student. Robert kept on bouncing his basketball down the street.

The next day, he saw the same thing. Mario saw him this time and waved. Robert waved back, but kept on his way to the basketball courts. The following day, Robert passed Mario and the other students in front of the school. Each day, the façade of the school was looking better and better.

On the fourth day he passed by the school as usual. This time he did not have his basketball. He walked up to the school.

Mario greeted him. "How's basketball going?" Mario asked.

"Okay," Robert replied. "Do you think they're still taking volunteers?"

"Of course! Ms. Blackwell said the more people that help, the faster we can get this done. Doesn't it look great?" Mario stepped back and admired his work.

"Yeah," Robert replied. "It is definitely an improvement!" He picked up a paintbrush and joined him. "So, you headed down to the baseball field after this?"

"You bet!" Mario replied, "I go every afternoon. Coach said with my arm, I may even have a chance at making pitcher next year!"

HOLLYWOOD HERE YOU COME

Step 1: Make a Movie

Today, because of amazing new technology, almost anyone can make movies. Digital video cameras, special computer software, and camera phones are available to beginning filmmakers.

Not all movies need to be elaborate mysteries or action-packed adventures. There are many different genres of movies. Some examples are comedy, history, documentary, and drama. Often the most creative movies break the mold and try something new.

Step 2: Choose a Script

Good movies start with good scripts, or screenplays. Scripts are the written version of the story. Dialogue, or what the characters in the movie say to each other, is the heart and soul of a movie script. Scripts are written in a unique way that makes them easy for actors to read. They also make it easy for the director to understand what each scene should look like. Sounds, special effects, and music are also important.

Step 3: Finding the People

Actors are important because they stay in the audience's memory long after the movie is over. You need to find the perfect person to play each character.

There are many kinds of movie directors. Regardless of directing style, it is the job of a director to help the actors deliver the finest performances they can.

Step 4: Build the Set

Getting ready to shoot a movie is a lot of work. A shoot, when a director and actors get together to film the scenes of a movie, can be done in a studio or on location. A studio is a place that can be changed to fit whatever scene you are shooting. On location is when you film in the place where your scene is really supposed to happen, or a place that looks like it.

Step 5: Edit the Movie

Once the shoot is over, editors and mixers use computers to add sounds, music, and special effects. Then the film companies make posters, create commercials, and have press conferences to promote the movie. However, many movies can be made with a crew of only a few people and a cast of just one person. That is the magic of the movies, especially today!

Now set up the camera, point the lens, and get the actors in their places. Ready! Set! Action!

A film being shot on location. You can tell from this photo that the film takes place some time ago.

CA Critical Thinking

Now answer numbers 1 through 4. Base your answers on the passage "A Helping Hand."

1. **Read the following sentence from the passage.**

> "It is definitely an <u>improvement</u>."

What is the base word for *improvement*?

A pavement

B improve

C rover

D mentally

2. **How did people in the story solve the problem of the school needing repairs?**

A They ignored the need for repairs.

B They hired a company to paint the school.

C They asked for volunteers to paint the school.

D They canceled summer vacation.

3. **Read the following sentences from the passage.**

> Mario <u>shrugged it off</u>. "I can do both. Besides, the school needs it."

In this sentence the idiomatic expression *shrugged it off* means

A he took off his shirt.

B he showed he didn't mind spending some time at school in the summer.

C he took off his backpack and put it down.

D he decided not to play baseball in the summer.

4. **What is the theme of this story? Use details from the passage to support your answer.**

Now answer numbers 1 through 4. Base your answers on the article "Hollywood Here You Come."

1. **Which of the following judgments can you make?**

   A   Making a movie is a complicated activity.
   B   A script is not important for a movie.
   C   Movie-making is an activity that does not cost much.
   D   You do not have to plan your filmmaking carefully.

2. **You could solve the problem of not having enough money to make your film by**

   A   making an elaborate mystery.
   B   not using a camera.
   C   using a simpler script.
   D   hiring movie stars.

3. **What seems to be the theme of this passage?**

   A   Movie-making has become easier over the years.
   B   Movie-making is an activity that cannot be done by amateurs.
   C   Making a movie is a very inexpensive and simple activity.
   D   Movie stars are most important in movie-making.

4. **What can you tell from the photo and caption?**

   A   The script has a lot of dialogue.
   B   The movie is being shot on location.
   C   The film is about selling cars.
   D   The cast and crew are filming in a studio.

Write on Demand

PROMPT What do you think it would be like to be a movie director? Write a journal entry in which you describe one day on a set. Write for 15 minutes. Write as much as you can as well as you can.

ATHENS 2004
PARALYMPIC GAMES
GUIDE
KENYA
ATHENS 2004
PARALYMPIC GAMES
1654

Unit 4
Achieving Dreams

The Big Question

How can we help others achieve their dreams?

Theme Launcher Video

LOG ON Find out more about organizations that help people at **www.macmillanmh.com**.

The Big Question

How can we help others achieve their dreams?

Some people need help to achieve their goals or dreams because they have extra challenges to overcome. They can get the help they need through organizations that are formed especially to help them.

You can help by donating money, time, or resources to one of the organizations that are dedicated to helping people achieve their goals. You can find out about these organizations through such sources as the Internet, public libraries, and the media.

Sharing what you have with those who need it is a time-honored way of helping people.

Research Activities

Throughout the unit, you will be learning about people who achieved their dreams with hard work and with the help of others. Focus your research on an organization that helps people reach their goals by helping them overcome challenges.

Keep Track of Ideas

As you read, keep track of all you are learning about people who achieved goals with the help of others. Use a Chart organizer. In the first section, write the unit theme: Achieving Dreams. In each section, write ideas you learn each week that will help you in your research and understanding of the unit theme.

FOLDABLES®
Study Organizer

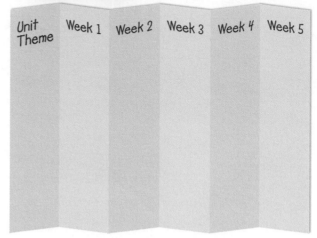

| Unit Theme | Week 1 | Week 2 | Week 3 | Week 4 | Week 5 |

Research Toolkit

Conduct Your Unit 4 Research Online with:

Research Roadmap
Follow step-by-step guide to complete your research project.

Online Resources
- Topic Finder and other Research Tools
- Videos and Virtual Fieldtrips
- Photos and Drawings for Presentations
- Related Articles and Web Resources

California Web Site Links

Go to **www.macmillanmh.com** for more information.

California People

Rudy Garcia-Tolson, Athlete
Rudy Garcia-Tolson is an amazing, differently abled athlete who competes in many events.

371

DETERMINATION DOES IT

CA **Talk About It**

All runners face challenges during races. How do you think this champion deals with challenges?

LOG ON ▶ Find out more about uncommon champions at **www.macmillanmh.com**.

BETHANY HAMILTON'S COMEBACK

by Cesar Aparicio

Bethany Hamilton has never been a **typical** surfer like all the others. She surfs "goofy footed," with her right foot in front. Now, even more so, she goes against the norm. She surfs with one arm!

One day in late October, Bethany was surfing at Hawaii's Tunnel Beach. Around 7:30 A.M., a tiger shark attacked Bethany, biting off her left arm. Bethany was rushed to the hospital where **specialists** in limb loss worked on her injury.

Before her attack, Bethany was ranked second from her area in amateur surfing and was thought of as one of the best new women surfers. She hoped to become a professional surfer. To further her plans, Bethany was homeschooled, which gave her more time to surf.

Bethany didn't put her plans for the future to the side. She would not let the attack put her in a **peripheral** position. Instead, she moved back into the limelight when she returned to the water about four weeks after the attack. Three months later, she received a prosthetic arm and competed nationally.

She competed in the National Scholastic Surfing Association meet in Hawaii and took fifth place. In worldwide competitions, she shows her **maturity**, or development, as a person and as a surfer, refusing to let her work before the attack represent the **summit**, or peak, of her surfing career. She continues to progress with each contest. "I'm an athlete first, with a great second story," Bethany said to a reporter.

With the help and **guidance** of both her coach and her father, Bethany has been encouraged to keep up the sport and she continues to improve. Because she returned so quickly and works so hard, her surfing skills have not **deteriorated**.

Bethany has received an award as best comeback athlete, which is proof of her athletic ability and a testament to her personal strength. This young woman is an **awesome** example for athletes around the world. She is a picture of courage and grace in the face of tremendous challenges.

Reread for **Comprehension**

Evaluate

Author's Perspective

One way to evaluate a text is to examine the author's perspective. How does Cesar Aparicio feel about Bethany Hamilton? Does he approve of what she is doing? How do you know?

Use the Author's Perspective Chart as you reread "Bethany Hamilton's Comeback" to identify the author's perspective.

Clues	Author's Perspective

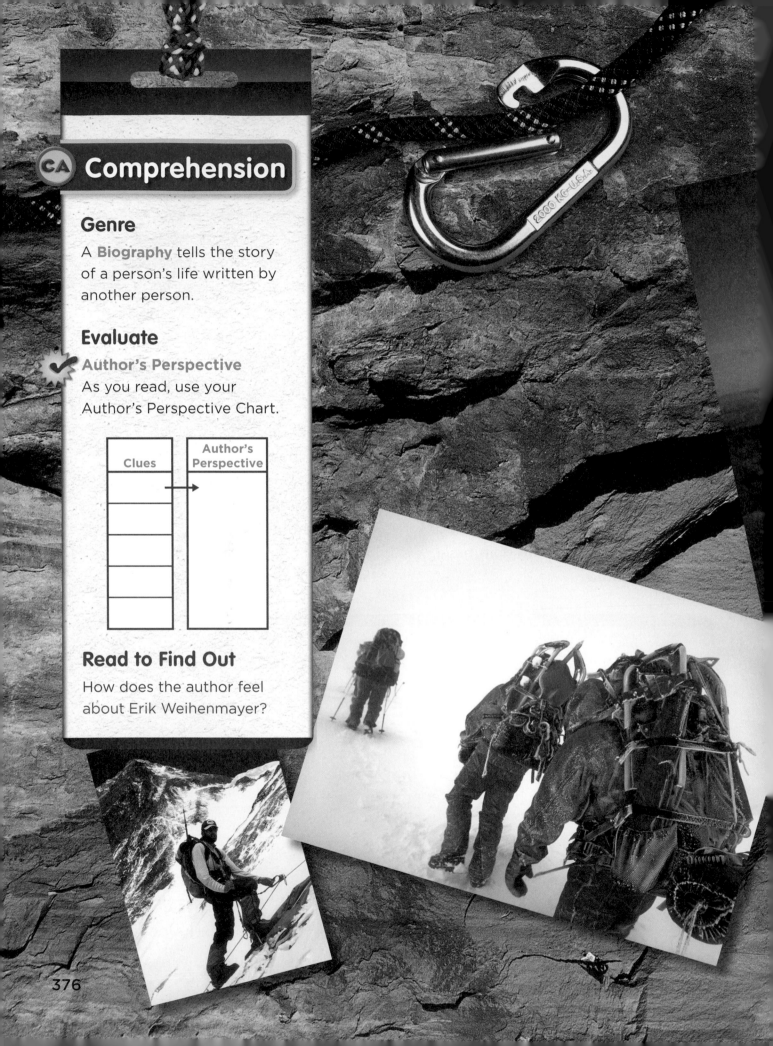

CA Comprehension

Genre
A **Biography** tells the story of a person's life written by another person.

Evaluate

Author's Perspective
As you read, use your Author's Perspective Chart.

Clues	Author's Perspective

Read to Find Out
How does the author feel about Erik Weihenmayer?

Seeing Things His Own Way

by Marty Kaminsky

377

Erik Weihenmayer thrust his ice ax into the deep snow, hoping to grip a hold long enough to catch his breath. The howling winds, gusting up to 100 miles per hour, roared like a fleet of jet planes. To communicate with his climbing partners, Erik had to scream to be heard. It was only 3,000 more feet to the **summit**, but Erik's team was hopelessly trapped for five days in a blizzard on the high slopes of Mt. McKinley.

At 20,320 feet, Alaska's Mt. McKinley is the highest peak in North America. Freezing temperatures, sudden avalanches, and devastating storms make it one of the most difficult mountains in the world to climb. Nearly one hundred climbers have lost their lives there after falling into deep crevasses or being blown off the face by gale-force winds. For even the most experienced mountaineers and rugged explorers, climbing McKinley is the challenge of a lifetime.

Imagine climbing such a treacherous peak without being able to see a single step. That is the task that Erik Weihenmayer faced in June 1995. Erik is completely blind, having lost his vision at age thirteen due to a condition he was born with called retinoschisis. But blindness has never stopped him from living an exciting life and pursuing adventures most of us only dream about.

"I am not a daredevil," Erik explains. "I have a healthy fear and respect of the mountains, but I believe with proper training and skill a blind person can tackle some **awesome** challenges."

From a young age, life itself proved to be a challenge for Erik. When he was a three-month-old baby, Erik's eyes began to quiver and shake. His parents were alarmed and brought him to teams of **specialists** over a year and a half. The doctors diagnosed his problem as retinoschisis, a rare condition that causes pressure to build in the retina until it disintegrates, eventually leading to blindness. To view something directly in front of him Erik would have to look up, down, or sideways. He relied on his **peripheral** (side) vision to navigate his neighborhood and to do daily chores and tasks.

Erik at a base camp on Mt. McKinley

But Erik hated to be treated differently, so he learned to compensate for his poor vision. When he played basketball with friends, they helped him cover the court by playing zone defenses. They also learned to feed him the ball with a bounce pass. "Erik would hear a bounce pass," his father, Ed Weihenmayer, explains. "But lots of passes hit him in the face anyway. After most games Erik had a bloody nose and looked as if he was playing football, not basketball."

With the help of family and friends, Erik was encouraged to find creative ways to participate in everyday activities. When his brothers raced their mountain bikes over a ramp, Erik joined in, but sometimes he rode off the edge, picking up scraped knees for his efforts. Though he rarely complained or showed his frustration, Erik's family was aware of his struggles. His father solved the bike problem by painting the ramp bright orange. After two more months of bike stunts on the ramp, however, Erik's eyesight had **deteriorated** to the point that the ramp became an orange blur. He rode off his driveway one day and broke his arm.

Despite his failing vision Erik continued his attempts to blend in and be like everyone else. Frequently he walked into trees or doors, and he had constant bruises and black-and-blue shins. "I guess it was a lack of **maturity** on my part," Erik admits. "It was a sense of denial. I refused to learn to read Braille or to use a cane, even though I needed one for my own safety."

By the time he was thirteen, Erik's eyesight was completely gone. At first he tried to function without the use of canes or visual aids, but that proved dangerous. While visiting his grandparents, he stepped off a dock and fell eight feet into a boat. Though unharmed by the incident, it shook him up. Out of sheer desperation, Erik came to accept his blindness.

"I realized that if I got good at using the systems for the blind I would blend in better and be more like everyone else," he says. "If I didn't use my cane I would be stumbling about, and that would make me stand out more."

Erik and his dog, Wizard

Machu Picchu

At fifteen Erik joined his high school's wrestling team. Because the sport depends on physical contact, strength, and instinct, Erik found he could compete on even terms with his opponents. He did not win a match as a freshman, but by his senior year he was chosen team captain and sported a 30-3-3 record. He was selected to represent Connecticut in the National Freestyle Wrestling Championships and went on to wrestle at Boston College.

Just as Erik was beginning to accept his blindness and learning to function in a sightless world, tragedy struck hard. While he was away at summer wrestling camp, Erik's mother was killed in an automobile accident. The loss was devastating, but Erik's father exerted extra efforts to spend more time with his children. As a way to bring the family closer, Ed Weihenmayer brought his children together for adventurous treks around the world. Among many other journeys, they visited the Batura Glacier in Pakistan and the Inca ruins at Machu Picchu in Peru.

"Facing his mother's death and blindness so close together was difficult," Ed recalls. "But Erik never used them as an excuse for not measuring up and going for it." Rock-climbing trips to New Hampshire and other travels with his family whet Erik's appetite for adventure. He soon became a skillful rock climber, scuba diver, and sky diver.

Erik with students

After getting his master's degree from Lesley College in Massachusetts, Erik was hired to teach at an elementary school in Phoenix, Arizona. Managing a class of lively fifth graders was a challenge equal to any Erik had undertaken, but he loved his work and handled it well. "My dad worked on Wall Street for thirty years," he says. "He struggled to find meaning in his work. I don't have that struggle as a teacher." The students in his classes quickly realize that Erik needs their help to make learning work for them. With his **guidance** they devise systems to communicate and get things done. Students pitch in taking turns writing on the board, hanging posters, and passing out papers. Although the class could take advantage of their sightless teacher, they rarely do. In fact, they fall over each other to be the first to fill his dog's water bowl.

As he settled into his teaching job, Erik and a buddy filled their weekends with climbing trips to the rock faces and mountains of Arizona. On the higher slopes Erik and his partners devised a climbing language that the lead climber would call out. If a teammate shouted, "Iceberg ahead," for example, Erik understood that a pointy rock sticking out of the ground was in his path. A cry of "ankle breaker" meant that little loose rocks lay ahead. By learning to follow in the footsteps of his partners and to rely on his other senses, Erik took on the tallest peaks in Africa and North and South America with his climbing friends.

> **Author's Perspective**
> What is the author's perspective, or attitude, toward Erik's teaching career? How do you know?

Erik rock climbing at the Phoenix, Arizona, Bouldering Competition

"Feeling the rock under my hand, feeling the wind and sensing I am hundreds of feet above tree line is an incredible experience," Erik says. "It's exciting to work on a team for a common goal." So great is his love of the mountains that Erik and his wife, Ellen, were wed at a rock altar 13,000 feet up the slopes of Mt. Kilimanjaro in Tanzania.

But pulling yourself up a sheer rock wall, balancing on an icy ridge, and handling sub-zero temperatures can prove frustrating for any mountaineer, particularly one who is blind. While climbing Mt. Rainier in 1985 Erik discovered he could not set up his tent in the freezing weather with his bulky gloves covering his hands. In **typical** fashion he refused to admit failure. "I was so embarrassed that I resolved never to let that happen again," he says. "When I returned to Phoenix I practiced setting up a tent in the one-hundred-degree heat with gloves on over and over. It is no longer a problem for me."

Careful planning and practice have always helped Erik work around the problems caused by his lack of vision. To prepare for the risky climb up Mt. McKinley, Erik's team practiced on Mt. Rainier in Washington and Long's Peak in Colorado. Back in Phoenix, Erik and a teammate strapped on fifty-pound packs and raced up and down the stairs of a forty-story skyscraper to build strength and endurance.

Before the McKinley trip Erik's climbing group, which called itself Team High Sights, secured the sponsorship of the American Foundation for the Blind. "I was hopeful that my climb would make a statement," Erik says.

> **Author's Perspective**
> What clues in the selection help reveal the author's perspective toward Erik's habit of refusing to admit failure?

Erik (right) in an igloo on Mt. McKinley at 17,000 feet

Huddling in their ice-coated tents at 17,000 feet, Team High Sights was forced to wait out a five-day storm on Mt. McKinley. Their food supply was dwindling and all that could be seen of the summit was a plume of snow blowing hundreds of feet into the air. Unless the storm let up, all hope of reaching the summit would have to be abandoned. On the sixth day they heard on their weather radio the news they'd been waiting for: There would be a twelve-hour period of clear weather in which to reach the summit and return before the next storm system closed off the mountain.

Strapping on their ice shoes and insulated gear, the climbers tied themselves together with sturdy rope. Pushing through thigh-deep snow was exhausting work, but Team High Sights carefully moved up the mountain. For Erik, the climb to the summit seemed endless. At the top of a knife-edge ridge his ski pole slipped and all he could feel was air. "I was concentrating very hard with each step," he explains. "Finally I took a step and my friend Stacey said, 'Congratulations, you're on the top of North America.'"

With tears in their eyes, the climbers embraced and snapped photographs of each other. Erik held aloft a pair of banners—one designed by a girl at his school, and one for the American Foundation for the Blind. After fifteen minutes at the peak, the team headed down, safely making their way back to a lower camp.

The climb to the top of Mt. McKinley was a proud accomplishment for Erik, and one that he hopes provides inspiration for others. "Before McKinley I never thought I was extremely tough," Erik says. "I always felt I had the potential to do much more. I hope my climb proves that we can all push beyond what we think we can do."

Having climbed McKinley, the highest mountain in North America, Erik is well on the way to meeting one of his climbing goals. In the next few years he plans to summit the highest peak on each continent, including Mt. Everest in Asia. He has learned to step around every obstacle in his path, and though it will be a difficult task, Erik knows there is no reason a blind man cannot sit atop the tallest mountain in the world.

Erik reached his goal of climbing Mt. Everest in 2001.

On Top of the World with Marty Kaminsky

Marty Kaminsky is an elementary school teacher who loves to write. He started by writing for magazines, such as *Highlights* and *Sports Illustrated for Kids*. When he heard stories about athletes who are physically challenged, he was hooked. He had to write about them, he said, for his children, and for the children he has taught through the years. He says, "They are the reason I write anything at all."

 LOG ON ▶ Find out more about Marty Kaminsky at **www.macmillanmh.com**.

(CA) Author's Purpose

This biography is full of Erik Weihenmayer's adventures. What was Marty Kaminsky's purpose in writing it?

# Critical Thinking

Summarize

Use the Author's Perspective Chart to summarize "Seeing Things His Own Way." Tell about the different situations that Erik Weihenmayer faced from childhood to adulthood.

Think and Compare

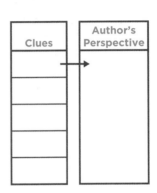

Clues	Author's Perspective

1. Use details from the **Author's Perspective** Chart to describe how the author feels about Erik Weihenmayer's accomplishments. Explain how the selection would change if the author felt differently about his subject. **Evaluate: Author's Perspective**

2. Of all of Erik Weihenmayer's accomplishments, which do you find to be the most inspiring? Why? Support your answer. **Analyze**

3. Think about a time when you overcame a difficulty. What obstacles did you encounter? How did your experience contribute to your **maturity**? **Evaluate**

4. What, above all, is the message of "Seeing Things His Own Way"? Use references from the text to support your answer. **Synthesize**

5. Read "Bethany Hamilton's Comeback" on pages 374–375. If Bethany Hamilton were to meet Erik Weihenmayer, what do you think they might discuss with each other? **Reading/Writing Across Texts**

Amazing Artificial Limbs

by Jackie Glassman

Your day is full of activities you probably don't think much about, such as brushing your teeth, eating breakfast, walking to school, and riding your bike. Now imagine how you would accomplish these tasks if you were missing a limb, an arm or a leg.

Some people have lost limbs because of accidents or have had them **amputated** because of a disease. Other people are just born that way.

Throughout history, inventors have been developing **artificial** limbs, known as prostheses. A mechanically-operated arm was invented as early as the 1940s.

Today's modern medical **technology** has led to the development of new materials, advances in computers, and a greater understanding of the body. Many body parts can now be replaced with artificial ones that work almost as well as the originals. The science of designing electronic limbs is called **bionics**. New electronic limbs make it possible for people to control their artificial limbs in highly effective ways. These high-tech devices are improving the lives of many people.

Diamond Excell and Her Bionic Arms

Diamond Excell had to write, eat, and even brush her teeth with her feet because she was born without shoulders or arms. Then on her eleventh birthday, Diamond received a wonderful gift. She was fitted with myoelectric arms designed by inventor Ivan Yaeger.

How an Artificial Arm Works

Reading a Diagram

This diagram shows an artificial arm. Inside are tiny electrical parts, motors, and batteries. Gears and motors inside allow the artificial arm to bend and work.

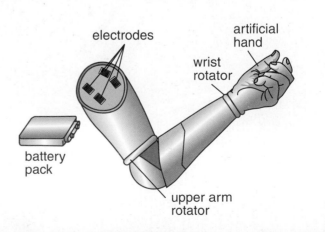

electrodes

artificial hand

wrist rotator

battery pack

upper arm rotator

The natural-looking limbs have tiny electrical parts and motors inside that made it possible for Diamond to hug her mother for the first time. By moving muscles in her back, Diamond creates electrical signals that control motors inside the prostheses. Each arm has motors that open and close the joints. The wrists and the elbows are designed so that when Diamond walks, her arms swing freely and naturally.

Until recently artificial legs were very low-tech. They were mainly controlled by the body's normal walking movements, which required a lot of energy. Today a myoelectric leg, like the myoelectric arm, is controlled by a person's muscles.

However, this is not as easy as it sounds. People with artificial limbs must go through lots of training to learn how to effectively control their replacement limbs. With the help of a myoelectric leg, many people can now participate in sports such as basketball and running.

With ongoing advances in science and technology, society can look forward to huge improvements in artificial limbs. For example, new materials allow prosthetic feet to press and spring much like real feet. One type of artificial foot transmits electronic information about pressure to the person using it. Feeling pressure helps people to balance because they can tell whether their weight is on the toes, heels, or sides of the feet.

Looking into the Future

In the very near future, scientists hope to create bionic limbs so that Diamond and others will have a first-rate sense of touch, making their artificial limbs that much closer to the real thing.

 Critical Thinking

1. Look at the text and diagram on page 391. How do you think the wrist rotator works? **Reading a Diagram**

2. What improvements do you think can still be made to artificial limbs? **Evaluate**

3. How is Erik Weihenmayer's determination in "Seeing Things His Own Way" like Diamond's? **Reading/Writing Across Texts**

 Science Activity

Research information about a high-tech innovation. Draw a diagram with accurate labels illustrating the innovation.

 Find out more about bionics at **www.macmillanmh.com**.

Writing

CA

✓ **Dialogue: Linked to Argument**

Writers use **dialogue** and **evidence** to link their **arguments** and prove their points.

Read the passage below. Notice how author Marty Kaminsky uses evidence to prove his argument.

An excerpt from
Seeing Things His Own Way

The author uses details to support his statement that Mt. McKinley is one of the most difficult mountains in the world to climb. Evidence such as the mountain's great height and fierce weather help make us willing to believe his statement.

At 20,320 feet, Alaska's Mt. McKinley is the highest peak in North America. Freezing temperatures, sudden avalanches, and devastating storms make it one of the most difficult mountains in the world to climb. Nearly one hundred climbers have lost their lives there after falling into deep crevasses or being blown off the face by gale-force winds. For even the most experienced mountaineers and rugged explorers, climbing McKinley is the challenge of a lifetime.

Seeing Things His Own Way
by Marty Kaminsky

Read and Find

Read Terrell's writing below. How did he use evidence to convince us his statement is true? Use the Writer's Checklist below to help you.

The MVP QB

by Terrell W.

"Devon is the best quarterback in our league. He has the most passing yards of anyone. He throws the ball so fast, all you can see is a blurry streak coming right at you! I've never seen anyone come close to sacking him, and you'd be a fool to think you could intercept one of those super passes," I told Jerome.

"We're going to win this year."

Read about the best quarterback ever.

Writer's Checklist

 Does the writer give a statement or an opinion?

 Does the writer use details as evidence to support his opinion?

 Are you able to understand why Terrell thinks Devon is a great quarterback?

CA Talk About It

How do you think Jackie Robinson felt when he became the first African American to play in the Major Leagues?

LOG ON ▶ Find out more about Jackie Robinson at **www.macmillanmh.com**.

Working TO WIN

Vocabulary

spectators
demonstration
prominent
luxury
prevail
maneuvered
collective
adept

Analogies

Analogies link pairs of words that relate in the same way.

Diners are to *eat* as *spectators* are to _____.

Answer: *watch*

Bike Ride, Anyone?

by Amy Leung

Some people might find it surprising that the present times are not considered the "Golden Age of Bicycling," since there are so many different bikes available. Believe it or not, this Golden Age occurred more than 100 years ago in the 1890s when horses were the main form of transport.

The first modern bicycle can be traced back to 1839 in Scotland. A variety of "bikes" followed. By the 1870s, James Starley of England was producing bikes. His bike, called the Ordinary, had a huge front and a small back wheel. Many **spectators** came to the 1876 U.S. Centennial Exhibition in Philadelphia to see a **demonstration** of how the Ordinary worked. Some models became more **prominent**, or well-known, than others. One bike designed in the United States was a real **luxury**. It cost more than some people made in a year!

In 1885 the Coventry Machinists Company in England produced a 50-pound machine called the Rover. It was built like the modern bicycle. By the 1890s the Ordinary and the Rover were pitted against each other. Eventually, the Ordinary faded from production and the Rover would **prevail**. The Rover was simply faster and more easily **maneuvered**, or controlled, up and down hills and around corners.

Bicycling really became popular in the 1890s because it was nearly as fast as a horse and required less care and expense. People rode their bikes through the country and the city. Changes began to take place as bicycling increased in popularity.

As more people began biking, they formed the League of American Wheelmen. The league had one **collective** goal: All members wanted to improve bicycling conditions. The league worked to get roads paved for easier passage in all types of weather. It also published a bicycling magazine and established bicycle etiquette.

Women were good cyclists, just as **adept** at riding as men. Susan B. Anthony, the famous women's rights advocate, said that the bicycle had done wonders for women's freedom. Isn't it wonderful that a bike could improve women's rights?

In the 1970s the mountain bike made bicycling even more popular. Adults joined kids and teenagers on their bikes. Biking is a fun pastime and a fantastic alternative to driving.

Reread for **Comprehension**

Make Inferences and Analyze
Fact and Opinion

A fact is a statement that can be proven true. An opinion is a statement of someone's feelings or beliefs. An opinion is not true or false. Making inferences and analyzing information can help you decide what is fact and opinion in a selection.

Use the Fact and Opinion Chart as you reread "Bike Ride, Anyone?"

Fact	Opinion

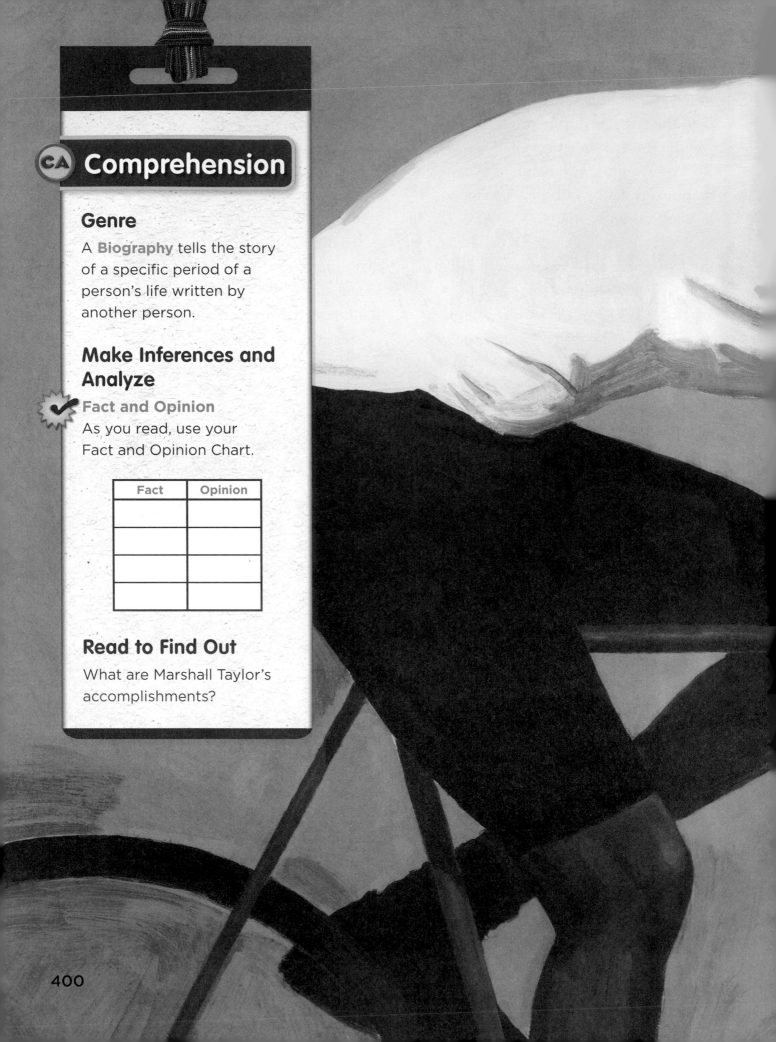

Genre

A **Biography** tells the story of a specific period of a person's life written by another person.

Make Inferences and Analyze

Fact and Opinion
As you read, use your Fact and Opinion Chart.

Fact	Opinion

Read to Find Out

What are Marshall Taylor's accomplishments?

MAJOR TAYLOR
CHAMPION CYCLIST

Award Winning Illustrator

BY **Lesa Cline-Ransome**
ILLUSTRATED BY **James E. Ransome**

In Indianapolis, Indiana, there was a street lined with bicycle shops from one end to the other. Visitors would marvel at each window displayed with the most up-to-date models along that stretch of North Pennsylvania Avenue locals called Bicycle Row.

Right at the center sat the Hay and Willits Bicycle Shop: Thomas Hay, Bert Willits, proprietors.

It was this shop young Marshall Taylor visited when his own bicycle needed fixing. Marshall was thirteen years old, and waiting patiently was not one of the things he did best. So while he waited, he kept himself busy trying out new stunts. Then, the repairs made, he used one of his fancy mounts to climb quickly onto his bicycle. If he hurried, he could still finish his newspaper route before supper.

As Marshall left, Mr. Hay shouted, "Hey, son, that was some stunt work."

"Oh, those," said Marshall. "I have a lot more, wanna see?"

And without waiting for an answer, he began his **demonstration** with an acrobatic mount. Round and round the store he rode, first backward, then forward on the handlebars, each move more daring than the last. By the time he'd finished, everyone in the store was applauding for more.

"How'd you get so good?" Tom Hay asked the boy.

Marshall explained that he'd taught himself quite a collection of tricks riding on the long stretches of country road between his newspaper stops.

"Are you looking for work? For six dollars a week, all you need to do is sweep, straighten, and show off some of those stunts, and you've got yourself a job."

"Six dollars to clean and do tricks?" Marshall asked. Why, that paid a dollar more than his paper route.

"Okay, okay, we'll throw in a new bike, too," countered Bert Willits.

"I'll take it!" Marshall shouted.

How did a thirteen-year-old black teenager in 1891 come to be such a crackerjack cyclist—or even to own a bicycle? Mr. Hay and Mr. Willits wondered. And so Marshall told them of his father's job as a coachman to the **prominent** Southard family and how at the age of eight he'd been hired as the live-in companion of their only son. It was then that Marshall began his new life of **luxury**: private tutoring, fine clothing, a playroom stacked with toys.

But what Marshall loved most was the bicycle the Southards had given him. He'd never seen anything like its smooth curved lines of metal, so shiny and new and so utterly modern. He jumped on at once, knowing those wheels could carry him faster than his legs ever could.

And sure enough, in no time he became the top cyclist in the neighborhood. Amongst stately Victorian houses and tree-lined streets, in each and every race, Marshall breezed by the other boys, aware only of the wind against his face and the road he left behind.

For the days when Marshall was to perform, Mr. Hay outfitted him in a uniform with elaborate braidings and shimmery gold buttons.

Crowds gathered afternoons at 4:00 P.M. sharp to watch Marshall on the sidewalk outside the store. They were amazed by the young man in military uniform so **adept** on two wheels.

"He looks like a little major!" they would marvel.

Then they'd filter into the store to request private lessons and try out the bicycles that could make that little major do his tricks.

Hay and Willits Bicycle Shop had finally made a name for itself, and the owners had the kid everyone now called Major Taylor to thank for it.

The annual ten-mile road race, sponsored by Hay and Willits, was one of the biggest sporting events in Indianapolis. Each year an elaborate gold medal for the winner was displayed in their window, on view for all. Marshall liked to put down his cleaning rags and stop to admire it. He'd adjust it, polish it, and hold it up to the light to watch it sparkle. Once, he even tried it on, smiling at his own reflection in the window.

"Major Taylor, Champion Cyclist," he whispered to himself.

Early on the morning of the race, Marshall took his place among hundreds of **spectators**. He'd never seen a bicycle race up close and he didn't want to miss a single detail.

When Mr. Hay spotted Marshall, he waved to him. "Come on over here, young man; you must start in this race," he insisted.

"I don't think I can do it," Marshall protested.

"Why, it's no different than riding with your friends," he encouraged. "Look, just start up the road and come back when you're tired. The crowd will love it."

Bang! The starting pistol sounded, and Marshall was off, pedaling hard and fast, hoping only to keep pace with the others.

"Just till I get tired . . . just till I get tired . . . ," he kept repeating, his legs pumping as fast as his heart. Gradually the rhythmic creaks of the other bicycles faded and all he could hear was his own panting. Time fell away as he struggled to maintain speed, and the wind whipped his face. Out of nowhere Mr. Hay appeared, shouting and dangling the gold medal.

"You're a mile ahead! Keep going!"

Now he thought he could make out a swell of spectators gathered at the finish. Pushing, pushing with everything he had, his legs cramped with exhaustion, he burst through the winning tape . . . and then collapsed.

When he came to, sore, stiff, and exhausted, the crowd's cheers were ringing in his ears.

At thirteen years old, Marshall Taylor had won his first race.

Back at the shop, Marshall's dreams now stretched far beyond the walls of Hay and Willits. More than anything, he wanted to be a professional cyclist.

> **Fact and Opinion**
> Identify one fact and one opinion about Marshall Taylor.

One by one, he committed to memory the names of racers who'd visited the shop—Arthur Zimmerman, Willie Windle of Massachusetts, and Louis "Birdie" Munger, who had recently opened a racing workshop in town.

As Marshall grew to know Munger, he began spending more and more time at his shop. He'd follow him to the track, pleading, "Tell me about the race when . . . "

Birdie was tickled by Marshall. In fact, the boy reminded him of a younger version of himself. "You've got talent, but you've got to keep working," Birdie instructed after one of Marshall's many wins. Soon Marshall had been hired as his assistant, running errands and doing chores.

When Birdie decided to move to Worcester, Massachusetts, he invited Marshall along. After a fond farewell to his family, Marshall set off with Birdie to begin training. To anyone who'd listen, he would boast, "I am going to make Major Marshall Taylor the fastest bicycle rider in the world."

Marshall's talent grew as fast as his popularity. It wasn't long before racing fans—although they may not have known the name Marshall Taylor—knew there was a young Negro causing quite a stir.

But by the time Marshall turned professional at age eighteen, challenges off the track began to trail him like a shadow. All of the large purses won in races all over the country couldn't buy him a meal in a restaurant or a room in a hotel.

Cities like Louisville, St. Louis, and even Indianapolis wouldn't permit a black man on their tracks—their entry forms read, "For White Riders Only." Still that couldn't keep Marshall down. As the only Negro granted membership in the League of American Wheelmen, he was entitled to compete on any track he chose.

"You're never going to finish this race!" riders would holler above the noise of the crowd, or "This race is going to be your last," they'd taunt. Working as a group, they'd box him out. Racing next to him, they'd poke and jab him. They agreed that if they defeated him, the winner would split the prize money with the others. But usually there was no prize money to split: For every trick they tried, Taylor had his own.

Marshall's style had always been to stay behind the pack. "Save it for the finish," he would recite to himself. Wearing his lucky number 13 armband, he'd keep pace, then ride full speed in the final yards. But when the competition turned crueler, he had to adjust his style. As soon as he'd spot a clearing in the pack, he'd cut through and make his way to the front. And that's where he stayed, all the way across the finish line.

The "Black Whirlwind," as he was called by the press, had his own set of rules: "Ride clean and ride fair." Asked by reporters how he managed to keep calm despite attacks by other cyclists, Marshall answered, "I simply ride away."

Munger's prediction years earlier had come true. Major Marshall Taylor was now the fastest bicycle rider in the world. After he won the 1899 World Championship title, beating out the Butler brothers, offers to compete abroad flooded his home. Promises of money and racing against the world's best cyclists were too much to resist.

In 1900 friends and family said good-bye as Marshall boarded the *Kaiser Wilhelm der Grosse*, proud to be representing his country on his first European racing tour.

From the moment he arrived in France, fans swarmed around him, welcoming "le Nègre Volant," the Flying Negro. At every Parisian café, hotel, and track, they followed for a chance to shake his hand. The press reported his every move, and he was invited into the homes of aristocracy. Halfway around the world, Marshall Taylor was finally getting the recognition and respect he had worked for his whole life.

It was not on a starting line but rather at the Café Esperance that Marshall met the French champion, Edmond Jacquelin. "Welcome to Paris, Monsieur Taylor!" he greeted, smiling broadly. And with that, the two became instant friends.

> **Fact and Opinion**
> Can the statement ". . . the two became instant friends" be verified? Explain your answer.

Jacquelin, winner of the 1900 World Championship, French Championship, and Grand Prix of Paris—the Triple Crown of racing—was a sharp contrast to the 1899 World Champion. Everyone wondered who would **prevail** in the next race—the quiet, gentlemanly Taylor or the explosive, larger-than-life Jacquelin?

Long before Taylor and Jacquelin arrived at Le Parc des Princes velodrome for their race, crowds had gathered, straining for a glimpse of the two rivals. Shivering against the cold, Taylor stood at the starting line dressed in layers to protect himself from the biting wind. Was this the Flying Negro from America the fans had heard so much about?

Meanwhile Jacquelin strode onto the track.

"Vive Taylor! Vive Jacquelin!" shouted the crowd as more fans huddled beyond the gates.

The race was on.

When it was over, roars of applause rang out to the beat of the French national anthem.

"Edmond Jacquelin, the victor in two straight heats," came the announcement.

To schedule a rematch so close to the first race was unheard of, but the crowds demanded it.

"Who will be king?" asked *L'Auto Velo*. Would it be the 1899 or the 1900 World Champion, America or France, Taylor or Jacquelin?

As the men took their positions at the start of the first heat and strapped their feet to their pedals, the crowd held one **collective** breath.

Bang!

Jacquelin jumped comfortably into the lead. Marshall concentrated on erasing all thoughts of their first race from his mind. He leaned lower over his handlebars, and from high in the stands fans looked down on the shadow of a figure lying almost flat, inching closer and closer to his rival.

For one brief moment the two became one. Side-by-side and wheel-by-wheel they sped to the finish. It was only in the final lengths that one seemed to edge ahead.

In the blink of an eye, the heat was over. Taylor had come from behind to cross the finish line first. The crowd roared, yet the victor was still to be decided: The winner had to take the best of three heats.

In the second heat, again Marshall waited for just the right moment.

When he noticed a shift in Jacquelin's closely guarded position, he **maneuvered** his bike as adeptly as he had in front of Hay and Willits Bicycle Shop years ago. And once again all eyes were on little Major Taylor.

The wind, which Marshall had once so loved against his face, now pushed at his back, carrying him well ahead of his rival and first through the winning tape.

Two races and two straight heats brought American fans to their feet. While Jacquelin quietly rode off the track, Marshall tied the American flag to his waist. As he rode his victory lap, he heard the familiar tune of "The Star Spangled Banner," and all the world watched the colors red, white, and blue billow and fly in the wind.

Take a Ride with Lesa Cline-Ransome and James E. Ransome

Lesa Cline-Ransome stood at the top of George Street, the hill in Worcester, Massachusetts, where Marshall Taylor trained. She visited the house he used to live in and read everything she could about his life. Her research helped this book feel real. Lesa wrote this book as a companion to *Satchel Paige*, her book about the renowned baseball player.

James E. Ransome started writing and illustrating books—about himself and his friends—in elementary school. He worked on this story with his wife, Lesa, and went with her to George Street. Seeing where Marshall Taylor trained, he says, "really brought him to life."

Another book by Lesa Cline-Ransome and James E. Ransome: *Satchel Paige*

 Find out more about Lesa Cline-Ransome and James E. Ransome at **www.macmillanmh.com**.

CA **Author's Purpose**

What do you think is the Ransomes' purpose for writing about Major Taylor? Give examples from the text that reveal their purpose.

CA Critical Thinking

Summarize

Use your Fact and Opinion Chart to help you summarize *Major Taylor*. What are the facts of Marshall Taylor's life leading up to his victory in France?

Fact	Opinion

Think and Compare

1. Reread the first paragraph on page 411. What **facts** does the author include? What **opinions** does the author state? **Make Inferences and Analyze: Fact and Opinion**

2. Do you think the author approves or disapproves of how Marshall Taylor was treated during his bicycle races? Use specific references from the text to support your answer. **Analyze**

3. Marshall Taylor was popular among **spectators** at races, but other racers used tricks to try to beat him. How did Taylor handle his competition? Use evidence from the text to support your answer. **Synthesize**

4. Why do you think we should remember Marshall Taylor? What can we learn from his achievements? **Evaluate**

5. Pretend you are Marshall Taylor. Write a letter to the author of "Bike Ride, Anyone?" on pages 398–399 telling the author how learning to ride a bicycle changed your life. **Reading/Writing Across Texts**

415

Lyric Poems are short and songlike and express the feelings of the speaker.

Concrete Poems are shaped to look like the poem's subject matter.

✔ Literary Elements

Assonance is the repetition of the same middle vowel sound in two or more closely grouped words.

Onomatopoeia is the use of words that sound like the action or thing they describe.

Bicycle Riding

by Sandra Liatsos

My feet rise
off the planet,
pedal wheels of steel
that sparkle as
they spin me through
the open space I feel
winging out
to galaxies
far beyond the sun,
where bicycles
are satellites,
their orbits never done.

The words *wheels* and *steel* repeat the middle vowel sound "ee" to create assonance.

The Sidewalk Racer or On the Skateboard

by Lillian Morrison

Skimming
an asphalt sea
I swerve, I curve, I
sway; I speed to whirring
sound an inch above the
ground; I'm the sailor
and the sail, I'm the
driver and the wheel
I'm the one and only
single engine
human auto
mobile.

Whirring is like the sound it is describing. This is an example of onomatopoeia.

 Critical Thinking

1. How does the assonance in "Bicycle Riding" appeal to your senses? Which sense does it appeal to most? **Assonance**

2. Lyric poems are written to express strong feeling. How do the poets feel about bicycle riding and skateboarding? **Analyze**

3. Do you think Marshall Taylor would agree with the feelings expressed in "Bicycle Riding" and "The Sidewalk Racer"? Why or why not? **Reading/Writing Across Texts**

 Find out more about assonance and onomatopoeia at **www.macmillanmh.com**.

Writing

CA

✓ **Dialogue: Linked to Argument**

Writers use **dialogue** and **evidence** to link their **arguments** and support their opinions.

Read the passage below. Notice how the author Lesa Cline-Ransome uses dialogue as evidence to support her opinion.

An excerpt from
Major Taylor: Champion Cyclist

The author uses examples of the unfair treatment Marshall had to put up with to support her statement that "challenges off the track began to trail him like a shadow." These pieces of evidence help convince us that she is right.

But by the time Marshall turned professional at age eighteen, challenges off the track began to trail him like a shadow. All of the large purses won in races all over the country couldn't buy him a meal in a restaurant or a room in a hotel.

Cities like Louisville, St. Louis, and even Indianapolis wouldn't permit a black man on their tracks—their entry forms read, "For White Riders Only."...

"You're never going to finish this race!" riders would holler above the noise of the crowd, or "This race is going to be your last," they'd taunt. Working as a group, they'd box him out. Racing next to him, they'd poke and jab him.

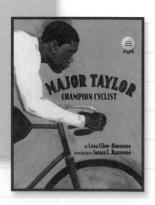

Read and Find

Read Lilah's writing below. How did she use dialogue to convince her sister to leave her things alone? Use the Writer's Checklist below to help you.

It Works!
by Lilah B.

"Carrie, I don't want you messing up my things in our room," I said to my little sister.

"But it's fun to play with your things," answered Carrie.

"I'll make a deal with you. If you can leave my side of the room alone during the day, I'll play or read with you for a whole hour after dinner."

Carrie loves to play with me, so this system has really worked. So far.

> Read about how I made a deal with my little sister.

Writer's Checklist

 Did the writer provide details to back up her argument?

 Is the connection between the details and the argument clear and strong?

☑ Do you find Lilah's argument convincing?

Talk About It

How do people accomplish extraordinary results in their lives? What special results are you hoping to achieve?

LOG ON ▶ Find out more about extraordinary results at **www.macmillanmh.com**.

Extraordinary Results

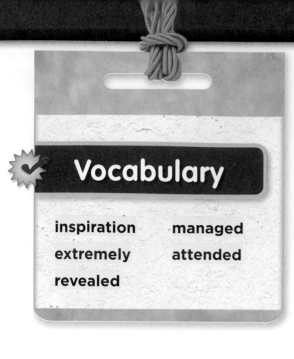

Dr. Boachie-Adjei in a New York City hospital. When he's in Ghana, he often sees 100 patients a day.

A Doctor's Dream

The story of Oheneba Boachie-Adjei is an **inspiration**. Growing up in the city of Kamasi in Ghana, all the odds were stacked against him. But through hard work, he achieved his life's goal.

When Boachie-Adjei was 8, he was stricken with a disease. **Extremely** ill, he grew ever weaker. A local healer did little to help. "I wasn't going to make it," he says.

It's a familiar story in Africa, where lack of medical care is common. Fortunately, Boachie-Adjei's family found one of the country's few physicians—a doctor who had trained in the United Kingdom. "I was lucky," he says, "to have a pediatrician who decided to come home."

This children's doctor inspired Boachie-Adjei to go to medical school. After high school he traveled to New York in 1972 with $12 in his pocket. While working in a factory, he studied hard and was accepted at Columbia University's medical school.

Now Boachie-Adjei is "paying back" the doctor who saved him. A top orthopedic surgeon, Boachie-Adjei runs an organization that has treated more than 500 bone disorders in Ghana and Barbados since 1998. He operates for free on people with serious back, hip, and foot problems.

What keeps Boachie-Adjei charged up are patients like Patience Affotey, an 18-year-old woman in Ghana whose back he repaired. "She was inspired by what we're doing and wants to be an orthopedic surgeon," says Boachie-Adjei. "Nothing could be any better than that."

Top 5 : Jobs That Parents Hope Their Kids Will Have

In a recent poll, 504 parents of kids ages 5 to 17 **revealed** what kind of job they hope their kids will have in the future. Here's what parents said those dream jobs are.

1.	Start a successful new business	25%
2.	Doctor	18%
3.	Teacher	11%
4. Tie *	Chief of a big company Professional athlete	9% 9%
5.	Lawyer	4%
6.	Other	24%

Source:
Survey by Harris Interactive

Against All Odds

Sang Tran's early years were spent in a war zone. When she was 5, her family fled Cambodia.

After terrible times, the family **managed** to relocate to Los Angeles. They arrived in the United States speaking almost no English. By the time Sang **attended** high school, she had shown a gift for teaching. Her specialty was helping new Asian immigrants.

Sang knew what she wanted in life, and she had the drive to achieve it. After graduating from college in Los Angeles, Sang landed her present job as a teacher in the city's Chinatown. She is helping kids like her achieve their dreams.

Sang Tran says her immigrant students in Los Angeles are going "through what I went through."

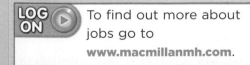

LOG ON ▶ To find out more about jobs go to **www.macmillanmh.com**.

CA Comprehension

Genre

Nonfiction: A nonfiction article in a newspaper or magazine presents facts and information.

Summarize

✓ **Main Idea and Details**
The main idea of an article is what the story is about. Details give more information about the main idea.

Sarah Chang's parents had much to do with her success.

Take a Bow

How did a young girl become a violin-playing superstar?

Even as a young girl, Sarah Chang wanted to be good at the violin. Now a young adult, Sarah is easily one of the best violin players on the planet. But she didn't become that all by herself.

Sarah was a child prodigy. A prodigy is the very rare child who performs on an adult level. Such incredible talent most often appears in math, chess, athletics, and, of course, music. Ability and intelligence are not enough—a gift must be detected and developed. It takes the support and teamwork of family, friends, and teachers to make talent grow.

Sarah Chang is a great example of a prodigy whose gift was nurtured by parents and teachers. Thanks in part to their hard work and sacrifice, she is an international superstar in the world of classical music.

424

A Star Is Born

Born in 1980, Sarah is the older child of violin teacher Min Soo Chang and his wife, Myoung. The couple settled in Philadelphia after leaving South Korea in 1979.

When Sarah was just three, her talent for music **revealed** itself. Her parents noticed that she was able to play the theme songs from cartoons on her piano. A year later Sarah moved on from the piano when she discovered her true calling: the violin.

"I always wanted to play my dad's violin," Sarah says, "but he wouldn't let me touch it. Little kids have sticky fingers."

Instead her father bought her a small, child-sized violin and began giving her lessons. He realized, however, that her talent could use all the support the family could give. After two years he sent a recording of Sarah's playing to violin teacher Dorothy DeLay. She taught at the Juilliard School—the nation's top school for the performing arts—in New York City. DeLay had trained Sarah's father and some of the greatest violin players in the world, including world-famous violinist Itzhak Perlman.

DeLay and others at Juilliard could see immediately that Sarah was **extremely** talented. But they worried she might be too young for the pressures of such high-level training. They asked her to wait a year until she turned seven. After that she **attended** classes taught by DeLay on the weekends.

Sarah's parents had to drive her to New York for the lessons. But they never made her feel like she owed them something for making those three-hour drives. Of course it helped that the lessons paid off—big time.

Sarah asked for a violin when she was 4 years old.

425

"Sarah plays like professionals in their twenties," said her teacher DeLay. Sarah not only played like an adult, she also practiced like one—rehearsing three hours each day.

When she was 9, Sarah was asked to perform with the New York Philharmonic on just a day's notice. The violinist who was supposed to play had canceled. No problem: Sarah was a huge success. Her playing earned her a standing ovation, bringing the crowd to its feet.

A Typical Teen?

By the time Sarah reached her teens, she had recorded a hit classical CD. She was also performing around the world. At age 12 she told an audience in London that "I can't really say what I'll be in 10 or 20 years. But I'm aiming to be a violinist."

To reach her goal, Sarah traveled a great deal and worked hard, yet she **managed** to live a normal life. Like many other 12-year-olds, she enjoyed roller-skating, sleepovers, and rock music.

One of Sarah's most amazing feats had nothing to do with music. Despite her busy schedule, she was able to keep up with her studies. As a sixth grader, she got her homework in on time by faxing it when she was on the road. And though she practiced violin four hours a day, she also watched about an hour or two of TV.

Sarah's parents didn't object to the TV watching. "She should have her childhood," said her mother.

Sarah is pictured with Sir Yehudi Menuhin, who had been a child prodigy on the violin himself.

Sarah's career is an inspiration to young musicians.

Sarah Today

Through her teen years, Sarah continued to practice the violin and do her homework in hotel rooms while she traveled. Still, she managed to graduate from Juilliard in 1999, when she was only 18.

Today Sarah is no longer a kid. She's in her late twenties, but she plays with that familiar boundless energy. Her bow moves with breathtaking speed over the strings. Sarah's music leaves audiences around the globe completely in awe.

To play that well, Sarah says she needs a lot of sleep. Why? She has such a busy schedule. In one recent year, she performed in Paris, London, Los Angeles, Minneapolis, New York, Philadelphia, Seattle, Madrid, and Berlin.

Sleep, however, is not the only secret to Sarah's success. She says it's the support she received from her "team"—her parents, teachers, the recording company, other musicians, and friends. Without them, she might never have achieved her dream.

 Critical Thinking

1. What is the main idea of this article?

2. In what way did Sarah's parents support her talent?

3. If you were good at something, what sacrifices would you make to improve? Why?

4. Dr. Boachie-Adjei in "A Doctor's Dream" and Sarah Chang had very different childhoods. What is common in each of them that let them realize their dreams?

Right There

You can put your finger on the answer. Look for key words in the question. Then find those key words in the selection.

Burt Rutan stands with his pilots in front of *SpaceShipOne* in Mojave, California.

The Sky's the Limit

Can you imagine taking a vacation on the moon? Burt Rutan can. He has dreamed of the day when space will be filled with tourists. By building his own spacecraft, he hopes his dream will finally come true.

Rutan's craft is called *SpaceShipOne.* It looks a lot like a small airplane. A cargo plane carries *SpaceShipOne* partway up, and then the spacecraft takes off on its own. Its rocket motor shoots it 70 miles into space. *SpaceShipOne* then uses its wings to float back to Earth.

Many people thought Rutan was out of his mind to design his own spacecraft. But he and his team believed in his project. In 2004, *SpaceShipOne* made two successful round-trips into space. Rutan's team won a $10 million prize for building the first privately owned craft to travel to space twice in two weeks.

SpaceShipOne is set to become part of a new line of craft for space tourists. A large airline company has ordered five spaceships from Rutan. But you better start saving your pennies if you want to take a ride. The price of a single ticket for a trip to space will be around $190,000!

Go on ▶

Now answer questions 1 through 5. Base your answers on the article "The Sky's the Limit."

1. Who designed *SpaceShipOne*?

   A   NASA
   B   Burt Rutan
   C   a large airline company
   D   Time For Kids magazine

2. Why did the team win a $10 million prize?

   A   They used a NASA-designed space shuttle to travel to space twice in two weeks.
   B   They flew a craft 70 miles into space and back again without using a rocket.
   C   They designed a craft that in the future will carry tourists into space for a price.
   D   They built the first privately owned craft to travel to space twice in two weeks.

3. How much will it cost to buy a ticket for a trip into space?

   A $10 million
   B $1 million
   C $190,000
   D $90,000

4. What was Burt Rutan's dream? What did he do to make his dream come true?

5. Do you think space tourism will be a success? Use details from the article to support your answer.

Tip
Look for key words.

Write on Demand

 CA People often look for extraordinary results in their lives. Think about a dream that you have and how you could achieve it. Write to <u>explain</u> how you plan to achieve your result.

Expository writing defines, or tells how to do something.

To figure out if a writing prompt asks for expository writing, look for clue words, such as <u>explain</u>, <u>tell how</u>, or <u>define</u>.

Below, see how one student begins a response to the prompt above.

The writer explains how to achieve an extraordinary result.

    I want to be a basketball player when I'm an adult. Here's how I plan to achieve this extraordinary result in my life. I practice basketball every day. I've found a local playground where I can practice and play in games with other kids. I try out for all the teams I can find and I listen carefully to coaches who give me pointers.
    I eat healthful foods and get plenty of sleep. I also keep myself in really good condition by running and lifting weights in the afternoon.
    Finally, I keep my grades up.
    I plan to be a professional player of a game I love and I will work hard to reach this extraordinary result.

Writing Prompt

Respond in writing to the prompt below. Write for 20 minutes. Write as much as you can, as well as you can. Review the hints below before and after you write.

CA Many people look for extraordinary results in their lives. Think of an extraordinary result you would like to achieve. Now write to explain how you plan to accomplish your extraordinary result.

Writing Hints for Prompts

- ☑ Carefully read the prompt.
- ☑ Organize your ideas to plan your writing.
- ☑ Support your ideas by giving reasons or using more details.
- ☑ Combine sentences to add variety and show emotions.
- ☑ Choose words that help readers understand your ideas.
- ☑ Review your writing and edit as needed.

FULFILLING A DREAM

CA Talk About It

César Chávez fulfilled his dream. How would you go about fulfilling yours?

LOG ON ▶ Find out more about people who fulfilled their dreams at **www.macmillanmh.com**.

433

Michelangelo's *David*

Vocabulary

Renaissance
commissioned
proportion
miniature
philosopher
elaborate
envisioned
recommend

Word Parts

Many English words have **Greek Roots**.

phil = love

soph = wise

Philosopher originally meant one who loves wisdom.

Suppose that you could travel back in time to the period of the **Renaissance**. This was an exciting age when there was a rebirth of interest in learning and the arts. It began in Italy in the 1300s and spread throughout Europe.

You arrive in Florence, a beautiful city in Italy. This is the city of the Medici family. The Medici are wealthy bankers and merchants who have **commissioned**, or sponsored, artists to create many paintings, statues, and buildings for the city. They have also supported poets and writers.

One of the people you meet is Michelangelo Buonarroti. Like fellow artist Leonardo da Vinci, he is a genius of many talents. Known for his beautiful paintings in the Sistine Chapel in Rome, he is also a great sculptor and is making sketches for a statue. Most artists of this period are concerned that parts of statues be in **proportion**. They want their work to show how one part of the body relates to other parts. Michelangelo's sketches show more than the figure's proportions, though. They show the power and spirit of the figure. Once Michelangelo is happy with his drawings, he will make a model of his statue. The model is a **miniature** version of the statue, which will be huge.

Another artist you meet is Leonardo da Vinci, also a leader of the Renaissance. One of his most famous paintings is the *Mona Lisa*. But Leonardo is more than a painter; he is a **philosopher** who studies the nature of the universe. He wants to know how everything works. He draws **elaborate** and detailed scientific pictures of plants, animals, humans, and the many inventions he has **envisioned** in his mind. Leonardo fills more than 4,000 pages in his notebooks with drawings. He shows you drawings of flying machines and undersea boats. How amazing for the fifteenth century!

A third artist of the Renaissance is Raphael. He is younger than Leonardo and Michelangelo and has studied their work. Some of the people you meet think his paintings are more delicate in color and have softer lines. Raphael shows you a work called *The School of Athens*.

Detail of Plato and Aristotle from *The School of Athens* by Raphael

It pictures an imaginary group of great thinkers. You are interested to see that included in the painting are Michelangelo, Leonardo, and Raphael.

When you return to the twenty-first century, you can't wait to tell your friends about these artists of the past. You **recommend**, or suggest, that they too pay a visit to the Renaissance Era.

Reread for Comprehension

Generate Questions
Make Generalizations
To make generalizations, combine key facts from the text and your prior knowledge. You can use this information to generate questions as you read.

Use a Generalizations Chart as you reread "Artists of the Past."

Important Information	Generalization

And he wouldn't eat meat. He liked animals too much to eat anything that had once been alive. Nor could he stand the sight of caged birds. If he saw a man selling birds, he would buy them all. Then he would open the cages and watch the birds fly away. What a flurry they made! How did they do it? All his life Leonardo tried to discover their secret of flying so he could make a flying machine for himself.

For a man who liked to ask questions, Leonardo da Vinci was born at the right time—April 15, 1452. Everybody was asking questions then. The age was called the **Renaissance**, a time of rebirth when people who had forgotten how to be curious became curious again. They were exploring new countries, discovering, inventing, looking at old things in new ways. What was the point, Leonardo asked, in copying what had already been done? He had to bring his own experience into whatever he painted. You wouldn't catch him putting a halo around the head of a saint. How could he? He had never seen a halo.

Leonardo da Vinci turned out to be a famous artist; still, he was not just an artist. He could never be just one thing. He was an engineer, an architect, a musician, a **philosopher**, an astronomer. Once he fashioned a special kind of flute made of silver in the shape of a horse's head. The ruler of Florence, Lorenzo de' Medici, asked him to deliver it as a gift to the duke of Milan. This was lucky for Leonardo. He had heard that the duke of Milan wanted to honor his father with a bronze horse in front of his palace. And Leonardo wanted to be the one to make it.

This would be his mark on history. Hundreds of years later people would point to the horse. "Leonardo made that," they would say.

> **Make Generalizations**
> Is the statement "Everybody was asking questions then" a valid generalization? Explain your answer.

Parachute

Catapult

So he wrote to the duke, listing all the things that he could do. He could make cannon, lightweight bridges, and covered chariots that couldn't be broken or harmed. On and on he went, but he saved the most important point for the last. He could make a bronze horse. In the end, he didn't send the letter. He simply left for Milan. Never mind that he was in the midst of painting a large religious picture in Florence. Let someone else finish it. He had planned the picture and that was the important part.

Leonardo was thirty years old now, handsome with curly blond hair. The duke gave him the job of working on the horse, but at the same time he was expected to take charge of entertainment in the palace. He had a beautiful singing voice, he could play musical instruments, he could juggle and ask riddles, and he was also asked to stage **elaborate** plays for special occasions. Whenever he had a chance, he went back to the horse.

He visited the stables, studying how a horse was put together.

He needed to understand everything about his subject. He measured and drew pictures until he knew where all the bones and muscles of a horse were. But you couldn't show all the muscles on a statue, he said, or the horse would look like a bag of turnips. You should show only those muscles the horse was using or getting ready to use.

He visited statues of horses. Many were shown in an amble— left front leg moving at the same time as the left back leg. This was not easy for a horse; he had to be taught to do it. Leonardo saw one horse, however, that he described as free—left front leg and right back leg moving together, in a trot. Moreover, both ears were pointed forward. (Some horses pointed one ear back to hear the rider's orders.)

Leonardo was ready to begin.

But the duke wasn't quite ready. He wanted a much bigger horse than the one he had originally planned. One three times larger than life. Could Leonardo manage anything that large? the duke wondered. He wrote to Lorenzo, asking him to **recommend** someone who could do the job.

Lorenzo replied: Leonardo da Vinci was the only one.

On April 23, 1490, Leonardo wrote in his notebook: "I resumed work on the horse." The hardest part would be the casting. He collected 58,000 pounds of metal—tin and copper—which would be heated until it was fluid. This would be turned into bronze and used to cast the horse. But should he pour the bronze all at once? No one had tried a single pouring of anything this large.

In November 1493, he had completed the clay model—twenty-four feet high. It was shown off at one of the duke's special occasions, and it was a sensation.

But Leonardo seemed to be in no hurry to start casting. Perhaps he wasn't sure how he'd do it. Besides, he was planning a new project. He had been **commissioned** to cover the wall of a convent with a picture of Jesus and his disciples at the Last Supper. Since he wanted to present the disciples realistically, each with his own personality, Leonardo walked the streets of Milan, looking for the right faces. He had trouble with Judas. He could never find anyone in Milan who looked evil enough. So he left Judas for someone else to do.

Later, in 1498, there were rumors that the French were preparing to invade Milan, and the duke wanted to be ready. And there was all the metal that Leonardo had collected. Just what the duke needed. So he sent it off to be made into cannon. Well, this is war, Leonardo reasoned. What else could they do?

When the French came in 1499, Leonardo and the duke fled. But the horse couldn't leave. There he was when the French arrived. The archers laughed. Never would they find as perfect a target, they said. Pulling back the strings on their bows, they let their arrows fly. Ping! Ping! Ping! The horse sagged. Ping!

Then it rained. And the horse became smaller and smaller.

At last it was nothing but a pile of mud stuck with arrows.

> **Make Generalizations**
> The author states that many statues showed horses in an amble. Is this a valid generalization? Explain.

Leonardo went back to inventing and painting, but he never forgot his horse.

He still wanted to invent a flying machine. But he still couldn't do it.

His greatest disappointment, however, was his horse.

As Leonardo became older, his hair turned white and grew down to his shoulders. His beard reached to his waist.

And he became depressed. What had he achieved? he asked himself. He complained to his notebook: "Tell me," he asked, "if anything has been achieved by me. Tell me. Tell me." It was especially hard when his rival, Michelangelo, taunted him.

"You," Michelangelo said, "who made a model of a horse you could never cast in bronze and which you gave up, to your shame."

In his notebook Leonardo mourned, "I have wasted my hours."

On May 2, 1519, Leonardo da Vinci died. It was said that even on his deathbed, Leonardo wept for his horse.

Leonardo has been remembered for hundreds of years, especially for his paintings *Mona Lisa* and *The Last Supper*. But not for his horse. That story was almost forgotten until 1977, when it was told in a magazine. And the right man read it. His name was Charles Dent. And Charlie loved art—reading about it, making it, looking at it, collecting it. Leonardo would have liked Charlie. They were both dreamers with big dreams. Yet Leonardo may have been envious. Charlie did what Leonardo had always longed to do. He flew, soaring through the sky like a bird freed from its cage. Charlie was an airline pilot, and whenever he traveled, he looked for art to take home.

The more Charlie read about Leonardo and his horse, the more he cared about Leonardo. When he read that Leonardo died still grieving for his horse, Charlie couldn't stand it. Right then he had the biggest dream of his life.

"Let's give Leonardo his horse," he said. It would be a gift from the American people to the people of Italy.

But could he really give Leonardo his horse? Could anyone? Charlie went to see famous scholars who had specialized in the study of Leonardo. When he came home, Charlie was smiling; he could go ahead.

But where would he build his horse? He needed a special building, he decided—a round building shaped like a dome, tall enough for a horse. On top there would be windows to let in the light.

Charlie didn't know a thing about domes, but luckily he found a man who did. When at last the Dome was finished, Charlie hung the pictures he had collected on the walls and arranged other art objects around the room.

All that was needed was the horse.

Every day Charlie could see the horse more clearly. Wherever he went, he carried a small piece of wax or a piece of clay and made **miniature** models of the horse. But he needed to be around real horses. He borrowed two champion Morgan horses and studied them for months, running his hands over their bodies so he could feel where the muscles and bones were. He measured every inch of the horses just as Leonardo would have done.

Then, in 1988, he began the eight-foot model of the horse. Over the wooden skeleton, he applied one thousand pounds of clay. To hold the horse steady, a post ran through the belly of the horse

to the ground. To fill the belly, the horse was stuffed with slats of wood and Styrofoam. So now the Dome had a clay horse—his left foreleg raised and bent, his right rear leg off the ground. Free. The muscles in his hindquarters were tense, his ears pointed forward, his nostrils were beginning to flare.

By 1993 the eight-foot plaster model of the clay horse was completed and ready to be cast into a twenty-four-foot bronze horse.

For that it would have to be sent to a foundry where it could be enlarged; a twenty-four-foot clay model sculpted; then the twenty-four-foot bronze horse cast.

In 1994, however, the people at the Dome were less concerned about the horse than they were worried about Charlie. He became sick and no one knew what was the matter. Then he was told that he had Lou Gehrig's disease and it could not be cured. He would not be alive when the horse arrived in Milan. All Charlie said was what he always said: He had never been interested in taking credit for the horse; the gift of the horse was a gesture of friendship from the American people to the Italian people, a salute across the centuries to Leonardo.

On December 13, Charlie's family and friends gathered around his bedside and promised him that the horse would be finished.

On Christmas morning 1994, Charlie died.

On August 1, 1995, the horse was ready to go to the foundry. He was hoisted into a van, tied, padded, and driven off for his great adventure.

At the Tallix Foundry in Beacon, New York, his transformation began. He was enlarged and cut up into sixty separate pieces. They were laid against the wall of the foundry while the Dome people gathered to watch the pieces being put together. It was certainly a huge horse, but was it as grand as Charlie had **envisioned**?

The Dome friends walked quietly around the horse. They seemed uneasy.

The horse wasn't right.

Art experts were called in. They shook their heads.

No, the horse wasn't right.

He looked awkward. Out of **proportion**. One of his rear legs appeared to be short. His eyes were not exactly parallel. He needed help.

Fortunately, a talented sculptor from New York City, Nina Akamu, agreed to try to fix him. But when she went to work on the twenty-four-foot horse, she found that the cementlike plaster that covered him resisted change. No matter how hard she tried, she couldn't fix him.

Everyone recognized that there was only one thing to do, but it took a while for anyone to say it out loud. Yet it had to be said. Nina would have to start from scratch and make another horse. For some, the idea of doing away with Charlie's horse was almost more than they could bear, yet they all knew that Charlie would want his horse to be as perfect as possible.

The horse would always be Charlie's dream, but as soon as Nina went to work, he had to become her horse, too. She had studied in Italy for eleven years. Her favorite Renaissance artist was Verrochio, Leonardo's teacher. It was lucky that she was there to carry on with Charlie's dream.

First Nina made an eight-foot clay horse. From it a second eight-foot horse was made of plaster. Using the plaster model as a guide, a twenty-four-foot horse was made in clay.

Everyone went to work to get the horse exactly right. Finally he was ready to be cast in bronze.

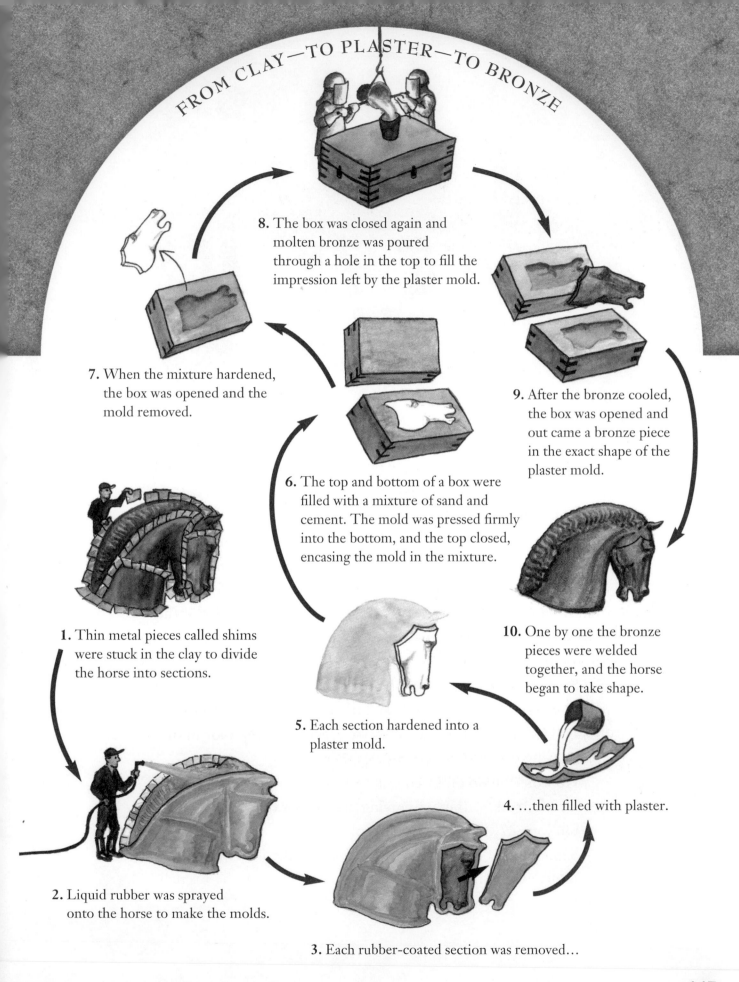

8. The box was closed again and molten bronze was poured through a hole in the top to fill the impression left by the plaster mold.

7. When the mixture hardened, the box was opened and the mold removed.

6. The top and bottom of a box were filled with a mixture of sand and cement. The mold was pressed firmly into the bottom, and the top closed, encasing the mold in the mixture.

9. After the bronze cooled, the box was opened and out came a bronze piece in the exact shape of the plaster mold.

1. Thin metal pieces called shims were stuck in the clay to divide the horse into sections.

5. Each section hardened into a plaster mold.

10. One by one the bronze pieces were welded together, and the horse began to take shape.

4. …then filled with plaster.

2. Liquid rubber was sprayed onto the horse to make the molds.

3. Each rubber-coated section was removed…

447

But how could such a large bronze sculpture stand on two legs? First they built a steel skeleton inside the body of the horse to support the sides, and then they inserted steel tubes in the two legs. The tubes were bolted to steel anchor plates below the hooves and embedded in concrete.

Finally, the horse was complete. Everyone stood back and looked up at him. They agreed that he was ready for his new home.

If Leonardo had finished his horse, he would only have had to move it from the vineyard where he worked to the front of the duke's palace. Charlie's horse had to cross the ocean to Italy. But he was too big.

So he was cut up into separate pieces, crated, and flown to Milan, where the Tallix people and the Dome people waited to reassemble him. Workers would crawl through a trapdoor in the horse's belly to fasten the pieces together.

He would stand on a pedestal in a small park in front of Milan's famous racetrack, within whinnying distance of the racing stable.

On June 27, 1999, the horse took off.

September 10, 1999, was the date set for the unveiling of the statue, exactly five hundred years to the day since the French invaded Milan and destroyed Leonardo's horse.

An enormous cloth was spread over the horse so he couldn't be seen. Two huge clusters of blue and white balloons were attached to either end of the cloth. On the pupil of one eye of the horse, Nina had written in tiny letters *Leonardo da Vinci*. On the other eye she had written *Charles Dent*. She had put her own name in the curly mane of the horse.

As a large crowd of Italians and Americans took their seats, the horse stayed in hiding. Speeches were made. The Italian national anthem was sung. Then the American national anthem.

Finally, the strings anchoring the balloons were cut and the cloth rose into the sky.

Ahhhhhhh!

At last Leonardo's horse was home.

Share a Historical Perspective with
Jean Fritz and Hudson Talbott

Jean Fritz lived in China until she was 13. "Having to wait to get to America," she says, "I needed to make up for lost time." That's one of the reasons she writes stories about America's history. When she gets letters from children saying she added the "fun" to history, she says she didn't add anything. There was as much fun in the past as there is today. One of the most exciting writing adventures she had was going to Italy for the celebration of the bronze horse in this story.

Another book by Jean Fritz: *Can't You Make Them Behave, King George?*

Hudson Talbott's

books have taken him to Africa, England, Ireland, and to the heart of the Amazon rain forest—by dugout canoe! What he loves the most about traveling is sharing his experiences with others.

 Find out more about Jean Fritz and Hudson Talbott at **www.macmillanmh.com**.

 Author's Purpose

What clues help you figure out the author's purpose for writing? Does she want to explain, inform, or persuade? Explain the reasons for your answers.

450

Critical Thinking

Summarize

Use your Generalizations Chart to summarize the story of *Leonardo's Horse*. Remember to include the most important details and retell them in your own words.

Think and Compare

Important Information	Generalization

1. What **generalizations** can you make about the method used to make the horse— from clay to plaster to bronze? Use your Generalizations Chart. **Generate Questions: Make Generalizations**

2. Do you think Charles Dent and Nina Akamu created the horse that Leonardo had **envisioned**? Use examples from the text. **Analyze**

3. How does the author describe a Renaissance person? Think about the talents and skills you possess today. What more do you think you would need to learn to be called a Renaissance person? **Synthesize**

4. The building of Leonardo's horse was meant to be a gift of friendship from the American people to the Italian people. Can great works of art bring cultures closer together? How? **Evaluate**

5. Read "Artists of the Past" on pages 434–435. What characteristics do Michelangelo, Leonardo da Vinci, and Nina Akamu have in common? **Reading/Writing Across Texts**

Leonardo da Vinci

by Diane Stanley

As an inventor, Leonardo is probably most famous for having tried to build a flying machine. He was convinced that "the bird is an instrument functioning according to mathematical laws, and man has the power to reproduce an instrument like this with all its movements." So he analyzed the flight patterns of birds and bats, studied the **anatomy** of their wings, and observed air currents.

Leonardo da Vinci wrote, "I believe that if this screw device is well manufactured, that is, if it is made of linen cloth, the pores of which have been closed with starch, and if the device is promptly reversed, the screw will engage its gear when in the air and it will rise up on high."

452

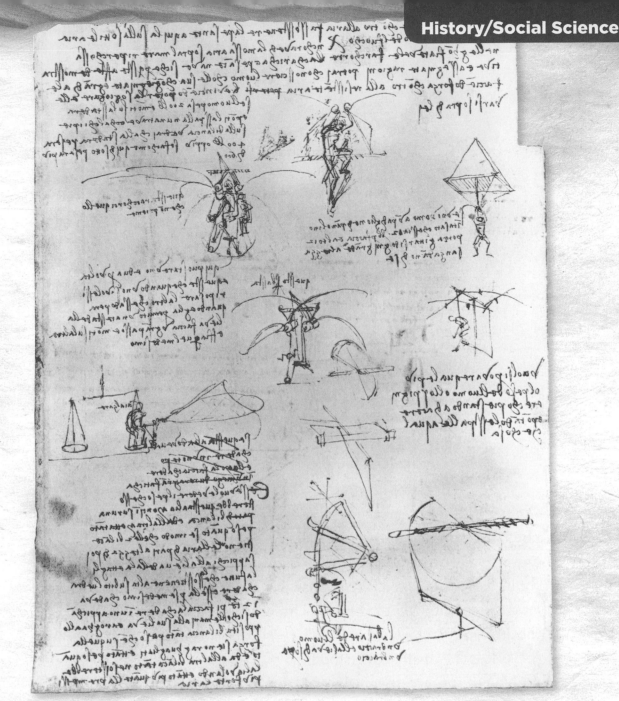

Drawings of *Parachute Experiments and Flying Machines* by Leonardo da Vinci

He sketched a variety of designs and finally, after years of preparation, built a model in a secret upstairs room at his workshop. On January 2, 1496, he wrote in his notebook, "Tomorrow morning, I shall make the strap and the attempt." Either he lost his nerve or it didn't work. At any rate, we have no record of it. But the next time he wrote of trying to fly, he was more cautious. "You will experiment with this machine over a lake," he wrote to himself, "and you will wear attached to your belt a long wineskin . . . so that if you fall in, you will not be drowned."

453

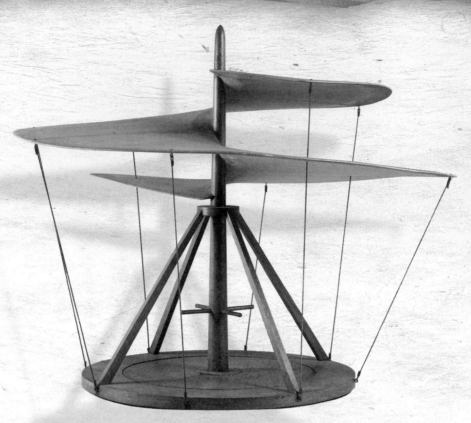

Model of airscrew built after sketch by Leonardo da Vinci

In 1503 he felt certain of success. Twice he wrote about it in his notebook, speculating grandly that the flight would dumbfound the universe and bring him eternal glory. Yet after years of work and study, Leonardo failed. We don't know any of the details, but much later the son of one of Leonardo's friends wrote these words about the attempt: "Vinci tried in vain."

At least he finally understood the problem. Birds are designed to fly—half the weight of their bodies is in the muscles of flight. Humans, on the other hand, with less than a quarter of their body weight in the arm and chest muscles, would never have the strength to fly like birds.

In his notes, Leonardo remarked that with this linen parachute, if it is held open, a person can jump without risk.

As a casual afterthought he designed a parachute as well as an airscrew, based on a toy, which some call the first helicopter. He also sketched the pattern of a leaf drifting to earth and under it showed a man on a winglike **glider**. If he had only worked along these lines instead of trying to imitate the flapping motion of birds, he might have been the first man to fly.

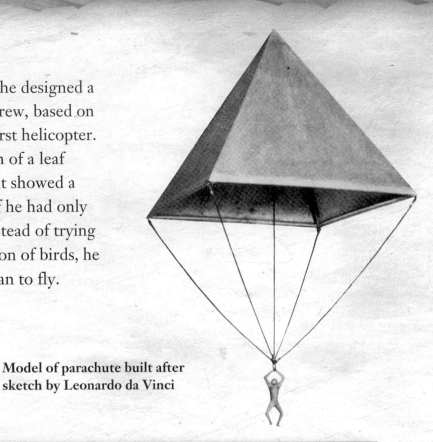

Model of parachute built after sketch by Leonardo da Vinci

CA Critical Thinking

1. How does the reader learn more about Leonardo da Vinci from his notebook entries and drawings? **Primary Source**

2. How does reading Leonardo da Vinci's own words help you understand his ideas and feelings? **Apply**

3. The notebook entries and *Leonardo's Horse* introduce you to Leonardo da Vinci. Which piece helped you get to "know" him better? Why? **Reading/Writing Across Texts**

History/Social Science Activity

Research other great minds from the Italian Renaissance. Select one and write a summary of this person's greatest innovation. Did this person keep a journal?

 Find out more about early flying machines at **www.macmillanmh.com**.

✔ **Dialogue: Credible and Cited**

Writers use **dialogue** and **evidence** that is **credible** and can be **cited** to link their arguments and support their opinions.

Reading and Writing Connection

Read the passage below. Notice how author Jean Fritz used evidence from Leonardo da Vinci's own journal to explain how he felt about his unfinished horse sculpture.

An excerpt from *Leonardo's Horse*

And he became depressed. What had he achieved? he asked himself. He complained to his notebook: "Tell me," he asked, "if anything has been achieved by me. Tell me. Tell me." It was especially hard when his rival, Michelangelo, taunted him.

"You," Michelangelo said, "who made a model of a horse you could never cast in bronze and which you gave up, to your shame."

In his notebook Leonardo mourned, "I have wasted my hours."

The author uses Leonardo da Vinci's own words as evidence to support her claim that he was depressed. She also makes sure to say where those words came from—his personal notebook—to show why we should believe them.

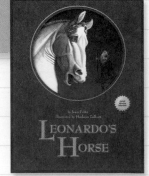

LEONARDO'S HORSE

Read and Find

Read Jamilla's writing below. How did she use a reliable source? Use the Writer's Checklist below to help you.

Papelbon's the Man!

by Jamilla S.

Bill Drake is a much better pitcher than Aiden. Bill may not be as big and as strong as Aiden, but he gets the job done. I looked up their stats on the league stats Web site yesterday. It listed Drake's ERA as 4.25, but Aiden's ERA was 1.77.

How can you argue with numbers like that?

Read how Jamilla uses evidence to support her opinion.

Writer's Checklist

 Did the writer provide evidence for her opinion about her favorite player?

 Does the writer use a source that can be trusted?

 Do the details and the source make you more likely to believe Jamilla?

CA Talk About It

In what ways do you count on relatives or family friends when you need help?

LOG ON ▶ Find out more about families and helping at **www.macmillanmh.com**.

HELP FROM WITHIN

An Aunt's Baseball Dreams

by Danielle Martin

Maybe it's my love of baseball that connects my great-aunt Helen and me. She has always kept me **enthralled** with her stories of playing baseball back in the 1940s. I would listen to these stories over and over. She used to say, "Go after what you want, Sarah. Don't be ashamed of failing. Real **embarrassment** comes from never trying."

Aunt Helen should know. In 1943, she was one of the young women who tried out for the All-American Girls Professional Baseball League, created to entertain fans. Women became **substitutes** because many of America's young men were fighting in World War II.

Aunt Helen had heard rumors that a team would play right in South Bend, Indiana. She dreamed of what it would be like to win a championship for her hometown! She imagined a large pennant hanging at the baseball field, and on this banner the name Helen Baker would be there for all to see.

On the day of the tryouts, Aunt Helen played baseball for hours with many young women. For this new league, some of the rules were different from the rules for regular softball. They still used a standard **regulation** softball, but the bases and pitcher's mound were placed at longer distances, for example.

Kenosha Comets

1946 YEAR BOOK

All the rules were explained by a **grouchy** man in a suit. Aunt Helen said that wearing a suit in the hot sun was what put him in a bad mood. But he had a **resemblance** to Aunt Helen's father. And if he looked like her father, she thought, he couldn't be bad.

About a week later, Aunt Helen collected the mail and found an envelope with her name **inscribed** in blue ink. The envelope was postmarked from Chicago. The letter was from the leaders of the girls' baseball league, who were located in Chicago! Aunt Helen tore it open and learned that she had been invited to the league's main tryouts!

But as the days went by, Aunt Helen became worried about traveling to Chicago alone. What if she went all that way and failed? When the day of the tryouts came, she was too afraid to go.

Team members go over the playbook.

Aunt Helen has spent the rest of her life wondering what would have happened if she had gone to those tryouts. Because of this, she has lived the rest of her life to its full **capacity**. She learned that every dream is worth chasing, even if you catch only a few of them.

Reread for Comprehension

Generate Questions

Make Inferences

Sometimes a writer does not tell you everything in a story. When you make inferences, you use clues from the story and what you already know to help you understand what is not directly stated in the story. Use the Inferences Chart as you reread "An Aunt's Baseball Dreams."

Text Clues and Prior Knowledge	Inference

Genre

Realistic Fiction is an invented story that could have happened in real life.

Generate Questions

Make Inferences
As you read, use your Inferences Chart.

Text Clues and Prior Knowledge	Inference

Read to Find Out

Why does Tía Lola's plan succeed?

How Tía Lola Came to Visit Stay

by **Julia Alvarez**
illustrated by **Lester Coloma**

Award
Winning
Author

Miguel and Juanita Guzmán have moved to Vermont
from New York City because their mother has taken a job
at a local college. Their mother's aunt, Tía Lola, arrives for a
visit from the Dominican Republic. Tía Lola soon impresses
Miguel's friends and Rudy, the owner of a local restaurant
and the coach of Miguel's baseball team. At the restaurant,
Tía Lola also charms the difficult Colonel Charlebois who
owns the farmhouse that Miguel's family rents.

The long, sweet, sunny days of summer come one after another after another. Each one is like a piece of fancy candy in a gold-and-blue wrapper.

Most nights, now that school is out, Tía Lola tells stories, sometimes until very late. The beautiful cousin who never cut her hair and carried it around in a wheelbarrow. The grandfather whose eyes turned blue when he saw his first grandchild.

Some nights, for a break, they explore the old house. In the attic, behind their own boxes, they find dusty trunks full of yellowing letters and photographs. Miguel discovers several faded photos of a group of boys all lined up in old-fashioned baseball uniforms. Except for the funny caps and knickers and knee socks, the boys in the photos could be any of the boys on Miguel's team. One photo of a boy with a baseball glove in his hand is **inscribed**, *Charlebois, '34.*

Miguel tries to imagine the **grouchy** old man at Rudy's Restaurant as the young boy with the friendly smile in the photograph.

But he can't see even a faint **resemblance**.

* * *

Since the team doesn't have a good place for daily practice, Miguel's mother suggests they use the back pasture behind the house. "But let me write Colonel Charlebois first, just in case."

Their landlord lives in a big white house in the center of town. He has already written them once this summer, complaining about "the unseemly shape of the vegetation," after Tía Lola trimmed the hedges in front of the house in the shapes of pineapples and parrots and palm trees.

"Can't you just call him and ask him, Mami?" Miguel asks. After all, the team is impatient to get started with practice. A letter will take several days to be answered.

"You try calling him," Miguel's mother says, holding out the phone. Miguel dials the number his mother reads from a card tacked on the kitchen bulletin board. The phone rings once, twice. A machine clicks on, and a cranky old voice speaks up: "This is Colonel Charles Charlebois. I can't be bothered coming to the phone every time it rings. If you have a message, you can write me."

"Let's write that letter, shall we?" Mami says, taking the phone back from Miguel.

> **Make Inferences**
> What inferences can you make about Colonel Charlebois based on his pre-recorded message?

465

Two days later, Colonel Charlebois's answer is in their mailbox. It has not been postmarked. He must have driven out and delivered it himself.

"I would be honored to have the team practice in my back pasture," he replies in a shaky hand as if he'd written the letter while riding in a car over a bumpy road.

"Honored!" Miguel's mother says, lifting her eyebrows. She translates the letter for Tía Lola, who merely nods as if she'd known all along that Colonel Charlebois is really a nice man.

And so every day Miguel's friends come over, and the team plays ball in the back field where only six months ago, Miguel wrote a great big welcome to Tía Lola. Twice a week, Rudy drops by to coach. They play all afternoon, and afterward when they are hot and sweaty, Tía Lola invites them inside for cool, refreshing smoothies, which she calls *frío-fríos*. As they slurp and lick, she practices her English by telling them wonderful stories about Dominican baseball players like Sammy Sosa and the Alou brothers and Juan Marichal and Pedro and Ramón Martínez. The way she tells the stories, it's as if she knows these players personally. Miguel and his friends are **enthralled**.

After a couple of weeks of practice, the team votes to make Miguel the captain. José, who is visiting from New York, **substitutes** for whoever is missing that day. Tía Lola is named manager.

"*¿Y qué hace el manager?*" Tía Lola wants to know what a manager does.

"A manager makes us *frío-fríos*," Captain Miguel says.

Every day, after practice, there are *frío-fríos* in a tall pitcher in the icebox.

It is a happy summer—

Until Tía Lola decides to paint the house purple.

* * *

Miguel and his friends have been playing ball in the back field—their view of the house shielded by the maple trees. As they walk back from practice, they look up.

"Holy cow!" Miguel cries out.

The front porch is the color of a bright bruise. Miguel can't help thinking of the deep, rich purple whose name he recently learned from his father in New York. "Dioxazine," he mutters to himself. The rest of the house is still the same color as almost every other house in town. "**Regulation** white," Papi calls it whenever he comes up to visit and drives through town.

In her high heels and a dress with flowers whose petals match the color of the porch stands Tía Lola, painting broad purple strokes.

For a brief second, Miguel feels a flash of that old **embarrassment** he used to feel about his crazy aunt.

"Awesome," his friend Dean is saying.

"Cool!" Sam agrees.

They wave at Tía Lola, who waves back.

"*¡Frío-fríos!*" she calls out. Today she has chosen grape flavor in honor of the new color of the house.

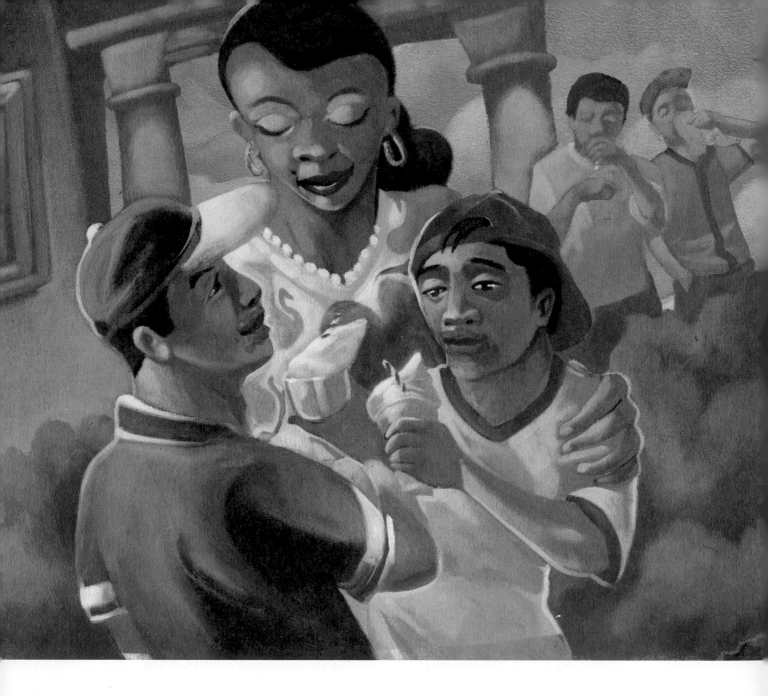

By the time Miguel's mother comes home from work, he and his friends look like they have helped Tía Lola paint the house: their mouths are purple smudges. When they open their mouths to say hello, their tongues are a pinkish purple.

"Okay, what is going on?" Mami asks, glancing from Miguel to Tía Lola. She looks as if she is about to cry, something she has not done in a long time.

Tía Lola speaks up. Don't the colors remind her of the island? *"La casita de tu niñez."* The house where Mami spent her childhood.

Miguel can see his mother's face softening. Her eyes have a faraway look. Suddenly, Mami is shaking her head and trying not to laugh. "Colonel Charlebois is going to throw a fit. Actually, he's going to throw us out."

"*El coronel, no hay problema,*" Tía Lola says, pointing to herself and Miguel and his friends. Miguel's mother looks from face to face as if she doesn't understand. Miguel and his friends nod as if they understand exactly what Tía Lola is up to.

* * *

The next afternoon, when Miguel's friends come inside from practice, Tía Lola takes their measurements. She has bought fabric with the money the team has collected and is making them their uniforms.

When it is Miguel's turn, he stands next to the mark that his mother made on the door frame back in January. He is already an inch taller!

"Tía Lola, what are you up to?" the team keeps asking. "Are we going to lose our playing field if Colonel Charlebois takes back his house?"

"*No hay problema,*" Tía Lola keeps saying. Her mouth curls up like a fish hook that has caught a big smile.

* * *

"Are you going to work magic on him?" Miguel asks his aunt that night.

"The magic of understanding," Tía Lola says, winking. She can look into a face and see straight to the heart.

She looks into Miguel's eyes and smiles her special smile.

As the house painting continues, several neighbors call. "What's happening to your house?" farmer Tom asks Miguel. "I don't believe I've ever seen a purple house. Is that a New York style or something?"

Their farming neighbors think of New York as a foreign country. Whenever Miguel and his family do something odd, Tom and Becky believe it is due to their having come from "the city."

"I've never seen a purple house in my life," Miguel admits.

"Neither have I," José adds, "and I live in the city!"

"I've seen one!" Juanita speaks up, showing off.

"Where?" Miguel challenges.

"In my imagination." She grins.

Miguel has been trying to imitate Tía Lola, looking for the best in people. He stares straight into Juanita's eyes, but all he can see is his smart-alecky little sister.

One afternoon, soon after José has returned to the city, Miguel is coming down the stairs to join his teammates in the back field. He pauses at the landing. The large window affords a view of the surrounding farms and the quaint New England town beyond.

A silver car Miguel doesn't recognize is coming down the dirt road to their house. Just before arriving at the farmhouse, it turns in to an old logging road at the back of the property. Behind a clump of ash trees, the car stops and the door opens.

Later, as he stands to bat, Miguel can make out a glint of silver among the trees. Who could it be? he wonders. He thinks of telling his mother about the stranger, but decides against it. She would probably think an escaped convict was lurking in the woods and not allow the team to practice in the back field anymore.

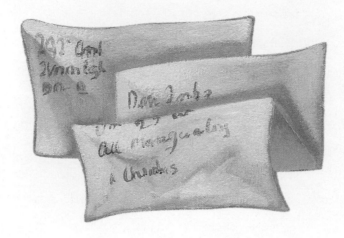

The next afternoon, Miguel watches from behind the curtain as the same silver car he saw in the woods yesterday comes slowly up the drive. His friends have already left after their baseball practice, and his mother is not home from work yet. He can hear Tía Lola's sewing machine humming away upstairs.

"Who is it?" Juanita is standing beside him, holding on to her brother's arm. All her smart-alecky confidence is gone.

"I think it's him—Colonel Charlebois," Miguel whispers. Now that the car is so close, he can make out the old man behind the wheel. The hood has a striking ornament: a little silver batter, crouched, ready to swing. "I'm going to pretend no one is home," Miguel adds.

But Colonel Charlebois doesn't come up to the door. He sits in his car, gazing up at the purple-and-white house for a few minutes, and then he drives away. Later that day, a letter appears in the mailbox. "Unless the house is back to its original white by the end of the month, you are welcome to move out."

"*Welcome* to move out?" Miguel repeats. He wrote ¡BIENVENIDA! to his Tía Lola when she moved in. It doesn't sound right to *welcome* someone to move out.

"We've got three weeks to paint the house back or move," their mother says in a teary voice at dinner. "I'm disappointed, too," she admits to Tía Lola. After all, she really loves the new color. That flaking white paint made the place look so blah and run-down. "But still, I don't want to have to move again," Mami sighs.

472

Tía Lola pats her niece's hand. There is something else they can try first.

"What's that?" her niece asks.

They can invite *el coronel* over on Saturday.

"But that's the day of our big game," Miguel reminds his aunt. They'll be playing against another local team from the next county over.

Tía Lola winks. She knows. *"Pero tengo un plan."* She has a plan. Miguel should tell his friends to come a little early so they can change.

"Change what?" Miguel's mother asks. "Change the color of the house?"

Tía Lola shakes her head. Change a hard heart. She'll need more grape juice from the store.

> **Make Inferences**
> What can you infer about Tía Lola's character? Support your answer.

The day dawns sunny and warm. The cloudless sky stretches on and on and on, endlessly blue with the glint of an airplane, like a needle sewing a tiny tear in it. Every tree seems filled to **capacity** with dark green rustling leaves. On the neighboring farms, the corn is as tall as the boys who play baseball in the fallow field nearby. Tía Lola's garden looks like one of Papi's palettes. But now, after living in the country for seven months, Miguel has his own new names for colors: zucchini green, squash yellow, chili-pepper red, raspberry crimson. The eggplants are as purple as the newly painted house. It is the full of summer. In a few weeks, up in the mountains, the maples will begin to turn.

Miguel's friends and their parents arrive early. The boys head upstairs behind Tía Lola and Rudy. Their parents stay downstairs, drinking grape smoothies and talking about how their gardens are doing. At last, the silver car rolls into the driveway.

Slowly, Colonel Charlebois climbs out. He stands, a cane in one hand, looking up at the house. One quarter of the house is purple. The other three-quarters is still white. Which color will the whole house end up being?

Miguel looks down at the old man from an upstairs window. Suddenly, he feels a sense of panic. What if Tía Lola's plan doesn't work? He doesn't want to move from the house that has finally become a home to him.

He feels his aunt's hand on his shoulder. *"No hay problema, Miguelito,"* she reassures him as if she can read his thoughts even without looking into his eyes.

Colonel Charlebois is still staring up at the house when the front door opens. Out file nine boys in purple-and-white-striped uniforms and purple baseball caps. They look as if the house itself has sprouted them! Miguel leads the way, a baseball in his hand. Behind them, Tía Lola and Rudy each hold the corner of a pennant that reads: CHARLIE'S BOYS.

Colonel Charlebois gazes at each boy. It is difficult to tell what is going through his mind. Suddenly, he drops his cane on the front lawn and calls out, "Let's play ball!" He stands, wobbly and waiting and smiling. Miguel looks into the old man's eyes and sees a boy, legs apart, body bent forward, a gloved hand held out in front of him.

He lifts his arm and throws the ball at that young boy—and the old man catches it.

Visiting With Julia Alvarez

Julia Alvarez wrote this story for her ten-year-old nephew. Julia thought back to when she was ten—the year her family moved from the Dominican Republic to the United States. What did she remember about growing up? Of course, she remembered the tías—her wonderful aunts, who had told her endless stories about their childhood. The story is set in Vermont, where Julia now lives. She said moving to the United States made her a writer, but the memory of her tías kept her first home alive.

 LOG ON ▶ Find out more about Julia Alvarez at **www.macmillanmh.com**.

CA Author's Purpose

Julia Alvarez wrote this selection to entertain. What makes her character Tía Lola so enjoyable to read about?

CA Critical Thinking

Summarize

Use your Inferences Chart to summarize *How Tía Lola Came to ~~Visit~~ Stay*. Think about how baseball is important to all the different elements of the story.

Think and Compare

Text Clues and Prior Knowledge	Inference

1. What does Tía Lola know about Colonel Charlebois that leads her to believe that he will not evict Miguel's family? **Make Inferences** to help you answer the question. **Generate Questions: Make Inferences**

2. Miguel sometimes feels brief **embarrassment** about the things Tía Lola says and does. Why, however, do you think Miguel so quickly realizes that Tía Lola has good solutions for problems? Explain your answer. **Evaluate**

3. Tía Lola is extremely helpful to Miguel and his family. Do you have a friend or relative who is helpful to you or your family? Compare that person with Tía Lola. **Synthesize**

4. Tía Lola used baseball to bring people together. How do you think sports can help bring a community together? **Analyze**

5. Read "An Aunt's Baseball Dreams" on pages 460–461. How is the author's great-aunt Helen like Tía Lola? If Tía Lola were to be offered a baseball tryout, do you think she would react the same way Helen did? Why or why not? **Reading/Writing Across Texts**

ROGER MARIS

Babe Ruth

Baseball
By the Numbers

Baseball fans love to read and discuss **statistics**. Statistics are individual facts, or **data**, expressed as numbers. You can compare these numbers to find out all kinds of interesting information: who had the most hits in a particular World Series or who pitched the most strikeouts in a lifetime career.

The most hits by a player in a single season was 262 by Ichiro Suzuki of the Seattle Mariners in 2004. He broke a record of 257 set by George Sisler way back in 1920.

Who hit the most **triples** in one season? A Pittsburgh Pirate named Owen Wilson set that record in 1912. In 1927 Babe Ruth earned the one-season home run crown by hitting 60. That record lasted until the end of the 1961 season, when Roger Maris rounded the bases after hitting his sixty-first homer. Maris's record has been broken a number of times since then, but that is the nature of records; they are challenges to be broken. Who will be the next to challenge the home run record?

Pos.	GP	St	AB	Run	Hits	2B	3B	HR	RBI	SF	SF
30	25	25	82	21	32	5	1	8	11	2	

Fact Finding
Reading an Almanac

Look at this segment of an almanac entry to discover who won the National League's Most Valuable Player (MVP) Award from the years 1997–2000. When did Sammy Sosa win? On what team did he play that year? In the year that Chipper Jones won MVP, how many home runs did he hit?

National League's Most Valuable Player Award Winners					
Year	Name	Team	Home Runs	RBIs	Avg.
1997	Larry Walker	Colorado Rockies	49	130	.366
1998	Sammy Sosa	Chicago Cubs	66	158	.308
1999	Chipper Jones	Atlanta Braves	45	110	.319
2000	Jeff Kent	San Francisco Giants	33	125	.334

Almanacs provide statistics on many different subjects.

 Critical Thinking

1. Look at the chart in the almanac entry. Find the player who hit the fewest home runs during the year he was awarded the National League's Most Valuable Player Award. **Reading a Chart**

2. What are some ways that you like to present information? Why are charts a useful way to present information? **Evaluate**

3. If Miguel in *How Tía Lola Came to Visit Stay* gave Colonel Charlebois a baseball almanac, how do you think the Colonel would respond? **Reading/Writing Across Texts**

 Math Activity

Research a major league baseball pitcher. Make a baseball card that includes statistics showing wins versus losses over his career.

 Find out more about baseball at **www.macmillanmh.com**.

Writing

✔ Dialogue: Credible and Cited

Writers use **dialogue** and **evidence** that is **credible** and can be **cited** to link their arguments and support their opinions.

Reading and Writing Connection

Read the passage below. Notice how the author gives details about the players' records that are taken from an article about baseball statistics.

An excerpt from
Baseball by the Numbers

The author provides facts about the players' records but doesn't mention where he found those records. By adding just one sentence stating the name of the reliable source where he got his information, the author could have made this passage even more convincing.

Who hit the most triples in one season? A Pittsburgh Pirate named Owen Wilson set that record in 1912. In 1927 Babe Ruth earned the one-season home run crown by hitting 60. That record lasted until the end of the 1961 season, when Roger Maris rounded the bases after hitting his sixty-first homer. Maris's record has been broken a number of times since then, but that is the nature of records; they are challenges to be broken. Who will be the next to challenge the home run record?

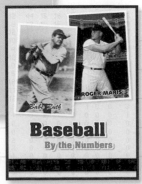

Baseball
By the Numbers

Read and Find

Read Stacia's writing below. How did she cite her reliable source? Use the Writer's Checklist below to help you.

Soldiers of the Emperor

by Stacia M.

Author Jane O'Connor tells how three farmers in China were trying to dig a well and happened to dig up a terra-cotta soldier's head. Archaeologists discovered more terra-cotta soldier figurines that had been buried. "The buried army is now considered one of the true wonders of the ancient world." *The Emperor's Silent Army* in *Treasures*, p. 137

Read how Stacia cites a reliable source for the evidence she uses.

Writer's Checklist

☑ Did the writer use a quotation or information from a known source to help support her idea?

☑ Does the writer refer to the source used in the writing or at the end in a bibliography?

☑ Can you look up this source yourself?

Review

Make Generalizations
Main Idea and Details
Author's Purpose
Suffixes
Diagrams and Labels

Chelsea's CHALLENGE

"Good evening, I'm Laurie Miller, and this is WYOU Channel 16 Local News." The woman on the television screen smiled. "This evening we take you to a breaking news story downtown. Larry, tell us what's happening."

Chelsea loved watching the news. There was Laurie Miller every night, with her perfect hair and smile. She always spoke beautifully and confidently. Chelsea wanted to be like her one day.

"G-Good ev-ev-evening." She mimicked. She shook her head. How was she ever going to be like Laurie Miller if she couldn't even get a word out?

Chelsea had been shy her whole life. It became worse when she started school, and especially when she had to speak in front of the class. Her face would turn red and her voice would come out low and soft, barely getting a word out. Every afternoon, while the class had activity time, Chelsea had to go to speech class where they would practice speaking.

"Think before you speak," her teacher instructed. "Say the words to yourself in your head. Speak slowly. There's no need to rush."

Every night she would practice after watching the evening news, imagining herself as Laurie Miller at her news desk. "Now back to L-Larry with the l-latest," she said. Better, she thought, I can do better. Laurie Miller wouldn't speak like that.

Chelsea continued her speech classes at school. Eventually she was able to talk to the other students more confidently. The class no longer snickered when she stumbled. As she walked back to her seat, the students encouraged her. "That was better, Chelsea," they said. "Keep it up."

Determined to overcome her self-consciousness, she joined the speech team in high school. This will force me to practice speaking in front of people, she thought. Still struggling with her shyness, she didn't win a single competition. In honor of her perseverance, however, she was awarded an honorable mention. Better, she thought, I can do better.

Chelsea went on to college to study journalism, still hoping to become a reporter. She joined the newspaper and wrote for the college radio program. She took acting classes and joined the theatre, determined to overcome the fear that haunted her. As she grew more confident in herself and her speech, her awkwardness slowly disappeared.

Years later, she sat behind a desk. The lights were warm on her face. She reviewed her notes. She mouthed the words slowly.

"Okay, ready? In 3-2-1."

Chelsea looked up and smiled. "Good evening. I'm Chelsea Johnson, and this is your local evening news."

Flying into Fire

A Different Kind of Courage

Most people agree that firefighters are heroes. But of all those American heroes, 450 have a very special responsibility and a special courage all their own. Smoke jumpers are a different kind of firefighter. They are the men and women to call when all other options have failed. When a fire burns out of control far from where cars and trucks can reach it, the smoke jumpers drop in.

The first "fire jumps" took place in 1940 in the state of Washington. The jumpers thought that using parachutes to get closer to fires could help keep these small blazes from spreading. It was a good idea but a deadly one. Ever since its beginnings, smoke jumping has been a very dangerous job. It takes training, discipline, and an adventurous spirit to join this special group of individuals.

The Fire Inside

First of all, people who want to be smoke jumpers must have experience fighting wilderness fires. They must also be in top physical condition. During their training they have to run for long distances while carrying heavy equipment. The intense heat adds another challenge. Even people who think they are in great shape suffer when exposed to the heat of a blazing forest fire. Then on top of that, add a heavy, padded jumpsuit and a helmet.

Rookies also brush up on other skills, such as map reading. During a jump, they might get caught dangling from a tree, so jumpers learn to cut themselves loose and climb safely to the bottom. They learn to pack supplies. Vital rations of food and water are included in this cargo, because jumpers need health and energy.

Learning to Fly

Parachute training is an important part of smoke jumper training. Special simulators give rookie jumpers a feel for what to expect during the fall. These simulators teach them how to steer their parachutes and make sure they open safely. The jumpers practice landing by jumping off towers that are built a short distance

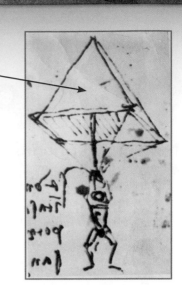

fabric

Parachute sketched by Leonardo da Vinci around 1483. It was made of fabric and wood. There was no harness and it was not tested until the year 2000.

from the ground. Many rookie jumpers limp away from their first landing, hoping that practice really does make perfect.

After several weeks of preparation, rookie jumpers are ready for the real thing and make their first jump from an airplane. They jump over and over again into different types of terrain.

Making the "Jump List"

After every test, some rookies stay and some quit. The people who pass graduate to the position of smoke jumper. They earn the right to be included on the "jump list," a team of firefighters who are qualified to parachute into fires. Then the rookies split up, and each member of the class goes his or her own way. They join different organizations and scatter all over the country.

When a fire breaks out, the call goes out and the smoke jumpers, wherever they are, spring into action. They fight fires when no one else can. The use of parachutes is what separates smoke jumpers from all other firefighters.

CA Critical Thinking

Now answer numbers 1 through 4. Base your answers on the story "Chelsea's Challenge."

1. **What is the main idea of the story?**

   A   Television helps people to be self-confident.
   B   Chelsea practiced all through school and college to overcome her shyness.
   C   Chelsea won many speech competitions.
   D   Chelsea had lots of friends in school.

2. **What was the author's purpose in writing this story?**

   A   The author wanted to inform the readers about working on television.
   B   The author wanted to entertain readers, but also to inform them about how practicing can help solve a problem.
   C   The author wanted to inform people how to give smooth speeches.
   D   The author wanted to persuade people to stop being shy.

3. **Read this sentence from the story.**

   > Determined to overcome her self-consciousness, she joined the speech team in high school.

   An example of a suffix in this sentence is:

   A   self
   B   ness
   C   come
   D   school

4. **How did Chelsea overcome her shyness? Use details from the story to support your answer.**

Now answer numbers 1 through 4. Base your answers on the article "Flying into Fire."

1. **What kind of person is a smoke jumper?**

   A   timid and cautious
   B   fearless and well-trained
   C   inexperienced and new at the job
   D   frivolous and light-hearted

2. **Why is training important for dangerous jobs?**

   A   to find out if the job is boring
   B   to increase your heartbeat
   C   because problems can occur without warning
   D   because it's exciting to work as a team

3. **What is the *best* reason for parachuting into a fire?**

   A   Smoke jumpers love to jump from planes.
   B   It's too hot for fire trucks to operate.
   C   The fire is at a low altitude.
   D   Firefighters on the ground can't get to the fire.

4. **Based on the diagram that Leonardo da Vinci drew, do you think the parachute he designed could be used by a smoke jumper?**

   A   Yes, because it would fit inside a plane.
   B   No, because parts of it are made from flammable materials.
   C   Yes, because it could be made inexpensively.
   D   No, because it is not the right shape.

Write on Demand

PROMPT Who would make a better smoke jumper: a city firefighter or a member of the Air Force trained in parachuting? Explain your choice. Use details from the article to support your answer. Write for 20 minutes. Write as much as you can as well as you can.

The Big Question

How do extreme acts of nature affect the Earth?

Theme Launcher Video

 Find out more about extreme acts of nature at **www.macmillanmh.com**.

How do extreme acts of nature affect the Earth?

Extreme acts of nature, such as volcanic eruptions, great floods, and earthquakes, can cause much destruction. They affect plants, animals, and humans. They also bring changes to Earth itself which are sometimes permanent. For example, volcanic eruptions have been known to destroy whole towns and create new islands. Some of these events have positive effects. Volcanic eruptions make the soil more fertile.

Learning about extreme acts of nature will help you better understand the natural world around you and changes that have occurred to Earth over time.

Research Activities

Throughout the unit, you will be gathering information about extreme acts of nature. Research a natural disaster that has affected the Earth and its resources. Write about its effects on nature and people.

Keep Track of Ideas

As you read, keep track of all you are learning about extreme acts of nature. Use the Accordion Book to organize your ideas. On the outside cover, write the unit theme: Our Incredible Earth. On each inside page, write information you learn each week that will help you in your research and understanding of the unit theme.

FOLDABLES®
Study Organizer

Unit Theme | Week 1 | Week 2 | Week 3 | Week 4 | Week 5

Research Toolkit

Conduct Your Unit 5 Research Online with:

Research Roadmap
Follow step-by-step guide to complete your research project.

Online Resources
• Topic Finder and other Research Tools
• Videos and Virtual Fieldtrips
• Photos and Drawings for Presentations
• Related Articles and Web Resources

California Web Site Links

Go to **www.macmillanmh.com** for more information.

California People

John Muir, Naturalist and Conservationist
John Muir is considered to be the first modern conservationist.

VOLCANOES

CA Talk About It

What do you think volcanoes can teach us about how Earth was formed?

 Find out more about volcanoes at **www.macmillanmh.com**.

Volcanoes from Outer Space!

Everyone knows that Earth has volcanoes. But did you know you can also find volcanoes in outer space? It's true! Scientists think the planet Venus may have more than 100,000 volcanoes. Astronomers have also found volcanoes on Jupiter's moons. And the planet Mars has the largest volcano in the solar system.

In some ways, the volcanoes **modern** astronomers have discovered in outer space are similar to the ones we know about on Earth. On our planet, an **active** volcano is also called a working volcano because it will **erupt** from time to time. When a volcano erupts, hot melted rock called lava and gases swell and **billow** up out of the volcano from deep below Earth's surface. The **energy** released by an eruption can equal millions of tons of dynamite.

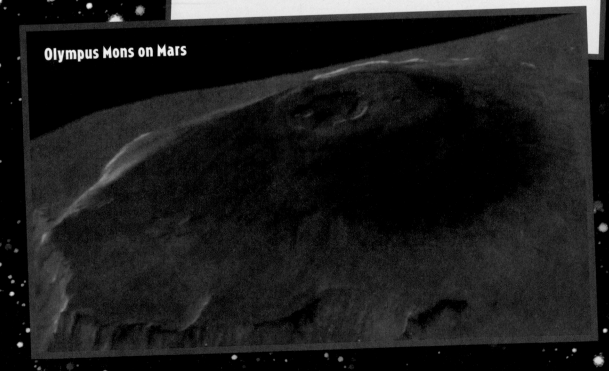

Olympus Mons on Mars

More than 80 percent of Earth's surface comes from volcanoes. Countless eruptions over billions of years created lava flows that formed the sea floor and even some mountains. In some areas, after the lava cooled, people came to **reclaim**, or move back into certain areas. The **ancient** city of Pompeii was built on a prehistoric lava field from the nearby volcano Mt. Vesuvius. It is the same on Mars, where three ancient volcanoes, millions of years old, have helped shape the surface of the planet.

Like many volcanoes on Earth, the volcanoes on Mars are shield volcanoes. This means they have a **crater**, or a large hole at the top, and gently sloping sides. The giant volcanoes on Mars, however, are truly huge. The largest, called Olympus Mons, is 16 miles high. Compare that to Mt. Everest, the tallest mountain on Earth, which is "only" a little more than five miles high. And while the largest volcano on Earth, Mauna Loa in Hawaii, is 70 miles across, Olympus Mons is more than 340 miles wide!

Why do volcanoes on Mars get so big? One reason is because Martian gravity is only about one third as strong as Earth's. Martian volcanoes can grow larger because, unlike volcanoes on Earth, they are not pulled down by gravity.

Reread for Comprehension

Analyze Text Structure

Compare and Contrast

When you compare and contrast characters or events you tell how they are alike and how they are different. This will help you to understand the text structure the author has used. To identify a compare-and-contrast text structure, look for signal words such as *like, just as, both,* and *similar* to signal that things are alike. Words such as *different, but,* and *unlike* signal that things are different.

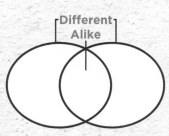

Use a Venn diagram to compare and contrast information as you reread "Volcanoes from Outer Space!"

Comprehension

Genre

Nonfiction presents facts about a subject in a direct, accurate, and up-to-date way.

Analyze and Contrast

Compare and Contrast As you read, fill in your Venn diagram.

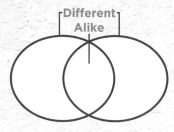

Read to Find Out

Choose two of the four types of volcanoes and examine the differences between them.

Volcanoes

by Seymour Simon

T hroughout history, people have told stories about volcanoes. The early Romans believed in Vulcan, their god of fire. They thought that Vulcan worked at a hot forge, striking sparks as he made swords and armor for the other gods. It is from the Roman god Vulcan that we get the word volcano.

The early Hawaiians told legends of the wanderings of Pele, their goddess of fire. Pele was chased from her homes by her sister Namaka, goddess of the sea. Pele moved constantly from one Hawaiian island to another. Finally, Pele settled in a mountain called Kilauea, on the Big Island of Hawaii. Even though the islanders tried to please Pele, she burst forth every few years. Kilauea is still an active volcano.

In early times, no one knew how volcanoes formed or why they spouted red-hot molten rock. In modern times, scientists began to study volcanoes. They still don't know all the answers, but they know much about how a volcano works.

Our planet is made up of many layers of rock. The top layers of solid rock are called the crust. Deep beneath the crust is the mantle, where it is so hot that some rock melts. The melted, or molten, rock is called magma.

Volcanoes are formed when magma pushes its way up through the cracks in Earth's crust. This is called a volcanic eruption. When magma pours forth on the surface, it is called lava. In this photograph of an eruption, you can see great fountains of boiling lava forming fiery rivers and lakes. As lava cools, it hardens to form rock that is also called lava.

Before

After

A volcano is a hill or mountain formed by erupted material that piles up around the vent. Mount Rainier in the state of Washington is an ice-covered volcano that last erupted in the nineteenth century.

Not far from Mount Rainier and another volcano, Mount Adams, is Mount St. Helens. Native Americans and early settlers in the Northwest had seen Mount St. Helens puff out some ash, steam, and lava in the mid-1800s. Yet for more than a century, the mountain seemed quiet and peaceful.

In March 1980, Mount St. Helens awakened from its long sleep. First there were a few small earthquakes that shook the mountain. Then, on March 27, Mount St. Helens began to spout ash and steam. Each day brought further earthquakes, until by mid-May more than ten thousand small earthquakes had been recorded. The mountain began to swell up and crack.

Sunday, May 18, dawned bright and clear. The mountain seemed much the same as it had been for the past month. Suddenly, at 8:32 A.M., Mount St. Helens erupted with incredible force. The energy released in the eruption was equal to ten million tons of dynamite.

The eruption of Mount St. Helens was the most destructive in the history of the United States. Sixty people lost their lives. Measurable ash fell over a huge area of more than 75,000 square miles. Hundreds of houses and cabins were destroyed, leaving many people homeless. Miles of highways, roads, and railways were badly damaged. The force of the eruption was so great that entire forests were blown down like rows of matchsticks.

Compare the way Mount St. Helens looked before and after the eruption. The top of the volcano and a large segment of its north face slid away. In its place is a huge volcanic crater.

Compare and Contrast
What are some differences between the way Mount St. Helens looked before the eruption of 1980 and after it?

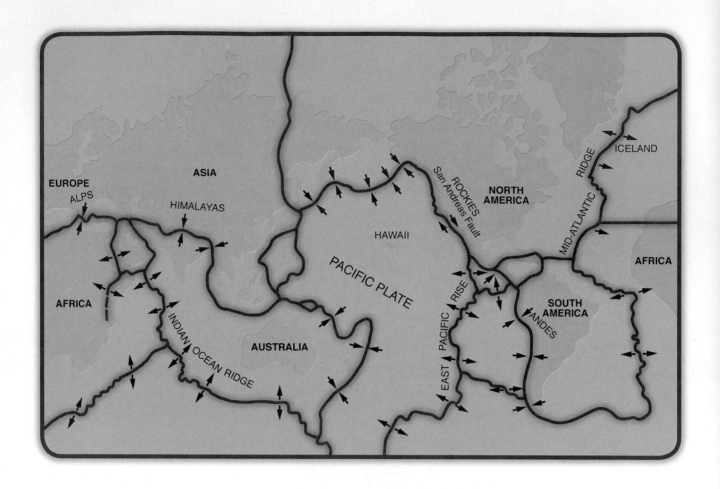

In 1982, the mountain and the area around it were dedicated as the Mount St. Helens National Volcanic Monument. Visitor centers allow people to view the actively growing lava dome that now partially fills the crater.

Volcanoes don't just happen anyplace. Earth's crust is broken into huge sections like a giant cracked eggshell. The pieces of the crust are called plates. The United States, Canada, Mexico, some of Russia, and the western half of the North Atlantic Ocean are all on the North American plate. Most of the world's volcanoes erupt in places where two plates meet.

Down the middle of the North Atlantic Ocean, two plates are slowly moving apart. Hot magma pushes up between them. A chain of underwater volcanoes runs along the line where the two plates meet. Some of the underwater volcanoes have grown so high that they rise from the ocean floor to above sea level as islands.

Iceland is a volcanic island in the North Atlantic. In 1963, an area of the sea near Iceland began to boil and churn. An undersea volcano was exploding and a new island was being formed. The island was named Surtsey, after the ancient Norse god of fire.

Ten years after the explosion that formed Surtsey, another volcano erupted off the south coast of Iceland on the island of Heimaey. Within six hours of the eruption, more than 5,000 people were taken off the island to safety. After two months, hundreds of buildings had burned down and dozens more had been buried in the advancing lava. Then the volcano stopped erupting. After a year's time, the people of Heimaey came back to reclaim their island with its new 735-foot volcano.

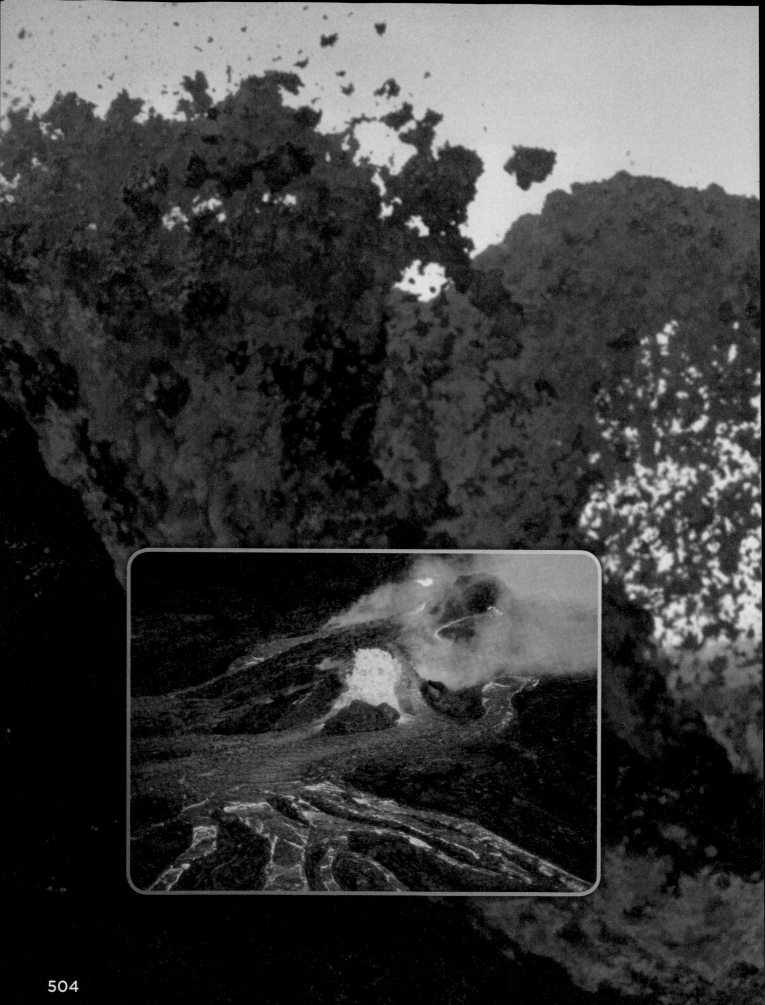

Many volcanoes and earthquakes are located along the margins of the large Pacific plate. Volcanoes and earthquakes are so numerous that these margins are called the "Ring of Fire." But a few volcanoes are not on the edge of a plate. The volcanoes in the Hawaiian Islands are in the middle of the Pacific plate.

These volcanoes have grown, one after another, as the Pacific plate slowly moves to the northwest to form the Hawaiian volcanic chain. Each volcano grew from the deep Pacific seafloor over several million years. Eruption followed eruption, and little by little, thin layers of lava hardened, one atop another. Thousands of eruptions were needed to build mountains high enough to reach from the deep sea bottom and appear as islands.

The largest Hawaiian volcano is Mauna Loa. It is seventy miles long and rises thirty thousand feet from the ocean floor. It is still growing and is one of Hawaii's most active volcanoes.

Hawaiian lava usually gushes out in red-hot fountains a few hundred feet high that feed lava rivers or lakes. Hawaiian volcanoes erupt much less violently than did Surtsey or Mount St. Helens. Only rarely does a Hawaiian volcano throw out rock and high clouds of ash.

Compare and Contrast
What are some differences between Hawaiian volcanoes and ones such as Surtsey or Mount St. Helens?

Steam clouds **billow** as a flow of hot lava enters the sea. Hawaii is constantly changing as frequent eruptions of the Mauna Loa and Kilauea volcanoes add hundreds of acres of new land to the Big Island. Old lava flows are quickly weathered by the waves into rocks and black sand.

Hawaiian lava is fluid and flows quickly. In some lava rivers, speeds as high as thirty-five miles per hour have been measured. In an eruption in 1986, a number of houses were threatened by the quick-moving lava. Firefighters sprayed water on the lava to slow down its advance.

When lava cools and hardens, it forms volcanic rocks. The kinds of rocks formed are clues to the kind of eruption. The two main kinds in Hawaii have Hawaiian names. Thick, slow-moving lava called aa (Ah-ah) hardens into a rough tangle of sharp rocks. Thin, hot, quick-moving lava called pahoehoe (pah-HO-ee-ho-ee) forms a smooth, billowy surface.

Types of Volcanoes

Shield

Cinder Cone

Composite or Strato

Dome

Earth scientists have divided volcanoes into four groups. **Shield** volcanoes, such as Mauna Loa and Kilauea, have broad, gentle slopes shaped like an ancient warrior's shield.

Cinder cone volcanoes look like piles of dry sand poured through an opening. They erupt explosively, blowing out red-hot ash and cinders. The ash and cinders build up to form the cone shape. A cinder cone on Pacaya volcano in Guatemala, Central America, has had frequent eruptions.

Most of the volcanoes in the world are **composite** or **stratovolcanoes**. Stratovolcanoes are formed by the lava, cinders, and ash from many eruptions. An eruption can be initially explosive, when ash and cinders fall to the ground. Later the eruption becomes less violent and lava slowly flows out, covering the layer of ash and cinders. Further eruptions add more layers of ash and cinders, followed by more layers of lava. Mount Shasta (left) in California and Mount Hood in Oregon are stratovolcanoes. They are still active even though they have not erupted for many years.

A fourth kind of volcano is called a **dome** volcano. Dome volcanoes have thick, slow-moving lava that forms a steep-sided dome shape. After an eruption, the volcano may be plugged with hardened lava. The plug prevents the gases from escaping, like a cork in a bottle of soda water. As the pressure builds up, the volcano eventually explodes, as Mount St. Helens did. Lassen Peak in California is a dome volcano that erupted violently in 1915. You can see the huge chunks of volcanic dome rock near the summit.

Around the world there are many very old volcanoes
that no longer erupt. Some of these volcanoes are dead and
will not erupt again. These are called extinct. Others can
be inactive for as long as 50,000 years and then reawaken.
These are called dormant. Crater Lake Volcano in Oregon is
currently considered dormant, but it is likely to erupt again.
Almost seven thousand years ago, its predecessor, Mount
Mazama, erupted and covered the ground for thousands of
miles around in a blanket of pumice and ash. Toward the
end of the eruption, the entire top of the volcano collapsed
inward. A huge crater, called a caldera, formed and was later
filled with water. Crater Lake reaches a depth of two thousand
feet, the deepest lake in North America.

After a volcano erupts, everything is buried under lava
or ash. Plants and animals are nowhere to be found. But
in a few short months, life renews itself. Plants grow in the
cracks between the rocks. Insects and other animals return.
Volcanoes do not just destroy. They bring new mountains,
new islands, and new soil to the land. Many good things
can come from the fiery explosions of volcanoes.

Volcano Watching
with Seymour Simon

Seymour Simon has written over 200 books, but he still calls himself a teacher. He started by teaching in a classroom, but now reaches more kids through his books. First, Seymour picks a topic he loved as a child. "Interests don't change," he says. "Kids still love spectacular things." After that, he researches and writes and rewrites the story until the explanations and descriptions are perfectly clear. Seymour wants his books to open up new worlds to the reader, not just answer questions. Then, when the books come out, he is back in the classroom, talking again to students and teachers.

Other books by Seymour Simon

TORNADOES
SEYMOUR SIMON

(CA) Author's Purpose
Authors of nonfiction often write to inform or explain. Why do you think Seymour Simon wrote *Volcanoes*? Use examples from the text to support your answer.

 LOG ON Find out more about Seymour Simon at **www.macmillanmh.com**.

CA Critical Thinking

Summarize

Use your Venn diagram to help you summarize *Volcanoes*. Be sure to include all the different types of volcanoes in your summary.

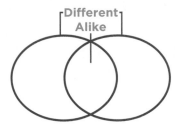

Think and Compare

1. **Compare and contrast** a volcano such as Mount St. Helens and the volcanoes found in the Hawaiian Islands. Use your Venn diagram to help you tell how these types of volcanoes are alike and how they are different. **Analyze Text Structure: Compare and Contrast**

2. The author concludes that many good things can come from volcanic eruptions. Does he present adequate evidence to support this conclusion? Explain. **Evaluate**

3. Would you want to study volcanoes someday? What aspect of volcano study, such as eruptions or the movement of Earth's plates, would you find most interesting? Why? **Apply**

4. What do you think scientists have learned about Earth from studying **active** volcanoes? Explain your answer. **Apply**

5. Reread "Volcanoes from Outer Space!" on pages 494–495. How are volcanoes on Mars similar to volcanoes on Earth? How are they different? Use evidence from each text to support your answer. **Reading/Writing Across Texts**

Mountain of FIRE:
A Native American Myth

retold by Grace Armstrong

Long ago when the world was new, there was one land and one people. All lived together by the great river in peace, worked well, and were happy.

Into this world were born two brothers who grew up quarreling. They argued over who was stronger and who had better land to work. Soon all the people had taken sides. The Great Spirit, Sahale, saw this quarreling and decided to end it.

> **This simile, comparing the voice to thunder, is an example of *figurative language*.**

In a voice like low, rumbling thunder, Sahale called the brothers together and gave each one an arrow for his bow. He said, "Wherever your arrow falls, that will be your land, and there you will be a chief." The first brother shot his arrow high in the air, and it landed to the south of the great river. He went there with his people, and they became known as the Multnomahs. The second brother shot his arrow into the air and it landed north of the river. There he went with his people, who became known as the Klickitats.

The brothers lived with their people in peace for some time. As time passed, though, envy began to cause quarrels. "The Klickitats have better land," some said. "The Multnomahs have more beautiful land," others cried. Sahale heard this bickering that seemed to grow like a storm and was unhappy with the two tribes. When violence threatened, Sahale stopped it by taking away all fire, even the sun, just as the autumn winds, cold, and snow were beginning.

Only one in all the land still had fire. She was Loo-Wit, an old, wrinkled woman with gray hair and quiet ways. She had stayed apart from all the quarrels. After the people had suffered and seemed to have mended their ways, Sahale asked Loo-Wit if she would like to share her fire with them. "For doing this," he told her, "you may have anything you wish."

"I wish to be young and beautiful," she said.

"Then that is what you will be," Sahale said.

Sahale led Loo-Wit to a great stone bridge over the river that joined the two lands. The people arrived at the bridge, led by their chiefs, to find the most beautiful woman they had ever seen. She began to give them fire. Loo-Wit kept the fire burning all day until fire was restored to all the people.

This was not to be the end of the quarreling. During this day the two chiefs had both fallen in love with Loo-Wit and wanted her for a wife. Loo-Wit could not choose between them, and once again, fighting erupted.

The two brothers refused to compromise or work on a solution. Because the brothers were unyielding in their positions, Sahale angrily changed the brothers into mountains. The chief of the Klickitats was turned into the mountain known today as Mount Adams. The chief of the Multnomahs was turned into the mountain known today as Mount Hood.

> **The use of the mountains, which are rock-hard and immovable, represents the brothers' stubbornness and is an example of *symbolism*.**

Loo-Wit, her heart broken over this, lost her desire to be young and beautiful. Sahale, in his pity, also changed her into a mountain, and placed her between the two brother mountains. She was allowed to keep inside her the fire she had shared with the people.

Because Loo-Wit was beautiful, her mountain was a beautiful cone of dazzling white. Today she is known as Mount St. Helens.

Loo-Wit wants to remind humans to care for Earth and for each other. When she is unhappy, she will awaken as she did in the 1980s.

Once her anger passes, though, the ground heals and plant and animal life have a chance to flourish once again.

CA Critical Thinking

1. What do you think of Sahale's decision to turn the quarreling brothers into mountains? What do mountains symbolize? **Symbolism**

2. What elements make this a myth? What would you choose to write a myth about? **Evaluate**

3. Compare the ways in which the narrator of "Mountain of Fire" and the author of *Volcanoes* view the eruption of Mount St. Helens. What is the value of having different versions of events? **Reading/Writing Across Texts**

 Find out more about myths at **www.macmillanmh.com**.

515

✔ **Setting and Context**

Writers use **setting** and **context** to establish their argument and to support their opinions.

Reading and Writing Connection

Read the passage below. Notice how author Seymour Simon uses the setting and the context of the aftermath of a volcano to support his argument.

An excerpt from
Volcanoes

Before showing us the remarkable life that can spring from a volcanic eruption, the author first reminds us of what we know about these eruptions. He starts with a setting and context of destruction and then shows how new life can spring from that context.

After a volcano erupts, everything is buried under lava or ash. Plants and animals are nowhere to be found. But in a few short months, life renews itself. Plants grow in the cracks between the rocks. Insects and other animals return. Volcanoes do not just destroy. They bring new mountains, new islands, and new soil to the land. Many good things can come from the fiery explosions of volcanoes.

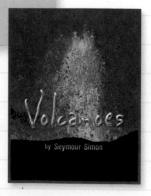

Volcanoes
by Seymour Simon

Read and Find

Read Pierre's writing below. Pierre helps us see why he could be so comfortable even though he was reading about sharks in *James and the Giant Peach.*

Cozy Comfort

by Pierre A.

I was reading a book in my soft, cozy bed, with two big fluffy pillows and comfy covers. The book was *James and The Giant Peach.* I was at the part where the peach was in the water and there were sharks being aggressive to it. I was comfortable because I had warm socks on my feet. I was so comfortable, in fact, that I started reading faster and faster.

Read about how reading in a comfortable place helps speed up the rate at which one student reads.

Writer's Checklist

 Can you see what the place looks like?

 Can you feel what Pierre feels like in this place?

 Does it make sense that being comfortable makes Pierre start reading faster?

517

POMPEII

 **Talk About It**

What do you think happened in this place?

LOG ON ▶ Find out more about Pompeii at **www.macmillanmh.com**.

519

✔ Vocabulary

ambitious   revived

drowsy   dwelling

lounge   pondering

agonized   vapors

✔ Dictionary

Many words have more than one meaning. Dictionaries define **Multiple-meaning Words**.

For example:

¹ *lounge (verb)* = to pass time lazily

² *lounge (noun)* = a room for lounging or being at ease

³ *lounge (noun)* = a couch or sofa

Voice from Vesuvius

by Isabel Kamsly

Tammi and Brian are in southern Italy with their parents. Their mother is an archaeologist, and their father heads a computer graphics company. Both are working at the excavations of Herculaneum on the Bay of Naples. It is an impressive, **ambitious** project.

The hot sun was making Tammi and Brian tired and **drowsy**. They had spent the morning watching a computer-generated exhibit of Herculaneum in A.D. 79 that their dad made. Now they decided to **lounge** on the ground at the archaeological site itself.

"Just think," said Brian, "about sixty-five feet of matter from Mt. Vesuvius fell on this city. That's much more than covered Pompeii."

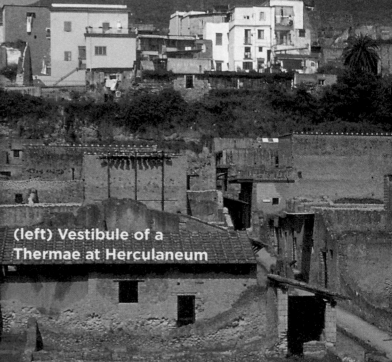

(left) Vestibule of a Thermae at Herculaneum

520

"Mom says that when it cooled, the volcanic ash covered the city like cement," added Tammi. "That's why things have been so well-preserved all these years."

"It was horrifying," said an **agonized** voice that sounded as if it were in pain.

Startled, the children turned to see who was speaking. No one was there. Suddenly, they were **revived** and wide awake. Was the voice coming from the ancient home in front of them?

"Some said the gods were punishing us," the voice said. "Is that what it was?"

Tammi peered into the **dwelling**, but the house was empty. Still she felt she should answer.

"I know people believed that," she said, "but it was really the volcano erupting. You know, Mt. Vesuvius."

"But why?" asked the voice.

"There's a scientific explanation," said Brian. "Earth is covered with large plates. They are always moving. When one plate pushes under another, it melts and becomes liquid rock called *magma*. This super-hot rock creates gas and steam. Then it can burst through Earth's surface as a volcano. Mt. Vesuvius has erupted more than seventy times since Herculaneum and Pompeii were covered in A.D. 79."

For a minute there was silence. Brian's scientific explanation required some **pondering**, or thinking about.

"There was so much ash, rock, and fumes. The **vapors** killed people as they ran for the sea," said the voice sadly.

"Er . . . you speak as if you were there," said Tammi.

"Yes, I was there . . . it was my fate." The voice trailed off, "I will always be there. . . ."

The children looked at one another. "It must be the sun," gasped Tammi. "Let's go find Mom and Dad."

Reread for **Comprehension**

Summarize

Theme
When you summarize what you read, it is helpful to identify the theme, or subject, of the story. Ask yourself how all the parts of the story relate to the theme.

A Theme Chart can help you summarize a story. Use the chart to identify the theme as you reread "Voice from Vesuvius."

Setting
What the Characters Want
Plot Problem
Outcome
Theme

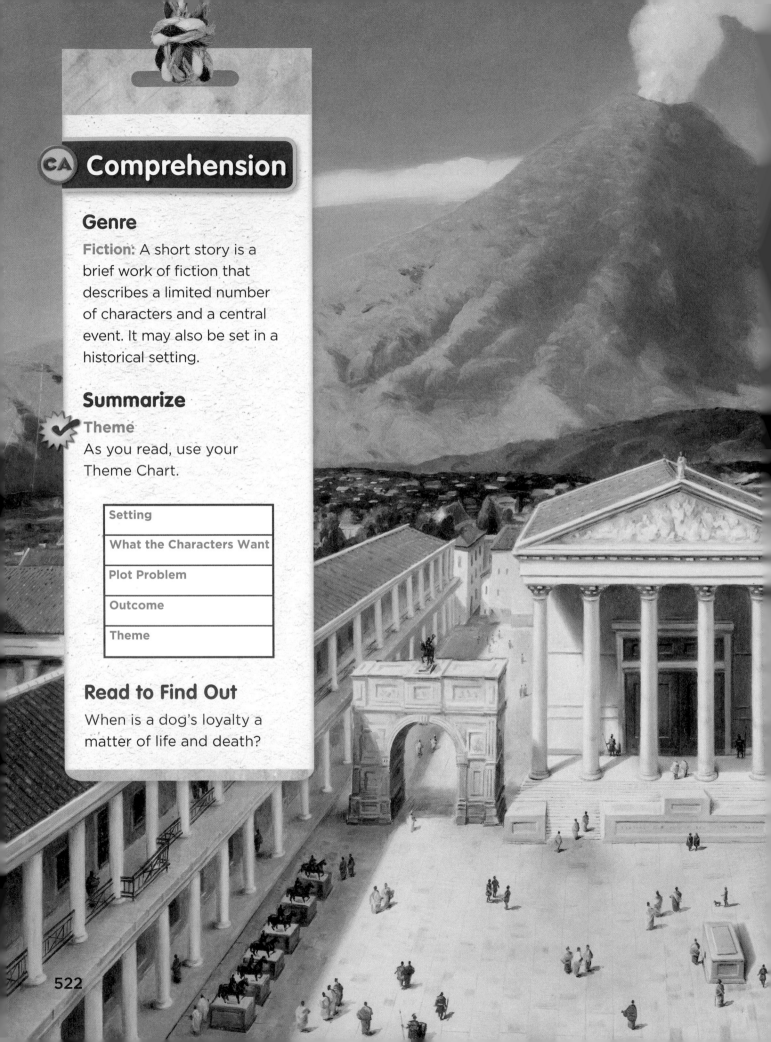

CA Comprehension

Genre

Fiction: A short story is a brief work of fiction that describes a limited number of characters and a central event. It may also be set in a historical setting.

Summarize

Theme

As you read, use your Theme Chart.

Setting
What the Characters Want
Plot Problem
Outcome
Theme

Read to Find Out

When is a dog's loyalty a matter of life and death?

522

THE DOG OF POMPEII

BY LOUIS UNTERMEYER
ILLUSTRATED BY MICHAEL JAROSZKO

Award Winning Author

523

Tito and his dog Bimbo lived (if you could call it living) under the wall where it joined the inner gate. They really didn't live there; they just slept there. They lived anywhere. Pompeii was one of the liveliest of the old Latin towns, but although Tito was never an unhappy boy, he was not exactly a merry one. The streets were always lively with shining chariots and bright red trappings; the open-air theaters rocked with laughing crowds; sham-battles and athletic sports were free for the asking in the great stadium. Once a year the Caesar visited the pleasure-city and the fire-works lasted for days; the sacrifices in the Forum were better than a show. But Tito saw none of these things. He was blind—had been blind from birth. He was known to every one in the poorer quarters. But no one could say how old he was, no one remembered his parents, no one could tell where he came from. Bimbo was another mystery. As long as people could remember seeing Tito—about twelve or thirteen years—they had seen Bimbo. Bimbo had never left his side. He was not only dog, but nurse, pillow, playmate, mother and father to Tito.

Did I say Bimbo never left his master? (Perhaps I had better say comrade, for if any one was the master, it was Bimbo.) I was wrong. Bimbo did trust Tito alone exactly three times a day. It was a fixed routine, a custom understood between boy and dog since the beginning of their friendship, and the way it worked was this: Early in the morning, shortly after dawn, while Tito was still dreaming, Bimbo would disappear. When Tito awoke, Bimbo would be sitting quietly at his side, his ears cocked, his stump of a tail tapping the ground, and a fresh-baked bread—more like a large round roll—at his feet. Tito would stretch himself; Bimbo would yawn; then they would breakfast. At noon, no matter where they happened to be, Bimbo would put his paw on Tito's knee and the two of them would return to the inner gate. Tito would curl up in the corner (almost like a dog) and go to sleep, while Bimbo, looking quite important (almost like a boy) would disappear again. In half an hour he'd be back with their lunch.

Sometimes it would be a piece of fruit or a scrap of meat, often it was nothing but a dry crust. But sometimes there would be one of those flat rich cakes, sprinkled with raisins and sugar, that Tito liked so much. At supper-time the same thing happened, although there was a little less of everything, for things were hard to snatch in the evening with the streets full of people. Besides, Bimbo didn't approve of too much food before going to sleep. A heavy supper made boys too restless and dogs too stodgy—and it was the business of a dog to sleep lightly with one ear open and muscles ready for action.

But, whether there was much or little, hot or cold, fresh or dry, food was always there. Tito never asked where it came from and Bimbo never told him. There was plenty of rain-water in the hollows of soft stones; the old egg-woman at the corner sometimes gave him a cupful of strong goat's milk; in the grape-season the fat wine-maker let him have drippings of the mild juice. So there was no danger of going hungry or thirsty. There was plenty of everything in Pompeii—if you knew where to find it—and if you had a dog like Bimbo.

Theme
What message about friendship does the author want readers to understand?

Breadseller in Public Square, from House of the Baker, Pompeiian fresco

Musicians. Street scene. Mosaic from Cicero's Villa, Pompeii

As I said before, Tito was not the merriest boy in Pompeii. He could not romp with the other youngsters and play Hare-and-Hounds and I-spy and Follow-your-Master and Ball-against-the-Building and Jack-stones and Kings-and-Robbers with them. But that did not make him sorry for himself. If he could not see the sights that delighted the lads of Pompeii he could hear and smell things they never noticed. He could really see more with his ears and nose than they could with their eyes. When he and Bimbo went out walking he knew just where they were going and exactly what was happening.

"Ah," he'd sniff and say, as they passed a handsome villa, "Glaucus Pansa is giving a grand dinner tonight. They're going to have three kinds of bread, and roast pigling, and stuffed goose, and a great stew—I think bear-stew—and a fig-pie." And Bimbo would note that this would be a good place to visit tomorrow.

Or, "H'm," Tito would murmur, half through his lips, half through his nostrils. "The wife of Marcus Lucretius is expecting her mother. She's shaking out every piece of goods in the house; she's going to use the best clothes—the ones she's been keeping in pine-needles and camphor—and there's an extra girl in the kitchen. Come, Bimbo, let's get out of the dust!"

Or, as they passed a small but elegant **dwelling** opposite the public-baths, "Too bad! The tragic poet is ill again. It must be a bad fever this time, for they're trying smoke-fumes instead of medicine. Whew! I'm glad I'm not a tragic poet!"

Or, as they neared the Forum, "Mm-m! What good things they have in the Macellum today!" (It really was a sort of butcher-grocer-market-place, but Tito didn't know any better. He called it the Macellum.) "Dates from Africa, and salt oysters from sea-caves, and cuttlefish, and new honey, and sweet onions, and—ugh!—water-buffalo steaks. Come, let's see what's what in the Forum." And Bimbo, just as curious as his comrade, hurried on. Being a dog, he trusted his ears and nose (like Tito) more than his eyes. And so the two of them entered the center of Pompeii.

The Forum was the part of the town to which everybody came at least once during each day. It was the Central Square and everything happened here. There were no private houses; all was public—the chief temples, the gold and red bazaars, the silk shops, the town hall, the booths belonging to the weavers and jewel merchants, the wealthy woolen market, the shrine of the household gods. Everything glittered here. The buildings looked as if they were new—which, in a sense, they were. The earthquake of twelve years ago had brought down all the old structures and, since the citizens of Pompeii were **ambitious** to rival Naples and even Rome, they had seized the opportunity to rebuild the whole town. And they had done it all within a dozen years. There was scarcely a building that was older than Tito.

Roman coins

Snake bracelet

527

Roman statue found in Pompeii

Tito had heard a great deal about the earthquake though, being about a year old at the time, he could scarcely remember it. This particular quake had been a light one—as earthquakes go. The weaker houses had been shaken down, parts of the out-worn wall had been wrecked; but there was little loss of life, and the brilliant new Pompeii had taken the place of the old. No one knew what caused these earthquakes. Records showed they had happened in the neighborhood since the beginning of time. Sailors said that it was to teach the lazy city-folk a lesson and make them appreciate those who risked the dangers of the sea to bring them luxuries and protect their town from invaders. The priests said that the gods took this way of showing their anger to those who refused to worship properly and who failed to bring enough sacrifices to the altars and (though they didn't say it in so many words) presents to the priests. The tradesmen said that the foreign merchants had corrupted the ground and it was no longer safe to traffic in imported goods that came from strange places and carried a curse with them. Every one had a different explanation—and every one's explanation was louder and sillier than his neighbor's.

They were talking about it this afternoon as Tito and Bimbo came out of the side-street into the public square. The Forum was the favorite promenade for rich and poor. What with the priests arguing with the politicians, servants doing the day's shopping, tradesmen crying their wares, women displaying the latest fashions from Greece and Egypt, children playing hide-and-seek among the marble columns, knots of soldiers, sailors, peasants from the provinces—to say nothing of those who merely came to **lounge** and look on—the square was crowded to its last inch. His ears even more than his nose guided Tito to the place where the talk was loudest. It was in front of the Shrine of the Household Gods that, naturally enough, the householders were arguing.

"I tell you," rumbled a voice which Tito recognized as bathmaster Rufus's, "there won't be another earthquake in my lifetime or yours. There may be a tremble or two, but earthquakes, like lightnings, never strike twice in the same place."

"Do they not?" asked a thin voice Tito had never heard. It had a high, sharp ring to it and Tito knew it as the accent of a stranger. "How about the two towns of Sicily that have been ruined three times within fifteen years by the eruptions of Mount Etna? And were they not warned? And does that column of smoke above Vesuvius mean nothing?"

"That?" Tito could hear the grunt with which one question answered another. "That's always there. We use it for our weather-guide. When the smoke stands up straight we know we'll have fair weather; when it flattens out it's sure to be foggy; when it drifts to the east—"

"Yes, yes," cut in the edged voice. "I've heard about your mountain barometer. But the column of smoke seems hundreds of feet higher than usual and it's thickening and spreading like a shadowy tree. They say in Naples—"

"Oh, Naples!" Tito knew this voice by the little squeak that went with it. It was Attilio, the cameo-cutter. "*They* talk while we suffer. Little help we got from them last time. Naples commits the crimes and Pompeii pays the price. It's become a proverb with us. Let them mind their own business."

"Yes," grumbled Rufus, "and others, too."

"Very well, my confident friends," responded the thin voice which now sounded curiously flat. "We also have a proverb—and it is this: Those who will not listen to men must be taught by the gods. I say no more. But I leave a last warning. Remember the holy ones. Look to your temples. And when the smoke-tree above Vesuvius grows to the shape of an umbrella-pine, look to your lives."

Tito could hear the air whistle as the speaker drew his toga about him and the quick shuffle of feet told him the stranger had gone.

"Now what," said the cameo-cutter, "did he mean by that?"

"I wonder," grunted Rufus, "I wonder."

Cameo

529

Theater mask mosaic

Tito wondered, too. And Bimbo, his head at a thoughtful angle, looked as if he had been doing a heavy piece of **pondering**. By nightfall the argument had been forgotten. If the smoke had increased no one saw it in the dark. Besides, it was Caesar's birthday and the town was in holiday mood. Tito and Bimbo were among the merry-makers, dodging the charioteers who shouted at them. A dozen times they almost upset baskets of sweets and jars of Vesuvian wine, said to be as fiery as the streams inside the volcano, and a dozen times they were cursed and cuffed. But Tito never missed his footing. He was thankful for his keen ears and quick instinct—most thankful of all for Bimbo.

They visited the uncovered theater and, though Tito could not see the faces of the actors, he could follow the play better than most of the audience, for their attention wandered—they were distracted by the scenery, the costumes, the by-play, even by themselves—while Tito's whole attention was centered in what he heard. Then to the city-walls, where the people of Pompeii watched a mock naval-battle in which the city was attacked by the sea and saved after thousands of flaming arrows had been exchanged and countless colored torches had been burned. Though the thrill of flaring ships and lighted skies was lost to Tito, the

Roman ships fresco from Pompeii

shouts and cheers excited him as much as any and he cried out with the loudest of them.

The next morning there were *two* of the beloved raisin and sugar cakes for his breakfast. Bimbo was unusually active and thumped his bit of a tail until Tito was afraid he would wear it out. The boy could not imagine whether Bimbo was urging him to some sort of game or was trying to tell something. After a while, he ceased to notice Bimbo. He felt **drowsy**. Last night's late hours had tired him. Besides, there was a heavy mist in the air—no, a thick fog rather than a mist—a fog that got into his throat and scraped it and made him cough. He walked as far as the marine gate to get a breath of the sea. But the blanket of haze had spread all over the bay and even the salt air seemed smoky.

He went to bed before dusk and slept. But he did not sleep well. He had too many dreams—dreams of ships lurching in the Forum, of losing his way in a screaming crowd, of armies marching across his chest, of being pulled over every rough pavement of Pompeii.

He woke early. Or, rather, he was pulled awake. Bimbo was doing the pulling. The dog had dragged Tito to his feet and was urging the boy along. Somewhere. Where, Tito did not know. His feet stumbled uncertainly; he was still half asleep. For a while he noticed nothing except the fact that it was hard to breathe. The air was hot. And heavy. So heavy that he could taste it. The air, it seemed, had turned to powder, a warm powder that stung his nostrils and burned his sightless eyes.

Then he began to hear sounds. Peculiar sounds. Like animals under the earth. Hissings and groanings and muffled cries that a dying creature might make dislodging the stones of his underground cave. There was no doubt of it now. The noises came from underneath. He not only heard them—he could feel them. The earth twitched; the twitching changed to an uneven shrugging of the soil. Then, as Bimbo half-pulled, half-coaxed him across, the ground jerked away from his feet and he was thrown against a stone-fountain.

Theater mask mosaic

531

The water—hot water—splashing in his face **revived** him. He got to his feet, Bimbo steadying him, helping him on again. The noises grew louder; they came closer. The cries were even more animal-like than before, but now they came from human throats. A few people, quicker of foot and more hurried by fear, began to rush by. A family or two—then a section—then, it seemed, an army broken out of bounds. Tito, bewildered though he was, could recognize Rufus as he bellowed past him, like a water-buffalo gone mad. Time was lost in a nightmare.

It was then the crashing began. First a sharp crackling, like a monstrous snapping of twigs; then a roar like the fall of a whole forest of trees; then an explosion that tore earth and sky. The heavens, though Tito could not see them, were shot through with continual flickerings of fire. Lightnings above were answered by thunders beneath. A house fell. Then another. By a miracle the two companions had escaped the dangerous side-streets and were in a more open space. It was the Forum. They rested here a while—how long he did not know.

Tito had no idea of the time of day. He could *feel* it was black—an unnatural blackness. Something inside—perhaps the lack of breakfast and lunch—told him it was past noon. But it didn't matter. Nothing seemed to matter. He was getting drowsy, too drowsy to walk. But walk he must. He knew it. And Bimbo knew it; the sharp tugs told him so. Nor was it a moment too soon. The sacred ground of the Forum was safe no longer. It was beginning to rock, then to pitch, then to split. As they stumbled out of the square, the earth wriggled like a caught snake and all the columns of the temple of Jupiter came down. It was the end of the world—or so it seemed.

To walk was not enough now. They must run. Tito was too frightened to know what to do or where to go. He had lost all sense of direction. He started to go back to the inner gate; but Bimbo, straining his back to the last inch, almost pulled his clothes from him. What did the creature want? Had the dog gone mad?

> **Theme**
> How do Bimbo's actions reinforce the theme of the story?

Submarine fauna, mosaic, 1st century from Pompeii

Then, suddenly, he understood. Bimbo was telling him the way out—urging him there. The sea gate of course. The sea gate—and then the sea. Far from falling buildings, heaving ground. He turned, Bimbo guiding him across open pits and dangerous pools of bubbling mud, away from buildings that had caught fire and were dropping their burning beams. Tito could no longer tell whether the noises were made by the shrieking sky or the **agonized** people. He and Bimbo ran on—the only silent beings in a howling world.

New dangers threatened. All Pompeii seemed to be thronging toward the marine gate and, squeezing among the crowds, there was the chance of being trampled to death. But the chance had to be taken. It was growing harder and harder to breathe. What air there was choked him. It was all dust now—dust and pebbles, pebbles as large as beans. They fell on his head, his hands—pumice-stones from the black heart of Vesuvius. The mountain was turning itself inside out. Tito remembered a phrase that the stranger had said in the Forum two days ago: "Those who will not listen to men must be taught by the gods." The people of Pompeii had refused to heed the warnings; they were being taught now—if it was not too late.

Suddenly it seemed too late for Tito. The red hot ashes blistered his skin, the stinging **vapors** tore his throat. He could not go on. He staggered toward a small tree at the side of the road and fell. In a moment Bimbo was beside him. He coaxed. But there was no answer. He licked Tito's hands, his feet, his face. The boy did not stir. Then Bimbo did the last thing he could—the last thing he wanted to do. He bit his comrade, bit him deep in the arm. With a cry of pain, Tito jumped to his feet, Bimbo after him. Tito was in despair, but Bimbo was determined. He drove the boy on, snapping at his heels, worrying his way through the crowd; barking, baring his teeth, heedless of kicks or falling stones. Sick with hunger, half-dead with fear and sulphur-fumes, Tito pounded on, pursued by Bimbo. How long he never knew. At last he staggered through the marine gate and felt soft sand under him. Then Tito fainted. . . .

Some one was dashing sea-water over him. Some one was carrying him toward a boat.

"Bimbo," he called. And then louder, "Bimbo!" But Bimbo had disappeared.

Voices jarred against each other. "Hurry—hurry!" "To the boats!" "Can't you see the child's frightened and starving!" "He keeps calling for some one!" "Poor boy, he's out of his mind." "Here, child—take this!"

They tucked him in among them. The oar-locks creaked; the oars splashed; the boat rode over toppling waves. Tito was safe. But he wept continually.

"Bimbo!" he wailed. "Bimbo! Bimbo!"

He could not be comforted.

Eighteen hundred years passed. Scientists were restoring the ancient city; excavators were working their way

through the stones and trash that had buried the entire town. Much had already been brought to light—statues, bronze instruments, bright mosaics, household articles; even delicate paintings had been preserved by the fall of ashes that had taken over two thousand lives. Columns were dug up and the Forum was beginning to emerge.

It was at a place where the ruins lay deepest that the Director paused.

"Come here," he called to his assistant. "I think we've discovered the remains of a building in good shape. Here are four huge millstones that were most likely turned by slaves or mules—and here is a whole wall standing with shelves inside it. Why! It must have been a bakery. And here's a curious thing. What do you think I found under this heap where the ashes were thickest? The skeleton of a dog!"

"Amazing!" gasped his assistant. "You'd think a dog would have had sense enough to run away at the time. And what is that flat thing he's holding between his teeth? It can't be a stone."

"No. It must have come from this bakery. You know it looks to me like some sort of cake hardened with the years. And, bless me, if those little black pebbles aren't raisins. A raisin-cake almost two thousand years old! I wonder what made him want it at such a moment?"

"I wonder," murmured the assistant.

MEET THE AUTHOR

LOUIS UNTERMEYER was a poet, an author, and a humorist. He was born in 1885 and lived to the age of 92. During his life, he took a trip to Italy, where he said these stories were waiting for him. When he saw the plaster cast of the dog in Pompeii, who had died almost 2,000 years before, he knew he must tell a story about it.

LOG ON ▶ Find out more about Louis Untermeyer at **www.macmillanmh.com**.

CA Author's Purpose

Louis Untermeyer wrote this story to entertain readers, but he also informs them about a spectacular historical setting. Describe the setting and its importance in the story.

CA Critical Thinking

Summarize

Use your Theme Chart to help you summarize "The Dog of Pompeii." What is the major event of the story? How does this event affect the main characters?

Setting
What the Characters Want
Plot Problem
Outcome
Theme

Think and Compare

1. The author uses much of the story to describe the wealth and beauty of Pompeii. The story ends with scientists amazed at finding an ordinary dog with a raisin cake. How do these two different story elements relate to the **theme**? **Summarize: Theme**

2. In the afterword, the author of this selection muses that Tito becomes a famous friend to and healer of animals. How is this idea an extension of the story's theme? **Synthesize**

3. Bimbo seems to be Tito's only comrade and ends up saving the boy from Vesuvius's suffocating **vapors**. What qualities do you think pets should possess? **Evaluate**

4. Tito uses Bimbo to see for him. How do animals today make life easier for the physically challenged? **Analyze**

5. Read "Voice from Vesuvius" on pages 520–521. How would the information presented in the story have helped Tito? **Reading/Writing Across Texts**

Encyclopedias

Encyclopedia articles are arranged alphabetically. Encyclopedia entries sometimes provide cross-references, often in capital letters.

Nonfiction: Encyclopedias provide information and facts about specific subjects that are listed alphabetically.

 Text Features

An **Encyclopedia** entry uses different type styles, such as bold or all capitals, to note topics and cross-references.

Content Vocabulary

excavation   **implement**

artifacts

POMPEII: archaeological finds

When the volcano Mt. Vesuvius erupted in the year A.D. 79, it destroyed the Roman cities of Pompeii and Herculaneum. For more than 1,500 years, they lay beneath heaps of cinders and ash. Then, in 1734, the first official **excavation** of Pompeii was begun under the direction of an Italian military engineer named Alcubierre.

Alcubierre was more interested in finding treasure than in finding answers to questions about what had happened to the buried city. Since the ancient site was not well guarded, artwork, historical objects, and other **artifacts** soon began to disappear. It became apparent that new methods would have to be put in place to uncover the rest of the city.

In 1860 the King of Italy, Victor Emmanuel II, chose Giuseppe Fiorelli to be the Director of Excavations at Pompeii. Fiorelli was an archaeologist who would **implement** important new methods for gathering information.

Fiorelli began by dividing the city into small quarters, or regions. He gave every block and building a number so it could be easily identified. This method is still used by archaeologists today. It helps them to keep track of the finds they have made. Fiorelli's workers were not allowed to proceed to another part of Pompeii until the area they were uncovering had been completely examined.

See also HERCULANEUM, MT. VESUVIUS

Encyclopedias come in different formats, including sets of books, CD-ROMs, and online. Online encyclopedias have links to topics mentioned in the article.

 Critical Thinking

1. What would you expect to find about the destructive power of volcanoes in the cross-reference information under "Herculaneum" and "Mt. Vesuvius"? **Reading an Encyclopedia Entry**

2. Compare and contrast the methods used by Alcubierre and Fiorelli. Which method was more successful at revealing the history of Pompeii? Explain your answer. **Evaluate**

3. How did reading the entry about Pompeii help you understand more about its history? **Reading/Writing Across Texts**

 History/Social Science Activity

Research the Roman city of Pompeii. What have archaeologists discovered about how people lived in that city? Write a brief report sharing the information that you learned.

 Find out more about Pompeii at **www.macmillanmh.com**.

539

✓ **Setting and Context**

Writers use **setting** and **context** to help them establish their argument.

Reading and Writing Connection

Read the passage below. Notice how author Louis Untermeyer uses the setting and the context to support his argument about the devotion of Tito's dog, Bimbo.

An excerpt from
The Dog of Pompeii

The author helps us see the chaos in Pompeii, showing us why it was so hard to escape. We see the loyal Bimbo in this context, leading his master to safety.

Then, suddenly, he understood. Bimbo was telling him the way out—urging him there. The sea gate of course. The sea gate—and then the sea. Far from falling buildings, heaving ground. He turned, Bimbo guiding him across open pits and dangerous pools of bubbling mud, away from buildings that had caught fire and were dropping their burning beams. Tito could no longer tell whether the noises were made by the shrieking sky or the agonized people. He and Bimbo ran on—the only silent beings in a howling world.

Read and Find

Read Anneke's writing below. How did she use setting and context to establish her argument? Use the Writer's Checklist to help you.

The Best Boat Ride

by Anneke R.

A real cool breeze is something that you experience when you're at the ocean. Set apart from the broiling world outside, the ocean is a winter of its own, but keeps the warm summer feeling inside you, too. Of all the ferry rides I have ever been on, this is probably the best. The waves are mild and low, keeping the boat steady without rocking. I am relaxed and happy,

Read about how the breeze and the waves on a ferry trip make the writer feel relaxed.

Writer's Checklist

 Can you see and feel the ocean and the breeze?

 Do the details help us understand why Anneke is so relaxed on the ferry?

 Does Anneke help us see even beyond the immediate setting?

541

Talk About It

What are some extreme forces of nature? Have you ever seen examples of them on TV or experienced them in person?

LOG ON ▶ Find out more about the destructive forces of nature at **www.macmillanmh.com**.

Earthquakes and Tsunamis

Making Waves

On December 26, 2004, a powerful undersea quake set off shock waves that were felt more than 3,000 miles away. Walls of water called a tsunami swept across the Indian Ocean, devastating several Asian countries and parts of East Africa—and killing more than 225,000 people in the **region**.

Tsunami means "harbor wave" in Japanese. It is a series of very long waves that race along the ocean at speeds that can reach 600 miles an hour. When the waves reach shore, they can grow to more than 30 feet high. They crash onto the shore with destructive force.

Tsunamis are not tidal waves, because they are not **affected** by the gravitational pull of the moon. Landslides and underwater volcanic eruptions can **trigger** tsunamis, but most are caused by earthquakes.

Birth of a Tsunami

This diagram shows how the 2004 Indian Ocean tsunami formed.

1. The tsunami started with an earthquake near Indonesia, at a place where two tectonic plates, or pieces of Earth's crust, meet.

When one plate pulls down on the other, stress builds.

2. The edge of the Burma plate snapped. This forced a massive movement of water in the Indian Ocean.

Sudden movement forces water up and down.

3. The waves spread in all directions, moving hundreds of miles per hour. They grew taller as they hit shallow waters near the shores.

As a tsunami nears shallow water, the waves slow down. But the outflow of water to the sea after the waves hit can be fast and destructive.

INDIAN PLATE

BURMA PLATE

Great Ball of Fire!

Nearly 250 million years ago, long before dinosaurs roamed, something terrible happened on Planet Earth. About 90 percent of all ocean species and 70 percent of those that lived on land were wiped out. It was the worst extinction ever. Huge coral reefs, forests of fernlike trees, and ferocious reptiles were killed.

What caused this devastation? Scientists at the University of Washington **undertook** a mission to find out. They say a giant asteroid or comet about four to seven miles across struck Earth. It was much like the one believed to have wiped out the dinosaurs 200 million years later.

The scientific team found and studied molecules—the most basic units of something—trapped in 250 million-year-old rock. The molecules are made from gases that could have come only from a comet or an asteroid.

The scientists say the ancient collision led to more than a thousand years of destruction. It caused volcanoes to erupt, heated up Earth's atmosphere, and led to a sharp drop in the level of oxygen in the oceans.

▲ An artist's vision of how an asteroid's collision with Earth might have looked. The impact touched off a catastrophe.

Top 5 Most Destructive Volcanic Eruptions

For billions of years, volcanoes have erupted all over the world. Despite this fact, every time another one blows its top, people are amazed at its fierce power. Here are the most destructive volcanoes in human history:

Volcano	Location	Year erupted
1. Krakatoa	Indonesia	1883
2. Mount Pelée	Martinique	1902
3. Nevada Del Ruiz	Colombia	1985
4. Mount Etna	Sicily, Italy	1669
5. Mount Vesuvius	Naples, Italy	A.D. 79

(Source: *The World Almanac for Kids*)

Krakatoa

LOG ON ▶ Find out more about volcanoes at **www.macmillanmh.com**.

545

The BIG ONE

How did an earthquake destroy a major American city—and could it happen again?

A San Francisco trolley operates several weeks after the 1906 earthquake.

More than a century ago, San Francisco was, as it is today, a gem of the Pacific Coast. It had a population of about 400,000 and was a bustling city full of businesses, homes, libraries, and restaurants. As citizens of San Francisco drifted to sleep on the night of April 17, 1906, all was well. But it wouldn't stay that way.

First the Shaking...

The devastation of San Francisco began at 5:12 A.M. on April 18, 1906. A horrible howling sound shattered the early morning. The earth suddenly rumbled, vibrated, heaved, pitched, and wobbled. "The whole street was undulating," recalled police sergeant Jesse Cook, who was there at the time.

The earthquake was the first major natural disaster recorded in photos and motion pictures.

The quake hit in two separate stages, each lasting a minute and five seconds. People woke up to showering plaster, breaking dishes, shifting furniture, toppling walls, and collapsing roofs. Houses lurched and fell apart, and buildings hopped off their foundations.

An added blast rattled the air, as the city gas plant blew up. Thousands of chimneys plunged through roofs. As a result of burst water mains, floods formed. Many people drowned in the waters.

The quakes suddenly ended in a strange stillness. Beyond view, the injured and trapped began to cry out. Soon those who were well enough **undertook** rescues and started to help them.

...Then the Flames

The major quakes were over, but the city's real troubles had just begun. About 90 percent of all buildings were made of wood. They were reduced to splinters. When stoves in houses overturned, the wood quickly caught on fire. Scattered blazes began to burn at once.

The broken water mains left the city without water. Because of that, the fire department couldn't help. Smaller blazes soon grew together into firestorms that ate up huge areas of the city.

The flames spread **despite** attempts to create firebreaks. Even though firefighters used dynamite to blow up whole blocks of homes and businesses, the fire leapt over the gaps and continued to burn the city.

In the first day, 250 city blocks were turned into ashes. Not until the third day did the last of the fires die down. By then 514 city blocks—or 4.1 square miles—had been destroyed, including 28,188 buildings.

Worst of all, about 2,500 people had died. More than 100,000 citizens had fled the city. Left behind were 250,000 homeless people. Rich and poor alike were **affected**. Everybody had to wait in line for food at quickly built soup kitchens and mess halls.

Keeping Hope Alive

The 1906 earthquake is still one of the greatest disasters suffered by a U.S. city.

San Franciscans, however, were not ready to give up. They worked together to make one of the greatest comebacks in history. By April 23, just five days after the quake, plans for the first new downtown building were compiled. In three years, 20,000 buildings went up, all bigger and stronger than the 28,000 that had burned.

Earthquake victims see more bad news: an approaching fire.

A Shaky Future

What lessons were learned from the collapse of San Francisco in 1906? The recent flooding from Hurricane Katrina in New Orleans is a reminder of what can happen when a city loses lives and housing. Today, even more is at risk in the Bay Area than in 1906. It now has about 7 million residents. It is also home to one of the nation's largest financial centers, busy ports, and a high concentration of scientific talent.

How can these resources be protected? Communities in and around San Francisco are constructing buildings and highways that may withstand an earthquake. They have also created routes that could be used for evacuation.

Many people believe that more needs to be done to protect the **region**. Older buildings in the Bay Area need to be updated to meet modern earthquake standards. A big quake would likely make them unusable.

Scientists say that stress deep below Earth's surface could be building again. They worry that this could **trigger** another earthquake—or a series of smaller quakes. This is news that makes earthquake preparedness even more important to everyone who lives in the City by the Bay.

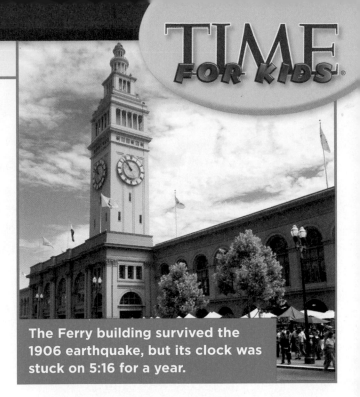

The Ferry building survived the 1906 earthquake, but its clock was stuck on 5:16 for a year.

 CA Critical Thinking

1. What are some of the ways that communities around San Francisco are protecting their resources?

2. What caused most of the damage to San Francisco after the earthquake?

3 How might you and your family try to stay safe if an earthquake hit your community?

4. Do you think being prepared for terrible natural disasters can save lives? How?

Her Job Is a BLAST

There are over 1,500 active volcanoes on Earth. Donna O'Meara, a volcano researcher, and her husband have visited about 100 of them. Time For Kids caught up with O'Meara to ask her a few questions about her job.

▲ Kilauea volcano gives off an exciting display of lava.

Question: Could you describe a typical day as a volcano researcher?

Answer: Once we arrive at an active volcano we try and get a local guide or geologist to give us some background about the volcano. Then, we pick a site to set up camp: tents, sleeping bags, cameras, video cameras, and such.

Q: What special equipment do you need out in the field?

A: We don our gas masks, hard hats, and fire retardant suits and monitor each eruption.

Q: What else do you use?

A: It's important to use all of your senses at an active volcano. Do you smell methane [a gas that might cause an explosion]? Get out of there fast. Feel the earth shake underfoot? Run.

▲ Donna and Steve O'Meara were married at Kilauea volcano in Hawaii.

Now answer questions 1 through 4. Base your answers on the article "Her Job Is a BLAST."

1. **How can you tell that this article is an interview?**

   A   The word interview appears in the introductory paragraph.

   B   The interviewer addresses Donna O'Meara by name.

   C   Donna O'Meara asks questions, which the interviewer answers.

   D   The article is set up in a question-and-answer format.

> **Tip**
> Look for information in more than one place.

2. **Why do the volcano researchers need camping equipment?**

   A   They plan to go camping after they finish their volcano research.

   B   They write reports to tell people where to camp near a volcano.

   C   They camp out to be close to the volcano they are researching.

   D   Camping out on an active volcano is a relaxing experience.

3. **What does the special equipment that O'Meara uses tell you about her job?**

   A   that the work can be very dangerous

   B   that the biggest concern is falling

   C   that it involves working in cold places

   D   that safety is not a major concern

4. **Why do you think researchers collect data from active volcanoes?**

5. **Would you want to be a volcano researcher? Why or why not? Use details from the article to support your answer.**

STOP 551

Write on Demand

CA Think of a topic you have read about that you would like to know more about. Research the topic and take notes about it. Then write a report, using your <u>research</u> notes.

Research reports give lots of facts about a subject.

To find out if a writing prompt asks for a research report, look for words such as <u>research</u>, <u>take notes</u>, and <u>report</u>.

Below, see how one student begins a response to the prompt above.

The writer uses details, found by doing research, to report on an interesting topic the class has read about.

I did research about supervolcanoes. The term supervolcano is now being used to describe something that can cause enormous destruction.

Supervolcanoes are formed when magma boils below the surface of the Earth. When it erupts, it causes the surrounding mountains to collapse and form a hole in Earth's surface called a caldera. The largest supervolcano in the United States lies under Yellowstone National Park. Some scientists think it could erupt again. Many people are paying attention and tracking it.

Writing Prompt

Respond in writing to the prompt below. Write for
25 minutes. Write as much as you can as well as you can.
Review the hints before and after you write.

Write about a topic you have recently read about.
Include as many details as you can about the subject.
Write as clearly as you can to make the information
understandable to readers.

Writing Hints for Prompts

☑ Read the prompt carefully.

☑ Organize your ideas to plan your writing.

☑ Support your ideas by giving reasons or using
   more details.

☑ Combine sentences to add variety and to
   smooth the flow of your writing.

☑ Choose words that help readers understand
   your ideas.

☑ Review your writing and edit it as needed.

Oceans

CA Talk About It

What are these people looking at?

LOG ON ▶ Find out more about oceans at **www.macmillanmh.com**.

Vocabulary

collision	century
mass	aerial
affects	methods
transported	established

Dictionary

Word Origins can be found in a dictionary. The definition may include information about the word. For example, the dictionary entry for *century* explains that it comes from the Latin word *centum* meaning "hundred."

A huge chunk of ice the size of a school bus breaks off from a glacier on a mountain peak. The gigantic, falling block of ice crashes into a valley on the side of the mountain that is filled with freshly fallen snow. What happens as a result of this **collision**? An avalanche!

This isn't an idea for a disaster movie. It really happened on April 12, 1981, on Mount Sanford in eastern Alaska. An avalanche is the very fast, sudden fall of a **mass** of snow or other material, such as rocks or mud. A snow avalanche begins when a large, unstable amount of snow breaks away from the side of a mountain and moves downhill. This can happen for a number of reasons. A sudden blast of air or even the vibration that may result from a loud noise can cause an avalanche. Many avalanches take place in early spring, when the snow on some mountains is softened by rain. This **affects** the bond between water molecules in the snow. As they weaken, an entire slope can sometimes begin to slide downward.

Ice, soil, rocks, and even shrubs and small trees may be carried and **transported** along with the snow. But snow alone can be very dangerous. For example, the snow in an avalanche can weigh hundreds of tons. It can roar down a slope at speeds of 200 miles per hour, burying people, cars, and houses.

The avalanche that took place on Mount Sanford was one of the biggest recorded during the last **century**, which covers the years 1901–2000. Airline pilots flying overhead when the avalanche occurred got an **aerial** view of the event, high above the mountain. One of them said the strong wind lifted layers of soil that had been exposed by the avalanche, and pushed them into a huge cloud.

This made it look as if a volcano had exploded. Luckily, few people live near Mount Sanford, so no one was hurt.

But avalanches do kill thousands of people every year. Scientists who study avalanches have come up with **methods**, or ways, to try to stop them. They have found that a thick grove of trees can keep some layers of snow from slipping and starting an avalanche. Rangers also sometimes blow up large slopes of snow before they can create an avalanche. Many safety patrols have been **established**, or begun, in countries and states that get a lot of snow, such as Alaska and Canada. They work hard to prevent as many avalanches as they can each year.

Reread for Comprehension

Analyze Text Structure

Description

Text structure is an organizational pattern an author uses to present information. Description is a type of text structure where the author classifies information by describing its characteristics. Authors often use signal words and phrases such as *for example* and *to begin with* to alert readers about an upcoming list of characteristics.

Fill in the Description Chart as you reread "Avalanche!"

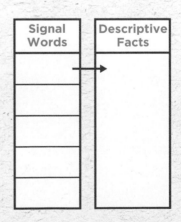

Signal Words	Descriptive Facts

Comprehension

Genre

Nonfiction presents facts about a subject in a direct, accurate, and up-to-date way.

Analyze Text Structure

Description

As you read, fill in your Description Chart.

Signal Words	Descriptive Facts
→	

Read to Find Out

What are some of the qualities of ice that make it so powerful?

Icebergs and Glaciers

by Seymour Simon

Award Winning Author

For most of us, spring means the return of warm weather. Snows melt and frozen lakes and rivers thaw. The icy scenes of winter begin to disappear.

But some places are cold all year round. This photo was taken at midnight during the middle of summer in Antarctica. At that time of year, the sun never sets during the night but remains low in the sky.

Antarctica is always covered by deep layers of ice and snow. So, too, are parts of Greenland, Canada, Alaska, and Iceland. Even when summer comes, ice and snow cover about one tenth of Earth's land surface.

The upper slopes and peaks of high mountains all over the world are also covered by ice and snow. These places of everlasting snow are said to be above the snow line. Summertime snowfields are found in the Rockies, the Himalayas, the Alps, the Andes, and even at the equator high atop Mount Kilimanjaro. It is in the constantly cold lands and above the snow line that glaciers are born.

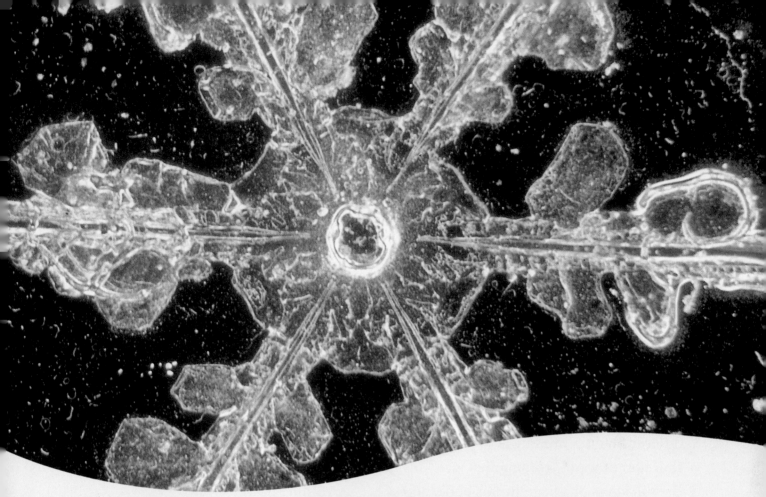

A single snowflake is a feathery crystal of ice about the size of your fingernail. Every snowflake is six-sided, yet each has a different shape.

Once the spinning flakes fall to the ground, they begin to clump together and lose their pointed beauty. Soon the snowflakes become rounded grains of ice with tiny bubbles of air trapped inside. As more snow falls, the weight of the snow and ice squeezes the grains of ice together, forcing out the trapped air. The color of the ice begins to change, too. The white of airy snow becomes the steel blue of airless ice. Finally, the blue ice crystals begin to pack together into a solid field of ice.

As more snow falls, the ice field becomes thicker and heavier, pressing downward with great force against the ground. As years go by, the ice field grows until it is about sixty feet deep. Then something strange happens.

> **Description**
> Describe what happens to single snowflakes as they become solid fields of ice.

561

The huge **mass** of ice begins to move. The ice bends and cracks and begins to slide over the ground, moving downhill. The ice moves slowly, usually less than two feet a day and sometimes only an inch or two. But however slowly, when an ice field begins to move, it has become a glacier.

Glaciers are sometimes called rivers of ice, but a glacier moves differently than a river. Water flows freely but ice is hard and can crack easily. For many years, scientists called glaciologists have studied how glaciers move. Some of their early findings were accidental. In 1827, one Swiss scientist built a hut on an alpine glacier. When he returned three years later, he found that the hut had moved more than one hundred yards downhill.

In recent years, scientists have found that glaciers move in two different ways. One way is by sliding across the ground on a very thin film of water from melted ice. This meltwater, sometimes only the thickness of a page in this book, allows the ice to slide more easily.

The second way that a glacier moves is called "creep." The tremendous weight of the glacier makes the crystals of ice slowly form layers one atop another. Then the layers begin gliding or creeping over one another.

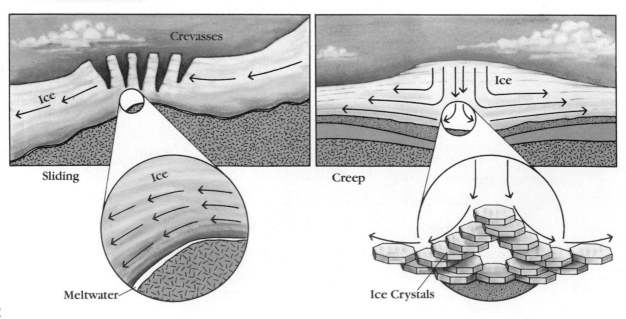

Sliding   Ice   Meltwater   Crevasses   Creep   Ice   Ice Crystals

All glaciers move in both ways. But some glaciers move more by sliding over the ground, while others move more by creeping. The photograph shows the Byrd Glacier in Antarctica. Antarctic glaciers move mostly by creeping.

Different parts of a glacier move at different speeds. Louis Agassiz, a nineteenth-**century** Swiss naturalist and scientist, once planted rows of stakes in straight lines across a glacier. The following year Agassiz found that the stakes had all moved down the valley. But the stakes in the middle of the glacier had moved the farthest. That showed that the ice in the middle of the glacier was moving faster than the ice along the sides.

In the early part of the twentieth century, Swiss and Italian scientists drilled holes straight down the thickness of a glacier. Then they placed iron rods in the holes. Over the years, the scientists found that the rods bent at the top. This showed that the ice at the top of a glacier moves more quickly than the ice at the bottom.

Nowadays, glaciologists use photography and other **methods** to learn about glaciers. The photo shows a scientist using an instrument called a transit to help find out the speed of a glacier.

The thicker the glacier the faster it moves. That's because the greater weight of the glacier causes the crystals of ice to creep more rapidly. Also a steep glacier will flow much more quickly than one on level land.

Temperature is a third factor that **affects** the speed of a glacier. The warmer the glacier the faster the ice moves because there is a greater amount of meltwater beneath the ice. In fact, scientists sometimes group glaciers together depending upon whether they are cold or warm. But even "warm" glaciers are still freezing.

Some glaciers move so slowly that you might not notice their movement for a long time. The cold Alaskan glaciers in this **aerial** photo creep downhill at only about six inches per year. But there are some steep, warm glaciers that flow more than one hundred feet a day.

As the glacier moves, the ice on top bends and sometimes cracks. The cracks in the ice are called crevasses. The crevasses can be deep and wide and very dangerous. This group of scientists exploring the Juneau Ice Field in Canada has to travel carefully.

When glaciers move, they grind and crush everything in their path. Small stones and huge rocks are pulled from the ground and carried along. Slowly, but with irresistible force, glaciers cut and carve the land. Trees, forests, hills, and even mountains are ground down over the years. The photo shows how most of the mountain has been carried away by the ice, leaving sharp peaks and ragged ridges.

As glaciers move, they often scratch lines into the layers of rock that lie beneath the soil. The scratches are made by smaller rocks carried along by the ice.

Sometimes glaciers wear down the bedrock to smooth, rounded humps. To some people, these rocks have the shapes of a flock of grazing sheep. So they are called *roches moutonnées*, French words that mean "sheep rocks."

The rocks carried along by a glacier are broken down and ground into smaller and smaller pieces. The smaller pieces are ground again and again until they are very tiny particles, almost too small for you to see. These particles, called rock flour, are carried away by a glacier's meltwater. The rock flour carried by the meltwater stream from a glacier has turned the seawater a grayish brown color.

Not all of the rocks carried by a glacier are ground into rock flour. Some of the rocks are left behind along the edges or at the end of a glacier. Sometimes these rocks build up into ridges or piles called moraines. You can see the moraines in this photo of the Worthington Glacier in Alaska.

There are many different kinds of glaciers. Mountain glaciers start in snowfields atop mountains. Then they begin to move downward following valleys until they reach the snow line and melt during the summer.

Mountain glaciers are often thousands of feet wide and many miles long. Avalanches of snow roar down their surfaces.

Sometimes mountain glaciers do not melt when they reach the bottom of the mountain. Instead, the glaciers flow over the countryside to form ice fields over the level ground.

Bigger than most mountain glaciers are ice caps—mountain glaciers that have become so thick that the mountain is almost buried. This computer-colored photo of Iceland was taken by satellite. The red spots are hot, active volcanoes. The green and the yellow areas are places where the temperatures are medium. The smaller white spots are mountain glaciers. The large white areas are ice caps.

Iceland's largest ice cap covers more than three thousand square miles. There is an active volcano buried beneath the western part of that ice cap. The heat from the volcano is always melting the ice above, forming a huge reservoir of meltwater. Every five years or so, the meltwater bursts out from under an edge of the cap. The roaring waters carry large boulders and giant blocks of ice. For miles around, the land is flooded and becomes a vast lake.

Ice sheets are the largest kind of glaciers. The Antarctic ice sheet is the biggest in the world. It is larger than the United States, Mexico, and Central America combined. In some places, the Antarctic ice sheet is more than fifteen thousand feet thick. That's about the height of ten Empire State Buildings stacked one atop another. Where an ice sheet meets the sea, it forms an ice shelf over the water.

Large masses of ice often break away from glaciers or ice shelves. The glacier is said to be calving and the floating blocks of ice are called icebergs.

The icebergs in the photo are eighty to one hundred feet high and several miles long. Each is a floating island of ice. The largest iceberg ever measured was about two hundred miles long and sixty miles wide. That's bigger than the state of Vermont or the country of Belgium.

As an iceberg floats, it melts, changes shape, and breaks apart. Until an iceberg melts and disappears completely, most of it is underwater.

Only a small part of an iceberg shows above the water. About seven eighths of the "berg" is hidden beneath the waves because glacial ice is slightly lighter than an equal amount of seawater. The large unseen part of an iceberg adds to the danger of a **collision** with a nearby ship.

On the night of April 14, 1912, the Titanic, the "safest ship in the world" according to its builders, was steaming across the North Atlantic. Yet in a few hours the ship had gone to the bottom of the ocean after striking a large iceberg. More than fifteen hundred people died in the icy waters that night. The next year, the International Ice Patrol was **established**, and it is still on the job. The patrol searches for dangerous icebergs and helps ships avoid them.

> **Description**
> Describe what makes icebergs particularly dangerous.

In the future, icebergs may prove to be useful as a source of fresh water for dry lands. One plan calls for mile-long Antarctic icebergs to be towed to distant countries by powerful tugboats and helicopters. The icebergs would be wrapped with layers of plastic insulation to protect them from melting on their journey. But there are still many problems with this idea, and it may be many years, if ever, before icebergs are **transported** in this way.

Twenty thousand years ago, ice sheets covered most of Canada, all of New England, and much of the midwestern and northwestern United States. Most of Great Britain and large parts of the former Soviet Union, Germany, and Poland, along with smaller parts of Austria, Italy, and France, were also covered by ice. Then, about ten thousand years ago, the ice began to melt. Today glaciers are found only in cold polar regions and high mountains.

During the past million years, glaciers and ice sheets have advanced and covered large parts of Earth at least four times and perhaps as many as ten times. Scientists call this time the Pleistocene ice ages. (Pleistocene comes from Greek words that mean "most recent.")

Today we can see the ways that the land was changed by the glaciers. The rivers of ice cut valleys through the land and made rolling hills. Rocks and boulders were dragged from one place and dropped in other places far away.

Perhaps the place where you live now was once covered by ice. If you look around, you may find clues to past ice ages: scratches on bedrock, a big boulder that stands alone, a round pond left behind as the ice melted.

Will the great ice ages ever return? Will ice sheets eventually bury New York, Chicago, London, Montreal, and other cities of the North? Or is our climate getting warmer, melting the huge polar ice fields and raising the level of the oceans?

Some scientists say that the last century has been the warmest in the past four thousand years, and it may become even warmer in the next century. But no one knows for sure. Many mysteries remain. Scientists are studying the ice ages and the glaciers of today. And little by little, the world of ice is yielding its secrets to science.

Meet the Author
Seymour Simon

Seymour Simon has written over 200 books about science. He has won many awards for his books, which include such topics as the human body, animals and animal behavior, climate and weather, earthquakes, volcanoes, mirrors, rocks and minerals, oceans, and stars. First, Seymour picks a topic he loved as a child. "Interests don't change," he says. "Kids still love spectacular things." After that, he researches and writes and rewrites the story until the explanations and descriptions are perfectly clear.

He visits schools to talk to adults and children and he still feels like a teacher. He wants his books to make science fun.

 LOG ON Find out more about Seymour Simon at **www.macmillanmh.com**.

Another book by Seymour Simon

WEATHER
SEYMOUR SIMON

CA Author's Purpose

Why do you think Seymour Simon chose photographs to illustrate *Icebergs and Glaciers* instead of drawings? How would the book be different if he had illustrated it with drawings?

572

 Critical Thinking

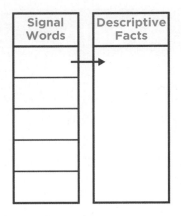

Signal Words	Descriptive Facts

Summarize

Use your Description Chart to help you summarize *Icebergs and Glaciers*. Think about all the information you learned about icebergs and glaciers and include the main points in your summary.

Think and Compare

1. Use the details on page 561 to give a **description** of the way single snowflakes can eventually become glaciers. **Analyze Text Structure: Description**

2. What are some of the factors that **affect** the way glaciers move, and how are they related? Use evidence from the text to support your answer. **Analyze**

3. If you were a scientist, would you rather study how glaciers move, or look for a method to get fresh water from icebergs? Explain your answer. **Apply**

4. Why might there be a greater danger of coming across icebergs in the North Atlantic Ocean than in seas farther south? **Apply**

5. Read "Avalanche!" on pages 556–557. Identify one way that a glacier might interact with snow to create an avalanche. **Reading/Writing Across Texts**

In her poem "Sierra," Diane Siebert traces the history of the Sierra Nevada Mountains. Here is an excerpt from the poem.

Sierra

by Diane Siebert

I am the mountain,

Tall and grand.

And like a sentinel I stand.

Surrounding me, my sisters rise

With watchful peaks that pierce the skies;

From north to south we form a chain

Dividing desert, field, and plain.

I am the mountain.

Come and know

Of how, ten million years ago

Great forces, moving plates of earth,

Brought, to an ancient land, rebirth;

Of how this planet's faulted crust

Was shifted, lifted, tilted, thrust

Toward the sky in waves of change

To form a newborn mountain range.

I am the mountain,

Young, yet old.

I've stood, and watching time unfold,

Have known the age of ice and snow

And felt the glaciers come and go.

> The mountain speaks. This is personification.

> The author repeats this phrase for rhythmic effect.

They moved with every melt and freeze;

They shattered boulders, leveled trees,

And carved, upon my granite rocks,

The terraced walls of slabs and blocks

That trace each path, each downward course,

Where through the years, with crushing force,

The glaciers sculpted deep ravines

And polished rocks to glossy sheens.

At last this era, long and cold,

Began to lose its frigid hold

When, matched against a warming sun,

Its final glacier, ton by ton,

Retreated, melting, making way

For what I have become today:

A place of strength and lofty height;

Of shadows shot with shafts of light;

Where meadows nestle in between

The arms of forests, cool and green. . . .

> The words *freeze* and *trees* rhyme.

ⒸⒶ Critical Thinking

1. Diane Siebert uses the phrase "I am the mountain" throughout the poem. What does this use of repetition contribute to the tone of the poem? **Repetition**

2. Do you think the poet's use of personification and rhyme in this poem is successful? Explain your answer. **Evaluate**

3. Compare the way the author Seymour Simon presents information in *Icebergs and Glaciers* with the way the poet Diane Siebert presents it in the poem "Sierra." How are these two different perspectives alike and different? **Reading/Writing Across Texts**.

LOG ON ▶ Find out more about poetry at **www.macmillanmh.com**.

Setting and Context

Writers **set a context** that will engage their audience and help to support their purpose.

Reading and Writing Connection

Read the passage below. Notice how author Seymour Simon uses a background story to help the reader feel a personal connection to the glaciologists.

An excerpt from
Icebergs and Glaciers

The author tells us this story about an accidental discovery regarding glaciers to help us see the scientist as a person, like one of us. He is trying to engage his audience so he can support his purpose of giving information about icebergs and glaciers.

Glaciers are sometimes called rivers of ice, but a glacier moves differently than a river. Water flows freely but ice is hard and can crack easily. For many years, scientists called glaciologists have studied how glaciers move. Some of their early findings were accidental. In 1827, one Swiss scientist built a hut on an alpine glacier. When he returned three years later, he found that the hut had moved more than one hundred yards downhill.

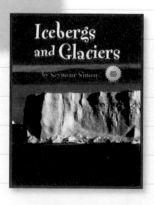

Icebergs and Glaciers
by Seymour Simon

Read and Find

Read Jason's writing below. How did he use the setting and the context to let the audience enjoy the fight? Use the Writer's Checklist below to help you.

Shakespeare

by Jason H.

We approached each other, shouting. We were at acting class doing a scene from *Romeo and Juliet*.

I stepped forward to swing my plastic sword at his head. He intercepted me. The imaginary swords engaged. I swung my sword at his neck where the imaginary armor had a gap. My opponent retreated. I won the fight.

Read how Jason sets the context to engage hs audience and support his purpose.

Writer's Checklist

 Did Jason explain where and why he was fighting his friend?

 Did he let us see the setting and the context as the fight progressed?

 Were you pretty sure this was not a real fight?

CA **Talk About It**

What can people learn about life on Earth by studying the sea?

LOG ON ▶ Find out more about underwater exploration at **www.macmillanmh.com**.

OCEAN EXPLORATION

Vocabulary

emerged	formations
clockwise	intact
hovering	severed
interior	wreckage

Word Parts

A **Suffix** is added to the end of a word to change its meaning.

edge + y = edgy: on edge; nervous

Waves

by Alicia Reese

Part of Earth's beauty comes from its oceans. Oceanographers study the chemical makeup of the ocean as well as the currents in water, weather patterns that have **emerged**, the geography of the ocean floor, and many other areas. Oceanographers' work is exciting, although sometimes it can be dangerous and cause them to become edgy. Using technology to do certain tasks helps. For example, robotic arms that rotate **clockwise** are sometimes used for the most dangerous tasks.

One basic part of oceanography is understanding waves and how they work. Sometimes ocean life can be seen in the wave. Creatures seem to be **hovering** within the **interior** of the wave, floating inside it as if they were weightless. Besides the beauty of waves, scientists are interested in their technical aspects. The diagram (right) shows how scientists examine waves.

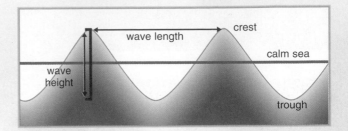

Waves are measured from the top (crest) to the bottom (trough). This allows scientists to find out the height of a wave. They also measure from crest to crest to determine the length of each wave.

Waves are classified by their height, length, and frequency. Some common kinds of waves are chop, swell, shallow, deep, and tsunami. Waves are created by specific conditions. The conditions that affect **formations** of waves include the ocean's temperature and depth, the wind's strength and speed, and the geological conditions of the area. Conditions must be favorable for certain kinds of waves to form, keep their shape, and remain **intact**.

A wave's height and length are directly related to its wind speed and duration, or how long it has been blowing. When it is really windy during a big storm, the waves grow in height and shrink in length.

During severe storms, huge and frequent waves might cut a sea vessel apart. Ships are at great risk of winding up as **severed** pieces after being hit by the force of a huge wave. By understanding the ocean, scientists can prevent this **wreckage** of ships by predicting when the water will be too dangerous for people and their ships.

The study of waves and the ocean also allows oceanographers to determine how certain beaches were formed. By studying the oceans a great deal can be learned about the surface we live on.

Reread for Comprehension

Evaluate

Fact and Opinion
A fact is something that can be proven true. An opinion is what someone thinks, feels, or believes. Nonfiction selections include facts, but may include some opinions, too. Knowing what information is fact and which is opinion can help you evaluate what you read.

Use your Fact and Opinion Chart as you reread "Waves."

Fact	Opinion

Comprehension

Genre

An **Autobiography** tells the story of a person's life written by that person.

Evaluate

Fact and Opinion
As you read, use your Fact and Opinion Chart.

Fact	Opinion

Read to Find Out

What is so fascinating about Robert D. Ballard's life?

The ocean liner R.M.S. *Titanic* was built in 1911 and deemed "virtually unsinkable." However, on its maiden voyage in 1912, the ship struck an iceberg in the North Atlantic and sank, killing 1,500 of the 2,200 passengers aboard. In 1985, Robert D. Ballard and his team discovered the remains of the *Titanic* on the ocean floor. A year later, the team returned to explore the ship in their submarine *Alvin*, with the help of *Jason Jr.*, or *JJ*, their robot.

Award Winning Selection

EXPLORING THE

TITANIC

by Robert D. Ballard

Our second view of the *Titanic* was breathtaking. As we glided soundlessly across the ocean bottom, the razor's edge of the bow loomed out of the darkness. The great ship towered above us. Suddenly it seemed to be coming right at us, about to run us over. My first reaction was that we had to get out of the way. But the *Titanic* wasn't going anywhere. As we gently brought our sub closer, we could see the bow more clearly. Both of her huge anchors were still in place. But the bow was buried more than sixty feet in mud, far too deep for anyone to pull her out of the ooze.

bow of the *Titanic*

It looked as though the metal hull was slowly melting away. What seemed like frozen rivers of rust covered the ship's side and spread out over the ocean bottom. It was almost as if the blood of the great ship lay in pools on the ocean floor.

As *Alvin* rose in slow motion up the ghostly side of the ship, I could see our lights reflecting off the still-unbroken glass of the *Titanic*'s portholes. They made me think of cats' eyes gleaming in the dark. In places the rust **formations** over the portholes looked like eyelashes with tears, as though the *Titanic* were crying. I could also see a lot of reddish-brown stalactites of rust over the wreck, like long icicles. I decided to call them "rusticles." This rust turned out to be very fragile. If touched by our sub, it disappeared like a cloud of smoke.

As we rose further and began to move across the mighty forward deck, I was amazed at the sheer size of everything: giant bollards and shiny bronze capstans that were used for winding ropes and cables; the huge links of the anchor chains. When you were there on the spot, the ship was truly titanic.

starboard railing

Fact and Opinion
Is the first sentence on this page fact or opinion? Explain.

strained to get a good look at the deck's wood planking, just four feet below us. Then my heart dropped to my stomach. "It's gone!" I muttered. Most of the *Titanic*'s wooden deck had been eaten away. Millions of little wood-eating worms had done more damage than the iceberg and the salt water. I began to wonder whether the metal deck below the destroyed wood planking would support our weight when *Alvin* landed.

We would soon find out. Slowly we moved into position to make our first landing test on the forward deck just next to the fallen mast. As we made our approach, our hearts beat quickly. We knew there was a real risk of crashing through the deck. The sub settled down, making a muffled crunching noise. If the deck gave way, we'd be trapped in collapsing **wreckage**. But it held, and we settled firmly. That meant there was a good chance that the *Titanic*'s decks would support us at other landing sites.

We carefully lifted off and turned toward the stern. The dim outline of the ship's superstructure came into view: first B Deck, then A, finally the Boat Deck—the top deck where the bridge was located. It was here that the captain and his officers had guided the ship across the Atlantic. The wooden wheelhouse was gone, probably knocked away in the sinking. But the bronze telemotor control to which the ship's wheel had once been attached stood **intact**, polished to a shine by the current. We then safely tested this second landing site.

This scale drawing shows the enormous distance between Ballard's search ship *Knorr* and the *Titanic* wreck.

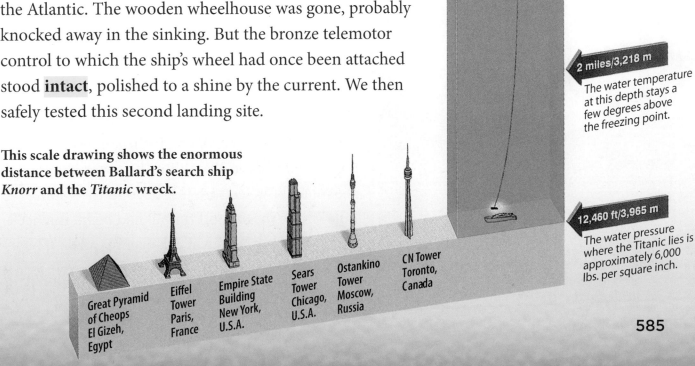

437 ft/133 m
This is the deepest a scuba diver has ever gone.

1,500 ft/465 m
Naval submarines dive no deeper than this. There is no light below this level.

3,028 ft/940 m
Pioneer underwater explorers William Beebe and Otis Barton reached this depth in a ball-shaped bathysphere in 1930.

1 mile/1,609 m
Many sea creatures here are transparent or can glow in the dark.

2 miles/3,218 m
The water temperature at this depth stays a few degrees above the freezing point.

12,460 ft/3,965 m
The water pressure where the Titanic lies is approximately 6,000 lbs. per square inch.

Great Pyramid of Cheops El Gizeh, Egypt

Eiffel Tower Paris, France

Empire State Building New York, U.S.A.

Sears Tower Chicago, U.S.A.

Ostankino Tower Moscow, Russia

CN Tower Toronto, Canada

the submarine *Alvin*

I had an eerie feeling as we glided along exploring the wreck. As I peered through my porthole, I could easily imagine people walking along the deck and looking out the windows of the ship that I was looking into. Here I was at the bottom of the ocean looking at a kind of time capsule from history.

Suddenly, as we rose up the port side of the ship, the sub shuddered and made a clanging noise. A waterfall of rust covered our portholes. "We've hit something!" I exclaimed. "What is it?"

"I don't know," our pilot replied. "I'm backing off." Unseen overhangs are the nightmare of the deep-sub pilot. Carefully, the pilot backed away from the hull and brought us slowly upward. Then, directly in front of our forward porthole, a big lifeboat davit slid by. We had hit one of the metal arms that held the lifeboats as they were lowered. This davit was one of the two that had held boat No. 8, the boat Mrs. Straus had refused to enter that night. She was the wife of the owner of Macy's department store in New York. When she had been offered a chance to save herself in one of the lifeboats, she had turned to her husband and said, "We have been living together for many years. Where you go, I go." Calmly, the two of them had sat down on a pile of deck chairs to wait for the end.

Now, as we peered out our portholes, it seemed as if the Boat Deck were crowded with passengers. I could almost hear the cry, "Women and children first!"

We knew from the previous year's pictures that the stern had broken off the ship, so we continued back to search for the **severed** end of the intact bow section. Just beyond the gaping hole where the second funnel had been, the deck began to plunge down at a dangerous angle. The graceful lines of the ship disappeared in a twisted mess of torn steel plating, upturned potholes, and

steering motor on the bridge of the *Titanic*

jumbled wreckage. We saw enough to know that the decks of the ship had collapsed in on one another like a giant accordion. With an unexpectedly strong current pushing us toward this twisted wreckage, we veered away and headed for the surface.

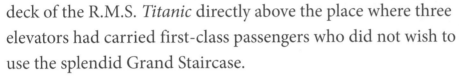

The next day we landed on the deck next to the very edge of the Grand Staircase, which had once been covered by an elegant glass dome. The dome hadn't survived the plunge, but the staircase shaft had, and to me it still represented the fabulous luxury of the ship. *Alvin* now rested quietly on the top deck of the R.M.S. *Titanic* directly above the place where three elevators had carried first-class passengers who did not wish to use the splendid Grand Staircase.

portside deck of the *Titanic*

We, however, would take the stairs with *JJ* the robot, our R2D2 of the deep. This would be the first deep-water test for our remote-controlled swimming eyeball, and we were very nervous about it. No one knew whether *JJ's* motors could stand up to the enormous ocean pressure of more than 6,000 pounds per square inch.

Using a control box with a joystick that operated like a video game, the operator cautiously steered *JJ* out of his garage attached to the front of *Alvin*. Slowly *JJ* went inching down into the yawning blackness of the Grand Staircase. More and more cable was let out as he dropped deeper and deeper.

We could see what *JJ* was seeing on our video in the sub. But at first *JJ* could see nothing. Then, as he dropped deeper, a room appeared off the portside foyer on A Deck. *JJ* swung around and our co-pilot saw something in the distance. "Look at that," he said softly. "Look at that chandelier."

the Grand Staircase in 1912

Now I could see it, too. "No, it can't be a chandelier," I said. "It couldn't possibly have survived."

I couldn't believe my eyes. The ship had fallen two and a half miles, hitting the bottom with the force of a train running into a mountain, and here was an almost perfectly preserved light fixture! *JJ* left the stairwell and started to enter the room, managing to get within a foot of the fixture. To our astonishment, we saw a feathery piece of coral sprouting from it. We could even see the sockets where the light bulbs had been fitted! "This is fantastic," I exulted.

Fact and Opinion
What facts and what opinions are stated in this second paragraph?

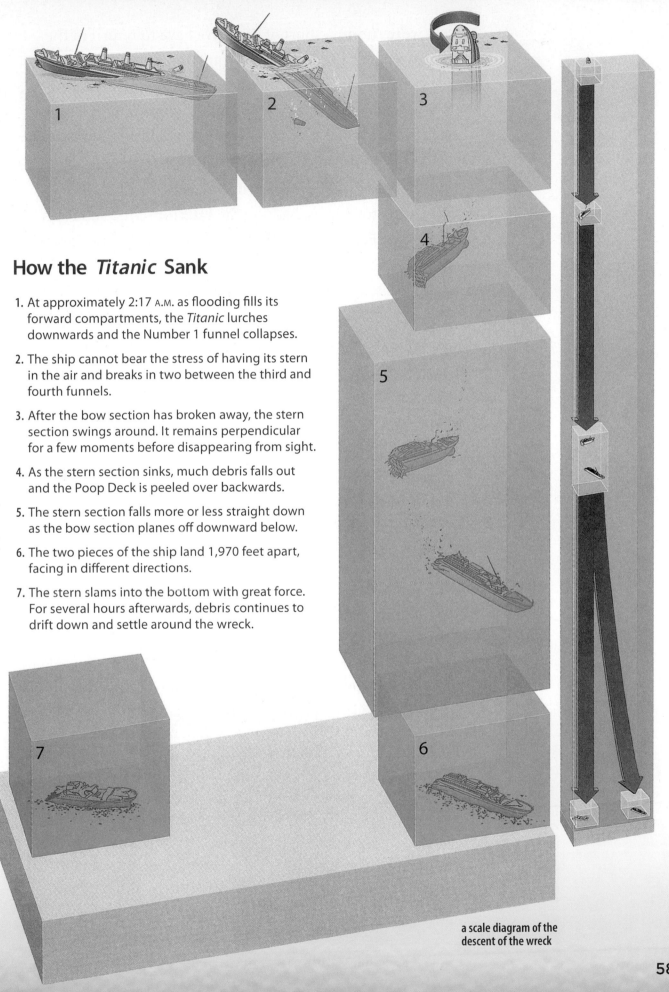

How the *Titanic* Sank

1. At approximately 2:17 A.M. as flooding fills its forward compartments, the *Titanic* lurches downwards and the Number 1 funnel collapses.

2. The ship cannot bear the stress of having its stern in the air and breaks in two between the third and fourth funnels.

3. After the bow section has broken away, the stern section swings around. It remains perpendicular for a few moments before disappearing from sight.

4. As the stern section sinks, much debris falls out and the Poop Deck is peeled over backwards.

5. The stern section falls more or less straight down as the bow section planes off downward below.

6. The two pieces of the ship land 1,970 feet apart, facing in different directions.

7. The stern slams into the bottom with great force. For several hours afterwards, debris continues to drift down and settle around the wreck.

a scale diagram of the descent of the wreck

"Bob, we're running short of time. We have to return to the surface." Our pilot's words cut like a knife through my excitement. Here we were deep inside the *Titanic*, actually going down the Grand Staircase, but we had used up all the time that we had to stay safely on the bottom. I knew our pilot was just following orders, but I still wanted to shout in protest.

Our little robot soldier **emerged** from the black hole and shone his lights toward us, bathing the **interior** of the sub in an unearthly glow. For a moment it felt as if an alien spaceship were **hovering** nearby. But that feeling quickly gave way to one of victory, thanks to our little friend. *JJ* had been a complete success.

On our next day's dive, we crossed over what had once been Captain Smith's cabin. Its outer wall now lay collapsed on the deck, as though a giant had brought his fist down on it. We passed within inches of one of the cabin's windows. Was this, I wondered, a window that Captain Smith had cranked open to let a little fresh air into his cabin before going to bed?

Suddenly a large piece of broken railing loomed out of the darkness. It seemed to be heading right for my viewport. I immediately warned the pilot who quickly turned *Alvin*'s stern around, rotating us free of the obstacle.

Now we began to drop onto the starboard Boat Deck. As we glided along, I felt as though I were visiting a ghost town where suddenly one day everyone had closed up shop and left.

An empty lifeboat davit stood nearby. Ahead I could see where the *Titanic*'s lifeboats had rested. It was on this very deck that the crowds of passengers had stood waiting to get into the boats.

the dining room in 1912; the dining room today

They had not known until the last moments that there were not enough lifeboats for everyone. It was also from this deck that you could have heard the *Titanic*'s brave band playing cheerful music to boost the crowd's spirit as the slope of the deck grew steeper and steeper.

Jason Jr. now went for a stroll along the Boat Deck. As he slowly made his way along, he looked in the windows of several first-class cabins as well as into some passageways, including one that still bore the words, "First-Class Entrance." As *JJ* passed by the gymnasium windows, I could see bits and pieces of equipment amid the rubble, including some metal grillwork that had been part of the electric camel, an old-fashioned exercise machine. We could also see various wheel shapes and a control lever. Much of the gym's ceiling was covered with rust. This was where the gym instructor, dressed in white flannel trousers, had urged passengers to try the gym machines. And, on the last night, passengers had gathered here for warmth as the lifeboats were being lowered.

JJ examines a bollard on the Forecastle Deck

I could see *JJ* far off down the deck, turning this way and that to get a better view inside doorways and various windows. It was almost as though our little robot had a mind of his own.

But now we had to bring him home. We had been on the *Titanic* for hours. Once again it was time to head back to the surface.

The morning of July 18 was lovely and warm, but I felt edgy about the day's mission. We had decided to visit the *Titanic*'s debris field. Along the 1,970 feet that separated the broken-off bow and stern pieces of the wreck, there was a large scattering of all kinds of objects from the ship. Everything from lumps of coal to wrought-iron deck benches had fallen to the bottom as she broke in two and sank. But I was anxious about what we might find down there among the rubble. I had often been asked about the possibility of finding human bodies. It was a chilling thought. We had not seen any signs of human remains so far, but I knew that if we were to find any, it would most likely be during this dive.

591

As the first fragments of wreckage began to appear on the bottom, I felt like we were entering a bombed-out museum. Thousands upon thousands of objects littered the rolling fields of ocean bottom, many of them perfectly preserved. The guts of the *Titanic* lay spilled out across the ocean floor. Cups and saucers, silver serving trays, pots and pans, wine bottles, boots, chamber pots, space heaters, bathtubs, suitcases, and more.

Then, without warning, I found myself looking into the ghostly eyes of a small, white smiling face. For a split second I thought it was a skull—and it really scared me. Then I realized I was looking at a doll's head, its hair and clothes gone.

My shock turned to sadness as I began to wonder who had owned this toy. Had the girl survived in one of the lifeboats? Or had she clutched the doll tightly as she sank in the icy waters?

We moved on through this amazing scenery. There were so many things scattered about that it became difficult to keep track of them. We came across one of the ship's boilers, and there on top of it sat an upright rusty metal cup like the ones the crew had used. It looked as though it had been placed there by a stoker moments before water had burst into the boiler room. It was astonishing to think that in fact this cup had just fluttered down that night to land right on top of a boiler.

Then in the light of *Alvin's* headlights, we spotted a safe ahead of us. I had heard about the story of fabulous treasure, including a leather-bound book covered with jewels, being locked in the ship's safes when she sank. Here was the chance of a lifetime, and I wanted to get a good look at it.

one of the ship's safes

The safe sat there with its door face up. The handle looked as though it was made of gold, although I knew it had to be brass. Next to it, I could see a small circular gold dial, and above both a nice shiny gold crest.

Why not try to open it? I watched as *Alvin*'s sample-gathering arm locked its metal fingers onto the handle. Its metal wrist began to rotate **clockwise**. To my surprise, the handle turned easily. Then it stopped. The door just wouldn't budge. It was rusted shut. I felt as if I'd been caught with my hand in the cookie jar. Oh, well, I thought, it was probably empty, anyway. In fact, when we later looked at the video footage we had taken, we could see that the bottom of the safe had rusted out. Any treasure should have been spread around nearby, but there was none to be seen. Fortunately, my promise to myself not to bring back anything from the *Titanic* was not put to the test.

robotic arm retrieves a leaded glass window

Two days passed before I went down to the *Titanic* again. After the rest, I was raring to go at it once more. This time we were going to explore the torn-off stern section that lay 1,970 feet away from the bow. It had been very badly damaged during the plunge to the bottom. Now it lay almost unrecognizable amidst badly twisted pieces of wreckage. We planned to land *Alvin* on the bottom directly behind the stern section and then send *JJ* in under the overhanging hull. Unless the *Titanic*'s three huge propellers had fallen off when she sank, I figured they still ought to be there, along with her enormous 101-ton rudder.

We made a soft landing on the bottom and discovered that one of *JJ*'s motors wouldn't work. Our dive looked like a washout. I sat glumly staring out of my viewport at the muddy bottom. Suddenly the mud started to move! Our pilot was slowly inching *Alvin* forward on its single ski right under the dangerous overhanging stern area. He was taking the sub itself to search for the huge propellers. Was he crazy? What if a piece of wreckage came crashing down? But our pilot was a professional, so I figured he must know exactly what he was doing.

In *Alvin* we explore under the overhanging deck of the *Titanic*'s severed stern section and photograph the buried rudder.

I could see an area ahead covered with rusticles that had fallen from the rim of the stern above. Until now we had had ocean above us. Crossing this point was like taking a dangerous dare. Once on the other side, there was no sure way of escaping if disaster struck. None of us spoke. The only sound in the sub was our breathing.

Slowly a massive black surface of steel plating seemed to inch down toward us overhead. The hull seemed to be coming at us from all sides. As we looked closely, we could see that like the bow, the stern section was buried deep in the mud—forty-five feet or so. Both the middle and the starboard propellers were under the mud. Only about sixteen feet of the massive rudder could be seen rising out of the ooze.

"Let's get out of here," I said. Ever so gently, *Alvin* retraced the path left by its ski. As we crossed over from the area covered with rusticles into the clear, we sighed with relief. We were out of danger. All of us were glad that this adventure was over.

Before we left the bottom this time, however, there was one mission that I wanted to complete. I wanted to place a memorial

plaque on the twisted and tangled wreckage of the stern, in memory of all those lost on the *Titanic*. Those who had died had gathered on the stern as the ship had tilted bow first. This had been their final haven. So we rose up the wall of steel to the top of the stern. With great care, *Alvin*'s mechanical arm plucked the plaque from where it had been strapped outside the sub, and gently released it. We watched as it sank quietly to the deck of the stern.

the plaque we placed on the stern in memory of those who died on the *Titanic*

As we lifted off and began our climb to the surface, our camera kept the plaque in view as long as possible. As we rose, it grew smaller and smaller, until finally it was swallowed in the gloom.

MEET THE AUTHOR

A doll's head and a man's patent leather shoe are usually not objects of wonder. But they were truly haunting images to explorer and oceanographer **Dr. Robert D. Ballard**, because of where they were found—among the wreckage of the *Titanic*. Ballard saw those objects through the eyes of a small robot operated from a three-man submarine. Searching a 150-square-mile area of the ocean floor for the *Titanic* "makes

finding a needle in a haystack seem trivial," he says.

Ballard continues to be intrigued by technology and by what lies in the depths of the ocean.

Another book by Dr. Robert D. Ballard: *Explorations*

  Find out more about Dr. Robert D. Ballard at **www.macmillanmh.com**.

CA Author's Purpose
This nonfiction piece informs readers. Identify some of the text features that convey information.

Critical Thinking

Summarize

Use your Fact and Opinion Chart to help you summarize *Exploring the* Titanic. Think about how the author's curiosity grew as he explored the *Titanic*.

Fact	Opinion

Think and Compare

1. Reread the first paragraph on page 584. What are the **facts** and what are the **opinions**? How do the facts help support the opinions? **Evaluate: Fact and Opinion**

2. According to the author, what are the advantages of using the *JJ* in the **interior** of the *Titanic*'s remains? **Evaluate**

3. If you wanted to be an oceanographer, what would you study in school? What special equipment would you have to learn to use? **Synthesize**

4. Do you think it was important to explore the remains of the *Titanic*? Why or why not? What can we learn from exploring ruins from the past? **Apply**

5. Read "Waves" on pages 580–581. Why would the information in "Waves" be important to the author of *Exploring the* Titanic? **Reading/Writing Across Texts**

Old Stormalong Finds a Man-Sized Ship

by Paul Robert Walker

Old Stormalong was the greatest sailor who ever sailed the seas. He stood four fathoms high, drank his soup from a Cape Cod dory, and ate a shark for dinner with ostrich eggs on the side. When he was finished, he stretched out on the deck and picked his teeth with an eighteen-foot oar.

Now, a fathom is the height of a good-sized man and a dory is a fair-sized rowboat. So Old Stormalong, well, he was a mighty big sailor. He had a hard time fitting on an ordinary ship, so he went from ship to ship, just trying to get comfortable. Finally he ended up as boatswain on the *Lady of the Sea*, the biggest ship in the Atlantic—at least that's what Stormy thought.

After a long voyage through the Caribbean, the *Lady* was heading for her home port of Boston. As she neared the Jersey coast, just off Barnegat Light, the weather turned bad, and the *Lady*—big as she was—tossed like a toy on the huge waves.

As Stormy peered through the growing tempest, he caught sight of something totally unexpected. A great new city was floating calm as could be on the stormy sea.

"It's unnatural!" he exclaimed. "How could the landlubbers build a city on the sea?" But as the *Lady* drew closer, he realized it wasn't a city at all. It was a ship! The biggest ship he'd ever seen—it made the *Lady of the Sea* look like a rowboat! Even from a distance he could read the name painted on the huge bow in letters twenty feet high: *Courser*.

Stormy leaned over the rail and gazed in admiration. "Now, that's a ship," he said with a sigh. "Aye, a man could stretch his legs on a ship like that."

Without bothering to take his gear from below, Stormy jumped over the side and swam toward the *Courser*. The seas were rough, but his powerful strokes brought him alongside the huge ship in a few minutes. He called for a rope and pulled himself aboard.

"And who might you be?" asked the captain.

"Alfred Bulltop Stormalong," Stormy replied. "At your service, sir."

"Well, sign the log," said the captain. "We can use a big man like you."

Stormy took a look around. The first thing he noticed was the horses—a whole stableful right on the deck!

"She's a horseboat, is she?" asked Stormy.

The captain laughed and patted Stormy on the back of the knee. "Horseboat, my eye!" he said. "Those are for the men on watch. The deck's so big, they have to ride around it."

This is a dialogue between Old Stormalong (Stormy) and the captain. Notice the quotation marks that surround each statement.

Stormy smiled and took a deep breath of the tangy salt air. "Aye," he said. "She's the ship for me."

And so she was. The *Courser* carried over six hundred men to keep her running trim. A man had to get out his compass to find his way from fore to aft. The sails were so big that they had to be made in the Sahara Desert—just to give the sailmakers room to spread them out. Bunkhouses and galleys were built up and down the masts, and the crow's nest was lost in the clouds. If a young man climbed the rigging, he was an old man by the time he came down.

Until Stormy came aboard, it took thirty-two men just to turn the wheel. But Old Stormalong could handle it steady by himself. Oh, he was a sight to see! A strong, handsome, four-fathom man in a peacoat as big as an ordinary sail. His black beard speckled with spray; his huge hands wrapped around the steering pegs; his dark eyes fixed on the horizon. Stormy was the only man aboard who could actually see where the ship was going.

The *Courser* could ride through an average storm as if she were floating on a millpond. In fact, during all the years that Old Stormalong handled the wheel, only two storms ever blew her off course.

The first was a September gale in the North Atlantic. The wind blew and blew—whipping the huge sails and spraying cold salt water across the decks until it was hard to tell whether a man was on the ship or in the sea. The fog was so thick that Stormy couldn't see the end of his beard. But he held the great wheel for two weeks straight—day and night—without eating or sleeping.

Finally, the winds died down and the fog lifted. When the sun rose over the cold blue water, the navigator discovered that they had been blown into the North Sea, and they were heading south—straight for disaster. You see, the *Courser* was much too big to turn around and a mite too big to pass through the English Channel.

Old Stormalong held the wheel steady while the officers rode around the deck shouting orders and watching the sides of the ship. As the *Courser* approached the narrowest point of the Channel—between Calais and the cliffs of Dover—the captain ordered the sails reefed and the men into the lifeboats.

"Hold fast!" shouted Stormy. "I think we can make it, sir."

"Are you sure?" asked the captain.

"It'll be close," said Stormy. "But if ye send all hands over and lay a coat of soap on the sides, we just might squeeze through. Better coat it extra heavy on the starboard—those Dover cliffs look mighty rough."

The captain ordered the crew to coat the sides as thick and slippery as they could. When the ship hit the bottleneck, she *just* squeezed through—it was so tight that the soap on the starboard side rubbed off against the cliffs. It's still there today, and that's why they're called the White Cliffs of Dover.

CA Critical Thinking

1. Find an example of hyperbole. How does hyperbole add humor to the story? **Hyperbole**

2. In what ways is Stormy a typical tall tale hero? Find examples in the text to support your answer. **Analyze**

3. What details would you add to *Exploring the* Titanic to make it a tall tale? **Reading/Writing Across Texts**

 Find out more about tall tales at **www.macmillanmh.com**.

Writing

CA

✓ **Setting and Context**

Writers **set a context** that will engage their audience and help to support their purpose.

Read the passage below. Notice how author Robert Ballard uses setting and context to make the audience feel sympathy for the doll's owner.

An excerpt from
Exploring the Titanic

The author mentions two of the elements of the setting, the lifeboats and the icy waters, to help us see the horror of the girl's experience.

Then, without warning, I found myself looking into the ghostly eyes of a small, white smiling face. For a split second I thought it was a skull—and it really scared me. Then I realized I was looking at a doll's head, its hair and clothes gone.

My shock turned to sadness as I began to wonder who had owned this toy. Had the girl survived in one of the lifeboats? Or had she clutched the doll tightly as she sank in the icy waters?

EXPLORING THE
TITANIC
by Robert D. Ballard

Read and Find

Read Janell's writing below. How did she use the setting and the context to help us make sense of what the kids did when they opened the freezer?

A Winter Wonderland

by Janell M.

One summer day my friend was over. It was hot and muggy in the house. We were sweating a lot, so we decided to get some ice cream. When we opened the freezer, the cold air smacked us in our faces. The freezer looked like Antarctica. So we stood there with the door open. It was like a winter wonderland.

Read how Janell used setting and context to make sense of what the kids did when they opened the freezer.

Writer's Checklist

 Could you picture how the kids felt before they opened the freezer?

 Can you feel how the cold air "smacked" them?

 Does Janell make it clear why the kids think the freezer is like a "winter wonderland"?

603

After Apple Picking

by Robert Frost

My long two-pointed ladder's sticking through a tree

Toward heaven still,

And there's a barrel that I didn't fill

Beside it, and there may be two or three

Apples I didn't pick upon some bough.   5

But I am done with apple-picking now.

Essence of winter sleep is on the night,

The scent of apples: I am drowsing off.

I cannot rub the strangeness from my sight

I got from looking through a pane of glass   10

I skimmed this morning from the drinking trough

And held against the world of hoary grass.

It melted, and I let it fall and break.

But I was well

Upon my way to sleep before it fell,   15

And I could tell

What form my dreaming was about to take.

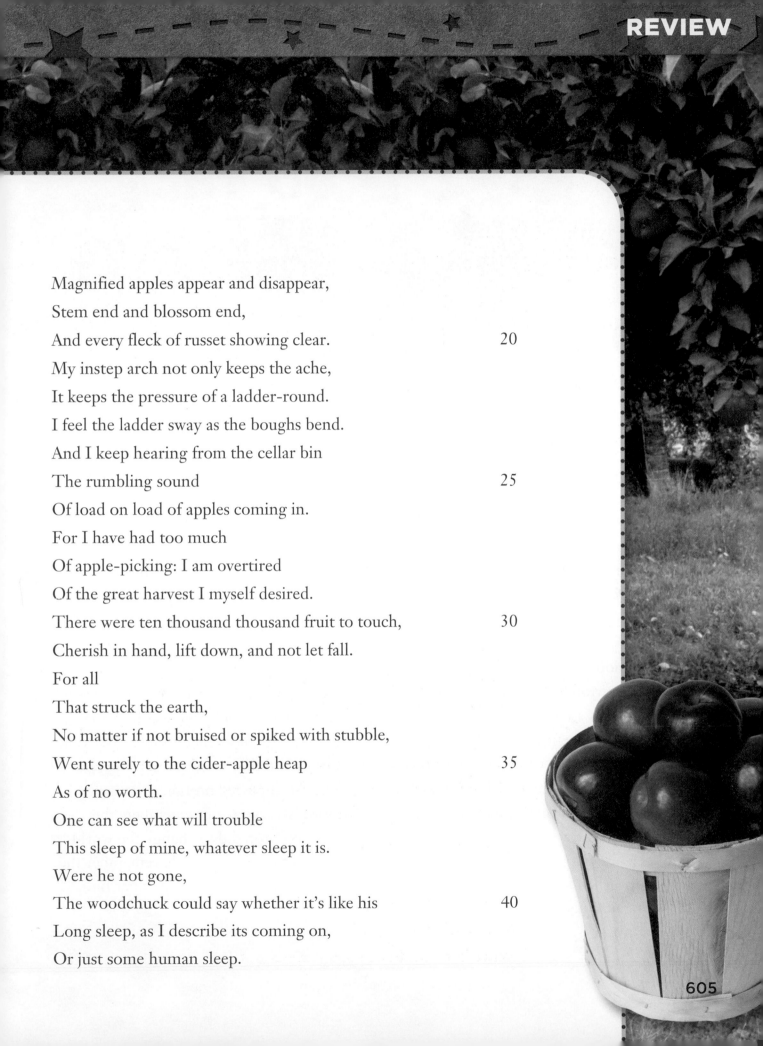

Magnified apples appear and disappear,

Stem end and blossom end,

And every fleck of russet showing clear.   20

My instep arch not only keeps the ache,

It keeps the pressure of a ladder-round.

I feel the ladder sway as the boughs bend.

And I keep hearing from the cellar bin

The rumbling sound   25

Of load on load of apples coming in.

For I have had too much

Of apple-picking: I am overtired

Of the great harvest I myself desired.

There were ten thousand thousand fruit to touch,   30

Cherish in hand, lift down, and not let fall.

For all

That struck the earth,

No matter if not bruised or spiked with stubble,

Went surely to the cider-apple heap   35

As of no worth.

One can see what will trouble

This sleep of mine, whatever sleep it is.

Were he not gone,

The woodchuck could say whether it's like his   40

Long sleep, as I describe its coming on,

Or just some human sleep.

A BUMP ON THE HEAD

Probably the most famous apple in history belonged to English physicist Sir Isaac Newton. His apple became the symbol for one of history's greatest scientific discoveries: the force of gravity.

However, some historians question whether or not the apple even existed. When examining history, people try to separate the fact from the fiction. And in Newton's case, his scientific work was the fact, and the story about the apple was all fiction.

Isaac Newton was born in 1642 in England. As a young man, he left home to study science at Cambridge University. One day while resting under an apple tree, an apple fell from a branch above and hit him right on the head. He looked at the apple and began to think. He thought about why the apple fell, applying some of his scientific knowledge from school.

Newton realized that forces inside Earth were always pulling objects toward its center. That's why the apple fell down and did not stay floating high up in the tree. When a person jumps, he or she does not go flying, soaring into space like a lost balloon. Gravity pulls everything toward the ground.

What's the problem with this famous and inspiring apple story? Most historians and scholars don't believe the bump on the head ever happened.

Then why did he tell this story? Today the general belief is that Newton invented that apple to make his work with gravity more memorable. Ask some people and they won't even remember why the apple fell on Isaac Newton's head. Not everyone remembers the work Newton did to change the world. Much of the time, people remember the apple more than they remember him.

Sir Isaac Newton at age 46 in 1689, painted by Godfrey Kneller

Would Newton live on in the minds of people without his famous story? Would we remember him at all without that apple? What if it had been a peach?

Sir Isaac Newton was the most famous scientist and thinker of his day. Most people think he was a genius. Some people believe that he contributed more to the development of science than any other single person in history. Besides his theory of gravity he invented many laws of physics, optics (the science of light), and mathematics. He was also a Member of Parliament and Master of the Royal Mint, where he prosecuted counterfeiters.

In his lifetime, Newton was famous and also controversial because he argued with other scientists about his and their inventions and philosophies. One of his famous quotes was "If I have been able to see further, it was only because I stood on the shoulders of giants."

Encyclopedia, by the way, comes from Latin words for Greek words that mean "in a circle of teaching." People say that a review of Newton in an encyclopedia of science would lead to two to three times more references than for any other scientist.

Here is a list of topics for Sir Isaac Newton in a typical general encyclopedia entry.

Sir Isaac Newton

Biography
 Early Years
 Middle Years
  Mathematics
  Optics
  Mechanics and Gravitation

Religious Views
 Views About the End of the World
 Newton and the Counterfeiters
 Enlightenment Philosophers
 Newton's Laws of Motion
 Newton's Apple
 Writings by Newton
 Fame
 Burial in Westminster Abbey
  References
  Further reading

CA Critical Thinking

Now answer numbers 1 through 4. Base your answers on the poem "After Apple Picking."

1. In the poem the poet is trying to show that

   A an apple a day keeps the doctor away.

   B picking apples is good exercise.

   C nature's seasons are like the stages in a person's life.

   D picking apples is like picking oranges.

2. You can infer that the season of the year the poet describes is

   A late fall because there was ice on the drinking trough in the morning.

   B summer because the poet is outside doing farm work.

   C spring because the poet mentions blossoms.

   D winter because there is snow on the ground.

3. When the poet says he is "done with apple picking now" he means

   A picking apples is hard work.

   B not every apple will get picked because he is tired and it is late.

   C the poet is a retired farmer and won't have to pick the apples any more.

   D there are a lot of apples in his orchard.

4. Explain why the theme of Robert Frost's poem "After Apple Picking" is a metaphor for life. Use details and phrases from the poem to support your answer.

Now answer numbers 1 through 4. Base your answers on the article "A Bump on the Head."

1. Why would a famous scientist invent a story like Newton's falling apple?

    A   to explain why apples grow on trees

    B   to help the cause of apple growers

    C   to help people understand a scientific principle

    D   to make people laugh

2. If the apple falling on Newton's head was the cause, then the effect was

    A   a very famous tree in England.

    B   a number of bad headaches that Newton suffered over his lifetime.

    C   one of Newton's most famous laws of science.

    D   a good idea for a play.

3. The Greek words that gave rise to the definition of *encyclopedia* represent

    A   another made-up story about famous scientists.

    B   a very good description of what is in an encyclopedia.

    C   a book about all kinds of bicycles.

    D   a book about things that are circular.

4. A good place to find more information about Newton's experience as Master of the Royal Mint would be in the encyclopedia section called

    A   Enlightenment Philosophers.

    B   Views About the End of the World.

    C   Fame.

    D   Newton and the Counterfeiters.

Write on Demand

PROMPT Would Sir Isaac Newton be a good subject to choose for a research paper? Why or why not? Use details from the article and from the encyclopedia listing to support your answer. Write for 25 minutes. Write as much as you can as well as you can.

The **Big** Question

How do people respond in desperate situations?

Theme Launcher Video

LOG ON ▶ Find out more about rescue efforts at www.macmillanmh.com.

The Big Question

How do people respond in desperate situations?

Earthquakes, wildfires, mudslides, heat waves, and floods! These, and many more, are all situations where humans or animals can be in severe danger and need relief.

Becoming aware of how to help others is a useful skill for you in case of future emergencies in your community. There are many organizations that conduct rescue operations to save people and animals that are in jeopardy.

Learning about different kinds of rescue efforts can teach us how to recognize and help those in desperate situations.

Research Activities

Throughout the unit, you will be gathering information about the ways in which people respond to difficult situations. Research an event in which people reacted and helped in a troubled or desperate situation. Write about the results of their efforts.

Keep Track of Ideas

As you read, keep track of all you are learning about rescue efforts. Use the Layered Book to organize your information. On the top section, write the unit theme: Rescue 9-1-1. On each layer, write information you learn each week that will help you in your research.

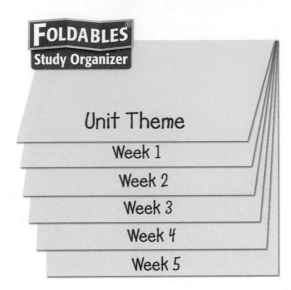

FOLDABLES®
Study Organizer

Unit Theme
Week 1
Week 2
Week 3
Week 4
Week 5

Research Toolkit

Conduct Your Unit 6 Research Online with:

Research Roadmap
Follow step-by-step guide to complete your research project.

Online Resources
- Topic Finder and other Research Tools
- Videos and Virtual Fieldtrips
- Photos and Drawings for Presentations
- Related Articles and Web Resources

California Web Site Links

Go to **www.macmillanmh.com** for more information.

California People

Henry R. Renteria, Director Governor's Office of Emergency Services

Mr. Renteria directs all OES services for the state of California.

613

CA Talk About It

How do people in families help one another during a disaster?

LOG ON ▶ Find out more about families helping each other at **www.macmillanmh.com**.

Saving a Family Member

Sam's Summer Search

by Kristi McGee

Sam **abruptly** stopped swinging. He jumped off the swing without even slowing down. He yelled, "Mommmm, where's Champ?" He realized he hadn't seen his new puppy for over an hour.

Sam looked around the yard, behind the bushes, and under the picnic table. No Champ! His mother heard the **anxiety** and fear build in his voice as he called her a second time. "Mom, I can't find Champ!" She was **conscious** of the mounting fear in her son.

She came outside quickly. "Let's look around the yard first. I'm sure he has just gone to take a nap."

"Champ! Champ! Come here, boy!" shouted Sam and his mother over and over. But still no Champ. They did get other responses, though. José, the next-door neighbor, immediately agreed to help Sam and his mom search for the lost dog. Then Sam's friend Tasha joined in the search, along with her older brother, Jamal.

The group decided to split up to look for Champ. They scoured the neighborhood from the main **intersection** of the big streets to the smallest alley. Still no Champ. Sam felt sadness and fear **engulf** him. He was sure that his best friend was gone forever. He was overwhelmed by the thought it was his fault.

After an hour, Tasha suggested they go home and make posters with pictures of Champ. It was the **procedure**, or way of doing things, animal rescue had suggested when she had lost her cat. She explained, "Somebody called the next day. He found Boots in his backyard. Posters really work!"

REWARD!
Lost Puppy
His name is Champ.
Please call Sam: 555-2610

Sam agreed. When they got home, Sam made a poster with a picture of Champ. It was a **souvenir** photograph from doggie kindergarten that Sam received to remind him of Champ's progress. Then Sam heard a noise and opened his bedroom door. He was greeted with a **cascade** of wet kisses. Champ had been locked in the bedroom this whole time! Sam's mom was right. Champ had been napping. Sam had never been so happy in his entire life!

Reread for **Comprehension**

Analyze Story Structure

Character, Setting, Plot
A story's structure is very often organized around the character's actions and how they affect the setting and plot. Sometimes there may be a problem that the character has to solve.

Use the Story Map as you reread "Sam's Summer Search."

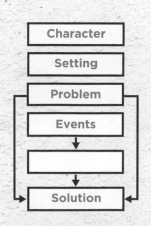

Character
Setting
Problem
Events
Solution

617

Comprehension

Genre

Realistic Fiction is an invented story that could have happened in real life.

Analyze Story Structure

Character, Setting, Plot
As you read, use your Story Map.

Character
Setting
Problem
Events
Solution

Read to Find Out

What does Sara learn about herself as she searches for Charlie?

THE SUMMER OF THE

SWANS

by Betsy Byars • illustrated by John Rowe

Sara and Joe must find Sara's little brother Charlie, a ten-year-old who suffered a brain injury as a small child and doesn't speak. Charlie leaves home during the night to find some swans he's seen on a nearby lake. After becoming lost in the woods near his home, Charlie doesn't know where to turn. In the morning Sara and her classmate Joe join the town's all-out search for the lost boy. But after frantically looking for hours, Sara and Joe have found only a slipper belonging to Charlie.

"**A**re you all right?"

"Yes, I just slipped."

She waited for a moment, bent over her knees, then she called, "Charlie! Charlie," without lifting her head.

"Oh, Charleeeeee," Joe shouted above her.

Sara knew Charlie would shout back if he heard her, the long wailing cry he gave sometimes when he was frightened during the night. It was such a familiar cry that for a moment she thought she heard it.

She waited, still touching the ground with one hand, until she was sure there was no answer.

"Come on," Joe said, holding out his hand.

He pulled her to her feet and she stood looking up at the top of the hill. Machines had cut away the earth there to get at the veins of coal, and the earth had been pushed down the hill to form a huge bank.

"I'll never get up that," she said. She leaned against a tree whose leaves were covered with the pale fine dirt which had filtered down when the machines had cut away the hill.

"Sure you will. I've been up it a dozen times."

He took her hand and she started after him, moving sideways up the steep bank. The dirt crumbled beneath her feet and she slid, skinned one knee, and then slipped again. When she had regained her balance she laughed wryly and said, "What's going to happen is that I'll end up pulling you all the way down the hill."

"No, I've got you. Keep coming."

She started again, putting one foot carefully above the other, picking her way over the stones. When she paused, he said, "Keep coming. We're almost there."

"I think it's a trick, like at the dentist's when he says, 'I'm almost through drilling.' Then he drills for another hour and says, 'Now, I'm really almost through drilling,' and he keeps on and then says, 'There's just one more spot and then I'll be practically really through.'"

"We must go to the same dentist."

"I don't think I can make it. There's no skin at all left on the sides of my legs."

"Well, we're really almost practically there now, in the words of your dentist."

She fell across the top of the dirt bank on her stomach, rested for a moment, and then turned and looked down the valley.

Character
Describe Sara's emotions at this point. Support your answer.

She could not speak for a moment. There lay the whole valley in a way she had never imagined it, a tiny finger of civilization set in a sweeping expanse of dark forest. The black treetops seemed to crowd against the yards, the houses, the roads, giving the impression that at any moment the trees would close over the houses like waves and leave nothing but an unbroken line of black-green leaves waving in the sunlight.

Up the valley she could see the **intersection** where they shopped, the drugstore, the gas station where her mother had once won a set of twenty-four stemmed glasses which Aunt Willie would not allow them to use, the grocery store, the lot where the yellow school buses were parked for the summer. She could look over the valley and see another hill where white cows were all grouped together by a fence and beyond that another hill and then another.

She looked back at the valley and she saw the lake and for the first time since she had stood up on the hill she remembered Charlie.

Raising her hand to her mouth, she called, "Charlie! Charlie! Charlie!" There was a faint echo that seemed to waver in her ears.

"Charlie, oh, Charlie!" Her voice was so loud it seemed to ram into the valley.

Sara waited. She looked down at the forest, and everything was so quiet it seemed to her that the whole valley, the whole world was waiting with her.

"Charlie, hey, Charlie!" Joe shouted.

"Charleeeeee!" She made the sound of it last a long time. "Can you hear meeeeee?"

With her eyes she followed the trail she knew he must have taken—the house, the Akers' vacant lot, the old pasture, the forest. The forest that seemed powerful enough to **engulf** a whole valley, she thought with a sinking feeling, could certainly swallow up a young boy.

"Charlie! Charlie! Charlie!" There was a waver in the last syllable that betrayed how near she was to tears. She looked down at the Indian slipper she was still holding.

"Charlie, oh, Charlie." She waited. There was not a sound anywhere. "Charlie, where are you?"

"Hey, Charlie!" Joe shouted.

They waited in the same dense silence. A cloud passed in front of the sun and a breeze began to blow through the trees. Then there was silence again.

"Charlie, Charlie, Charlie, Charlie, Charlie."

She paused, listened, then bent **abruptly** and put Charlie's slipper to her eyes. She waited for the hot tears that had come so often this summer, the tears that had seemed so close only a moment before. Now her eyes remained dry.

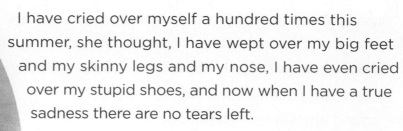

I have cried over myself a hundred times this summer, she thought, I have wept over my big feet and my skinny legs and my nose, I have even cried over my stupid shoes, and now when I have a true sadness there are no tears left.

She held the felt side of the slipper against her eyes like a blindfold and stood there, feeling the hot sun on her head and the wind wrapping around her legs, **conscious** of the height and the valley sweeping down from her feet.

"Listen, just because you can't hear him doesn't mean anything. He could be—"

"Wait a minute." She lowered the slipper and looked down the valley. A sudden wind blew dust into her face and she lifted her hand to shield her eyes.

"I thought I heard something. Charlie! Answer me right this minute."

She waited with the slipper held against her, one hand to her eyes, her whole body motionless, concentrating on her brother. Then she stiffened. She thought again she had heard something—Charlie's long high wail. Charlie could sound sadder than anyone when he cried.

In her **anxiety** she took the slipper and twisted it again and again as if she were wringing water out. She called, then stopped abruptly and listened. She looked at Joe and he shook his head slowly.

She looked away. A bird rose from the trees below and flew toward the hills in the distance. She waited until she could see it no longer and then slowly, still listening for the call that didn't come, she sank to the ground and sat with her head bent over her knees.

Beside her, Joe scuffed his foot in the dust and sent a **cascade** of rocks and dirt down the bank. When the sound of it faded, he began to call, "Charlie, hey, Charlie," again and again.

Charlie awoke, but he lay for a moment without opening his eyes. He did not remember where he was, but he had a certain dread of seeing it.

There were great parts of his life that were lost to Charlie, blank spaces that he could never fill in. He would find himself in a strange place and not know how he had got there. Like the time Sara had been hit in the nose with a baseball at the ice cream shop, and the blood and the sight of Sara kneeling on the ground in helpless pain had frightened him so much that he had turned and run without direction, in a frenzy, dashing headlong up the street, blind to cars and people.

By chance Mr. Weicek had seen him, put him in the car, and driven him home, and Aunt Willie had put him to bed, but later he remembered none of this. He had only awakened in bed and looked at the crumpled bit of ice-cream cone still clenched in his hand and wondered about it.

His whole life had been built on a strict routine, and as long as this routine was kept up, he felt safe and well. The same foods, the same bed, the same furniture in the same place, the same seat on the school bus, the same class **procedure** were all important to him. But always there could be the unexpected, the dreadful surprise that would topple his carefully constructed life in an instant.

The first thing he became aware of was the twigs pressing into his face, and he put his hand under his cheek. Still he did not open his eyes. Pictures began to drift into his mind; he saw Aunt Willie's box which was filled with old jewelry and buttons and knickknacks, and he found that he could remember every item in that box—the string of white beads without a clasp, the old earrings, the tiny book with **souvenir** fold-out pictures of New York, the plastic decorations from cakes, the turtle made of sea shells. Every item was so real that he opened his eyes and was surprised to see, instead of the glittering contents of the box, the dull and unfamiliar forest.

He raised his head and immediately felt the aching of his body. Slowly he sat up and looked down at his hands. His fingernails were black with earth, two of them broken below the quick, and he got up slowly and sat on the log behind him and inspected his fingers more closely.

Then he sat up straight. His hands dropped to his lap. His head cocked to the side like a bird listening. Slowly he straightened until he was standing. At his side his fingers twitched at the empty air as if to grasp something. He took a step forward, still with his head to the side. He remained absolutely still.

Then he began to cry out in a hoarse excited voice, again and again, screaming now, because he had just heard someone far away calling his name.

At the top of the hill Sara got slowly to her feet and stood looking down at the forest. She pushed the hair back from her forehead and moistened her lips. The wind dried them as she waited.

Joe started to say something but she reached out one hand and took his arm to stop him. Scarcely daring to believe her ears, she stepped closer to the edge of the bank. Now she heard it unmistakably—the sharp repeated cry—and she knew it was Charlie.

"Charlie!" she shouted with all her might.

She paused and listened, and his cries were louder and she knew he was not far away after all, just down the slope, in the direction of the ravine.

"It's Charlie, it's Charlie!"

A wild joy overtook her and she jumped up and down on the bare earth and she felt that she could crush the whole hill just by jumping if she wanted.

She sat and scooted down the bank, sending earth and pebbles in a cascade before her. She landed on the soft ground, ran a few steps, lost her balance, caught hold of the first tree trunk she could find, and swung around till she stopped.

She let out another whoop of pure joy, turned and ran down the hill in great strides, the puce tennis shoes slapping the ground like rubber paddles, the wind in her face, her hands grabbing one tree trunk after another for support. She felt like a wild creature who had traveled through the forest this way for a lifetime. Nothing could stop her now.

At the edge of the ravine she paused and stood gasping for breath. Her heart was beating so fast it pounded in her ears, and her throat was dry. She leaned against a tree, resting her cheek against the rough bark.

Character
How have Sara's emotions changed from the beginning of the story to when she hears Charlie?

She thought for a minute she was going to faint, a thing she had never done before, not even when she broke her nose. She hadn't even believed people really did faint until this minute when she clung to the tree because her legs were as useless as rubber bands.

There was a ringing in her ears and another sound, a wailing siren-like cry that was painfully familiar.

"Charlie?"

Charlie's crying, like the sound of a cricket, seemed everywhere and nowhere.

629

She walked along the edge of the ravine, circling the large boulders and trees. Then she looked down into the ravine where the shadows lay, and she felt as if something had turned over inside her because she saw Charlie.

He was standing in his torn pajamas, face turned upward, hands raised, shouting with all his might. His eyes were shut tight. His face was streaked with dirt and tears. His pajama jacket hung in shreds about his scratched chest.

He opened his eyes and as he saw Sara a strange expression came over his face, an expression of wonder and joy and disbelief, and Sara knew that if she lived to be a hundred no one would ever look at her quite that way again.

She paused, looked down at him, and then, sliding on the seat of her pants, went down the bank and took him in her arms.

"Oh, Charlie."

His arms gripped her like steel.

"Oh, Charlie."

She could feel his fingers digging into her back as he clutched her shirt. "It's all right now, Charlie, I'm here and we're going home." His face was buried in her shirt and she patted his head, said again, "It's all right now. Everything's fine."

She held him against her for a moment and now the hot tears were in her eyes and on her cheeks and she didn't even notice.

MEET THE AUTHOR

Betsy Byars's first book was rejected eleven times! But she kept reading (a book a day) and writing, and now she has many published books. *The Summer of the Swans* won the Newbery Medal, a distinguished honor. All of Byars's stories come from her life. She calls them scrapbooks because they bring back memories from her past. When Betsy is not reading or writing, she is flying in her plane, parked at the end of her airstrip outside her front door!

LOG ON ▶ Find out more about Betsy Byars at **www.macmillanmh.com**.

Other books by Betsy Byars: *The Midnight Fox* and *The 18th Emergency*

 Author's Purpose
Authors write to inform, persuade, entertain, or explain. In describing the longest day in Sara's life, Byars both entertains and informs. Give examples of each.

Critical Thinking

Summarize

Use your Story Map to summarize *The Summer of the Swans*. Tell about the different emotions that Sara feels while searching for Charlie.

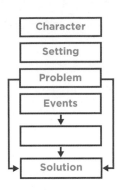

| Character |
| Setting |
| Problem |
| Events |
| |
| Solution |

Think and Compare

1. How do you think Charlie's reaction to Sara's finding him changes the way Sara feels about herself? Does this affect her **character**? **Analyze Story Structure: Character**

2. Why does Sara feel **anxiety** when she looks at the forest **setting**? Use evidence from the text to support your answer. **Analyze Story Structure: Setting**

3. Reread Charlie's flashback on page 625. If you saw the world as Charlie does, how would you handle being lost? **Evaluate**

4. The **plot** of the story presents many obstacles for Sara to overcome. If you were to plan a search for Charlie, what would you need in order to overcome these obstacles? **Analyze Story Structure: Plot**

5. Read "Sam's Summer Search" on pages 616–617. How do friends help in the two situations? **Reading/Writing Across Texts**

A **Folktale** is a traditional story handed down through generations of a particular culture.

✔ **Literary Elements**

A **Simile** is a comparison of two things that are alike, using words such as *like* and *as* to make the comparison. For example, *as cold as ice* is a simile.

A **Metaphor** is a direct comparison of two things without any connecting words. For example, *the wind is an imp* is a metaphor.

Zlateh

the Goat

by Isaac Bashevis Singer

At Hanukkah time the road from the village to the town is usually covered with snow, but this year the winter had been a mild one. Hanukkah had almost come, yet little snow had fallen. The sun shone most of the time. The peasants complained that because of the dry weather there would be a poor harvest of winter grain. New grass sprouted, and the peasants sent their cattle to pasture.

For Reuven the furrier it was a bad year, and after long hesitation he decided to sell Zlateh the goat. She was old and gave little milk. Feyvel the town butcher had offered eight gulden for her. Such a sum would buy Hanukkah candles, potatoes and oil for pancakes, gifts for the children, and other holiday necessaries for the house. Reuven told his oldest boy Aaron to take the goat to town.

Aaron understood what taking the goat to Feyvel meant, but he had to obey his father. Leah, his mother, wiped the tears from her eyes when she heard the news. Aaron's younger sisters, Anna and Miriam, cried loudly. Aaron put on his quilted jacket and a cap with earmuffs, bound a rope around Zlateh's neck, and took along two slices of bread with cheese to eat on the road. Aaron was supposed to deliver the goat by evening, spend the night at the butcher's, and return the next day with the money.

While the family said good-bye to the goat, and Aaron placed the rope around her neck, Zlateh stood as patiently and good-naturedly as ever. She licked Reuven's hand. She shook her small white beard. Zlateh trusted human beings. She knew that they always fed her and never did her any harm.

When Aaron brought her out on the road to town, she seemed somewhat astonished. She'd never been led in that direction before. She looked back at him questioningly, as if to say, "Where are you taking me?" But after a while, she seemed to come to the conclusion that a goat shouldn't ask questions. Still, the road was different. They passed new fields, pastures, and huts with thatched roofs. Here and there a dog barked and came running after them, but Aaron chased it away with his stick.

The sun was shining when Aaron left the village. Suddenly the weather changed. A large black cloud with a bluish center appeared in the east and spread itself rapidly over the sky. A cold wind blew in with it. The crows flew

low, croaking. At first it looked as if it would rain, but instead it began to hail as in summer. It was early in the day, but it became dark as dusk. After a while the hail turned to snow.

In his twelve years Aaron had seen all kinds of weather, but he had never experienced a snow like this one. It was so dense it shut out the light of the day. In a short time, their path was completely covered. The wind became as cold as ice. The road to town was narrow and winding. Aaron no longer knew where he was. He could not see through the snow. The cold soon penetrated his quilted jacket.

At first Zlateh didn't seem to mind the change in weather. She too was twelve years old and knew what winter meant. But when her legs sank deeper and deeper into the snow, she began to turn her head and look at Aaron in wonderment. Her mild eyes seemed to ask, "Why are we out in such a storm?" Aaron hoped that a peasant would come along in his cart, but no one passed by.

The snow grew thicker, falling to the ground in large, whirling flakes. Beneath it Aaron's boots touched the softness of a plowed field. He realized that he was no longer on the road. He had gone astray. He could no longer figure out which was east or west, which way was the village, the town. The wind whistled, howled, whirled the snow about in eddies. It looked as if white imps were playing tag on the fields. A white dust rose above

> **Simile**
> "It looked as if white imps were playing tag on the fields" is a simile describing the falling snow.

the ground. Zlateh stopped. She could walk no longer. Stubbornly she anchored her cleft hooves in the earth and bleated as if pleading to be taken home. Icicles hung from her white beard, and her horns were glazed with frost.

Aaron did not want to admit the danger, but he knew just the same that if they did not find shelter they would freeze to death. This was no ordinary storm. It was a mighty blizzard. The snowfall had reached his knees. His hands were numb, and he could no longer feel his toes. He choked when he breathed. His nose felt like wood, and he rubbed it with snow. Zlateh's bleating began to sound like crying. Those humans in whom she had so much confidence had dragged her into a trap. Aaron began to pray to God for himself and for the innocent animal.

Suddenly he made out the shape of a hill. He wondered what it could be. Who had piled snow into such a huge heap? He moved toward it, dragging Zlateh along after him. When he came near it, he realized that it was a large haystack which the snow had blanketed.

Aaron realized immediately that they were saved. With great effort he dug his way through the snow. He was a village boy and knew what to do. When he reached the hay, he hollowed out a nest for himself and the goat. No matter how cold it may be outside, in the hay it is always warm. And hay was food for Zlateh. The moment she smelled it she became contented and began to eat. Outside the snow continued to fall. It quickly covered the passageway Aaron had dug. But a boy and an animal need to breathe, and there was hardly any air in their hideout. Aaron bored a kind of a window through the hay and snow and carefully kept the passage clear.

Zlateh, having eaten her fill, sat down on her hind legs and seemed to have regained her confidence in man. Aaron ate his slices of bread and cheese, but after the difficult journey he was still hungry. He looked at Zlateh and noticed her udders were full. He lay down next to her, placing himself so that when he milked her he could squirt the milk into his mouth. It was rich and sweet. Zlateh was not accustomed to being milked that way, but she did not resist. On the contrary, she seemed eager to reward Aaron for bringing her to a shelter whose very walls, floor, and ceiling were made of food.

Through the window Aaron could catch a glimpse of the chaos outside. The wind carried before it whole drifts of snow. It was completely dark, and he did not know whether night had already come or whether it was the darkness of the storm. Thank God that in the hay it was not cold. The dried hay, grass, and field flowers exuded the warmth of the summer sun. Zlateh ate frequently; she nibbled from above, below, from the left and right. Her body gave forth an animal warmth, and Aaron cuddled up to her. He had always loved Zlateh, but now she was like a sister. He was alone, cut off from his family, and wanted to talk. He began to talk to Zlateh. "Zlateh, what do you think about what has happened to us?" he asked.

"Maaaa," Zlateh answered.

"If we hadn't found this stack of hay, we would both be frozen stiff by now," Aaron said.

"Maaaa," was the goat's reply.

"If the snow keeps on falling like this, we may have to stay here for days," Aaron explained.

"Maaaa," Zlateh bleated.

"What does 'Maaaa' mean?" Aaron asked. "You'd better speak up clearly."

"Maaaa. Maaaa," Zlateh tried.

"Well, let it be 'Maaaa' then," Aaron said patiently. "You can't speak, but I know you understand. I need you and you need me. Isn't that right?"

"Maaaa."

Aaron became sleepy. He made a pillow out of some hay, leaned his head on it, and dozed off. Zlateh too fell asleep.

When Aaron opened his eyes, he didn't know whether it was morning or night. The snow had blocked up his window. He tried to clear it, but when he had bored through it to the length of his arm, he still hadn't reached the outside. Luckily he had his stick with him and was able to break through to the open air. It was still dark outside. The snow continued to fall and the wind wailed, first with one voice and then with many. Sometimes it had the sound of devilish laughter. Zlateh too awoke, and when Aaron greeted her, she answered, "Maaaa." Yes, Zlateh's language consisted of only one word, but it meant many things. Now she was saying, "We must accept all that God gives us—heat, cold, hunger, satisfaction, light, and darkness."

Aaron had awakened hungry. He had eaten up his food, but Zlateh had plenty of milk.

For three days Aaron and Zlateh stayed in the haystack. Aaron had always loved Zlateh, but in these three days he loved her more and more. She fed him with her milk and helped him keep warm. She comforted him with her patience. He told her many stories, and she always cocked her ears and listened. When he patted her, she licked his hands and his face. Then she said, "Maaaa," and he knew it meant, I love you too.

The snow fell for three days, though after the first day it was not as thick and the wind quieted down. Sometimes Aaron felt that there could never have been a summer, that the snow had always fallen, ever since he could remember. He, Aaron, never had a father or mother or

sisters. He was a snow child, born of the snow, and so was Zlateh. It was so quiet in the hay that his ears rang in the stillness. Aaron and Zlateh slept all night and a good part of the day. As for Aaron's dreams, they were all about warm weather. He dreamed of green fields, trees covered with blossoms, clear brooks, and singing birds. By the third night the snow had stopped, but Aaron did not dare to find his way home in the darkness. The sky became clear and the moon shone, casting silvery nets on the snow. Aaron dug his way out and looked at the world. It was all white, quiet, dreaming dreams of heavenly splendor. The stars were large and close. The moon swam in the sky as in a sea.

On the morning of the fourth day Aaron heard the ringing of sleigh bells. The haystack was not far from the road. The peasant who drove the sleigh pointed out the way to him—not to the town and Feyvel the butcher, but home to the village. Aaron had decided in the haystack that he would never part with Zlateh.

Aaron's family and their neighbors had searched for the boy and the goat but had found no trace of them during the storm. They feared they were lost. Aaron's mother and sisters cried for him; his father remained silent and gloomy. Suddenly one of the neighbors came running to their house with the news that Aaron and Zlateh were coming up the road.

> **Metaphor**
> "He was a snow child, born of the snow, and so was Zlateh" is a metaphor for their snowbound condition.

640

There was great joy in the family. Aaron told them how he had found the stack of hay and how Zlateh had fed him with her milk. Aaron's sisters kissed and hugged Zlateh and gave her a special treat of chopped carrots and potato peels, which Zlateh gobbled up hungrily.

Nobody ever again thought of selling Zlateh, and now that the cold weather had finally set in, the villagers needed the services of Reuven the furrier once more. When Hanukkah came, Aaron's mother was able to fry pancakes every evening, and Zlateh got her portion too. Even though Zlateh had her own pen, she often came to the kitchen, knocking on the door with her horns to indicate that she was ready for a visit, and she was always admitted. In the evening Aaron, Miriam, and Anne played dreidel. Zlateh sat near the stove watching the children and the flickering of the Hanukkah candles.

Once in a while Aaron would ask her, "Zlateh, do you remember the three days we spent together?"

And Zlateh would scratch her neck with a horn, shake her white bearded head and come out with a single sound which expressed all her thoughts, and all her love.

CA Critical Thinking

1. Why does the author use so many similes to describe the blizzard in this story? Use examples from the text to support your argument. **Similes**

2. Traditional folktales are told over and over because they contain truths for every generation. What is the main theme of this story and how do you know that? **Synthesize**

3. Compare Charlie in *The Summer of the Swans* to Aaron in this selection. Do you think the difference in their circumstances made a difference in the way they felt when they were separated from their families? **Reading/Writing Across Texts**

 Find out more about folktales at **www.macmillanmh.com**.

✔ **Varying Sentence Types**

Writers **vary the types of sentences** they use to make their writing interesting and engaging.

Reading and Writing Connection

Read the passage below. Notice how author Betsy Byars varies the types of sentences to help us follow Charlie from his dreams into his reality.

Author Betsy Byars describes Charlie when he first wakes up. She mixes sentence lengths and begins sentences in different ways to show us the range of feelings that Charlie experiences.

An excerpt from
Summer of the Swans

The first thing he became aware of was the twigs pressing into his face, and he put his hand under his cheek. Still he did not open his eyes. Pictures began to drift into his mind; he saw Aunt Willie's box which was filled with old jewelry and buttons and knickknacks, and he found that he could remember every item in that box—the string of white beads without a clasp, the old earrings, the tiny book with souvenir fold-out pictures of New York, the plastic decorations from cakes, the turtle made of sea shells. Every item was so real that he opened his eyes and was surprised to see, instead of the glittering contents of the box, the dull and unfamiliar forest.

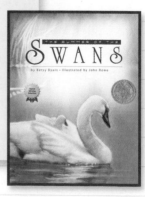

Read and Find

Read Andrew's writing below. How did he begin sentences in different ways and mix sentence lengths? Use the Writer's Checklist below to help you.

Tough Stuff

by Andrew P.

An official tournament. I was so nervous that I thought I had forgotten all the tricks I knew.

I came out and saw hundreds of people clapping. I put the skateboard on the ground. I could feel the wheels under my feet kissing the floor as I went through the route. The first ramp was close and the first opportunity to perform a trick was approaching.

Read how one student uses varying sentence styles to make his writing interesting.

Writer's Checklist

 Does the writer begin sentences in different ways?

 Does the writer mix sentence lengths, alternating long sentences with shorter ones?

 Does the writer repeat sentence types to emphasize or contrast information?

Talk About It

In what ways do people protect wildlife? What kinds of things can harm wildlife?

LOG ON Find out more about protecting wildlife at **www.macmillanmh.com**.

Saving Animals

Protecting the Clouded Leopard

by Amrik Singh

Not many people know about the clouded leopard. Even scientists don't know much about the animal in the wild because it is so private. We do know that the clouded leopard isn't actually a leopard. It is a species of its own. However, it does have spots like a leopard. They help it blend into the background in the forest.

What else do we know about the cat? It is one of the best climbers of all wild cats. This skill is clearly imprinted in the kittens early on by their mothers and by instinct. In the wild, the cat lives in the tropical rain forests of Asia. It hunts small animals, such as squirrels and monkeys. It is listed on the United States Endangered Species Act. This protects it from being hunted. Scientists have **speculated** that the wild population is getting smaller, but no actual numbers are available.

The Clouded Leopard Project works to **conserve** and protect the population of these cats. The project teaches about clouded leopards, **analyzing** their habits in captivity by watching their behaviors and interactions. The project realizes it is **vital** to the cats' survival to breed the animals in zoos. If more clouded leopards aren't born, the population will be **propelled** quickly into extinction.

The Clouded Leopard Project has recently begun a conservation effort in Thailand. It is a natural home of the clouded leopard. Funds will be given to the Khao Kheow Open Zoo to help with the breeding of these cats. Part of the money also will help save the habitat of the wild cats. People will work to monitor these wild cats. They will be photographed instead of being **sedated**, or drugged, to be tagged. Sedating clouded leopards could cause the cats' bodies to lose too much water and become **dehydrated**, or worse.

The project has had some great successes in the last few years. Two cubs were born in the United States, and two were born in Thailand.

Members of the Clouded Leopard Project hope the urge to protect such species will become **embedded** in people. They sponsor several education programs at zoos. They also sponsor programs to directly help the cats. Through their work they ultimately will increase the population of this species.

Reread for Comprehension

Make Inferences and Analyze

Main Idea and Details
Understanding the main idea will help readers make inferences about what they read. Authors include details to support the main idea.

Use a Main Idea Chart to help you record the main idea and details as you reread "Protecting the Clouded Leopard."

Main Idea _____
_____
_____
Detail 1 _____
_____
Detail 2 _____
_____

Summary _____
_____
_____
_____

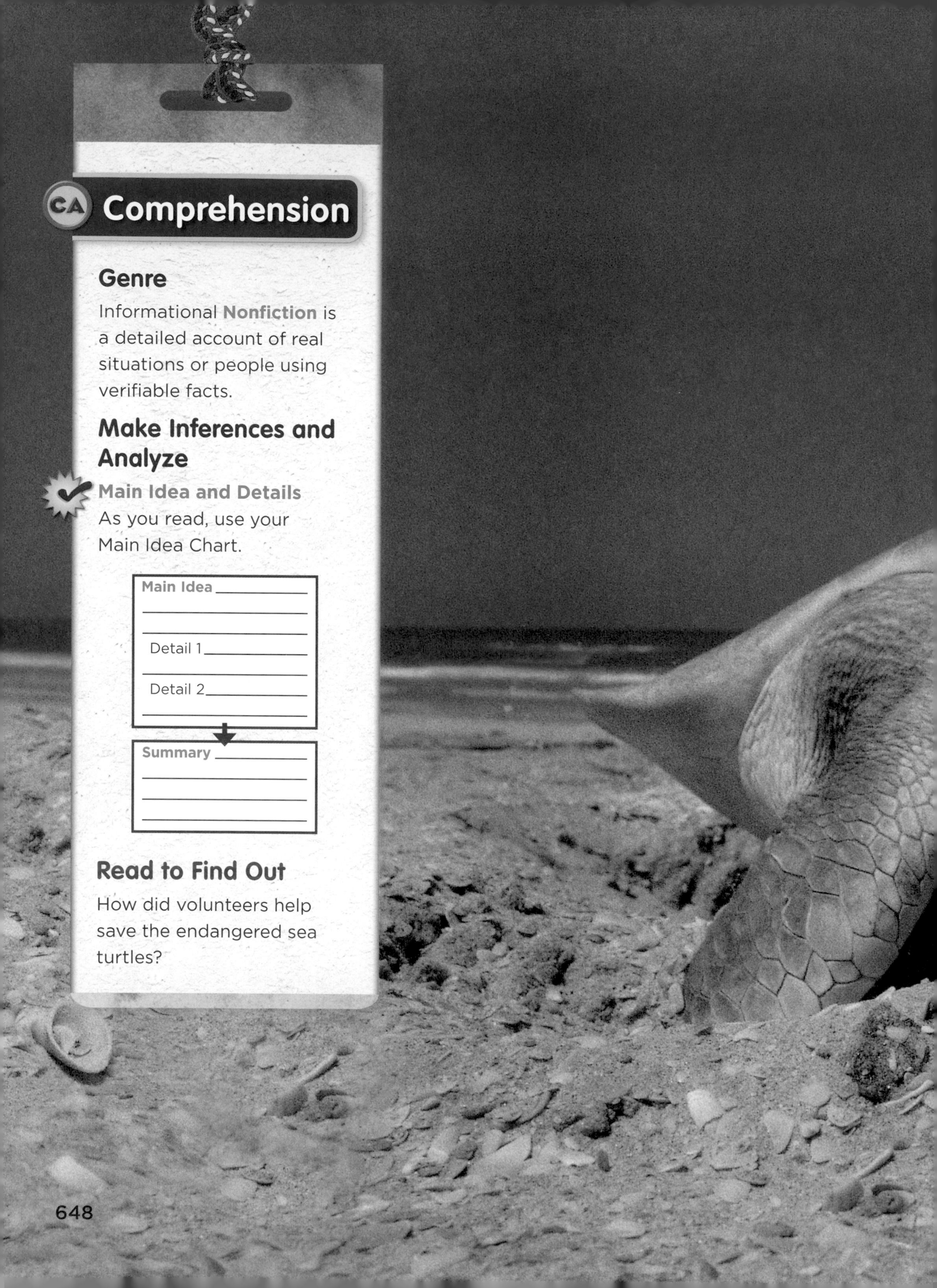

Genre

Informational **Nonfiction** is a detailed account of real situations or people using verifiable facts.

Make Inferences and Analyze

Main Idea and Details
As you read, use your Main Idea Chart.

Main Idea _____
_____
_____

Detail 1_____

Detail 2_____
_____

Summary _____
_____
_____
_____

Read to Find Out

How did volunteers help save the endangered sea turtles?

INTERRUPTED
JOURNEY
Saving Endangered Sea Turtles

by KATHRYN LASKY
photographs by CHRISTOPHER G. KNIGHT

Award
Winning
Selection

Stranded

The young turtle has been swimming for three months now in the same warm shallow bay, grazing on small crabs and plankton, basking in an endless dream of calm water and plentiful food. But as the days begin to shorten and the light drains out of the sky earlier and earlier, the water grows colder. It drops to fifty degrees Fahrenheit. The turtle is confused. Swimming is harder. Its heartbeat slows—and almost stops.

Ten days before Thanksgiving, on a beach where Pilgrims once walked, Max Nolan, a ten-year-old boy, and his mother begin their patrol. The Nolans are among volunteers who walk Cape Cod's beaches during November and December to search for turtles who are often cold and stunned and seem dead—turtles whose lives they may be able to save.

It is a blustery day on Ellis Landing Beach. At twenty-five knots the bitter northwest wind stings Max's face like sharp needles. It makes his eyes water but he keeps looking—looking above the high-water mark through the clumps of seaweed, looking below the tide line where the sand is hard and sleek and lapped by surf—looking for a dark greenish-brown mound about the size of a pie plate, looking for a Kemp's ridley turtle that is dying and perhaps can be saved.

Max and his mother and the other volunteers work for a **vital** cause. All sea turtles are threatened or endangered; Kemp's ridleys are the most endangered of all. Right now on our planet there are fewer than eight thousand Kemp's ridley turtles left. They are a vanishing species.

On Ellis Landing Beach, snow squalls begin to whirl down. The waves are building, and as they begin to break, the white froth whips across their steep faces. So far there is no sign of a turtle.

Max is far ahead of his mother when he sees the hump in the sand being washed by the surf. He runs up to it and shouts to his mom, "Got one!" The turtle is cold. Its flippers are floppy. Its eyes are open, but the turtle is not moving at all. It might be dead, but then again, it might not.

> **Main Idea**
> What is the main idea on pages 650–651? What details support it?

651

Max remembers the instructions given to all rescuers. He picks up the turtle, which weighs about five pounds, and moves it above the high-tide mark to keep it from washing out to sea. Then he runs to find seaweed to protect it from the wind. He finds a stick to mark the spot, and next, he and his mother go to the nearest telephone and call the sea-turtle rescue line of the Massachusetts Audubon Society.

Within an hour the turtle has been picked up and taken to the Wellfleet Bay Wildlife Sanctuary on Cape Cod. Robert Prescott, the director of the Sanctuary, examines the turtle. "It sure does look dead," he says softly. "But you never can tell." If the turtle is really alive, it must be brought out of its cold, stunned condition. That is a task for the New England Aquarium with its medical team who, over the years, have made a specialty of treating turtles.

Robert puts the new turtle in a plastic wading pool with another turtle that is quite lively. Max crouches by the edge and watches his turtle. It is as still as a stone. He gently touches a flipper. Nothing moves. Then after about twenty minutes, he thinks he might see a flicker in the turtle's left eyelid. He leans closer. "Hey, it's moving!" It wasn't just the eyelid. He saw the right rear flipper move a fraction of an inch. Over the next five minutes, he sees the turtle make three or four microscopically small motions with its right rear flipper. Soon, the rescue team from the New England Aquarium arrives.

Emergency

Beth Chittick is a vet at the New England Aquarium. When the turtles arrive she is ready for them. The turtles are taken immediately into the examination room. Beth is joined by head veterinarian, Howard Crum. They insert a thermometer into the cloaca, the opening under the turtle's tail. The temperature of the turtle Max found is fifty degrees Fahrenheit. Normal temperature for a turtle is usually about seventy-five degrees. Howard next tries to find a heartbeat. He listens intently. "I think I can hear a faint sound . . . " He holds the stiff turtle against his ear as one might hold a seashell. "Why, gee whiz, I can hear the ocean," he jokes.

> **Main Idea**
> What is the main idea of this paragraph? Find two details to support your answer.

Howard is still not convinced that the turtle is dead. "With turtles," Howard says, "death is a relative term." Turtles can operate, can survive, even when their hearts slow down for periods of time. Events that might damage the larger, more complicated brains of other animals will not always prove fatal to turtles.

In fact, a turtle's heartbeat naturally slows down at times to just one or two beats per minute in order to **conserve** oxygen and keep vital organs like the brain working. So Howard won't give up on this turtle yet. The turtle does not seem **dehydrated**. The skin on its limbs is not wrinkled—a good sign.

An assistant swabs down an area on the turtle's neck, from which a blood sample will be taken. By **analyzing** the blood, Howard and Beth will be able to see how the turtle's kidneys and other organs are functioning.

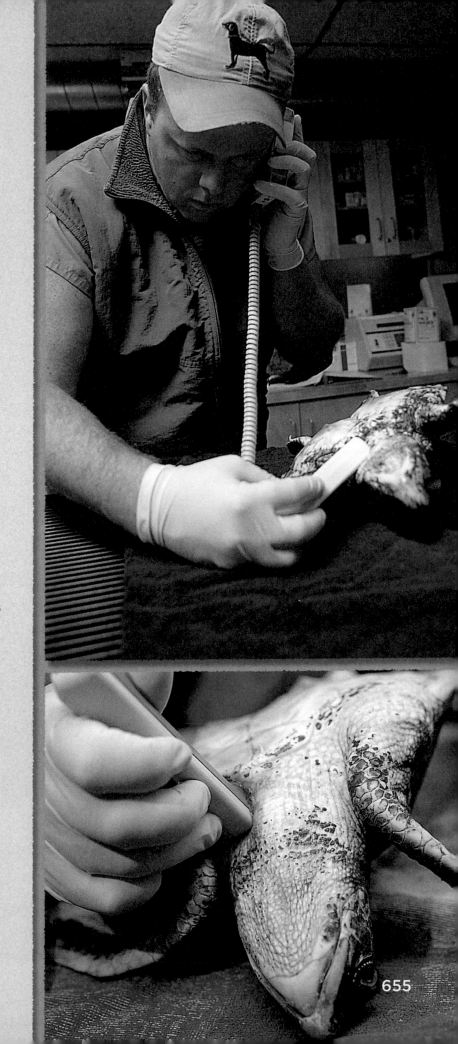

655

Next the turtle is cleaned. The algae are washed and wiped from its shell. The doctors detect movement in its tail and then see some of the same movements that Max saw in its flippers. They are the motions a turtle makes when it swims. They do not necessarily mean that it is alive, though. It has been **speculated** that these movements could be what are sometimes called vestigial motions, echoes of long-ago actions, fossil behaviors **embedded** in the brain of an ancient creature. The turtle could be swimming in death or swimming toward life.

Nonetheless, the vets hook up the turtle to an intravenous needle through which fluids will be pumped very slowly at a temperature slightly higher than the turtle's body. Beth and Howard have learned much about the condition of this turtle but they are still not sure if it is really alive or dead.

Finally the turtle is tagged with a yellow-blue band. It will be known as Yellow-Blue. It is put in the Intensive Care Unit, a large temperature-controlled stainless steel box with a glass window. Inside, the turtle is placed on a soft pile of towels so its shell is supported and it will not have to rest on its ventrum, or bottom shell.

Then the team turn their attention to another turtle, which is definitely alive. Howard picks up the turtle and talks to it as its flippers thrash madly. "Okay, little man!" This turtle's temperature is sixty-two degrees. When they take its blood, the sample appears much redder than the nearly brownish blood of Yellow-Blue, which indicates that there is more oxygen in it.

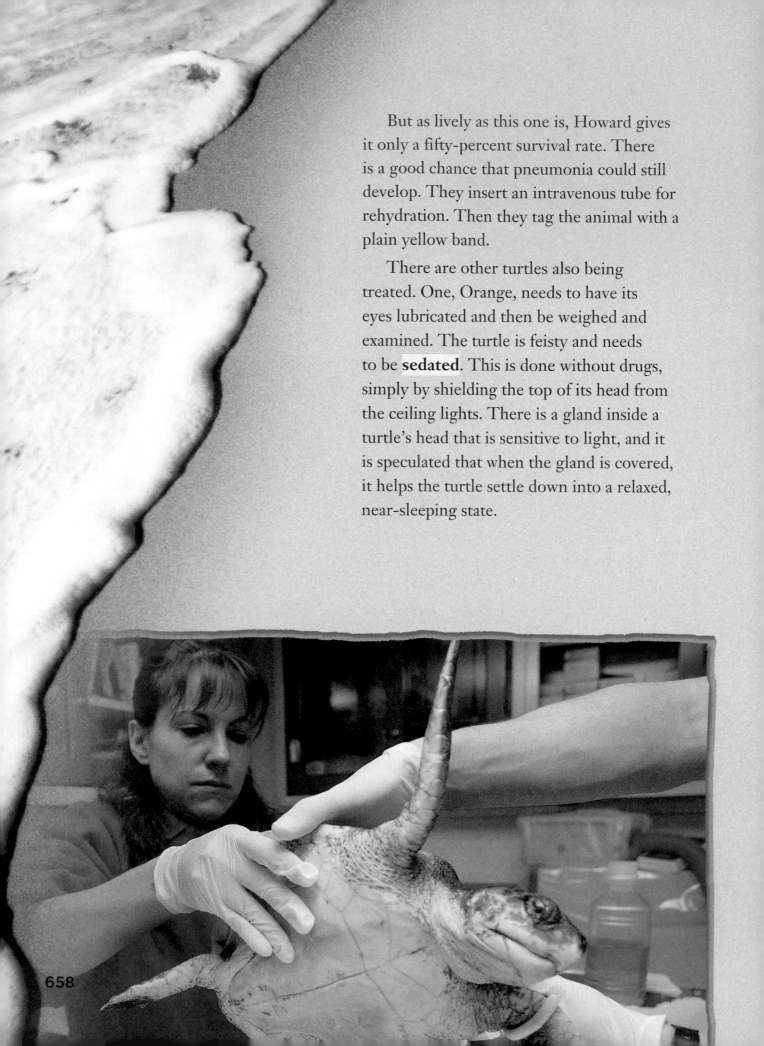

But as lively as this one is, Howard gives it only a fifty-percent survival rate. There is a good chance that pneumonia could still develop. They insert an intravenous tube for rehydration. Then they tag the animal with a plain yellow band.

There are other turtles also being treated. One, Orange, needs to have its eyes lubricated and then be weighed and examined. The turtle is feisty and needs to be **sedated**. This is done without drugs, simply by shielding the top of its head from the ceiling lights. There is a gland inside a turtle's head that is sensitive to light, and it is speculated that when the gland is covered, it helps the turtle settle down into a relaxed, near-sleeping state.

In this peaceful state, Orange begins to "swim" on the table, its flippers making the paddling motions that have since birth **propelled** it through thousands of miles of sea. Its heart rate, at thirty-six beats a minute, is good. Its respiration rate is still slow. It takes only one breath every minute. Its temperature is near seventy degrees. Orange is x-rayed for signs of pneumonia. The lungs are clear.

Whatever the outcome for these three turtles, Beth, Howard, Robert, Max, and his mother all know they are doing their part to help return the turtles to health, to help return them to the sea.

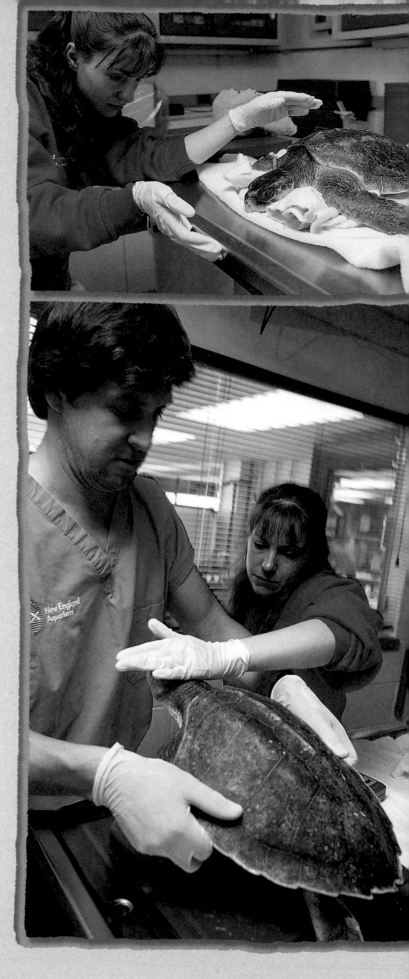

Take a Journey with Kathryn Lasky and Christopher G. Knight

Kathryn Lasky has written more than 100 books in all genres. You would think she wouldn't have time for anything else, but twice she has sailed with her husband across the Atlantic Ocean in a small sailboat. Even when she was seasick, Kathryn loved watching the birds and the dolphins . . . and maybe she even saw a sea turtle!

Christopher G. Knight is Kathryn Lasky's husband. He is also a photographer and an adventurer. He has paddled a kayak from Alaska to Seattle and canoed through seven countries in Europe. Then he met Kathryn. They have two children and have done seventeen books together.

Other books by Kathryn Lasky:
The Man Who Made Time Travel and
A Voice of Her Own

CA Author's Purpose

Kathryn Lasky's purpose here is to inform. She tells about real people doing real things and documents those acts with photographs. How do the photos add to the text?

LOG ON Find out more about Kathryn Lasky and Christopher G. Knight at **www.macmillanmh.com**.

CA Critical Thinking

Summarize

Use your Main Idea Chart to help you summarize *Interrupted Journey*. State the main idea in one or two sentences.

Main Idea _____
_____
Detail 1 _____
Detail 2 _____
_____

↓

Summary _____
_____
_____
_____

Think and Compare

1. What are some important **details** that Kathryn Lasky includes to support the **main idea** of the article? **Make Inferences and Analyze: Main Idea and Details**

2. Do you think the yellow-blue turtle will live? Explain why or why not. Use information from the text to support your answer. **Evaluate**

3. Max and his mother are volunteers. What kind of volunteer work would you like to do? Are volunteers **vital** to your community? Why or why not? **Synthesize**

4. What facts from *Interrupted Journey* would you choose to show if you were to give a presentation about conservation? Explain your choices. **Apply**

5. Read "Protecting the Clouded Leopard" on pages 646–647. Compare and contrast the conservation project detailed in that selection with the one in *Interrupted Journey*. How are the two projects similar? How are their methods different? **Reading/Writing Across Texts**

Free Verse has irregular lines and lacks a metrical pattern and rhyme scheme.

Song Lyrics are the written words of a song. Long ago poems were not just recited but were often sung.

✔ Literary Elements

Alliteration is the repetition of initial consonant sounds.

Imagery is the use of words to create a picture in the reader's mind.

Birdfoot's Grampa

by Joseph Bruchac

The old man
must have stopped our car
two dozen times to climb out
and gather into his hands
the small toads blinded
by our lights and leaping,
live drops of rain.

The rain was falling,
a mist about his white hair
and I kept saying
you can't save them all,
accept it, get back in
we've got places to go.

But, leathery hands full
of wet brown life,
knee deep in the summer
roadside grass,
he just smiled and said
*they have places to go to
too.*

The words *lights*, *leaping*, and *live* all begin with *l* to create alliteration.

The poet creates a picture when he describes the toads as "live drops of rain."

662

This Land Is Your Land

lyrics by Woody Guthrie

This land is your land, this land is my land
From California to the New York island;
From the redwood forest to the Gulf Stream waters,
This land was made for you and me.

As I was walking that ribbon of highway,
I saw above me that endless skyway;
I saw below me that golden valley,
This land was made for you and me.

The lyricist uses imagery when he compares a highway to a ribbon.

(CA) Critical Thinking

1. Find another example of imagery in "Birdfoot's Grampa" or "This Land Is Your Land." How does the image appeal to one of your senses? **Imagery**

2. What kind of person is Birdfoot's grandfather? Give examples from the poem. **Analyze**

3. How are Max Nolan's attitudes toward wildlife in *Interrupted Journey* and the grampa's attitudes in "Birdfoot's Grampa" similar? **Reading/Writing Across Texts**

LOG ON ▶ Find out more about poetry at **www.macmillanmh.com**.

Writing

✔ Varying Sentence Types

Good writers use **varying styles of sentences** to add interest to their writing.

Reading and Writing Connection

Read the passage below. Notice how author Kathryn Lasky begins sentences in different ways. Do you think she is trying to create an interesting rhythm in the writing?

An excerpt from
Interrupted Journey

The author shows us how the director of the Wellfleet Bay Wildlife Sanctuary on Cape Cod, and Max spend time watching carefully the sea turtle that Max found along the shore. She varies sentence types throughout the writing to make it more interesting.

Robert puts the new turtle in a plastic wading pool with another turtle that is quite lively. Max crouches by the edge and watches his turtle. It is as still as a stone. He gently touches a flipper. Nothing moves. Then after about twenty minutes, he thinks he might see a flicker in the turtle's left eyelid. He leans closer. "Hey, it's moving!" It wasn't just the eyelid. He saw the right rear flipper move a fraction of an inch. Over the next five minutes, he sees the turtle make three or four microscopically small motions with its right rear flipper. Soon, the rescue team from the New England Aquarium arrives.

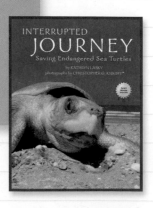

664

Read and Find

Read Rizan's writing below. How did he use different types of sentences to enhance the action? Use the Writer's Checklist below to help you.

Ultimate Flying Disc

by Rizan L.

He pulled his hand back and then—fling—the disc went shooting into the sky. We darted across the field, but none of us got it. Daniel leaped into the air. He snatched the disc and shot it at Carli. Success! Other team's throw. Sara got the disc and whizzed it across the field to Daniel. Daniel passed it back to Carli, and she shot it to Sara in the end zone.

Read how one person describes a very fast flying disc game.

Writer's Checklist

- ✓ Did the writer begin sentences in different ways?

- ✓ Did the writer choose different sentence lengths to show us how fast the game was being played?

- ◻ Did the writer vary sentence styles to add interest to the writing?

Why are people around the world working hard to find new sources of energy?

LOG ON ▶ Find out more about energy at www.macmillanmh.com.

Energy

SOURCES OF ENERGY

Vocabulary

nonrenewable

renewable

adverse

generate

apparatus

The energy we use in just about all aspects of our daily lives comes from two types of sources: nonrenewable and renewable.

Solar collectors

NONRENEWABLE Sources of Energy

Most of the energy we use comes from deposits of fossil fuels in the earth. These include coal, natural gas, and petroleum. Once these natural resources are used up, they are gone forever. Getting fossil fuels out of the earth involves drilling, mining, building pipelines, and other processes that can have **adverse** effects on the environment. Releasing the energy in fossil fuels requires combustion. This burning process releases pollutants that can contribute to acid rain and global warming.

Oil-drilling platform

RENEWABLE Sources of Energy

Renewable sources of energy are everlasting. Using them does not use them up. They generate much less pollution—both in gathering and production—than nonrenewable sources.

* Solar energy comes from the sun. Solar panels on buildings convert sunlight to electricity.

* Wind can **generate** electricity by turning a turbine, an **apparatus** with blades similar to a giant windmill.

* Geothermal energy comes from heat in Earth's core. Engineers use the heat to create steam to generate electricity.

* Dams and rivers generate hydropower. Water flowing through a dam activates a turbine that runs an electric generator.

LOG ON ▶ Find out more about energy sources at www.macmillanmh.com.

ENERGY PRODUCERS AND CONSUMERS

Here's a look at the world's top 10 energy consumers and producers.

TOP 10 ENERGY PRODUCERS	TOP 10 ENERGY CONSUMERS
1. United States	1. United States
2. Russia	2. China
3. China	3. Russia
4. Saudi Arabia	4. Japan
5. Canada	5. Germany
6. United Kingdom	6. India
7. Iran	7. Canada
8. Norway	8. France
9. Australia	9. United Kingdom
10. Mexico	10. Brazil

(**Source:** *Energy Information Administration, U.S. Dept. of Energy*)

WIND POWER

Wind exists because the sun warms Earth's surface air unevenly. Warm air expands and rises. Cool air rushes in to take its place. The resulting air movement is wind. Technology can turn this wind—and the sun— into pollution-free energy.

Wind "farm"

* The wind that blows through North Dakota, South Dakota, and Texas could create enough electricity to meet the needs of the entire country.

* More than 10,000 U.S. homes are totally powered by solar energy.

* The largest wind farm in the world is in Altamont Pass, California. It has 6,500 windmills!

* If every shopping mall in the U.S. had solar panels on its roof, the panels would produce enough power for every house in the country!

(Sources: Solar Energy Research and Education Foundation; *The Wind at Work* by Gretchen Woelfle)

BUILDING GREEN

How can homes be made more environmentally friendly?

Water-filled drums in a south-facing glass wall absorb heat from the sun and release it slowly at night to warm this New Mexico home in winter.

If Earth could talk, it might not call everyone's house "home sweet home." Instead, it would probably point out that many of our houses are not so "sweet." They can actually have an **adverse** effect on the health of the planet. Imaginative builders are out to change that by dreaming up new ways to make our homes more "green," a term that means "ecologically friendly."

HOME, GREEN HOME

Recently, a new house built near Houston, Texas, was so efficient that it didn't need a furnace. The hot-water heater kept the house warm enough in the relatively mild Texas winter. This, combined with reduced air-conditioning costs, saved enough money to offset the cost of the house's extra-thick insulation and high-performance windows.

This solar-powered house in Germany has transparent insulation and solar panels facing south to collect and store solar energy for everyday use.

Unfortunately the successful project, part of a Department of Energy program, hasn't much changed the habits of many homebuilders. "It's hard for big companies to change their way of doing things," says Bill Zoeller. He works with the firm that designed the Houston home.

But some builders are changing. For instance, Habitat for Humanity is building energy-efficient homes that rely less on **nonrenewable** sources of energy. It is working with the Environmental Protection Agency to clean up former industrial sites for affordable housing. Improved insulation and construction techniques are part of the plan. Zoeller sees significant gains in all this. He says, "In some parts of the country, even average homes are now 30 percent more efficient than a few years ago."

DRIVING HOME CHANGE

Many Californians claim they practically live in their cars. John Picard, 34, goes a step further: He lives in a lot of cars, literally.

"These are cars from the '60s that were in the junkyard," he says, indicating his 2,400-square-foot ultramodern home in Marina del Rey, California. "Now they are my house."

Picard's walls aren't made from hubcaps and fenders. They are made by a company that manufactures recycled-steel framing material from junked cars and discarded cans and washing machines. In fact, Picard's entire house—a space-age, two-story metal cube—was built using recycled material and modern technology. The result is a home that's environmentally correct and comfortable, too. The woodless construction alone, Picard estimates, "saved about 100 trees."

Other "ecohouse" features include filtered air and an **apparatus** that monitors the interior temperature and energy-efficient lighting. Plus there is a roof-mounted solar panel that can **generate** most of his home's energy needs. "My house," he notes proudly, "has the potential for zero utility bills."

Designing Picard's ecohouse took a year. Construction took four months. "I wanted to do an energy-efficient house that everybody could construct," Picard explains. He hopes that his ecohouse will inspire similar construction in the future. "I know it changes people when they see and understand it," he says. "It brings quality back into building, and it's good for the environment."

THE LATEST STRAW (NOT THE LAST!)

Straw seems like an improbable home-building material. After all, there is that story about the three pigs. And there's another story about a straw house that was eaten by cows.

Judy Knox, 50, and her husband Matts Myhrman, 54, have a different view. They are spreading the news that straw-bale construction, once used on the tree-barren American prairie, is ripe for a comeback. In this building technique, straw is stacked in bales, often bound by

John Picard's "metal cube" home

Charcoal-color flooring absorbs heat and helps warm the house.

chicken wire, and sealed with stucco or adobe. Straw is a cheap, energy-efficient resource, say Knox and Myhrman. Plus, new straw grows every year—so it is a **renewable** resource.

In 1990, the two launched their Tucson-based company, Out On Bale, to conduct workshops for straw builders. They've overseen construction of 20 straw structures, from a sauna to a bunkhouse. "It's an annually renewable

waste product," says Myhrman, that's "right for the planet."

Knox is a longtime environmental activist from New Hampshire. Myhrman is a Maine native and former ecology teacher. They became excited about straw houses after visiting two of them in New Mexico in the 1980s. With their two-foot-thick walls, the houses provided "a quiet restful kind of feeling," says Knox. "It felt friendly." Walls can be raised in a day or two. Quick-to-erect straw houses could, say Knox and Myhrman, shelter disaster victims or homeless people.

Straw, however, does have one drawback: When wet, it attracts fungi, so builders must take care to keep bales dry. And sometimes during construction "the straw bales break up, like shredded wheat," notes local architect Tom Greenwood, who recently designed a straw cabin. What then? Greenwood jokes, "Don't add milk."

CA Critical Thinking

1. What does the term "building green" mean?

2. What makes the building techniques described in this article environmentally friendly?

3. If you were building a "green" house, which building technique would you want to use? Why?

4. "Sources of Energy" on page 668 outlines the consequences of relying on nonrenewable energy sources. How do the people in "Building Green" avoid these drawbacks?

Building a straw house

Show What You Know

CA

Think and Search

Read on to find the answer. Look for information in more than one place.

The Kennebec River flows freely now.

LEARNING TO GO WITH THE FLOW

Dams are a source of energy in the United States and around the world. But damming rivers also causes environmental damage. In 1887, the Edwards Dam was built across the Kennebec River near Augusta, Maine, to generate electricity. Even back then, there was concern that the dam would interfere with the life cycle of fish in the area.

The concern was justified. It wasn't long after the dam was built that salmon, herring, shad, and other fish pretty much disappeared from the river. The dam blocked the fish from swimming to the upstream areas where they reproduce.

In 1997 the government concluded that the benefits the dam provided were outweighed by the environmental damage it caused. In 1999 the old dam was destroyed and the Kennebec came roaring back to life. Within weeks, native fish species returned by the hundreds. Edwards was the first U.S. hydroelectric dam ordered destroyed against its owners' wishes. It signaled the start of a successful campaign to remove other river dams around the country that were causing environmental damage.

Restoring rivers to their natural paths is hard work. But environmentalists say the effort always pays off—in expected as well as surprising ways, it turns out. The Edwards Dam had trapped hundreds of logs at its base that were salvaged and recycled into musical instruments, furniture, and other products.

Go on ▶

Now answer questions 1 through 5. Base your answers on the article "Learning to Go with the Flow."

1. **What environmental damage did the Edwards Dam cause?**

   A   The dam changed the water temperature in the river.

   B   Fish were unable to swim upstream, which affected their life cycle.

   C   The electricity produced by the dam killed the fish.

   D   The dam was a source of pollution that killed the fish.

> **Tip**
> Look for information in more than one place.

2. **For how long did the Edwards Dam exist?**

   A   just over 100 years

   B   two years

   C   two decades

   D   more than 150 years

3. **What were the benefits of removing the Edwards Dam?**

   A   Fish returned, and logs were retrieved and reused.

   B   Tourism and fishing increased in the Augusta, Maine area.

   C   The local electric utility received an increase in revenues.

   D   The Kennebec River became a source of energy again.

4. **What was the significance of the decision to tear down the Edwards Dam for other hydroelectric dams over rivers in the U.S.?**

5. **The article refers to the benefits of the Edwards Dam as well as the damage it caused. Explain what you think the benefits were and why the government decided to tear down the dam. Use details from the article in your answer.**

Write on Demand

People often have strong opinions about issues. Think about an issue about which you have strong feelings. Now write a persuasive essay to <u>convince</u> others to <u>agree with</u> your opinion.

Persuasive writing tries to influence the reader to agree with an opinion.

To figure out if a prompt calls for persuasive writing, look for clue words such as <u>convince</u> or <u>agree with</u>.

Below, see how one student begins a response to the prompt above.

The Good Side of a Dam

Sometimes scientists make demands that are unreasonable. Tearing down a dam is an example of what I'm referring to.

I'm all for protecting the environment, but I'm not for letting a fish cause the destruction of a dam. People's rights are "righter" than animals' rights. A hydroelectric dam generates much-needed electricity for an area. We need electricity to keep people working and help the economy.

So I say no, let's not sacrifice dams and our economy to help plants and animals.

The writer uses details to support an opinion about tearing down a dam.

Writing Prompt

Respond in writing to the prompt below. Write for 25 minutes. Write as much as you can, as well as you can. Review the hints below before and after you write.

 Some people believe the government should ban certain kinds of cars that use a lot of gas. Others think the government should not restrict the kinds of cars people buy. Write a persuasive essay on this topic, stating your opinion and supporting it with details.

Writing Hints for Prompts

☑ Read the prompt carefully.

☑ Organize your ideas to plan your writing.

☑ Support your opinion by giving reasons and using details.

☑ Combine sentences to add variety and show emotions.

☑ Choose precise words that help readers understand your ideas.

☑ Review your writing and edit as needed.

CA **Talk About It**

What do you know about sled dogs? How could a sled dog become a hero?

LOG ON ▶ Find out more about sled dogs saving people at **www.macmillanmh.com**.

SAVING A TOWN

THE LAST
GREAT RACE
ON EARTH

by David Goldberg

Life is different in Anchorage, Alaska, at the beginning of March. Every year at this time, the downtown streets become crowded with people. But these are not just regular **pedestrians**. In addition to the people walking through the streets, there are hundreds of dogs. It is time for the Iditarod—the famous dogsled race of Alaska.

The name of the race comes from the name of an Alaska gold rush town, Iditarod. It means "distant" or "distant place." It comes from one of the languages of native Alaskans.

More than sixty sled teams begin the race in Anchorage. When the teams reach the **outskirts** of town, they get a taste of Alaska's wilderness. For about two weeks, they will fight the **unbearable** cold, wind, snow, and ice to finish the race. The temperature on the trail is often well below zero degrees.

The Iditarod trail stretches for about a thousand miles. It has many **rendezvous** points. At these meeting places, race teams "check in" to let officials know how they are doing. Some teams get into trouble along the way. Officials will **intercept** them on the trail and give them the help they need. For example, officials might stop a team's progress to give first aid or to collect an injured or tired dog. These dogs are cared for and reunited with their owners after the race.

The Iditarod trail is an important part of Alaska's history. A part of the trail was used by some heroic dogs and humans in 1925. In Nome, Alaska, many people were catching the deadly disease diphtheria. The whole town was in **quarantine**, or isolation, in order to stop this **epidemic**. The only way to get medicine to Nome was by dogsled. About twenty "mushers," or dogsled drivers, offered to help. They wanted to save the people of Nome from this terrible **plight**.

Today the Iditarod race honors this heroic journey and all of the journeys on the famous trail. As the race organizers say, the Iditarod is "the last great race on Earth."

Reread for Comprehension

Summarize
Sequence
Knowing the order, or sequence, of events in a story will help you better understand the narrative. A Sequence Chart can help you organize the events in the order that they happened. This will help you summarize the story.

Use a Sequence Chart to list the events as you reread "The Last Great Race on Earth."

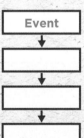

Event

Genre

Nonfiction is a detailed account of real people or situations using verifiable facts.

Summarize

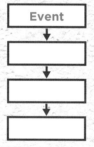

Sequence

As you read, use your Sequence Chart.

Event
↓
↓
↓

Read to Find Out

What role did the sled dogs play in the sequence of events?

THE GREAT SERUM RACE

Nome

Anchorage

BLAZING THE IDITAROD TRAIL

BY DEBBIE S. MILLER

ILLUSTRATIONS BY JON VAN ZYLE

*I*n March every year, dog sled teams and drivers from all over the world compete in the *Iditarod Trail Sled Dog Race*. This race, over a thousand miles from Anchorage to Nome, Alaska, commemorates the famous serum run of 1925. It is the longest sled dog race in the world. In this selection, you will read about how it all began.

On a dusky January afternoon in 1925, Dr. Welch walked quickly toward the **outskirts** of Nome. Sled dogs howled from their yards. Outside a small cabin, a worried Inupiat Eskimo mother greeted the doctor. She led him into her home where two small children lay in bed, struggling to breathe.

"Can you open your mouth?" Dr. Welch asked the three-year-old boy.

The weak child tried to open his mouth, but it was too painful for his swollen throat. His fever was extremely high. Dr. Welch comforted the mother and children, but there was little he could do. The next day, both children died.

Soon after, another girl, Bessie Stanley, was miserable with the same symptoms. But this time, Dr. Welch could examine Bessie's throat. He immediately recognized the symptoms of diphtheria. Poor Bessie would not live through the night.

Diphtheria. Dr. Welch had not seen a case in twenty years. This fast-spreading disease could wipe out the entire community of more than 1,400 people. Dr. Welch immediately met with the city council and recommended a **quarantine**. The schools and other public places were closed. Community leaders told people to stay in their homes.

There was only one way to fight diphtheria. The town needed a supply of antitoxin serum. Dr. Welch sent out a desperate plea for help by radio telegraph. The message soon reached Governor Bone in Juneau and other important officials. Newspapers across the nation picked up word that the historic gold rush town needed emergency help.

The nearest supply of serum was at a hospital in Anchorage, 1,000 miles away, across a snowbound wilderness. Officials considered flying the serum to Nome, but it was too dangerous to operate open cockpit planes in extreme cold temperatures. In those days, planes were used only during the summer. Nome was an icebound port, so boats were not an option. The serum could travel partway by train, and then the only safe means of transport was by sled dog team.

On January 26, an Anchorage doctor carefully packed the glass bottles of serum for the long journey. The bottles had to be protected to keep the serum from freezing. He gave the twenty-pound bundle to the conductor at the train station.

Sequence
What event started the great serum race? When did it take place?

Soon, steam engine 66 began to chug its way north to Nenana, the closest railroad link to Nome. Nenana lay nearly 300 miles away, beyond the tallest mountains of North America.

On the frozen Tanana River, five-year-old Alfred John could hear the distant roar of the steam engine. His Athabaskan Indian family lived in a cabin near the train station in Nenana. Although it was late at night and nearly fifty degrees below zero, Alfred and his mother bundled up in their warmest caribou legskin boots and fur-lined parkas and walked to the station to greet the train.

As they waited by the tracks in the moonlight, Alfred watched the huge locomotive hiss steam into the frozen sky and slow to a screeching halt. He saw men unload the freight, and the conductor hand the serum package to Bill Shannon. Bill was the first of twenty mushers to carry the serum in a dog team relay to Nome. These brave men and their best dogs would travel nearly 700 miles on a snow-packed mail trail.

Bill covered the serum with a bear hide and lashed it to the sled. His strongest team of nine malamutes barked and were anxious to move. Just before midnight on January 27, Bill waved good-bye to Alfred and shouted to his dogs. *Swoosh!* Into the winter night, the dog team sped toward Tolovana, the first relay stop some fifty-two miles away.

Bill knew every turn of the trail. Like many of the mushers, his regular job was to transport mail and freight with his dog team. Traveling long distances in the extreme cold was a dangerous challenge. If the dogs ran too fast and breathed too deeply, they could frost their lungs. When the team reached bitter-cold stretches along the river, Bill slowed his dogs to protect them. He often ran behind the sled to keep himself warm.

Hundreds of miles away, Togo leaned into his harness and waited patiently for Leonhard Seppala to position Scotty and the other huskies. Togo, now twelve years old, was a proven leader for one of the strongest dog teams in the world. Leonhard, dressed in his warmest squirrel parka, sealskin pants, and reindeer mukluks, had carefully chosen twenty of his best dogs. Officials had asked the famed Norwegian musher to **intercept** the serum at Nulato, a village located halfway between Nome and Nenana.

Jingle, jangle—the bells on Leonhard's sled rang as the team rounded the corner. There were so many dog teams in Nome that mushers were required to carry bells to warn **pedestrians**. Togo led the team down Front Street while friends wished them good luck.

In Tolovana, Edgar Kalland, the twenty-year-old Athabaskan Indian mail driver, ate breakfast and waited anxiously for Bill Shannon. The Tolovana Roadhouse was a favorite rest stop for Edgar. Outside the roadhouse, Edgar's dogs pricked up their ears, and some began to howl. Bill's team drew closer.

The team looked exhausted when their frosted faces came into view. Two of the dogs would later die from frozen lungs. Following the doctor's instructions, Bill carefully removed the serum. He hurried into the roadhouse to warm the container and prevent the serum from freezing. As the two men talked about the weather, Edgar put on three pairs of socks and his boots.

Once the serum warmed, Edgar took off for Manley Hot Springs with his team of seven dogs. The thirty-one-mile trip to the next relay point was brutally cold. Temperatures fell to fifty-six degrees below zero. At one point the dogs had to wade through slushy overflow, a place where the river seeped through a crack in the ice. When the team reached Manley Hot Springs, the dogs could barely lift their ice-crusted legs. Edgar's mitts were frozen stiff to the sled handle. A roadhouse worker poured a kettle of hot water over the mitts to melt the ice and free Edgar's hands.

The relay continued from musher to musher, roadhouse to roadhouse, with teams pushing west through the biting cold. At each relay point, the mushers warmed the serum over wood-fired stoves. Following the winding rivers, the teams covered an average of thirty miles each, at a speed of six or seven miles per hour. The mushers traveled around the clock, usually by moonlight or twilight. In the middle of Alaska's winter, only a few hours of sunshine fell on the teams each day.

When the twelfth dog team headed for the village of Nulato, waves of northern lights flowed across the sky. Musher Charlie Evans faced the coldest temperatures at sixty-four degrees below zero. He wrapped the serum in a rabbit skin robe for extra protection. Charlie's nine-dog team moved slowly. Near open stretches of water on the Yukon River, a layer of eerie ice fog blanketed the valley. The ice fog, a mist of ice particles, was so dense that Charlie could barely see his wheel dogs, the ones closest to the sled. The experienced dogs followed the trail by scent rather than sight.

Nearing Nulato, two of the dogs moved stiffly and dragged their paws. The skin was beginning to freeze. Charlie stopped the team and gently loaded the poor dogs into the sled. In their struggle to save the lives of Nome's residents, these two dogs would fall victim to the deadly weather.

When the team reached the halfway point, conditions in Nome had grown worse. Five people had died from the disease, and more than twenty cases had been diagnosed. Another thirty people were suspected of having diphtheria. Newspapers across the country reported Nome's **plight** and the progress of the serum run.

The relay teams pressed onward. Togo and team worked their way east to intercept the serum. When Leonhard passed villages, he told residents about the **epidemic** and advised them to stay away from Nome. As the team approached the village of Shaktoolik, Togo picked up the scent of another dog team and sprinted forward. Leonhard could see a musher in the distance trying to untangle his string of dogs.

"On by!" Leonhard shouted to Togo.

Togo followed the familiar directions and steered the team away from the confusion.

"Serum—turn back!" shouted Henry Ivanoff, one of the relay mushers.

In the howling wind Leonhard barely heard the words. Luckily, he looked over his shoulder to see the musher waving frantically at him. Leonhard was surprised to see the relay team. After he set out for Nulato, twenty more mushers were chosen to travel short relays to speed up the serum run. Out in the wilderness, Leonhard had no idea that his **rendezvous** point was now 130 miles closer.

"Gee!" Leonhard yelled to Togo.

Togo gradually turned right and the swing dogs helped pull the sled toward the waiting team. The two men greeted each other briefly, shouting in the gale. Within minutes Leonhard had secured the serum package to his sled and instructed Togo to head home.

Togo and his teammate had traveled more than forty miles that day with the wind at their backs. Now the fierce gale blew in their faces with thirty below zero temperatures. Blowing snow plastered the team as they approached Norton Bay. Leonhard considered the risks. If they crossed the frozen bay, the sea ice might break up in the powerful gale. They could be stranded from shore on drifting ice. If they skirted the bay on land, the trip would take much longer. Leonhard thought of the children in Nome who were suffering from the disease. He decided to take the shorter route and cross the treacherous sea ice.

Leonhard believed that Togo could lead the team across twenty miles of frozen sea. As they pressed into the wind the dogs hit slick stretches of glare ice. They slipped, fell, and struggled to move forward. But mile after mile, Togo kept his course through the wall of wind. At day's end, Togo picked up the scent of food that drifted from the Inupiat sod house at Isaac's Point. After traveling eighty-four miles, they rested for the night. The dogs devoured their rations of salmon and seal blubber.

The following morning, Leonhard discovered that the previous day's trail had vanished. The ice had broken up and drifted out to sea. Worried about the unstable conditions, Leonhard decided to hug the shoreline for safety.

Togo led the way toward Dexter's Roadhouse in Golovin, about fifty miles away. Along the coast, the wind's force became **unbearable**. Blowing snow blasted the dogs' faces like buckshot. Some of the dogs began to stiffen up. Leonhard stopped the sled and gently massaged the freezing muscles of Togo, Scotty, and the others. When they finally reached Golovin, the dogs collapsed and buried their ice-coated faces beneath their tails. Togo and team had traveled farther than any other relay team.

Now it was another dog's turn to lead a fresh team of seventeen malamutes to Bluff, the final relay point. With a shout from musher Charlie Olson, lead dog Jack charged off into the blowing snow. After struggling through four hours of whiteout conditions, the experienced leader faintly heard a dog barking through the gale. It was Balto.

At Bluff, Balto and Fox waited for Gunnar Kaasen to adjust the leather harnesses and secure the serum package. Then the pair of leaders heard their musher's shout through the raging wind. Balto and Fox led the strong team of thirteen huskies into the swirling snow. Mile after mile, they trotted steadily toward Nome. During the final leg of the run, the wind assaulted them. A violent gust flipped the sled over, and the dogs went flying.

Sequence
What happened after Gunnar Kaasen received the serum?

Gunnar struggled to his feet against the might of the wind. After he fought to untangle the dogs, he checked the sled to make sure the serum was securely fastened. Gunnar felt the bottom of the sled in disbelief. The serum package was gone!

In the dark, he crawled around the sled. Since he couldn't see his surroundings, he took off his mitts and felt through the snow with his bare hands. After more than 600 hard-won miles and twenty teams risking their lives, could it be that the serum was lost forever?

Panicked, Gunnar ran his numb hands across the windswept bumps of snow. All he could do was hope. Suddenly, he felt something hard. It was the serum! His frostbitten fingers struggled to tie the package onto the sled. Then the wind-battered team ran off.

They struggled on through the night. With less than twenty miles remaining, two of the dogs ran stiffly and appeared to be freezing. Gunnar anchored the sled and put rabbit-skin covers on the dogs to protect their undersides from frostbite.

Through the darkness, Balto and Fox smelled familiar scents. At last the exhausted team reached Nome. They drove into town as most people slept through the blizzard. When Gunnar knocked on the door, Dr. Welch greeted him with a stunned face. How could a musher and team have fought their way through such a storm?

With stiff hands, Gunnar gave the shocked but thankful doctor the life-saving serum.

Twenty brave mushers and more than 160 strong dogs traveled hundreds of miles in the worst conditions. The incredible relay took less than six days. Four dogs perished and several others grew lame because of the lethal weather. Yet their struggle saved many lives in Nome.

One month after the epidemic first began, the quarantine was lifted. The schools reopened and children hugged their old friends. The whole town celebrated by holding a dance and watching a movie at the theater. Togo, Scotty, Balto, Fox, Jack, and all the other dogs were true heroes.

ON THE TRAIL WITH

Debbie

Jon

Debbie S. Miller can look out her window and see a moose, a fox, and piles of snow. She lives in Alaska and used to teach school in an arctic village in the Brooks Mountain Range, near the Arctic Circle. Ideas for her books are all around her—the ice and snow, the polar bears, and, of course, those amazing husky dogs.

Jon Van Zyle and his wife live with twenty husky dogs and a black cat named Dickens near Eagle River, Alaska. Jon is the official artist for the Iditarod Trail Sled Dog Race. He has even competed twice in the race himself—all 1,049 miles of it!

Other books by Debbie S. Miller: *Disappearing Lake* and *Flight of the Golden Plover*

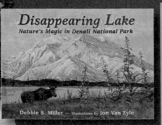

CA **Author's Purpose**

Debbie Miller is informing the reader about the origins of the Iditarod. The text is full of verifiable facts such as dates and distances. What are some examples?

 Find out more about Debbie S. Miller and Jon Van Zyle at **www.macmillanmh.com**.

 Critical Thinking

Summarize

Use your Sequence Chart to help you summarize *The Great Serum Race*. What were the series of events that led to the serum getting safely to Nome?

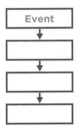

Think and Compare

1. When the serum traveled to Nome during the **epidemic**, what was the **sequence** in which the mushers handed off the serum? **Summarize: Sequence**

2. In your opinion, who made the biggest contribution to the successful delivery of the serum to the people of Nome? Use specific examples from the text to support your answer. **Synthesize**

3. Think about a time when you had to work with a team of people to get something important done. How was working as a team important to achieving your goal? **Analyze**

4. The mushers and dog sled teams involved in the serum race are heroes. What do you think makes a hero? Compare the heroes in *The Great Serum Race* to other heroes you know or have read about. What do they have in common? **Evaluate**

5. Read "The Last Great Race on Earth" on pages 680–681. Why is it important that the Iditarod feature the checkpoints and medical assistance described in this selection? Use specific evidence from *The Great Serum Race* to support your answer. **Reading/Writing Across Texts**

Poetry

Haiku

Haiku is an unrhymed form of Japanese poetry that is three lines long. The first line often has five syllables; the second line, seven syllables; the third line, five syllables. Haiku often describes something in nature.

✓ Literary Elements

Symbolism is the use of an everyday thing to stand for something more meaningful.

Metaphor is a comparison of two essentially unlike things.

Snow-swallowed valley,
Only the winding river . . .
Black fluent brush stroke.
　　　　—Boncho

The winding river is compared to a painting's single brush stroke.

A storm-wind blows—
out from among the grasses
the full moon grows.
　　　　—Chora

The sound of water symbolizes renewal and the coming of spring.

A mountain village:
Under piled-up snow
the sound of water.
　　　　　　—Shiki

 **Critical Thinking**

1. What else might Shiki have used to symbolize the coming of spring? **Symbolism**

2. How does the choice of season help convey the mood of these poems? How do the poems make you feel? **Evaluate**

3. Compare and contrast the weather and feelings of isolation described in these poems with that portrayed in *The Great Serum Race*. **Reading/Writing Across Texts**

 Find out more about haiku at **www.macmillanmh.com**.

Writing

✔ Subjects and Predicates

Good writers are clear in their use of **subjects and predicates**.

Reading and Writing Connection

Read the passage below. Notice how author Debbie Miller starts with a simple sentence in which Bill is the subject. As she shows the complexity of his challenge, she introduces complex sentences.

The author uses complex subjects and predicates to help us see how skilled Bill has to be to survive as a musher.

An excerpt from
The Great Serum Race

Bill knew every turn of the trail. Like many of the mushers, his regular job was to transport mail and freight with his dog team. Traveling long distances in the extreme cold was a dangerous challenge. If the dogs ran too fast and breathed too deeply, they could frost their lungs. When the team reached bitter-cold stretches along the river, Bill slowed his dogs to protect them. He often ran behind the sled to keep himself warm.

Read and Find

Read Jeff's writing below. How did Jeff use particular subjects to move our attention from him to the people watching him and then back to him?

The Dancing Lesson

by Jeff L.

Sweat poured down my head as I struggled to move to the rhythm of the song. The music sounded funny to me, and I lost my concentration. When I couldn't move correctly, the teacher had to help me. I felt embarrassed. It felt as if all eyes were on me. I followed the steps. When I was done, everyone clapped.

Read how one student grappled with a dancing lesson.

Writer's Checklist

✓ Does the writer choose subjects that focus on the critical elements of the piece?

✓ Does the writer use predicates that help you understand each subject?

☑ Do subjects and predicates add meaning?

Rebuilding

CA **Talk About It**

What and why are these people rebuilding?

LOG ON ▶ Find out more about fires at www.macmillanmh.com.

⚡ Vocabulary

structures	**volunteered**
exterior	**perished**
residents	**consumed**
flee	**exhaustion**

✔ Context Clues

Surrounding words **within a paragraph** can help you find the meaning of unfamiliar words. Find *exterior* in the first paragraph. Use another word in the same sentence to figure out what *exterior* means. Where was the wood used for decoration?

The Great London Fire

By Jonathon Drysdale

Accidental fires were common in London, England, during the 1600s. This was because open fires burned in houses, shops, workshops, and other **structures** all the time. People used fire to cook, keep warm, and to make pottery and metal objects. Wood was the most common building material. It was also used for **exterior**, or outside decoration. Straw for horses was stored in stables on almost every street. Many people also laid straw on their floor. Both of these materials burn very easily.

In the early hours of Sunday morning, September 2, 1666, a fire broke out in the king's own bakery on Pudding Lane. This was a narrow street with very few houses and **residents**, because most of the buildings were shops. As a result, once fire took hold in the bakery kitchen, it spread very quickly.

One young woman who lived above the bakery tried to **flee** from the flames and get away by jumping from the roof onto another building. She became the fire's first victim.

There was no fire department in London in the 1600s. Local people usually **volunteered** to put out fires without pay, filling leather buckets with water or beating the flames with rugs or brooms. But because of the strong wind that night, this fire was soon burning out of control. In no time the fire spread to other nearby streets.

By Sunday morning 300 buildings had **perished**. They had been destroyed and **consumed** by the flames. Only ashes remained. Londoners poured out of their homes, trying to save what they could from the blaze. The writer Samuel Pepys noticed that many people chose to save their musical instruments. People with valuables buried them or hid them in city sewers before finding their way to safety.

On Tuesday the fire headed west and destroyed Old St. Paul's Cathedral. The writer John Evelyn described melting lead running down the pavement in a stream, "glowing with fiery redness." After almost three days, many people fighting the fire were tired and suffering from **exhaustion**. By Wednesday, however, the wind died down and the fire was finally put out on Thursday night.

More than 13,000 houses were destroyed in the fire of 1666. Luckily, only five people were killed by the flames. The fire left over 200,000 people homeless, and now they faced a great task: rebuilding the city of London.

Reread for Comprehension

Analyze Text Structure

Cause and Effect

A cause is why an event happens. The effect is what happens. Visualizing the events that an author writes about will help you to better understand the cause-and-effect relationships between events and the organization of the story.

Use your Cause and Effect Chart to record important causes of events as you reread "The Great London Fire."

Cause ➜ Effect
➜
➜
➜
➜

CA Comprehension

Genre

Nonfiction is a detailed account of real situations or people using verifiable facts.

Analyze Text Structure

Cause and Effect
As you read, fill in your Cause and Effect Chart.

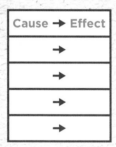

Cause ➔ Effect
➔
➔
➔
➔

Read to Find Out

What made it possible for some people to survive the disastrous fire which destroyed Chicago?

The Great Fire

by Jim Murphy

On the evening of Sunday, October 8, 1871, a fire began in a small barn on the far west side of Chicago, Illinois. The wind, which had been strong all day, picked up the flames, and for over 31 hours drove them through the very heart of the city.

Panic and fear swept through the city as over 100,000 people were forced to flee what would later become known as the "Great Fire." Joseph Chamberlin, a reporter, covered the fire for the *Chicago Evening Post*. Many survivors later wrote about their experiences. Among them were Julia Lemos, a mother who had to save her five children, and Alexander Frear, who rushed to rescue his relatives with help from their friend Mr. Wood.

James Hildreth came up with a bold plan to save the city. He used explosives to blow up empty houses and create firebreaks. These cleared areas would help stop the spread of the fire. Claire Innes, a 12-year-old girl, was separated from her family by the flames. She later described being locked inside an alley, trapped, with the fire coming at her from all sides . . . .

$\mathcal{C}$laire wasted little time in being frightened. Her first thought was to see if one or the other of the alley openings might be passable despite the billowing smoke. She got within thirty feet of the thick smoke only to be driven back. "The heat was like that of an oven. I tried to open the door to a building but found it bolted. Smoke was escaping from under the other doors, so I gave up hope of finding safety through them."

As the roofs and then the interiors of the surrounding **structures** were **consumed** by flames, a scorching wind swept around the alley. The rain of burning embers grew heavier and more unbearable. Claire retreated, seeking the safest, coolest place, and found herself back at the construction site.

"I cannot say that I actually decided to hide behind the bricks since I could not hear myself think in the terrible noise. I did not even look at the fire, but hid my face in the dirt and pulled my bundle, which I had retrieved, over my head."

For understandable reasons, Claire did not spend much time observing the burning buildings around her, so her description of what happened is limited. It can reasonably be assumed that she was surrounded by a frightening cacophony of sounds—wood igniting and burning wildly, the glass of windows exploding, stairways and ceilings collapsing. When the interior support framing of a building had been eaten through and weakened enough, parts of the **exterior** brick walls would fall with a ground-rumbling roar.

The pile of bricks Claire hid behind shielded her from the severest heat and most of the flying debris. But there is little doubt that she had a great deal of luck on her side as well. For one thing, it's likely that most of the building walls did not collapse to release a wave of fire and heat; those walls that did give way, fell far enough from her that she was not crushed. Other factors may have contributed to her survival. The buildings that ringed the construction site might have had few windows, thus containing the baking heat of their

Crosby's Opera House burns while pedestrians scamper to safety. Just moments before this scene, a restaurant in the opera house was still serving customers. (*Harper's Weekly*, October 28, 1871)

fires to some extent. Most important, a deadly convection column never established itself in the immediate area so a blanket of killing heat and fire did not cover her.

Exactly how long it took for the buildings to burn is not clear; Claire only says that it took "many minutes." It probably took much longer, an hour or more for the fires to completely gut the structures that lined the alley. During all of this time, "[I] kept my head hidden beneath the bundle and said my prayers."

Cause and Effect
What were some of the reasons that Claire survived the fire?

Once the main force of the fires began to lessen, Claire peeked out. What she saw must have astonished her. Sturdy brick structures had been transformed into blackened skeletons whose insides continued to burn brightly. Still, Claire had more immediate concerns.

"My legs and arms and back [were] all burnt where my dress caught fire. . . . I put out the fire and made ready to leave which was not easy as the [alleyway] openings were blocked with brick and burning wood and smoke. I called [for help] again and again and at last a voice called back to me through the smoke. He told me to stand away from there as a wall of the building might fall on me, and that was all. This made me even more alarmed, but I did not want to stay in the alley alone, so I began climbing. The bricks were still

The streets of Chicago are jammed with frightened people trying to escape the flames. In this kind of confusion, it is easy to understand how Claire Innes was separated from her family.

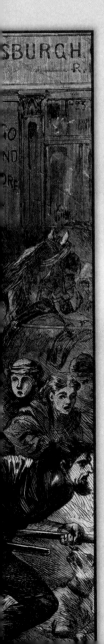

hot—very hot—but I found that if I did not stop [moving] my feet were not burnt so bad."

Claire scrambled over the smoldering pile of debris and made it to the street. She was by no means safe. Buildings up and down the block were burning and collapsing, punctuated every so often by the explosion of flammable liquids. Abandoned pieces of furniture on the street and sidewalk were fiery torches, while shadowy figures darted through the night seeking a safe escape. Claire made her way along the street with single-minded purpose. "Now," she said, sensing the enormity of the task facing her, "I had to find my family in all of this."

During the night, James Hildreth and his men were hard at work trying to prevent the fire from spreading south. After the first few blasts failed to bring down the structures, Hildreth figured out precisely how much powder was needed. Soon he and his helpers were blasting apart house after house along Harrison Street. By the time they had reached the Wabash Avenue Methodist Episcopal Church, they were capable of setting off a powerful charge every five minutes.

With the houses leveled, local **residents** grabbed buckets and kept the debris soaked until the threat of fire passed. Hildreth's methods appeared harsh to many people, especially those who saw their homes blown up while the fire was still blocks away. But there is little doubt that the firebreaks he created halted the southward creep of the fire and saved several blocks of homes from destruction.

While the fire was being contained in the south, to the north another story was unfolding. The width and speed of the fire made it impossible for weary firemen to work in an organized or coordinated way. Besides, they were now beyond **exhaustion**. Two nights of fire fighting and little rest or food had pushed many to the brink of collapse. Several had to be taken from the area in wagons. One tired fireman sat down on a street corner to catch his breath and promptly fell asleep despite the roar of the fire around him.

At six o'clock on Monday morning, the fire had been burning over nine hours, and seemed capable of continuing its march north unless more help could be found. Chicago's mayor, Robert B. Mason, had been up all night receiving reports about the spread of the fire and praying for a miracle. Finally, he gave up hope and sent urgent telegrams to the surrounding cities and towns. "CHICAGO IS IN FLAMES," read his message to the mayor of Milwaukee. "SEND YOUR WHOLE DEPARTMENT TO HELP US."

Aid came pouring in from Milwaukee, Cincinnati, Dayton, Louisville, Detroit, Port Huron, Bloomington, Springfield, Janesville, Allegheny, and Pittsburgh. Some cities sent steamers and ladder wagons, others sent badly needed hose and fresh firefighters. And many did so at great risk. Milwaukee put three steamers and their crews onboard a train, leaving that city with only one working engine.

The sun rose on Monday, and Chicago continued to burn. The fire went largely unchecked because the additional men and equipment took many hours to arrive.

After narrowly escaping the flames the night before, Joseph Chamberlin had gone to the North Division to watch the fire there. Just before seven o'clock, he went back to the West Division. "Then a curious-looking crimson ball came out of the lake, which they said was the sun; but oh, how sickly and insignificant it looked! I had watched the greatest of the world's conflagrations from its beginning . . . and although the fire was still blazing all over the city with undiminished luster, I could not look at it. I was almost unable to walk with exhaustion and the effects of a long season of excitement, and sought my home for an hour's sleep."

Chamberlin went up Madison Street into an area untouched by the fire and was startled when he met "scores of working girls on their way 'down town' as usual, bearing their lunch-baskets, as if nothing had happened. They saw the fire and smoke before them, but could not believe that the city, with their means of livelihood, had been swept away during the night."

Because telephones, radios, and televisions did not exist, people in the distant portions of Chicago did not know very much about the fire. Many people had seen the bright glow in the distance, but the true degree of disaster was not known until burned-out friends and relatives began knocking on their doors. Then, telegraph lines hummed with brief accounts of the tragedy, and these details were passed from city to city. Fuller accounts would follow. Before the end of Monday, the Chicago *Evening Journal* managed to get a one-page edition onto the streets. In searing headlines, it announced:

THE GREAT CALAMITY OF THE AGE!

Chicago in Ashes!!

Hundreds of Millions of Dollars' Worth of Property Destroyed

The South, the North and a Portion of the West Divisions of the City in Ruins.

All the Hotels, Banks, Public Buildings, Newspaper Offices and Great Business Blocks Swept Away.

The Conflagration Still in Progress.

Fury of the Flames.

Details, Etc., Etc.

Alexander Frear probably wished he could turn his back on the fire and find a cozy bed. Unfortunately, his adventures with the fire were far from over.

After fleeing across the burning bridge, Frear went directly to where his sister-in-law's house had been, his heart filled with grief. He had long ago decided that her three children had **perished** in the fire; now, on top of this, he had lost track of his sister-in-law, Mr. Wood, and another nephew in the chaos of the night. He presumed the worst.

He must have been pleasantly shocked not just to discover the house intact but to be greeted at the door by his nephew and Mr. Wood. What's more, they "informed me that Mrs. Frear had been taken to a private house in Huron Street, and was perfectly safe and well cared for."

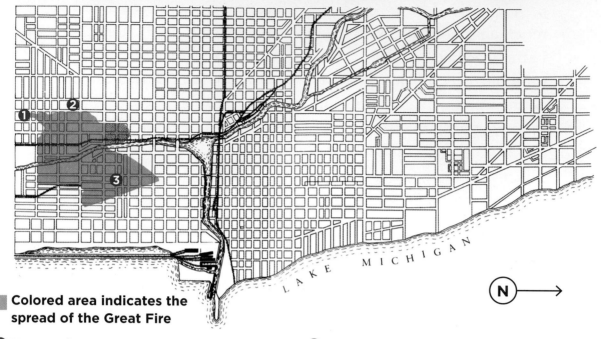

BEGINNING STAGES OF THE GREAT FIRE IN CHICAGO

Colored area indicates the spread of the Great Fire

❶ House of Patrick and Catherine O'Leary, where the fire started

❷ Home of Alexander Frear's sister-in-law

❸ Neighborhood where Claire Innes and her family lived

At this point, Frear gave in to his physical exhaustion. "I was wet and scorched and bedraggled. My clothes were burnt full of holes on my arms and shoulders and back. . . . I fell down in the hallway and went to sleep."

Less than a half hour later, Frear was shaken awake and told that "Mrs. Frear must be moved again."

Mr. Wood knew exactly where she was on Huron Street and **volunteered** to lead Frear there. They went as quickly as possible up Des Plaines Street. For most of the way, houses blocked their view of the burnt and burning section of the city, but when they neared a bridge crossing to the North Division, the view opened up before them.

"It was about eight-thirty o'clock," Frear recalled. "We could see across the river at the cross streets that where yesterday was a populous city was now a mass of smoking ruins. All the way round we encountered thousands of people; but the excitement had given way to a terrible grief and desolation."

For the first time since the start of the fire, the light of day allowed everyone to see and feel the true extent of damage. Alfred Sewell noted the stunned emotions of the vast majority of citizens: "O, what a horrible scene was presented to the view of the spectator on that gloomy [morning]. . . . Heaps of ruins, and here and there a standing wall, as far as the eye could reach, and far beyond, for a stretch of four miles. . . . We walked through the streets, covered everywhere with heaps of debris and parts of walls, and could not help comparing ourselves to ghosts wandering through a vast grave-yard. 'Am I really awake, or am I having a horrible dream?' is a question we seriously asked ourselves many times. . . ."

People were stunned and overwhelmed, and probably feared the worst about relatives and friends who might have been in the path of the Great Fire. But Frear had to push aside his emotions and exhaustion—his sister-in-law was still somewhere near the burning fire, and he had to act if she was to be saved.

"Luckily Wood knew where to find Mrs. Frear, and [we] arrived at the house just in time to get her into a baker's wagon, which Wood and I pulled for half a mile."

His sister-in-law was still distraught over the loss of her children, and grew even more agitated when they passed a wagon loaded with frightened children. Frear and Wood hurried away as quickly as possible, weaving around the piles of personal property abandoned in the road.

Once back at his sister-in-law's home, Frear tried to make her comfortable, aided by the capable hands and kind words of neighbors. The shock of his experiences began to set in and he was overtaken by a pounding headache and fever. He had run the gauntlet of flames, risked his life several times in a futile effort to locate his young nieces and nephew, and barely managed to escape.

Imagine his feelings when, at four in the afternoon, the solemn, sad whispers in the house were replaced by loud, joyous shouts. A second later, Frear discovered that "word came from the Kimballs that the children were all safe out at Riverside." It was then that Frear could drag himself to a bedroom, climb into a bed, and pull a quilt over his head to shut out the fire.

As Frear slept, the fire went north with little opposition. House after house ignited and burned to the ground, leaving behind blackened foundations and charred heaps of wood. This area contained some of the city's largest, most stately homes, but the fire treated them with the same disdain it did the humblest wooden cottages on De Koven Street.

With the water supply gone, firemen could do very little unless they were near the river or lake and could draw water directly from those sources. Not even Hildreth's special talent with powder prevailed. After creating an effective firebreak in the south, Hildreth took his powder and scooted north to get in front of the fire. He took with him only two helpers, assuming that residents of the threatened blocks would eagerly volunteer. He tried to stop a number of men hurrying to escape, but none responded.

"I grabbed hold of them, took right hold of them with more force than if I'd been sheriff . . . but they would leave me, just as soon as I would take my hands off them, and cut. The word 'powder' was a terror to them."

Finally, Hildreth, frustrated and weary, admitted defeat and headed home.

The same chaos and flight took hold of the northern section of the city. Alfred Sewell remembered the panic in the North Division: "Like an immense drove of panic-

stricken sheep, the terrified mass ran, and rushed, and scrambled, and screamed through the streets. . . ."

Men who wrote about the Great Fire generally portrayed women as passive and helpless, waiting for their husbands, brothers, or some other man to save them. This seemed to go doubly for women who were wealthier. But if we look beyond the condescending references, a remarkable picture of strong and active women emerges. Sewell might describe women as "weak and delicate [and] accustomed to no toil or trial" but they still managed to flee "with their arms full of treasures rescued from their doomed homes, and some even shouldered valises and trunks with the strength of strong men, and bore and dragged them through the crowd."

Chicago is blackened and burned, and several ships on Lake Michigan are in flames. The fire would continue to burn until it reached Fullerton Avenue, which is to the right almost two miles from the front wall of the fire shown here.

A slightly elevated view looking along Clark Street (to the left). Most of the buildings have collapsed or been completely consumed; those still standing in the distance have been gutted and will have to be leveled.

Or take the case of Julia Lemos. Lemos was a recent widow and the mother of five. In addition, she was taking care of her ailing mother and elderly father, all while holding down a job as an artist in a lithographer's shop. At the end of September, Lemos found the burden of caring for all of these dependents overwhelming, and, reluctantly and tearfully, she placed four of her children in the nearby Half-Orphan Asylum. She hoped that her mother would recover quickly so that the separation would be a very short one.

Lemos found the situation very hard emotionally. While the chores were a bit easier, she missed her children and worried about them constantly. On the weekend of the fire, Lemos went to the asylum to get her children back, but was told that it was against official policy to release them just then.

Monday morning, Lemos woke to discover that the fire was heading toward their block. Her first course of action was to march to the asylum to demand that her children be turned over to her without any official mumbo jumbo. With her children in tow, she hurried home to organize their flight.

Since Lemos had little money, she went next door to her landlord's house and asked for the twelve dollars she had given him for that month's rent. He refused to give back any money, but when she didn't leave, he offered a compromise: he would take a load of her possessions to the prairie for the rent money. Lemos agreed and got two large trunks packed and on the wagon, plus a mattress and a featherbed.

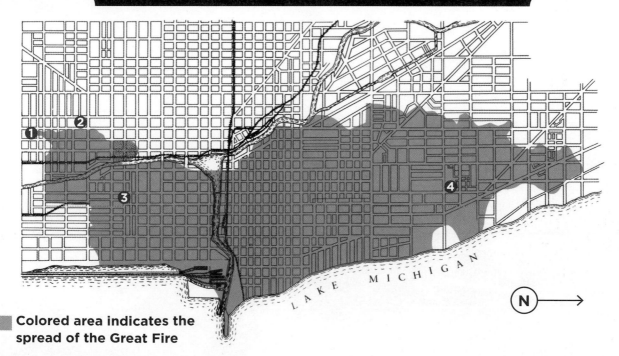

FINAL STAGES OF THE GREAT FIRE IN CHICAGO

Colored area indicates the spread of the Great Fire

❶ House of Patrick and Catherine O'Leary, where the fire started

❷ Home of Alexander Frear's sister-in-law

❸ Neighborhood where Claire Innes and her family lived

❹ Approximate location of Julia Lemos's home

At this point, her aged father balked at leaving the house, insisting that the fire would change direction before it got to them. Lemos paced the house, baby in her arms and four children following closely, all the time trying to convince her father to leave. She was looking out the door as others fled up the street when a woman hurried by with three children behind her. "Madam," the woman yelled sharply, "ain't you going to save those children?"

This question jolted Lemos into action. After insisting her parents leave the house, she guided the group out of the city and into the empty prairie where their possessions had been left. Thirty minutes after settling down for the night, wind-driven debris from the fire ignited the dry grass nearby, forcing them to abandon their things and retreat farther north.

Cause and Effect
What was the incentive that finally made Julia Lemos leave her house?

The title of this photo might have been "Ruins and Reconstruction." The burned-out buildings in the rear seem to be watching as workers lay the beams for a new structure. Note the piles of bricks that line the street. Brick was the only building material that survived the fire and could be reused.

Lemos remembered feeling the heat of the flames on her back as she urged her parents and children along.

They stopped a mile from the first spot and formed a tight circle. Lemos cradled her baby in her arms while her nine-year-old son, Willy, slept with his head in her lap. Suddenly, he began to cry.

Lemos looked up. In the distance she could see the city on fire, the orange-red flames reaching toward the sky. She was about to say something comforting to Willy, when she saw a church steeple sag, then topple over into the dark smoke and flames. It certainly did seem like the Last Day, but she was sure of one thing: Despite all sorts of opposition, she had kept her family together and now they were truly safe.

INTO THE PAST WITH
Jim Murphy

Jim Murphy

Jim Murphy grew up in a small town in New Jersey. He is an award-winning author who has written more than 20 books, many of them historic nonfiction. He says that, "One of my goals in writing about events from the past is to show that children weren't just observers of our history. They were actual participants and sometimes did amazing and heroic things."

He was doing research for a book one day when he came across a letter written by a 12-year-old girl, Claire Innis. The letter described her experience of being trapped in an alley with burning buildings all around her during the Chicago fire in 1871. He made a copy of the letter and did not think about it again until he happened to come across a copy of *The Great Conflagration*, which was published in December of 1871 and had many eyewitness accounts of the Great Fire. Claire's letter and other firsthand accounts in *The Great Conflagration* inspired him to write the award-winning *The Great Fire*.

LOG ON ▶ Find out more about Jim Murphy at **www.macmillanmh.com**.

Another book by Jim Murphy

BY THE AUTHOR OF *THE GREAT FIRE*
BLIZZARD!
JIM MURPHY
SCHOLASTIC

CA **Author's Purpose**

Why do you think author Jim Murphy included eyewitness accounts in his book *The Great Fire*?

722

Critical Thinking

Summarize

Use your Cause and Effect Chart to help you summarize *The Great Fire*. Think about some of the reasons why the fire was so devastating for Chicago.

Cause ➜ Effect
➜
➜
➜
➜

Think and Compare

1. The author uses a **cause-and-effect** text structure to present information in this story. Reread the information on pages 708–709. What series of events were behind the causes that allowed Claire Innis to escape the fire? **Analyze Text Structure: Cause and Effect**

2. Why do you think many city **residents,** such as Julia Lemos and the women Joseph Chamberlin saw on their way to work Monday morning, found it difficult to believe that the fire would have any effect on their lives? **Analyze**

3. What was James Hildreth's plan to stop the fire? Do you think it was a good idea? What might you have suggested to try to stop the spread of the flames? **Apply**

4. Why do you think people who have never experienced this kind of disaster are still interested in reading about it, even though it took place over 130 years ago? **Apply**

5. Reread "The Great London Fire" on pages 704–705. Identify some of the conditions in the London of 1666 that were also present in Chicago in 1871, and that contributed to the fires that nearly destroyed each city. **Reading/Writing Across Texts**

History/ Social Science
CA

Genre

Nonfiction: Some newspaper articles tell about events and ask who, what, where, when, and why.

✔ Text Features

A **Primary Source** is information that comes from the time being studied. It could be a newspaper or magazine article, letters, photographs, or an official document.

Applications are special forms with blank spaces that need to be filled in when applying for something such as a library card.

Content Vocabulary

conflagration	**cornices**
sustenance	**quoins**

FIRE!
Destruction of Chicago !
2,600 Acres of Build-ings Destroyed.
Eighty Thousand People Burned Out.
All the Hotels, Banks

Primary Sources can bring historical events to life. This excerpt is from an article about the Chicago Fire that comes from the Chicago Tribune, October 11, 1871.

DURING SUNDAY NIGHT, Monday, and Tuesday, this city has been swept by a **conflagration** which has no parallel in the annals of history, for the quantity of property destroyed, and the utter and almost irremediable ruin which it wrought. A fire in a barn on the West Side was the insignificant cause of a conflagration which has swept out of existence hundreds of millions of property, has reduced to poverty thousands who, the day before, were in a state of opulence, has covered the prairies, now swept by the cold southwest wind, with thousands of homeless unfortunates, which has stripped 2,600 acres of buildings, which has destroyed public improvements that it has taken years of patient labor to build up, and which has set back for years the progress of the city, diminished her population, and crushed her resources. But to a blow, no matter how terrible, Chicago will not succumb. Late as it is in the season, general as the ruin is, the spirit of her citizens has not given way, and before the smoke has cleared away, and the ruins are cold, they are beginning to plan for the future. Though so many have been deprived of homes and **sustenance**, aid in money and provisions is flowing in from all quarters, and much of the present distress will be alleviated before another day has gone by.

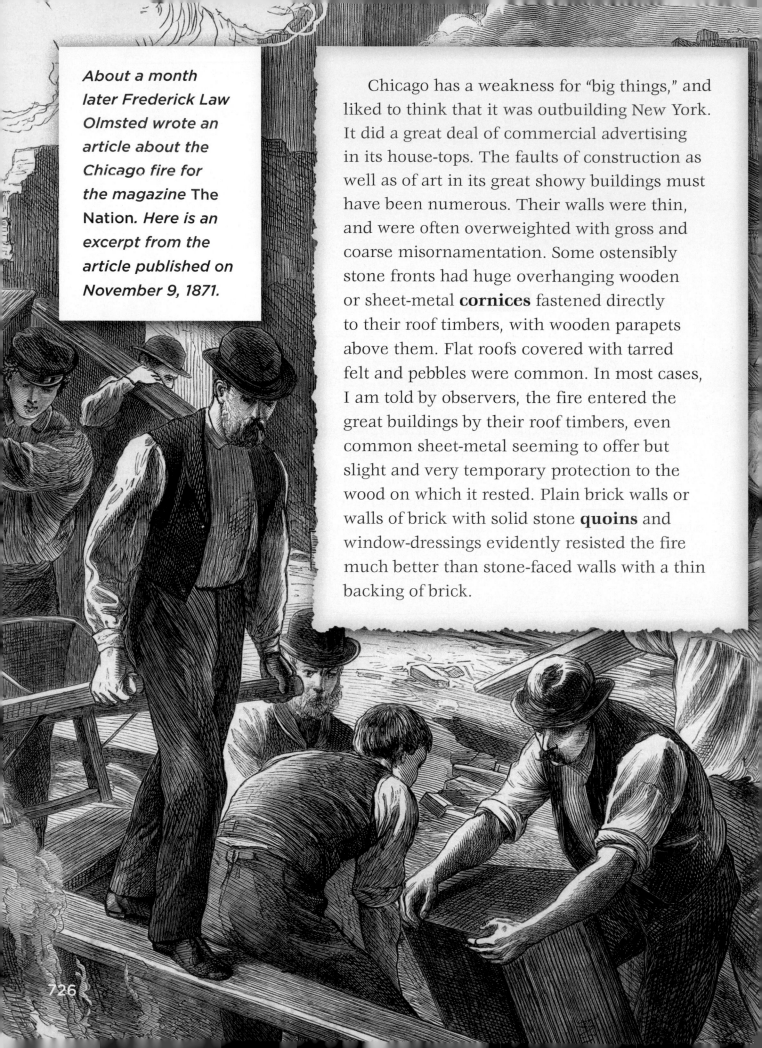

About a month later Frederick Law Olmsted wrote an article about the Chicago fire for the magazine The Nation. *Here is an excerpt from the article published on November 9, 1871.*

Chicago has a weakness for "big things," and liked to think that it was outbuilding New York. It did a great deal of commercial advertising in its house-tops. The faults of construction as well as of art in its great showy buildings must have been numerous. Their walls were thin, and were often overweighted with gross and coarse misornamentation. Some ostensibly stone fronts had huge overhanging wooden or sheet-metal **cornices** fastened directly to their roof timbers, with wooden parapets above them. Flat roofs covered with tarred felt and pebbles were common. In most cases, I am told by observers, the fire entered the great buildings by their roof timbers, even common sheet-metal seeming to offer but slight and very temporary protection to the wood on which it rested. Plain brick walls or walls of brick with solid stone **quoins** and window-dressings evidently resisted the fire much better than stone-faced walls with a thin backing of brick.

A public library is a good place to do research. Here is a sample of an application for a library card.

Springfield Public Library
Card Application

INSTRUCTIONS: Please fill in the information requested. Your new library account will be assigned a barcode ID. To obtain your card you must bring to the library a photo ID (or provide two other forms of identification such as a utility bill, bank statement, etc.) to verify your name and address and to sign this printed form in the presence of a librarian. Applications must also be signed by a parent or guardian for all children under 12 years of age.

Name — Last, First, Middle:	CA Driver's License #
	Date of Birth:
Home Address:	Mailing Address (if different from home address):
City, State, Zip:	City, State, Zip:
Home Phone:	Parent Name (if applicant under 18):

 Critical Thinking

1. If you are under 12 years of age, who else must sign your library card application? Why is it important to be accurate when filling in the information? **Reading an Application**

2. How does the reporter who wrote the article for the *Chicago Tribune* feel about the citizens of Chicago? How can you tell? **Analyze**

3. How do the articles from the *Chicago Tribune* and *The Nation* add to the information that the author presented in the excerpt from *The Great Fire*? **Reading/Writing Across Texts**

 History/Social Science Activity

The Royal Library of Alexandria in Alexandria, Egypt, was once the largest library in the world. It was thought to have been destroyed by a fire. Research the destruction of the Royal Library by fire and create a fact card.

 Find out more about the ancient city of Alexandria at **www.macmillanmh.com**.

CA Writing

✓ Subjects and Predicates

Good writers use compound **subjects and predicates** to add interest to a piece of writing.

Reading and Writing Connection

Read the passage below. Notice how author Jim Murphy weaves the fire and its characteristics into the subjects and predicates of many of the sentences.

An excerpt from
The Great Fire

The author uses "fire" and "the width and speed of the fire" to focus attention on the power of the fire. The predicates that go with the subjects of his sentences are complex and interesting.

While the fire was being contained in the south, to the north another story was unfolding. The width and speed of the fire made it impossible for weary firemen to work in an organized or coordinated way. Besides, they were now beyond exhaustion. Two nights of fire fighting and little rest or food had pushed many to the brink of collapse. Several had to be taken from the area in wagons. One tired fireman sat down on a street corner to catch his breath and promptly fell asleep despite the roar of the fire around him.

Read and Find

Read Sarah's writing below. How did she use a variety of subjects and predicates to draw you into her experience of drinking the Chinese tea? Use the Writer's Checklist below to help you.

Chinatown

by Sarah M.

As the liquid goes down my throat, the ginger hits with full force. It is overwhelmingly strong. The more sips I take, the more powerful this sensation is, as if a rope is being yanked through my throat. It is as if I am taking in the smells and sights of China with every sip that slides through my mouth.

Read how one person experienced drinking special Chinese tea.

Writer's Checklist

 Is there a subject that is repeated in the same or in different forms?

✓ Is the author choosing predicates that focus attention on the cause of the action?

 Do the predicates help define the subjects?

✓ **Review**

Main Idea and Details
Character, Setting, Plot
Fact and Opinion
Multiple-Meaning Words
Application

Sybil Ludington rallying the colonial militia on April 26th, 1777

The Midnight Ride of Sybil Ludington

"Who goes there?"

Sixteen-year-old Sybil Ludington tried to sound brave, but her fear betrayed her. Her voice trembled as she spoke. She had been awakened by the hoofbeats of a horse that had stopped in front of her house. With her father away in the Continental army, and her mother ill, there was only Sybil to defend the farm. She hung her head out her bedroom window on that rainy April night of 1777 and again challenged the rider to identify himself.

"I say, who goes there?" she repeated.

"Is that you, Mistress Sybil?" came the soft reply.

"Yes, 'tis I. But who are you?"

"Edward Ogden."

"Edward! I shall be right down!"

Edward Ogden was a boy Sybil knew well. As a friend and neighbor, he had come to the Ludington farm many times. When New York joined the War for Independence, Sybil had watched Edward, along with his father and her own, march off to join the cause. Sybil raced down the stairs and unlatched the door. Edward blew in with the wind and the rain.

"Edward! Why have you returned? Is it Father? Is he well?"

Sybil lit a lantern and held it to the boy's face. He was wet and dirty. He trembled from the cold. But there was something more. He was pale. Sickly pale. Sybil pulled aside the soaked cloak he held around himself and saw the blood spreading over his shoulder.

"You're wounded!"

"I was injured in a skirmish last week. I was on the mend, but I have been riding all night. I am afraid I have reopened the wound. I've lost some blood."

Sybil led Edward to the kitchen in the back of the house. She rekindled the flame in the fireplace and sat Edward in a chair before the fire.

"Now," she said, "let us tend to your wound."

"There is no time, Sybil. I came to your farm because my horse is too cold and tired to go any farther. I need to take your horse and be on my way at once."

"But why?" asked Sybil, frightened by his urgency.

"Because the British have attacked Danbury, Connecticut. Danbury is but fifteen miles from here. The local militia must be warned and summoned to fight!" Edward rose with his words but quickly fell back to his seat.

"Edward, you are as weak as a kitten. You can go no farther." Sybil was prepared to argue but did not have to. Edward had fainted. Sybil quickly cleaned and rebandaged his wound. She wrapped the boy in blankets, and stoked the fire with enough wood to last until morning. Then she dressed and went out into the rain. Sybil led Edward's horse to the barn and saddled her own.

"It is for us to do now, my girl," she said to her horse as she galloped off into the night. Sybil rode from farm to farm, rousing the citizens of Putnam County. She covered forty miles of country roads, spreading the alarm as she went. The local militia successfully marched to take back Danbury and protect the little town of Fredericksburg. Today that town is called Ludingtonville in honor of the brave girl who rode through the night to protect its freedom.

731

Portable Music:
Taking It with You

In July 1979, life for the music lover was about to change. The portable music tape player arrived on the music scene and changed the world. Music, and how people listened to it, would never be the same.

The Music in Your Head

Before the birth of the portable tape player, people were stuck having to listen to whatever was playing. Before it was portable, music was something that groups of people shared, whether they liked it or not. The radio or tape player was too big to carry from room to room.

The first transistor radio went on sale in 1954 and allowed the buyer to take his or her music anywhere. There was even an earpiece for private listening. People got their first taste of listening to music on their own terms and they liked it. Change was a good thing!

An Amazing Accident

The invention of the portable tape player in 1979 became the foundation for the shift in how people listened to music. There is a legend that suggests it was more the result of an accident than smart business sense. The president of a small Japanese electronics company asked his designers to make him a small tape player to take with him on a long airplane trip. The designers at the company took one of their older devices, a tape player and recorder, and removed the record feature and speaker. In its place they gave the player a plug for earphones.

As soon as the rest of the company heard about the new product, they were already planning its release to the public. They perfected it and within months of its release, the portable tape player became a cultural phenomenon. Music had been set free.

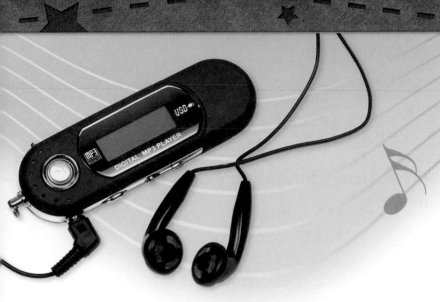

Going Digital

The freedom of music depends on how it is played. When the popularity of computers began to make the world a digital planet, portable music had to catch up. In the 1980s and the 1990s, compact discs proved that digital music was superior to old-fashioned tape recordings. Slimmer, better sounding CDs were taking over. Portable CD players became the toys of choice.

MP3 computer files are the newest trend in music. They are individual recordings that have been created for storage on a computer. These files can be played on special players called DAPs, or digital audio players. MP3 files make it possible to have more music in less space because they exist only inside the memory of a computer chip. What happens now? One small portable music player can hold thousands of MP3 songs in a machine the size of a credit card. Music freedom has exploded in a way no one had ever dreamed possible. It's only a matter of time until a DAP is in the pocket of every music lover.

DAP MUSIC CLUB

Join today to discuss all kinds of music and where to obtain recordings. You do not have to own a **DAP** to be a member.

Name_____

Address_____

City and State_____

Phone number_____

E-mail address (optional)_____

CA Critical Thinking

Now answer questions 1 through 4. Base your answers on the story "The Midnight Ride of Sybil Ludington."

1. What is this story mostly about?

    A a young boy who is injured

    B a militia that saves a town

    C a town that changes its name

    D a girl who demonstrates bravery

2. Although Sybil was frightened, she rode through the night to warn her neighbors. What can you conclude about Sybil's character?

    A Sybil was a good rider.

    B Sybil was a courageous girl who did what had to be done.

    C Sybil wanted to have a town named after her.

    D Sybil liked to ride alone at night.

3. Read the following sentences from the story.

> "Edward! Why have you returned?
> Is it Father? Is he well?"

What is another meaning for the word *well*?

    A hurt

    B a source of water

    C maybe

    D a short form of *we will*

4. This story about Sybil Ludington is historical fiction. Parts of it are true and can be proven.

Other parts are made up. Which parts of the story do you think are made up? Use details and information from the story to support your answer.

Now answer questions 1 through 4. Base your answers on the article "Portable Music: Taking It with You."

1. **Which *best* describes the theme of this article?**

   A   Change is a good thing in portable music.
   B   Music never changes.
   C   Portable tape players are never outdated.
   D   Everyone should have an MP3 player.

2. **Which of the following statements is a fact, not an opinion?**

   A   Change was a good thing!
   B   Music had been set free.
   C   In July 1979, life for the music lover was about to change.
   D   It's only a matter of time until a DAP is in the pocket of every music lover.

3. **The invention of the portable tape player**

   A   was the well-thought-out idea of an engineer.
   B   made television popular.
   C   took more than ten years.
   D   became the foundation for the change in how people listened to music.

4. **Why would a music club application ask for an e-mail address?**

   A   The club meets online.
   B   The club sends notices of meetings via e-mail.
   C   The club plays music online.
   D   You can only join the club if you have an e-mail address.

Write on Demand

PROMPT Now that we can take our music with us, we can play it anywhere at any time. Is this always a good thing? Use details from the article and your own experience to support your answer. Write for 25 minutes. Write as much as you can as well as you can.

Glossary

What Is a Glossary?

A glossary can help you find the **meanings** of words in this book that you may not know. The words in the glossary are listed in **alphabetical order**. **Guide words** at the top of each page tell you the first and last words on the page.

Each word is divided into syllables. The way to pronounce the word is given next. You can understand the pronunciation respelling by using the **pronunciation key**. A shorter key appears at the bottom of every other page. When a word has more than one syllable, a dark accent mark (´) shows which syllable is stressed. In some words, a light accent mark (´) shows which syllable has a less heavy stress. Sometimes an entry includes a second meaning for the word.

summit

chameleon

Guide Words

First word on the page — Last word on the page

Sample Entry

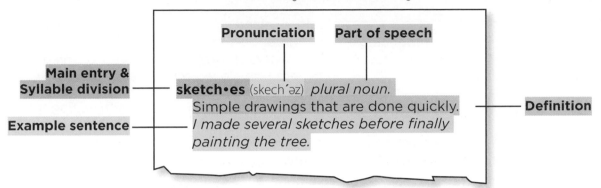

Pronunciation

Part of speech

Main entry & Syllable division — **sketch•es** (skech´əz) *plural noun.*

Definition — Simple drawings that are done quickly.

Example sentence — *I made several sketches before finally painting the tree.*

Pronunciation Key

Phonetic Spelling	Examples
a	**a**t, b**a**d, pl**ai**d, l**au**gh
ā	**a**pe, p**ai**n, d**ay**, br**ea**k
ä	f**a**ther, c**a**lm
âr	c**are**, p**air**, b**ear**, th**eir**, wh**ere**
e	**e**nd, p**e**t, s**ai**d, h**ea**ven, fri**e**nd
ē	**e**qual, m**e**, f**ee**t, t**ea**m, p**ie**ce, k**ey**
i	**i**t, b**i**g, g**i**ve, h**y**mn
ī	**i**ce, f**i**ne, l**ie**, m**y**
îr	**ear**, d**eer**, h**ere**, p**ier**ce
o	**o**dd, h**o**t, w**a**tch
ō	**o**ld, **oa**t, t**oe**, l**ow**
ô	c**o**ffee, **a**ll, t**au**ght, l**aw**, f**ou**ght
ôr	**or**der, f**or**k, h**or**se, st**or**y, p**our**
oi	**oi**l, t**oy**
ou	**ou**t, n**ow**, b**ou**gh
u	**u**p, m**u**d, l**o**ve, d**ou**ble
ū	**u**se, m**u**le, c**ue**, f**eu**d, f**ew**
ü	r**u**le, tr**ue**, f**oo**d, fr**ui**t
ù	p**u**t, w**oo**d, sh**ou**ld, l**oo**k
ûr	b**ur**n, h**ur**ry, t**er**m, b**ir**d, w**or**d, c**our**age
ə	**a**bout, tak**e**n, penc**i**l, lem**o**n, circ**u**s
b	**b**at, a**b**ove, jo**b**
ch	**ch**in, su**ch**, ma**tch**

Phonetic Spelling	Examples
d	**d**ear, so**d**a, ba**d**
f	**f**ive, de**f**end, lea**f**, o**ff**, cou**gh**, ele**ph**ant
g	**g**ame, a**g**o, fo**g**, e**gg**
h	**h**at, a**h**ead
hw	**wh**ite, **wh**ether, **wh**ich
j	**j**oke, en**j**oy, **g**em, pa**g**e, e**dge**
k	**k**ite, ba**k**ery, see**k**, ta**ck**, **c**at
l	**l**id, sai**l**or, fee**l**, ba**ll**, a**ll**ow
m	**m**an, fa**m**ily, drea**m**
n	**n**ot, fi**n**al, pa**n**, **kn**ife, **gn**aw
ng	lo**ng**, si**ng**er
p	**p**ail, re**p**air, soa**p**, ha**pp**y
r	**r**ide, pa**r**ent, wea**r**, mo**r**e, ma**rr**y
s	**s**it, a**s**ide, pet**s**, **c**ent, pa**ss**
sh	**sh**oe, wa**sh**er, fi**sh**, mi**ss**ion, na**ti**on
t	**t**ag, pre**t**end, fa**t**, dresse**d**
th	**th**in, pan**th**er, bo**th**
<u>th</u>	**<u>th</u>**ese, mo**<u>th</u>**er, smoo**<u>th</u>**
v	**v**ery, fa**v**or, wa**v**e
w	**w**et, **w**eather, re**w**ard
y	**y**es, on**i**on
z	**z**oo, la**z**y, ja**zz**, ro**s**e, dog**s**, hou**s**es
zh	vi**s**ion, trea**s**ure, sei**z**ure

Aa

a•brupt•ly (ə bruptʹlē) *adverb.* Happening in a quick way or without warning. *Ben **abruptly** dropped the hot potato.*

ac•ces•si•ble (ak sesʹə bəl) *adjective.* Able to be reached, entered, or approached. *Ramps make buildings **accessible** to those who cannot climb stairs.*

ac•com•pa•nied (ə kumʹpən ēd) *verb.* Went along with. *A dog always **accompanied** Mr. Granger on his walk.*

ac•qui•si•tion (aʹkwi zishʹən) *noun.* The act of receiving or aquiring a possession. *The museum was very proud of its new **acquisition**.*

ac•tive (akʹtiv) *adjective.* Producing action or movement. *The puppy was extremely **active** and seemed to tire out its mother.*

a•dept (ə deptʹ) *adjective.* Highly skilled, expert. *Bonnie is **adept** on the balance beam in gymnastics.*

ad•verse (ad vûrsʹ, adʹvûrs) *adjective.* Not helpful to what is wanted; not favorable. *The game was played under **adverse** conditions because of heavy rain.*

aer•i•al (ârʹē əl) *adjective.* Of or in the air. *Because we were so close to the **aerial** show, we were looking straight up.*

aer•o•nau•tics (ârʹə nôʹtiks) *noun.* The science or art of flight. *The pilots studied **aeronautics**.*

af•fect•ed (ə fĕkʹtid) *adjective.* 1. Acted upon or influenced. 2. Assumed for show in an artificial way. 1. *The strong rains in August **affected** the vineyard grapes negatively.*

af•fects (ə fĕktsʹ) *verb.* Acts upon. *Every spice you add **affects** the soup's taste.*

ag•o•nized (aʹgə nīzdʹ) *verb.* Experienced great discomfort, pain, or stress. *The owner **agonized** over money problems after he closed the store for the day.*

am•bi•tious (am bishʹəs) *adjective.* Eager to succeed. *The **ambitious** assistant would work all weekend in hopes of becoming a manager someday.*

am•pu•tat•ed (amʹpyə tāʹtid) *verb.* Having had any limb or digit cut off by surgery. *After her arm was crushed in the car accident, it was **amputated**.*

an•a•lyz•ing (aʹnə līʹzing) *verb.* Examining carefully and in detail in order to understand something. *By **analyzing** the soil sample, the scientist learned that the land was safe for a playground.*

a•nat•o•my (ə naʹtə mē) *noun.* The branch of science dealing with the structure of animals or plants and the relationships of their parts. *The teacher held classes in **anatomy**.*

an•cient (ān(t)ʹshənt) *adjective.* Relating to a very early time. *The displays in the museum were from **ancient** times.*

a•non•y•mous (ə noʹnə məs) *adjective.* Of unknown origin or authorship; without any name given. *All the donations were **anonymous**, so the hospital did not know whom to thank for all the money.*

Word History

Anonymous comes from Greek words. *Onyma* means "name," and the *a-* placed at the beginning means "without."

an•thro•pol•o•gists (an´thrə pol´ə gists) *noun,* plural. Students or experts in the science that deals with physical, cultural, and social development of humans. *Several* **anthropologists** *showed up at the site after the workers found the artifacts.*

an•tic•i•pat•ed (an tis´ə pā´tid) *verb.* Expected or looked forward to. *All day we* **anticipated** *getting our test scores from our teacher.*

anx•i•e•ty (ang zī´i tē) *noun.* A feeling of fearful uneasiness or worry about what may happen. *The family felt* **anxiety** *when no one could find the lost dog.*

ap•pa•rat•us (a´pə rat´əs, a´pə rā´təs) *noun.* A mechanism used for a particular purpose. *The* **apparatus** *in the gym needs repairing.*

aq•ue•ducts (a´kwə dukts´) *noun,* plural. Large pipes that carry water over a long distance. **Aqueducts** *were built for easier access to the water supply to the village.*

ar•ray (ər ā´) *noun.* A large collection or display. *The shop window offered a wide* **array** *of objects for the home.*

ar•ti•facts (är´ti fakts´) *noun,* plural. Anything made or changed by humans. *The tools were Viking* **artifacts**.

ar•ti•fi•cial (är´tə fi´shəl) *adjective.* Produced by humans; made in imitation or as a substitute. *The* **artificial** *knee my uncle received worked as well as his natural one.*

as•pir•ing (ə spīr´ing) *verb.* Wanting or trying very hard to achieve some goal. *John is* **aspiring** *after fame and fortune.*

auc•tion (ôk´shən) *noun.* A public sale at which property or possessions are sold to the highest bidder. *My brother bid twenty dollars for some lamps at an* **auction**.

awe•some (ô´səm) *adjective.* Inspiring great wonder combined with fear or respect. *The Grand Canyon is an* **awesome** *sight.*

Bb

be•wil•der•ing (bi wil´də ring) *verb.* Confusing or puzzling. *This math problem is* **bewildering** *to me.*

bi•ased sam•ple (bī´əst sam´pəl) *noun.* A group of subjects in a survey that does not represent the total group. *In order for Kim to get the results she wanted in her survey, she polled a* **biased sample**.

bil•low (bil´ō) *verb.* To rise in waves. *Watch the curtains* **billow** *in the breeze.*

bi•on•ics (bī o´niks) *noun.* The study of the parts of the bodies of humans and other animals in order to devise improvements in various machines, especially computers and artificial limbs. *Since I am so interested in sports and computers, I decided to study* **bionics** *at college.*

at; āpe; fär; câre; end; mē; it; īce; pîerce; hot; ōld; sông; fôrk; oil; out; up; ūse; rüle; pu̇ll; tûrn; chin; sing; shop; thin; this; hw in white; zh in treasure.

The symbol ə stands for the unstressed vowel sound in about, taken, pencil, lemon, and circus.

board (bôrd) *noun.* Meals provided regularly for pay or in exchange for services. *The student got free room and board.*

bol•ster (bōl´stər) *verb.* To support or strengthen. *The sight of land can bolster a sailor's low spirits after many days at sea.*

Cc

ca•pac•i•ty (kə pa´sə tē) *noun.* The maximum amount that can be contained. *The restaurant had a capacity of 38 people.*

cas•cade (kas kād´) *noun.* A waterfall or series of small waterfalls; anything resembling this. *The clothes fell out of the suitcase in a cascade down the staircase.*

cha•me•leon (kə mēl´yən) *noun.* Any of various small, slow-moving lizards that can change the color of their skin to match their surroundings. Also used in reference to a person who is very changeable. *Since he tended to look different every time we saw him, we called him a chameleon.*

char•is•mat•ic (kar´əz ma´tik) *adjective.* Having the quality of attracting the loyalty and devotion of a large following of people. *People are drawn to charismatic politicians.*

civ•i•lized (si´və līzd´) *adjective.* No longer savage or primitive. *He was a civilized young man with excellent manners.*

clock•wise (klok´wīz´) *adverb.* Going in the direction that the hands of a clock move. *The popular new dance involved spinning around clockwise several times.*

co•in•ci•den•ces (kō in´si dən ses) *noun,* plural. Occurrences of circumstances or events at the same time and apparently by chance. *A series of coincidences led me to meet my group of friends in the museum.*

col•lec•tive (kə lek´tiv) *adjective.* Of, relating to, or done by a group of persons; united. *The book was written by a collective effort; all the writers added something.*

col•li•sion (kə li´zhən) *noun.* A coming together with solid impact. *The noise from the collision of the cars was loud.*

com•mis•sioned (kə mish´ənd) *verb.* Being assigned to create a work of art. *My art teacher was commissioned to paint a huge mural at the new hotel.*

com•mit•ment (kə mit´mənt) *noun.* The act of devoting oneself; an obligation. *Since joining the drama club was a huge time commitment, I had to think twice before signing up.*

con•cen•trate (kon´sən trāt) *verb.* 1. To focus on. 2. To come closely together. *1. Distractions make it difficult to concentrate. 2. Orange juice concentrate is usually found in the freezer section.*

con•fla•gra•tion (kon´flə grā´shən) *noun.* A large fire causing much damage. *The conflagration consumed much of the warehouse.*

con•nec•tion (kə nek´shən) *noun.* The act or state of linking. *I checked the connection of my computer when it did not start up.*

con•quis•ta•do•res (kon kēs´tə dôr´ēz) *noun,* plural. The Spanish conquerors in Mexico and Peru during the sixteenth century. *In history class we are learning about Hernando Cortés and the conquistadores who conquered the Aztec Empire.*

con•scious (kon´shəs) *adjective.* 1. Knowing or realizing; aware. *Linda was* **conscious** *of her own tendency to exaggerate.* 2. Awake. *Despite the blow to his head, Al remained* **conscious***.*

con•serve (kən sûrv´) *verb.* To preserve. **Conserve** *your strength.*

con•sumed (kən sūmd´) *verb.* 1. To have used up. 2. To have eaten or drunk up. *The fire* **consumed** *the forest.*

cor•nic•es (kôr´nis əs) *noun,* plural. Ornamental building moldings. *Birds like to build nests in the tower's* **cornices***.*

cra•ter (krā´ tər) *noun.* A cuplike depression. *There is a* **crater** *on the moon that can be seen from Earth.*

Dd

da•ta (dā´tə, da´tə) *noun,* plural. Information from which conclusions can be drawn; facts and figures. *The* **data** *from the reports must be accurate.*

dec•ades (de´kādz) *noun,* plural. Periods of ten years. *At my grandmother's party, she told stories that spanned the eight* **decades** *of her life.*

Word History

The word **decade** comes from the Greek word, *deka,* which means "ten."

de•crease (di kres´) *verb.* To lessen or reduce. *Our class made a list of ways to* **decrease** *pollution in our state.*

de•hy•drat•ed (dē hī´drā tid) *adjective.* To have had water or moisture removed. *The marathon runner was* **dehydrated** *after the race because she sweated so much.*

de•ject•ed•ly (di jek´tid lē) *adverb.* Showing disheartened, downcast, or low spirits. *I* **dejectedly** *kicked the ball against the wall after we lost the soccer game.*

dem•on•stra•tion (de´mən strā´shən) *noun.* Something that proves clearly; an explaining or showing by the use of visible examples. *It's a thrill when scientists prove a new theory in a* **demonstration***.*

de•ny (di nī´) *verb.* To declare something to be untrue. *Because I was not late for class, I will* **deny** *being tardy.*

de•spite (di spīt´) *preposition.* In spite of. **Despite** *the monster's long fangs and scary features, it was really quite friendly.*

de•spon•dent•ly (di spon´dənt lē) *adverb.* In a depressed or dejected way. *As the team lost more points, they walked* **despondently** *along the sidelines.*

des•ti•na•tion (des´tə nā´shən) *noun.* A place to which a person or thing is going. *The train conductor asked us what our* **destination** *was when we boarded.*

de•te•ri•o•rat•ed (di tîr´ē ə rā´tid) *verb.* Lessened in character, quality, condition, or value; worsened. *The newspaper* **deteriorated** *rapidly in the rain.*

de•vot•ed (di vō´tid) *adjective.* Loyal; faithful. *Mr. and Mrs. Martinez were* **devoted** *to each other their entire lives.*

---

at; āpe; fär; câre; end; mē; it; īce; pîerce; hot; ōld; sông; fôrk; oil; out; up; ūse; rūle; pull; tûrn; chin; sing; shop; thin; this; hw in white; zh in treasure.

The symbol ə stands for the unstressed vowel sound in about, taken, pencil, lemon, and circus.

di·lap·i·dat·ed (də laʹpi dā´tid) *adjective.* Fallen into ruin or decay. *Everyone on our street decided to help paint the **dilapidated** old house on the corner.*

drow·sy (drouʹzē) *adjective.* Feeling sleepy. *The guard was **drowsy** after working extra shifts every day of the week.*

dwell·ing (dwelʹing) *noun.* A place where a person lives. *While walking along the beach, the children found an old **dwelling** made of wood and canvas.*

Ee

e·lab·o·rate (i laʹbər it) *adjective.* Worked out with great care and great detail. *The committee spent one year planning the **elaborate** ceremony.* (i laʹbər rāt) *verb.* To give additional or fuller treatment to something spoken or written. *I was too tired to **elaborate** on the events of the trip, so I just gave a basic account of it.*

em·barked (em bärktʹ) *verb.* To have begun or set out, as on an adventure. *The vacationers **embarked** on a two-week cruise in the Caribbean.*

em·bar·rass·ment (em barʹəs mənt) *noun.* The act or state of feeling uncomfortable or ashamed. *Aunt Tillie's behavior at the party was an **embarrassment** to the family.*

em·bed·ded (em beʹdid) *verb.* To have set in surrounding matter; to have placed or planted firmly. *The seeds were deeply **embedded** in the soil.*

e·merged (i mûrjdʹ) *verb.* Came into view. *New understanding **emerged** as soon as the reports were released.*

em·ploy·ee (em ploiʹē) *noun.* A person who works for a person or business for pay. *A good **employee** is one who always does his or her best on the job.*

en·coun·ter (en kounʹtər) *noun.* A meeting between friends, enemies, or colleagues. *My grandfather told me about a violent **encounter** during the war.*

en·er·gy (eʹnər jē) *noun.* The ability to act with force or power. *Drinking orange juice gives me **energy**.*

en·gulf (en gulfʹ) *verb.* To swallow up or completely surround. *The flames may **engulf** the whole hillside unless we put the fire out soon.*

en·thralled (en thrôldʹ) *verb.* Held spellbound; charmed. *The crowd was **enthralled** by the magician and his bag of magic tricks.*

en·vi·sioned (en vizhʹənd) *verb.* Formed a picture in the mind. *The principal **envisioned** a big, new gym for his school.*

ep·i·dem·ic (eʹpə deʹmik) *noun.* 1. The rapid spread of a disease among people at the same time. *The elementary school experienced an **epidemic** of chicken pox last winter.* 2. The rapid spread or sudden, widespread appearance of anything. *An **epidemic** of burglaries hit our town.*

erupt (i ruptʹ) *verb.* To throw forth violently. *The scientists quickly withdrew from the vicinity of the volcano, because they feared it would **erupt**.*

es·cort (esʹkôrt) *noun.* A person or persons who go along with another as a courtesy or for protection. *Cinderella's stepsisters wanted the prince to be their **escort** to the ball.*

es·tab·lished (i staʹblisht) *verb.* Set up permanently. *The restaurant where we ate lunch was **established** in 1897!*

es·tab·lish·ment (i staʹblish mənt) *noun.* A place of business. *Before the **establishment** could open, the lease needed to be signed.*

es•ti•mate (es′tə māt′) *verb.* To come to a conclusion by reasoning or an educated guess. *We* **estimate** *that the trip will take an hour, but it might take longer if there is heavy traffic.* (es′tə mit) *noun.* An approximate judgment or calculation. *The painters gave me an* **estimate** *of what the job would cost.*

ex•ca•va•tion (ek′skə vā′shən) *noun.* The process of planned digging. *The historical* **excavation** *was made more difficult because of heavy rains.*

ex•cel (ek sel′) *verb.* To do very well; to succeed. *The teacher told us that it takes a lot of studying to* **excel** *in our classes.*

ex•cep•tion•al (ek sep′shə nəl) *adjective.* Unusual or out of the ordinary. *I liked the* **exceptional** *architecture of the building.*

ex•haus•tion (ig zôs′chən) *noun.* A lack of strength or energy. *The jogger collapsed from* **exhaustion***.*

ex•te•ri•or (ek stîr′ē ər) *noun.* The outside surface. *The building* **exterior** *suffered damage from the storm.*

ex•trav•a•gant (ek stra′və gənt) *adjective.* Lavish or wasteful in the spending of money. *Mary made many* **extravagant** *purchases that she really could not afford.*

Ff

fam•ine (fam′in) *noun.* A great lack of food in an area or country. *The* **famine** *affected nearly all the people in the village.*

feat (fēt) *noun.* An act or deed that shows great courage, strength, or skill. *Climbing that mountain was quite a* **feat***.*

fea•ture (fē′chər) *noun.* A distinctive part of something. *My grandmother's favorite* **feature** *of her new car is the comfortable driving seat.*

fidg•et (fij′it) *verb.* To be nervous or make restless movements. *The girl tried not to* **fidget** *in the long line.*

flee (flē) *verb.* To run away from danger. *The park ranger warned that if we disturb a wasp nest, we should* **flee** *immediately.*

fleet•ing (flē′ting) *adjective.* Passing very quickly. *We had only a* **fleeting** *look at the famous actress as she hurried away.*

flour•ish (flûr′ish) *verb.* To grow or develop strongly or prosperously; thrive. *In order for a child to grow and* **flourish***, he or she must eat nutritious food and get lots of rest and exercise.*

fore•man (fôr′mən) *noun.* A worker who supervises a group of workers, as in a factory or on a farm. *The* **foreman** *was in charge of seeing that the cars came off the assembly line on time.*

fore•told (fôr tōld′) *verb.* Told of ahead of time. *The game played out just as my coach* **foretold***: we won the championship!*

for•mal•ly (fôr′mə lē) *adverb.* Acting with stiff, proper, or polite behavior. *The governor* **formally** *welcomed the guests to the party.*

for•ma•tions (fôr mā′shəns) *noun,* plural. Something that is formed. *The tourists took a boat to see the strange rock* **formations** *in the lake.*

---

at; āpe; fär; câre; end; mē; it; īce; pîerce; hot; ōld; sông; fôrk; oil; out; up; ūse; rüle; púll; tûrn; chin; sing; shop; thin; this; hw in white; zh in treasure.

The symbol ə stands for the unstressed vowel sound in about, taken, pencil, lemon, and circus.

743

foun·da·tion (foun dā'shən) *noun.* A basis on which something stands. *First, the construction crew poured the building's* **foundation**.

ful·fill (ful fil') *verb.* To carry out or bring to completion; cause to happen. *Miguel was able to* **fulfill** *his promise as a musician by mastering the piano.*

Gg

gen·er·ate (jen'ə rāt') *verb.* To bring about or produce. *That machine will* **generate** *electricity.*

gen·er·os·i·ty (jen'ə ros'i tē) *noun.* Willingness to give or share freely. *We thanked the community for its* **generosity** *and helpfulness during the crisis.*

glee·ful·ly (glē'fə lē) *adverb.* In a joyous or merry way. *The children* **gleefully** *ran toward the ice-cream truck.*

glid·er (glī'dər) *noun.* An aircraft that flies without a motor and rides on currents of air. *We entered a contest to see who could build a model* **glider** *that could fly the farthest.*

gloat·ed (glō'tid) *verb.* Thought about with satisfaction or, sometimes, mean-spirited pleasure. *The town* **gloated** *over its team's victory in the state tournament.*

gri·maced (gri'məst) *verb.* Twisted the face to show disgust, pain, or displeasure. *The carpenter* **grimaced** *when he stepped on a nail.*

grouch·y (grou'chē) *adjective.* In a bad mood; irritable; sulky. *Working with* **grouchy** *people is no fun at all.*

guid·ance (gī'dəns) *noun.* The act or process of guiding; giving direction or leading. *Before embarking on a law career, Maria sought* **guidance** *from lawyers she had met.*

Hh

ham·per[1] (ham'pər) *verb.* To interfere or slow the action or progress of something. *The rain did not* **hamper** *people from enjoying themselves at the outdoor concert.*

ham·per[2] (ham'pər) *noun.* A large basket or container, usually with a cover. *After getting caught in the rain, I threw my wet clothes in the laundry* **hamper**.

hob·bled (ho'bəld) *verb.* Moved or walked awkwardly with a limp. *After he sprained his ankle, Brad* **hobbled** *around for three weeks.*

hon·or·a·ble (on'ər ə bəl) *adjective.* Characterized by or having a sense of what is right or moral. *The young girl was considered very* **honorable** *when she returned the wallet she found.*

hov·er·ing (hu'və ring) *verb.* Remaining in the same spot for a period of time. *The bees were* **hovering** *above the chocolate cake at our picnic.*

Ii

il·le·gal·ly (i lē'gə lē) *adverb.* Acting in an unlawful manner. *The police officer wrote tickets for all the cars that were parked* **illegally**.

im·mense (i mens') *adjective.* Very large or huge. *The crowd at the outdoor concert left an* **immense** *amount of garbage on the ground.*

im•mi•grants (i′mi grənts) *noun,* plural. People who leave one country to live in another. *There are* **immigrants** *from many different countries living in my neighborhood.*

im•mi•grat•ed (i′mi grā′tid) *verb.* Entered a country or region in which one was not born in order to make a permanent home there. *Saskia's parents* **immigrated** *here from Russia about fifteen years ago.*

im•ple•ment (im′plə mənt) *1. noun.* A tool used to perform a task. *The student used a writing* **implement** *to complete the test. 2. verb.* To put into effect. *The school would* **implement** *the new rules in the next year.*

in•duct•ed (in duk′tid) *verb.* To have formally been placed into office or membership. *The retired baseball player was finally* **inducted** *into the Hall of Fame.*

in•scribed (in skrībd′) *verb.* Written, carved, engraved, or marked on something. *The stone walls were* **inscribed** *with the names of people who had given money to the museum.*

in•stinc•tive•ly (in stingk′tiv lē) *adverb.* Of or relating to a natural tendency. *Birds* **instinctively** *feed their young in the nest.*

in•tact (in takt′) *adjective.* Not damaged and in one whole piece. *The flower vase was still* **intact** *after it was found in the bottom of the box.*

in•ter•cept (in′tər sept′) *verb.* To stop on the way; to stop the course or progress of. *The defensive back managed to* **intercept** *the quarterback's pass.*

Word History

Intercept comes from the Latin, *interceptus,* which is the past participle of *intercipere,* meaning "interrupt" or "to catch between."

in•te•ri•or (in tîr′ē ər) *noun.* The inside of something. *The* **interior** *of the building was very cool compared to the outside.*

in•ter•pret•er (in tûr′pri tər) *noun.* One who helps to make something clear or understandable. *The* **interpreter** *at the United Nations translated English into Swahili.*

in•ter•sec•tion (in′tər sek′shən) *noun.* A place of intersecting, especially where two or more roads or streets meet or cross. *We stopped our car at the* **intersection** *of 70th Street and Second Avenue.*

i•so•lat•ed (ī′sə lā′tid) *verb.* Being or feeling alone. *New students sometimes feel* **isolated** *at the beginning of the school year.*

at; āpe; fär; câre; end; mē; it; īce; pîerce; hot; ōld; sông; fôrk; oil; out; up; ūse; rüle; pu̇ll; tûrn; chin; sing; shop; thin; <u>th</u>is; hw in white; zh in treasure.

The symbol ə stands for the unstressed vowel sound in about, taken, pencil, lemon, and circus.

Ll

la•ment•ed (lə men′təd) *verb.* Expressed sorrow, grief, or regret. *We all **lamented** the loss of the best player on the team to a knee injury.*

leg•a•cy (le′gə sē) *noun.* Something handed down by custom or tradition. *The mansion was passed down to my uncle by a **legacy** specifying that he never modernize it.*

lounge (lounj) *verb.* To lean, sit, or lie lazily. *During the summer, I love to **lounge** around the pool.* —*noun.* 1. A place for sitting, waiting, or relaxing within a public setting. *In the Victorian era, there was a ladies' and a gentlemen's **lounge** at the railway station.* 2. A couch or sofa. *I sat on a comfortable **lounge**.*

lux•u•ry (luk′shə rē, lug′zhə rē) *noun.* Something that adds to a person's comfort or pleasure but is not really necessary. *A yacht is a **luxury** that most of us cannot afford.*

Mm

main•tain (mān tān′) *verb.* To safeguard or hold the condition of. *One way to stay healthy is to **maintain** a healthy diet.*

ma•neu•vered (mə nü′vərd) *verb.* Used skillful or clever moves or plans. *Jackson **maneuvered** the large boat skillfully past the smaller ones.*

mass (mas) *noun.* A body of matter. *The fog looked like a large gray **mass** creeping up the coast.*

ma•tu•ri•ty (mə chür′ə tē) *noun.* The state or quality of reaching full physical and mental development, or full growth. *The crops are ready to be harvested when they have reached **maturity**.*

me•di•e•val (mē′dē ē′vəl, mid ē′vəl) *adjective.* Belonging to or happening in the Middle Ages, the period of European history from about the fifth century to the middle of the fifteenth century. *James came to class in a **medieval** costume to present his report on tenth-century Europe.*

mem•o•ra•bil•i•a (me′mə rə bil′ē ə) *noun, plural.* Things that are worth being collected or recorded. *At the flea market there was a lot of **memorabilia**.*

meth•ods (me′thəds) *noun, plural.* Ways of doing something. *The professor's teaching **methods** were considered new and progressive.*

mi•grant (mī′grənt) *adjective.* Moving from one region to another in search of work. *The **migrant** worker returned every April.*

mim•ics (mi′miks) *verb.* To imitate the speech, manners, or gestures of; to copy closely or reproduce. *The way Lucy **mimics** Harpo Marx is a classic bit of comedy.*

min•i•a•ture (min′ē ə chər) *adjective.* Greatly reduced in size or very small. *On their vacation, my parents bought me a **miniature** model of the Eiffel Tower.*

mis•treat•ed (mis trē′tid) *verb.* Treated badly. *The veterinarian said the dog we found had been **mistreated** by its owner.*

mod•er•ate (*adjective*, mod′ər it; *verb*, mod′ə rāt) *adjective.* Not extreme; balanced. *We have had **moderate** temperatures this winter.* —*verb.* To preside over or at. *My class wanted me to **moderate** the middle school debate, but I was too shy.*

mod•ern (mo′dərn) *adjective.* Of or relating to the present. *The new apartment complex was a totally **modern** design.*

myth•o•log•i•cal (mith′ə loj′i kəl) *adjective.* Of, relating to, or found in mythology. *The **mythological** character of Zeus was the ruler of all the gods on Mount Olympus.*

Nn

non•re•new•a•ble (nonʹri nüʹə bəl, nonʹri nüʹə bəl) *adjective.* Easily used up or exhausted. *Coal and petroleum are* **nonrenewable** *natural resources.*

nour•ish•ing (nûrʹi shing) *adjective.* Promoting health and growth. *So that I could grow up to be healthy and strong, my mother made me eat many* **nourishing** *foods.*

nui•sance (nüʹsəns, nūʹsəns) *noun.* A person, thing, or action that annoys or offends. *The bees were a huge* **nuisance** *during the picnic.*

Oo

or•deals (ôr dēlzʹ) *noun,* plural. Very difficult tests or painful experiences. *Auditioning for the two ballet companies made for exhausting* **ordeals***.*

or•i•gin (ôrʹi jin, orʹi jin) *noun.* 1. The source from which something begins. *What is the* **origin** *of that folk song?* 2. Parentage; ancestry. *Settlers of European* **origin** *arrived in Plymouth, Massachusetts, in 1620.*

out•skirts (outʹskûrts) *noun,* plural. The regions or sections surrounding or at the edge of an area, as in a city. *On the* **outskirts** *of the town we discovered beautiful woodland.*

Pp

par•tic•i•pate (pär tisʹə pātʹ) *verb.* To take part in an activity with others. *My teacher asked me to* **participate** *in the class discussion about NATO.*

pa•thet•ic (pə theʹtik) *adjective.* Bringing about pity, sadness, or sympathy. *The lost puppy looked so* **pathetic***, we brought him home.*

ped•es•tri•ans (pə desʹtrē ənz) *noun,* plural. Persons who travel on foot; walkers. *At busy intersections,* **pedestrians** *must cross only when the light stops traffic.*

Word History

The word **pedestrians** stems from the Latin word *pedester,* that originally comes from the Latin *pes,* meaning "foot."

pe•riph•er•al (pə riʹfə rəl) *adjective.* Relating to, located at, or forming the outermost part or edge. *Even though Ivan was facing the window, he saw in his* **peripheral** *vision that Karen had come in the door.*

per•ished (perʹishd) *verb.* To have died. *Many people* **perished** *in the earthquake.*

per•suade (pər swādʹ) *verb.* To cause someone to believe or do something by pleading or arguing. *The manager tried to* **persuade** *her employees to work extra hours during the holidays.*

---

at; āpe; fär; câre; end; mē; it; īce; pîerce; hot; ōld; sông; fôrk; oil; out; up; ūse; rüle; pùll; tûrn; chin; sing; shop; thin; <u>th</u>is; hw in white; zh in treasure.

The symbol ə stands for the unstressed vowel sound in about, taken, pencil, lemon, and circus.

phase (fāz) *noun.* A stage of development of a person or thing. *On the third* **phase** *of the journey, we traveled by sea.*

phi•los•o•pher (fə los′ə fər) *noun.* An expert in or student of the purpose of humanity, the universe, and life itself. *Many people showed up to listen to the* **philosopher** *speak on the human condition.*

plight (plīt) *noun.* A bad situation or condition. *The drought created a terrible* **plight** *for farmers.*

pon•der•ing (pon′dər ing) *noun.* The act of thinking something through. *Before deciding which summer camp to attend, Lisa spent a week of* **pondering***.*

pores (pôrz) *noun,* plural. Very small openings. *The* **pores** *in skin occur naturally.*

port•a•ble (pôr′tə bəl) *adjective.* Able to be moved easily or carried by hand. *The manager brought a* **portable** *television to the store so he could watch the baseball game while he worked.*

poverty (pov′ər tē) *noun.* The state of being poor. *Malnutrition can often be the direct result of* **poverty***.*

pre•car•i•ous (pri kâr′ē əs) *adjective.* Dependent on chance or circumstance; dangerous. *The climber was in a* **precarious** *position on the cliff.*

pre•cede (pri sēd′) *verb.* To go or come before or ahead of. *The bridesmaids* **precede** *the bride down the aisle.*

pref•er•enc•es (pre′fər əns əz) *noun,* plural. That which is preferred, liked better. *My* **preferences** *didn't seem to count when my family opted to go to the seashore rather than the mountains.*

pre•sum•a•bly (pri zü′mə blē) *adverb.* Likely, probably, or taken for granted. *Many students* **presumably** *stayed home when they saw all the snow this morning.*

pre•vail (pri vāl′) *verb.* 1. To be greater in power or influence; triumph or succeed. *We must try to* **prevail** *over everyday obstacles.* 2. To be widespread; persist. *Colds still* **prevail** *in our school during the winter.*

prin•ci•pal (prin′sə pəl) *adjective; noun.* 1. Greatest or first in importance, or value. *The fisher's* **principal** *objective was locating abundant tuna.* 2. The head or leader of an elementary or secondary school. *The* **principal** *of my school can be strict, but is very respectful of everyone.*

prob•a•bly (pro′ bə blē) *adverb.* Most likely. *If the traffic doesn't clear, we will* **probably** *miss our flight.*

pro•ce•dure (prə sē′jər) *noun.* A particular course of action, especially one that follows a definite series of steps. *The children followed the correct* **procedure** *during the fire drill.*

pro•hib•it (prō hib′it) *verb.* To forbid or prevent. *We need to* **prohibit** *smoking on the bus.*

pro•long (prə lông′) *verb.* To make longer, especially in time. *The host was happy to* **prolong** *the dinner, since the guests were having such a good time.*

prom•e•nade (pro′mə nād′, prom′ə näd′) *noun.* A leisurely walk, especially one taken in a public place for pleasure or display. *The ladies made their evening* **promenade** *to show off their finery.*

prom•i•nent (pro′mə nənt) *adjective.* Well-known or important; very noticeable. *Mr. Rodriguez and Mr. Johnson are* **prominent** *community leaders.*

pro•mot•ed (prə mō′tid) *verb.* 1. To have raised in rank. *The corporal was* **promoted** *to sergeant.* 2. To have tried to sell or make popular. *The advertisers* **promoted** *the new supermarket on television and in newspapers.*

pro•pelled (prə peld´) *verb.* Caused to move forward or onward; kept in motion. *The engine blast **propelled** the rocket into space.*

pro•por•tion (prə pôr´shən) *noun.* The relation of one thing to another with respect to size, number, degree, or amount. *The number of seats in the gym was not in **proportion** to the number of students.*

pros•pered (pros´pərd) *verb.* Having had success, wealth, or good fortune. *The owners of the business finally **prospered** after years of hard work.*

pur•su•ing (pər sū´ing) *verb.* To follow in order to overtake or capture. ***Pursuing** criminals is only one aspect of what police do.*

Qq

quar•an•tine (kwôr´ən tēn´, kwor´ən tēn´) *noun.* The isolation of persons, animals, ships, or goods exposed to infectious disease, to prevent the spread of the disease. *The doctors placed the family under **quarantine** when influenza broke out.*

quick•ened (kwi´kənd) *verb.* To have moved more rapidly. *Sally **quickened** her pace so she wouldn't miss her bus.*

quoins (koins, kwoins) *noun,* plural. Outside angles of a wall or building. *The **quoins** facing west were made of granite.*

Rr

raft•ers (raf´tərz) *noun,* plural. The sloping beams that support a roof. *Termites caused a lot of damage to the **rafters** in our house.*

ran•chos (ranch´ōs) *noun,* plural. The Spanish term for ranches. *The **ranchos** of Old California were known for their fertile land.*

ran•dom sam•ple (ran´dəm sam´pəl) *noun.* A sampling technique where a group of subjects (*sample*) is selected by chance from a larger group (*population*) for study. Every sample that can be selected has the same probability of being selected. *We conducted a survey on opinions about recycling, so we used a **random sample** of men and women.*

re•claim (ri klām´) *verb.* To bring back into a useful condition. *The new tenants decided to **reclaim** the backyard by throwing away garbage, removing cement slabs, and replanting grass and trees.*

at; āpe; fär; câre; end; mē; it; īce; pîerce; hot; ōld; sông; fôrk; oil; out; up; ūse; rüle; pùll; tûrn; chin; sing; shop; thin; this; hw in white; zh in treasure.

The symbol ə stands for the unstressed vowel sound in about, taken, pencil, lemon, and circus.

rec•om•mend (re′kə mend′) *verb.* To suggest or advise favorably. *I would recommend pizza if you go to that restaurant.*

re•gions (rē′jəns) *noun,* plural. Geographic areas with characteristics that set them apart. *The scientist traveled to different regions to take water and soil samples.*

reg•u•late (reg′yə lāt′) *verb.* To control, manage, or set. *The mayor wanted to regulate the amount of traffic on streets.*

reg•u•la•tion (reg′yə lā′shən) *adjective.* Required by law or rule. *The teacher issued regulation PE uniforms to the students.* —*noun.* A rule or order prescribed by authority. *There was a regulation dealing with excessive lateness at the elite prep school.*

re•li•a•ble (ri lī′ə bəl) *adjective.* Trustworthy; can be depended on. *The mechanic recommended buying the reliable sedan over the sporty convertible.*

re•mote (ri mōt′) *adjective.* Located out of the way, secluded. *It was a remote part of the mountains where few ever go.*

Ren•ais•sance (ren′ə säns′) *noun.* A revival of art, intellect, and scientific learning that took place in Europe from the fourteenth through the sixteenth centuries. *This weekend I need to finish my paper on the Italian Renaissance.*

ren•dez•vous (rän′di vü′) *adjective, noun.* Of or relating to an appointment to meet at a fixed place or time; the place chosen for such a meeting. *The rendezvous point for the sewing club was set for the local café.*

Word History

Rendezvous comes directly from the French *rendezvous* which also means "appointment" or "place of meeting."

re•new•a•ble (ri nü′ə bəl) *adjective.* Able to be replaced or restored. *The lease to the apartment was renewable after three years.*

rep•re•sent•a•tive sam•ple (rep′ri zen′tə tiv sam′pəl) *noun.* In statistics, when the group sampled represents a typical example or specimen. *Our survey was about school activities, so we chose a representative sample from all grades.*

rep•u•ta•tion (rep′yə tā′shən) *noun.* The public's opinion or reception of something or someone. *The scholar's reputation was ruined when he was caught cheating.*

re•sem•blance (ri zem′bləns) *noun.* A similarity, as of physical appearance; likeness. *There is often a close physical resemblance among members of the same family.*

res•i•dents (rez′i dənts) *noun,* plural. People who reside at the same place. *There were a number of residents that owned dogs.*

re•stored (ri stôrd′) *verb.* Reestablished. *The clock was restored after 20 years.*

re•strict•ed (ri strik′tid) *adjective.* Confined or limited. *The restricted area had a tall fence and a security guard to prevent trespassing.*

re•vived (ri vīvd′) *verb.* Gave new strength or freshness. *It was so humid that I felt revived when I drank the glass of iced tea.*

rum•maged (rum′ijd) *verb.* Having searched through (something) thoroughly by moving about its contents. *We rummaged around the attic until we found Grandma's old toys.*

rup•tured (rup′chərd) *verb.* Broken open or apart. *The pipe ruptured in the basement and caused a flood that ruined the carpet.*

Ss

scroung•ing (skroun´jing) *verb.* Gathering or collecting with effort or difficulty. *After school, I found my brother* **scrounging** *around the cupboards for something to eat.*

se•dat•ed (si dā´tid) *verb.* Made calm. *The nervous patient was* **sedated** *so she could sleep.*

sen•sa•tion•al (sen sā´shə nəl) *adjective.* Arousing or intending to arouse great excitement or interest; outstanding or extraordinary. *The* **sensational** *news story was, in fact, an exaggeration.*

sev•ered (se´vərd) *verb.* Separated by cutting or breaking. *The hose was* **severed** *when the gardener hit it by accident.*

shak•i•ly (shā´ki lē) *adverb.* Moving quickly to and fro, up and down, or side to side. *The little boy* **shakily** *picked up the heavy box.*

sheep•ish•ly (shē´pish lē) *adverb.* In an awkward, shy, or embarrassed way. *After slipping on the floor, the man* **sheepishly** *got up and left the room.*

sig•nif•i•cance (sig ni´fi kəns) *noun.* Of special value or importance. *The flag of any nation holds* **significance** *for its people.*

sleuth•ing (slü´thing) *verb.* The act of detecting or investigating. *Ramona's* **sleuthing** *led her to solve the mystery.*

sou•ve•nir (sü´və nîr´) *adjective.* Reminder of a person, place, or event; keepsake. *Mom kept the* **souvenir** *baseball we bought at the championship game.*

spe•cial•ists (spe´shə lists) *noun,* plural. Persons who focus on or specialize in a particular branch of a profession or field of study. *When faced with a disease, it is helpful to consult* **specialists**.

spec•ta•tors (spek´tā tərz) *noun,* plural. People who observe. *The* **spectators** *cheered for their team.*

spec•u•lat•ed (spek´yə lā´tid) *verb.* Thought carefully or seriously about; thought of reasons or answers for. *Because there were so few fish in the lake, the community* **speculated** *on the possibility of pollution.*

spon•sor•ing (spon´sə ring) *verb.* Assuming responsibility for or support of another person or thing. *Ms. Kaplan will be* **sponsoring** *the newspaper next year.*

spon•ta•ne•ous (spon tā´nē əs) *adjective.* On the spur of the moment; unplanned. *Since I like to control everything, I am not a* **spontaneous** *person.*

starch (stärch) *noun.* A carbohydrate used for stiffening cloth. *Stiffen that tablecloth with* **starch**.

sta•tis•tics (stə tis´tiks) *noun.* Numerical facts or data or the study of such. **Statistics** *show that American women vote in greater numbers than do American men.*

stead•fast•ly (sted´fast´lē) *adverb.* In an unchanging, unwavering way; faithfully. *The crew was* **steadfastly** *loyal to their captain.*

structures (struk´chərz) *noun,* plural. Anything built. *The huge* **structures** *were impressive.*

---

at; āpe; fär; câre; end; mē; it; īce; pîerce; hot; ōld; sông; fôrk; oil; out; up; ūse; rüle; pùll; tûrn; chin; sing; shop; thin; this; hw in white; zh in treasure.

The symbol ə stands for the unstressed vowel sound in about, taken, pencil, lemon, and circus.

sub•sti•tutes (sub'sti tūtz') *noun,* plural. Persons or things used in place of another. *My grandmother will sometimes use honey or maple syrup as sugar* **substitutes.**

sum•mit (sum'it) *noun.* The highest part or point. *The climbers reached the* **summit** *of the mountain and had a fabulous view.*

sump•tu•ous (sum'chü əs) *adjective.* Expensive and lavish, richly done. *The castle had* **sumptuous** *furnishings.*

su•per•sti•tious (sü'pər stish'əs) *adjective.* Having beliefs based on an unreasoning fear of the unknown. *Many architects of tall buildings are* **superstitious** *and never include a thirteenth floor.*

sus•te•nance (səs'tə nənts) *noun.* Nourishment. *Many nutritious foods offer* **sustenance** *to people and animals.*

sweet•en (swē'tən) *verb.* To make or become sweet or sweeter. *Because the batter was bitter, the cook had to* **sweeten** *it with honey.*

swiv•eled (swi'vəld) *verb.* Turned something on a base. *The principal* **swiveled** *around in her chair when she heard me enter her office.*

sym•me•try (sim'ə trē) *noun.* An arrangement of parts that are alike on either side of a central line; proportion and harmony of form. *The starfish shows a lovely* **symmetry** *in its shape.*

Tt

tech•nol•o•gy (tek nol'ə jē) *noun.* Methods and machines used in doing things in science or industry. *The surgeons used the newest* **technology** *during the operation.*

ter•rac•ing (ter'ə sing) *verb.* To form raised, level platforms of earth with vertical or sloping fronts or sides. *The farmers were* **terracing** *their land to conserve the soil.*

tink•er•ing (ting'kə ring) *verb.* To busy oneself in a trifling or aimless way; putter. *The farmer had been* **tinkering** *with the engine of his tractor all morning.*

trans•por•ted (trāns pôr'tid) *verb.* Brought or carried something. *The products were* **transported** *by truck across the country.*

trig•ger (trig'ər) *noun; verb.* 1. A small lever on a gun or firearm. 2. To start or cause. *The mountain climbers were quiet, so they would not* **trigger** *an avalanche.*

tri•ples (trip'əlz) *noun,* plural. Hits in baseball when a batter reaches third base. *Sara hit two* **triples** *during the game.*

typ•i•cal (tip'i kəl) *adjective.* Showing the qualities of a particular type; usual. *Jake's joking response was* **typical;** *he likes to get me to laugh about my problems.*

Uu

un•bear•a•ble (un bâr'ə bəl) *adjective.* That which cannot be endured or tolerated. *When there are presents to open, the wait can be* **unbearable***!*

un•der•took (un'dər tŭk') *verb.* To have agreed to accept a task. *The team* **undertook** *a new project even though they were not finished with another one.*

un•de•tec•ted (un'di tek'tid) *verb.* Not being noticed or discovered. *The secret plot was* **undetected** *for some time, but the police soon learned the truth.*

un•i•mag•i•na•ble (un´i maj´ə nə bəl) *adjective.* Unable to be imagined; hard to imagine. *That the whole class could fail the test was **unimaginable**.*

u•ni•ver•sal•ly (ū´nə vûr´sə lē) *adverb.* In every instance or place; without exception. *The movie was **universally** criticized for its horrible acting and ridiculous plot.*

un•stead•y (un sted´ē) *adjective.* Shaky or not firm. *I was nervous when Michael climbed up the **unsteady** ladder to get on the roof.*

u•ten•sils (ū ten´səlz) *noun,* plural. Objects that are useful in doing or making something. *One third of the world eats with its fingers, one third with chopsticks, and one third with metal **utensils**.*

ut•tered (ut´ərd) *verb.* Expressed aloud. *The teacher got very upset when someone **uttered** the answer during the test.*

Vv

va•pors (vā´pərz) *noun,* plural. Visible particles of matter suspended in the air, such as mist or smoke. *Our teacher told us that some of the **vapors** from the science experiment were harmful.*

veg•e•ta•tion (vej´i tā´shən) *noun.* Plant life. *The fields and forests are full of **vegetation**.*

ven•om•ous (ven´ə məs) *adjective.* Able to inflict a poisonous wound, especially by biting or stinging. *Some snakes are **venomous**, so be careful not to get close!*

vic•to•ri•ous (vik tôr´ē əs) *adjective.* Having won a contest or conflict. *The **victorious** team was given a parade when they returned home.*

vig•or•ous•ly (vig´ər əs lē) *adverb.* Done in a powerful or forceful way; with healthy strength. *The lawyer **vigorously** defended the U.S. Constitution.*

vi•tal (vī´təl) *adjective.* Of greatest importance. *The information was **vital** to everyone who wanted the project to succeed.*

vol•un•teered (vol´ən tîrd´) *verb.* Gave or offered. *The entire family **volunteered** to hand out water at the marathon.*

Ww

with•stood (with stud´) *verb.* Held out against or fought against. *The beach house **withstood** the force of the hurricane.*

wrath (rath) *noun.* Extreme or violent anger. *The football player tried extra hard in the game to avoid the **wrath** of his coach.*

wreck•age (re´kij) *noun.* The remains of anything that has been destroyed. *A lot of **wreckage** from the sunken ship washed up on the beach.*

---

at; āpe; fär; câre; end; mē; it; īce; pîerce; hot; ōld; sông; fôrk; oil; out; up; ūse; rüle; pùll; tûrn; chin; sing; shop; thin; <u>th</u>is; hw in white; zh in treasure.

The symbol ə stands for the unstressed vowel sound in about, taken, pencil, lemon, and circus.

Acknowledgments

The publisher gratefully acknowledges permission to reprint the following copyrighted material:

"After Apple Picking" by Robert Frost is from NORTH OF BOSTON. Copyright © 1915. Reprinted by permission of Henry Holt and Company.

"Amazing Artificial Limbs" includes information from "Bionic Arms for 11-Year-Old." BBC News. March 15, 2001. http://news.bbc.co.uk/1/hi/health/1222642.stm.

"Baseball by the Numbers" chart is from THE NEW YORK TIMES 2004 ALMANAC edited by John W. Wright. Copyright © 2003 by The New York Times Company. Used by permission of the Penguin Group Penguin Putnam Inc.

"Bicycle Riding" is from CRICKET by Sandra Liatsos. Copyright © 1984 by Sandra Liatsos. Reprinted by permission of Marion Reiner for the Author.

"Birdfoot's Grampa" is from NATIVE AMERICAN STORIES by Joseph Bruchac, illustrated by John Kahionhes Fadden. Text copyright © 1991 by Joseph Bruchac. Illustrations copyright © 1991 by John Kahionhes Fadden.

"Breaking Through" is from BREAKING THROUGH by Francisco Jiménez. Copyright © 2001 by Francisco Jiménez. Reprinted by permission of Houghton Mifflin Company.

"The Crow and the Pitcher" is from AESOP'S FABLES by Jerry Pinkney. Copyright © 2000 by Jerry Pinkney. Reprinted by permission of SeaStar Books, a division of North-South Books, Inc.

"Daily Life in Ancient Greece" is from Ancient Greece Daily Life by Stewart Ross. Copyright © 2007 by Bailey Publishing Associates Ltd. Used by permission of Compass Points Books.

"The Dog of Pompeii" is from THE DONKEY OF GOD by Louis Untermeyer, illustrated by James MacDonald. Text copyright © 1999 The Estate of Louis Untermeyer. This permission is expressly granted by Laurence S. Untermeyer.

"The Emperor's Silent Army: Terracotta Warriors of Ancient China" is from THE EMPEROR'S SILENT ARMY: TERRACOTTA WARRIORS OF ANCIENT CHINA by Jane O'Connor. Copyright © Jane O'Connor, 2002. Reprinted by permission of Viking, a division of Penguin Putnam Books for Young Readers.

"Empire in the Andes" includes information from LOST CITY OF THE INCAS by Hiram Bingham and New World News. Copyright © 2001 by Labyrinthina.

"Exploring the Titanic" is from EXPLORING THE TITANIC by Robert D. Ballard, cover illustration by Ken Marshall. Text copyright © Odyssey Corporation 1998. Illustration copyright © 1988 Madison Publishing Inc. Used by permission of Scholastic Inc.

"Fire! Destruction of Chicago!" is from the Chicago Tribune, 1871. Copyright © 1996 Chicago Historical Society and the Trustees of Northwestern University. Used by permission.

"The Golden Touch: The Story of Bacchus and King Midas" is from FAVORITE GREEK MYTHS by Mary Pope Osborne. Copyright © 1989 by Mary Pope Osborne. Reprinted by permission of Scholastic Inc.

"The Great Fire" by Jim Murphy. Copyright © by Jim Murphy. Used by permission of Scholastic Paperback Nonfiction, an imprint of Scholastic Inc.

"The Great Serum Race: Blazing the Iditarod Trail" is from THE GREAT SERUM RACE: BLAZING THE IDITAROD TRAIL by Debbie S. Miller, illustrations by Jon Van Zyle. Text copyright © 2002 by Debbie S. Miller. Illustrations copyright © 2002 by Jon Van Zyle. Used by permission of Walker & Company.

"Haiku" is from JAPANESE HAIKU by Boncho. Translated by Peter Beilenson. Copyright © 1955, 1956 by Peter Pauper Press. Reprinted by permission of Peter Pauper Press.

"Honus and Me" is from HONUS AND ME by Dan Gutman. Copyright © 1997 by Dan Gutnam. Used by permission of HarperCollins Children's Books.

"How Tía Lola Came to Visit Stay" is from HOW TÍA LOLA CAME TO VISIT STAY by Julia Alvarez. Text copyright © 2001 by Julia Alverez. Jacket Illustration copyright © by Sally Wern Comport. Reprinted by permission of Alfred A. Knopf, a division of Random House.

"How to Conduct a Survey" is from MACMILLAN/McGRAW-HILL MATH. Copyright © 2005 by Macmillan/McGraw-Hill. Illustration credits: p. 140: Brian Dugan.

"Icebergs and Glaciers" by Seymour Simon. Text copyright © by Seymour Simon. Used by permission of William Morrow & Company, Inc.

"Interrupted Journey: Saving Endangered Sea Turtles" is from INTERRUPTED JOURNEY: SAVING ENDANGERED SEA TURTLES by Kathryn Lasky. Copyright © 2001 by Kathryn Lasky. Used by permission of Candlewick Press.

"In the Days of the Vaqueros: America's First True Cowboys" is from IN THE DAYS OF THE VAQUEROS: AMERICA'S FIRST TRUE COWBOYS by Russell Freedman. Text copyright © 2001 by Russell Freedman. Reprinted by permission of Houghton Mifflin Company.

"Juan Verdades: The Man Who Couldn't Tell a Lie" is from JUAN VERDADES: THE MAN WHO COULDN'T TELL A LIE by Joe Hayes, illustrated by Joseph Daniel Fiedler. Text copyright © 2001 by Joe Hayes. Illustrations copyright © 2001 by Joseph Daniel Fiedler. Used by permission of Orchard Books, an imprint of Scholastic.

"LAFFF" is from LAFFF by Lensey Namioka, illustrations by Raúl Colón. Copyright © 1993 by Lensey Namioka. Used by permission.

"Leonardo da Vinci" is from LEONARDO DA VINCI by Diane Stanley. Copyright © 1996 by Diane Stanley. Used by permission of William Morrow and Company, Inc.

"Leonardo da Vinci" caption from http://www.museoscienza.org/english/leonardo/vitc.html.

"Leonardo's Horse" is from LEONARDO'S HORSE by Jean Fritz, illustrated by Hudson Talbott. Text copyright © 2001 by Jean Fritz. Illustrations copyright © 2001 by Hudson Talbott. Reprinted by permission of G.P. Putnam's Sons, a division of Penguin Putnam Books for Young Readers.

"Lost City: The Discovery of Machu Picchu" is from LOST CITY: THE DISCOVERY OF MACHU PICCHU by Ted Lewin. Copyright © 2003 by Ted Lewin. Reprinted by permission of Philomel Books, a division of Penguin Putnam Books for Young Readers.

"The Magic Gourd" is from THE MAGIC GOURD by Baba Wagué Diakité. Text and art copyright © 2003 by Baba Wagué Diakité. Used by permission of Scholastic Press, a division of Scholastic Inc.

"Major Taylor: Champion Cyclist" is from MAJOR TAYLOR: CHAMPION CYCLIST by Lesa Cline-Ransome, illustrated by James E. Ransome. Text copyright © 2004 by Lesa Cline-Ransome. Illustrations copyright © 2004 by James E. Ransome. Reprinted by permission of Atheneum Books for Young Readers, an Imprint of Simon & Schuster Children's Publishing Division.

"Nothing Ever Happens on 90th Street" is from NOTHING EVER HAPPENS ON 90TH STREET by Roni Schotter, illustrated by Kyrsten Brooker. Text copyright © 1997 by Roni Schotter. Illustrations copyright © 1997 by Kyrsten Brooker. Reprinted by permission of Orchard Books.

"Old Stormalong Finds a Man-Sized Ship" is from BIG MEN, BIG COUNTRY by Paul Robert Walker, illustrations by James Bernardin. Text copyright © 1993 by Paul Robert Walker. Illustration copyright © 1993 by James Bernardin. Reprinted by permission of Harcourt, Inc.

"The Origin of Ghana" is from THE ROYAL KINGDOMS OF GHANA, MALI, AND SONGHAY: LIFE IN MEDIEVAL AFRICA by Patricia and Fredrick McKissack. Copyright © 1994 by Patricia and Fredrick McKissack. Reprinted by permission of Henry Holt and Company.

"Rumpelstiltskin's Daughter" is from RUMPELSTILTSKIN'S DAUGHTER by Diane Stanley. Copyright © 1997 by Diane Stanley. Used by permission of Morrow Junior Books, a division of William Morrow & Company, Inc.

"Seeing Things His Own Way" is from UNCOMMON CHAMPIONS: FIFTEEN ATHLETES WHO BATTLED BACK by Marty Kaminsky. Copyright © 2000 by Marty Kaminsky. Reprinted by Boyds Mills Press, Inc., a Highlights Company.

"The Sidewalk Racer or On the Skateboard" is from THE SIDEWALK RACER AND OTHER POEMS OF SPORTS AND MOTION by Lillian

Morrison. Copyright © 1977 by Lillian Morrison. Reprinted by permission of the author in Macmillan McGraw-Hill Reading (Grade 5) copyright © 2003, 2001.

SIERRA by Diane Siebert. Text © 1991 by Diane Siebert. Reprinted by permission of HarperCollins.

"The Storm" by Chora, and "Winter" by Shiki are from AN INTRODUCTION TO HAIKU by Harold G. Henderson. Copyright © 1958 by Harold G. Henderson. Reprinted by permission of Random House.

"The Summer of the Swans" is from THE SUMMER OF THE SWANS by Betsy Byars. Copyright © 1970 by Betsy Byars. All rights reserved. Used by permission of Puffin Books.

"TA-NA-E-KA" by Mary Whitebird, illustrated by Shonto Begay. Published in SCHOLASTIC VOICE, December 13, 1973. Copyright © 1973 by Scholastic, Inc.

"This Land is Your Land" by Woody Guthrie. Copyright © 1956, 1958, and 1970 Ludlow Music Inc. Used by permission of Ludlow Music, Inc., New York.

"Volcanoes" by Seymour Simon. Copyright © 1988 by Seymour Simon. Used by permission of Collins, an imprint of HarperCollins Publishers.

"Zlateh the Goat" is from ZLATEH THE GOAT AND OTHER STORIES by Isaac Bashevis Singer. Text copyright © 1966 by Isaac Bashevis Singer, renewed 1994 by Alma Singer. Used by permission of HarperCollins Publishers.

ILLUSTRATIONS

Cover Illustration by John Rowe

8-9: Antonio Cangemi. 10-27: Kyrsten Brooker. 36-37: Colin Bootman. 72-73: Ned Shaw. 74-87: Raúl Colón. 96-97: Peter Thornton. 98-113: Nicole Tadgell. 154: Lydia Hess. 155: Adam Hook. 157-165: Adam Hook. 175: Charles Reasoner. 188-203: Ted Lewin. 212-213: Stephan Daigle. 214-227: Baba Wagué Dakité. 228-229: Jennifer Hewitson. 248-265: Joseph Daniel Fielder. 267: John Hovell. 267: (b) Arvis Stewart. 276-292: Diane Stanley. 296: Carol Heyer. 316-333: Shonto Begay. 334-335: Jerry Pinkney. 342-352: Ron Mazellan. 355-356: Ron Mazellan. 400-401: James E. Ransome. 403-407: James E. Ransome. 409: James E. Ransome. 412-413: James E. Ransome. 437-439: Hudson Talbott. 440: Hudson Talbott. 443-444: Hudson Talbott. 447-451: Hudson Talbott. 462-474: Lester Coloma. 476-477: Lester Coloma. 522-523: Michael Jaroszko. 574-575: Warren Gebert. 582-583: Ken Marschall. 585: Pronk&Associates. 588: Ken Marschall. 589: Pronk&Associates. 594: Ken Marschall. 596-597: Pronk&Associates. 598-601: Carol Heyer. 618-633: John Rowe. 660: Courtesy of Candlewick Press. 682-695: Jon Van Zyle. 684-685: Jon Van Zyle. 696-697: Jon Van Zyle. 698-699: Oki Han.

PHOTOGRAPHY

All photographs are by Macmillan/McGraw-Hill (MMH) or Ken Karp for MMH except as noted below:

Inside Front and Back Cover: The McGraw-Hill Companies/John A. Karachewski, photographer; iv: (b) Courtesy of Francisco Jimenez. v: (t) Don Smetzer/PhotoEdit. vi: (c) Wolfgang Kaehler. vii: (t) Sissie Brimberg/National Geographic/Getty Images, Inc. ix: (t) David Young-Wolff/PhotoEdit Inc. x: (c bkgd) Photodisc/Getty Images, Inc.; (c inset) Jamie Bloomquist Photography. xi: (t) David Young-Wolff/PhotoEdit. xii: (c) National Park Service; (b) Erich Lessing/Art Resource, NY. xiii: (t) Reuters/Landov; (c) Dr. Charles Swithinbank/Scott Polar Research Institute. xiv: (b) Christopher G. Knight. xv: (t) ML Sinibadi/CORBIS; (b) John Thompson. 2-3: Noboru Hashimoto/CORBIS. 3: Ronnie Kaufman/CORBIS. 4: Lawrence Manning/CORBIS. 5: Sean Masterson/Courtesy, Pam Ryan. 6-7: Frederic Neema/ CORBIS SYGMA. 26: Wendy Goldberg. 28: (l) Courtesy of Karen Odom; (r) Courtesy of Perry Faulkner. 30: Paul Barton/CORBIS. 33: Gabe Palmer/CORBIS. 34-35: Joe Cornish/Stone/Getty Images. 38: Courtesy of Francisco Jimenez. 38-39: Getty Images. 39: Courtesy of Francisco Jimenez. 41: Library of Congress. 43: (t) Getty Images; (b) Courtesy of Francisco Jimenez; (bkgd) Library of Congress. 44: (t) Courtesy of Francisco Jimenez; (bkgd) Getty Images. 45: (bkgd) Library of Congress; (l, r) Courtesy of Francisco Jimenez; (b) ImageFarm, Inc. 47: (t) Bettmann/CORBIS. 49: (bkgd) Library of Congress; (t) Courtesy of Francisco Jimenez; (frame) Getty Images. 50: (t) Courtesy of Francisco Jimenez; (frame) Photodisc/Getty Images. 50-51: Ed Young/CORBIS. 52: David Young-Wolff/Getty Images, Inc. 56: Courtesy, Francisco Jimenez. 57: David Schmidt/Masterfile. 58-59: Don Smetzer/Photo Edit. 60: Melanie Weiner. 61: (t) Coral Von Zumwalt; (b) Jurgen Vogt/Getty Images. 62-63: Cantomedia. 64: Frank Cantor and (cover design) Alex Camlin. 65: Frank Cantor. 66: (l) Reuters/CORBIS; (r) Anne Frank Fonds-Basel/Anne Frank House Amsterdam/Getty Images. 69: (bkgd) Ana de Sousa/Shutterstock; (tr) PhotoLink/Getty Images; (bl) Ryan McVay/Getty

Images; (br) Stockbyte/PunchStock. 70-71: A. Hansen/Getty Images, Inc. 86: (l) Courtesy of Lensey Namioka; (r) Courtesy of Morgan Gaynin Inc. 88: (bkgd) Roger Harris/Photo Researchers, Inc.; (b) Jeff Greenberg/The Image Works, Inc. 89: (t) Aaron Horowitz/CORBIS; (l) STScI/NASA/Ressmeyer/CORBIS; (cr) Julian Baum/SPL/Photo Researchers, Inc.; (br) Bettmann/CORBIS. 90: (tl) Rykoff Collection/CORBIS; (bl) Bettmann/CORBIS. 90-91: (c) Aaron Horowitz/CORBIS; (c) STScI/NASA/Ressmeyer/CORBIS. 91: Erich Schrempp/SPL/Photo Researchers, Inc. 93: Rubberball Productions/Getty Images, Inc. 94-95: Pixtal/AGE FotoStock. 112: (l) Courtesy of Karen English; (r) Courtesy of Nicole Tadgell. 114-115: (bkgd) Michael Pole/CORBIS; (t) Cydney Conger/CORBIS. 117: Fabio Cardoso/AGE Fotostock. 118: Jose Luis Pelaez, Inc./CORBIS. 118-119: Royalty-Free/CORBIS. 120: Visual Arts Library (London)/Alamy. 124-125: Diehm/Stone/Getty Images. 126: Petr Bonek/Alamy. 127: Courtesy, Mark Hylkema. 128-129: Miles Ertman/Masterfile. 130: AP-Wide World Photos. 131: Bojan Brecelj/CORBIS. 132-133: Wolfgang Kaehler. 133: Patrick Aventurier/GAMMA. 134: O. Louis Mazzatenta/National Geographic Image Collection. 135: Wolfgang Kaehler. 136: Zhou Kang (c) copyright 2001. Imaginechina.com. All rights reserved. 137: The Art Archive/British Library. 139: Bridgeman-Giraudon/Art Resource, NY. 140: Bonhams, London, UK/Bridgeman Art Library. 141: Jiang Ren/Private Collection/Imaginechina.com. 142-143: The Art Archive/Genius of China Exhibition. 144: Jim O'Connor. 144-145: Wolfgang Kaehler. 146-147: K.M. Westermann/CORBIS. 148: Patrick Aventurier/GAMMA. 149: Rubberball Productions/Getty Images, Inc. 150-151: Adrain Buck/Alamy. 152-153: Ted Spiegel/CORBIS. 156: John Hios/AKG Images. 158: Erich Lessing/Art Resource. 160: Museo Capitonlino, Rome/Dagli Orti/Art Archive. 163: Ashmolean Museum, Oxford/Bridgeman Art Library. 164: Dagli Orti/Art Archive. 166: Courtesy, Stewart Ross. 168: Siede Preis/Getty Images. 168-169: L. Hobbs/PhotoLink/Getty Images. 171: Joe McBride/Stone/Getty Images, Inc. 172-173: Sissie Brimberg/National Geographic/Getty Images, Inc. 174: Science Magazine/AFP/NewsCom. 175: Bettman/CORBIS. 176-177: Gallo images-Denny Allen/Digital Vision/Alamy. 177: Kenneth Garrett/National Geographic. 178: Michele Molinari/Danita Delimont/Alamy. 178-179: Gallo images-Denny Allen/Digital Vision/Alamy. 179: (t) Penny Tweedie/CORBIS. 180: Shelly Katz. 183: (bkgd) John Clines/Shutterstock; (tr) PhotoLink/Getty Images; (l) Stockbyte/PunchStock; (br) Tracy Montana/PhotoLink/Getty Images. 184-185: Jeremy Horner/Stone/Getty Images. 186: Adalberto Rios Szalay/Sexto Sol/Getty Images, Inc. 186-187: Frank Siteman/AGE Fotostock. 187: Werner Forman/Art Resource. 202: Courtesy, Ted Lewin. 204: Jamie Marshall - Tribaley Images/Alamy. 204-205: Galen Rowell/CORBIS. 206: The Granger Collection, New York. 206-207: (t) Kevin Schafer/CORBIS; (b) Pablo Corral Vega/CORBIS. 207: Wolfgang Kaehler. 209: AGE Fotostock. 210-211: Steve Allen/Brand X Pictures/PictureQuest. 213: Dana White/PhotoEdit Inc. 226: Leo Arfer. 231: The Art Archive. 233: AGE Fotostock. 234: Scala/Art Resource. 235: F. Jack Jackson/Alamy. 236: Bettmann/CORBIS. 240-241: Jonathan Nourok/PhotoEdit Inc. 241: Allen Brown/Dbimages/Alamy. 242: Vincent Besnault/Digital Vision/Getty Images. 243: Michael Smith/Newsmakers/Getty Images. 244-245: Dana White/PhotoEdit. 246: Dewitt Jones/CORBIS. 246-247: George H.H. Huey/CORBIS. 264: (l) Jack Kotz for MMH; (r) Courtesy of Joseph Daniel Fiedler. 266-267: David Stoecklein/CORBIS. 268: Christie's Images/CORBIS. 268-269: Tom Bean/Getty Images, Inc. 271: PhotoDisc/Getty Images, Inc. 272-273: Michael Newman/PhotoEdit. 292: Karen Sachar. 299: Comstock/Getty Images, Inc. 300-301: David Young-Wolff/PhotoEdit Inc. 302: James Keyser/Time-Life Pictures/Getty Images, Inc. 303: (t) Freddy Lea; (b) Alex McKnight; (b) Katherine Lambert. 304: (t) Ann States; (b) Oseoloa McCarty, Courtesy Southern Mississippi University. 305: Timothy Greenfield-Sanders. 306: (t) Terry Ashe/Time-Life Pictures/Getty Images, Inc.; (b) John Chiasson. 307: Ann States. 308: Nancy Palmieri. 311: (bkgd) John Clines/Shutterstock; (tr) PhotoLink/Getty Images; (l) Stockbyte/PunchStock; (br) Tracy Montana/PhotoLink/Getty Images. 312-313: Stephanie Maze/CORBIS. 314: Joanna B. Pinneo/Aurora. 315: Bill Aron/PhotoEdit Inc. 332: Tom Alexander. 337: Alan Levenson/AGE Fotostock. 338-339: Philip Rostron/Masterfile. 356: Courtesy of Dan Gutman. 358: (l) Royalty-Free/CORBIS; (r) AP Photo/Kathy Willens. 361: AGE Fotostock. 362: Peter Griffin/Alamy. 362-363: Royalty-Free/CORBIS. 363: Ingram Publishing (Superstock Limited)/Alamy. 364: Royalty-Free/CORBIS. 365: (t) Comstock/Punchstock; (r) Royalty-Free/CORBIS; (b) Morril/Index Stock Imagery. 368-369: Bob Daemmrich/PhotoEdit Inc. 369: George S. De Blonsky/Alamy. 370: moodboard/Alamy. 371: AllStar Picture Library/Alamy. 372-373: Bob Daemmrich/CORBIS. 374: Noah Hamilton Photography. 375: AP-Wide World Photos. 376: (t) Duomo/CORBIS; (bl) Didrick Johnck/CORBIS; (br) Jamie Bloomquist Photography. 376-377: (t) Jamie Bloomquist Photography; (bkgd) Photodisc/Getty Images, Inc. 378: Royalty-free/CORBIS. 378-379: Photodisc/Getty Images, Inc. 379: Jamie Bloomquist Photography. 380-381: Photodisc/Getty Images, Inc. 381: (l) Ed Weinhenmayer; (r) Danny Lehman/CORBIS. 382: Jamie Bloomquist Photography. 382-383: Photodisc/Getty Images, Inc. 383: Phoenix Country Day School. 384: C Squared Studios/Getty Images, Inc. 384-385: Photodisc/Getty Images, Inc. 385: Jamie Bloomquist Photography. 386: Didrick Johnck/CORBIS. 386-387: Photodisc/Getty Images, Inc. 387: Duomo/CORBIS. 388: (l)

Reading/Language Arts
CA California Standards
Grade 6

READING

1.0 Word Analysis, Fluency, and Systematic Vocabulary Development
Students use their knowledge of word origins and word relationships, as well as historical and literary context clues, to determine the meaning of specialized vocabulary and to understand the precise meaning of grade-level-appropriate words.

Word Recognition

1.1 Read aloud narrative and expository text fluently and accurately and with appropriate pacing, intonation, and expression.

Vocabulary and Concept Development

1.2 Identify and interpret figurative language and words with multiple meanings.

1.3 Recognize the origins and meanings of frequently used foreign words in English and use these words accurately in speaking and writing.

1.4 Monitor expository text for unknown words or words with novel meanings by using word, sentence, and paragraph clues to determine meaning.

1.5 Understand and explain "shades of meaning" in related words (e.g., *softly* and *quietly*).

2.0 Reading Comprehension (Focus on Informational Materials)
Students read and understand grade-level-appropriate material. They describe and connect the essential ideas, arguments, and perspectives of the text by using their knowledge of text structure, organization, and purpose. The selections in *Recommended Literature, Kindergarten Through Grade Twelve* illustrate the quality and complexity of the materials to be read by students. In addition, by grade eight, students read one million words annually on their own, including a good representation of grade-level-appropriate narrative and expository text (e.g., classic and contemporary literature, magazines, newspapers, online information). In grade six, students continue to make progress toward this goal.

Structural Features of Informational Materials

2.1 Identify the structural features of popular media (e.g., newspapers, magazines, online information) and use the features to obtain information.

2.2 Analyze text that uses the compare-and-contrast organizational pattern.

READING (continued)

Comprehension and Analysis of Grade-Level-Appropriate Text

2.3 Connect and clarify main ideas by identifying their relationships to other sources and related topics.

2.4 Clarify an understanding of texts by creating outlines, logical notes, summaries, or reports.

2.5 Follow multiple-step instructions for preparing applications (e.g., for a public library card, bank savings account, sports club, league membership).

Expository Critique

2.6 Determine the adequacy and appropriateness of the evidence for an author's conclusions.

2.7 Make reasonable assertions about a text through accurate, supporting citations.

2.8 Note instances of unsupported inferences, fallacious reasoning, persuasion, and propaganda in text.

3.0 Literary Response and Analysis Students read and respond to historically or culturally significant works of literature that reflect and enhance their studies of history and social science. They clarify the ideas and connect them to other literary works. The selections in *Recommended Literature, Kindergarten Through Grade Twelve* illustrate the quality and complexity of the materials to be read by students.

Structural Features of Literature

3.1 Identify the forms of fiction and describe the major characteristics of each form.

Narrative Analysis of Grade-Level-Appropriate Text

3.2 Analyze the effect of the qualities of the character (e.g., courage or cowardice, ambition or laziness) on the plot and the resolution of the conflict.

3.3 Analyze the influence of setting on the problem and its resolution.

3.4 Define how tone or meaning is conveyed in poetry through word choice, figurative language, sentence structure, line length, punctuation, rhythm, repetition, and rhyme.

3.5 Identify the speaker and recognize the difference between first-and third-person narration (e.g., autobiography compared with biography).

3.6 Identify and analyze features of themes conveyed through characters, actions, and images.

3.7 Explain the effects of common literary devices (e.g., symbolism, imagery, metaphor) in a variety of fictional and nonfictional texts.

Literary Criticism

3.8 Critique the credibility of characterization and the degree to which a plot is contrived or realistic (e.g., compare use of fact and fantasy in historical fiction).

WRITING

1.0 Writing Strategies Students write clear, coherent, and focused essays. The writing exhibits students' awareness of the audience and purpose. Essays contain formal introductions, supporting evidence, and conclusions. Students progress through the stages of the writing process as needed.

Organization and Focus

1.1 Choose the form of writing (e.g., personal letter, letter to the editor, review, poem, report, narrative) that best suits the intended purpose.

1.2 Create multiple-paragraph expository compositions:
   a. Engage the interest of the reader and state a clear purpose.
   b. Develop the topic with supporting details and precise verbs, nouns, and adjectives to paint a visual image in the mind of the reader.
   c. Conclude with a detailed summary linked to the purpose of the composition.

1.3 Use a variety of effective and coherent organizational patterns, including comparison and contrast; organization by categories; and arrangement by spatial order, order of importance, or climactic order.

Research and Technology

1.4 Use organizational features of electronic text (e.g., bulletin boards, databases, keyword searches, e-mail addresses) to locate information.

1.5 Compose documents with appropriate formatting by using word-processing skills and principles of design (e.g., margins, tabs, spacing, columns, page orientation).

Evaluation and Revision

1.6 Revise writing to improve the organization and consistency of ideas within and between paragraphs.

2.0 Writing Applications (Genres and Their Characteristics) Students write narrative, expository, persuasive, and descriptive texts of at least 500 to 700 words in each genre. Student writing demonstrates a command of standard American English and the research, organizational, and drafting strategies outlined in Writing Standard 1.0.

Using the writing strategies of grade six outlined in Writing Standard 1.0, students:

2.1 Write narratives:
   a. Establish and develop a plot and setting and present a point of view that is appropriate to the stories.
   b. Include sensory details and concrete language to develop plot and character.
   c. Use a range of narrative devices (e.g., dialogue, suspense).

WRITING (continued)

2.2 Write expository compositions (e.g., description, explanation, comparison and contrast, problem and solution):
  a. State the thesis or purpose.
  b. Explain the situation.
  c. Follow an organizational pattern appropriate to the type of composition.
  d. Offer persuasive evidence to validate arguments and conclusions as needed.

2.3 Write research reports:
  a. Pose relevant questions with a scope narrow enough to be thoroughly covered.
  b. Support the main idea or ideas with facts, details, examples, and explanations from multiple authoritative sources (e.g., speakers, periodicals, online information searches).
  c. Include a bibliography.

2.4 Write responses to literature:
  a. Develop an interpretation exhibiting careful reading, understanding, and insight.
  b. Organize the interpretation around several clear ideas, premises, or images.
  c. Develop and justify the interpretation through sustained use of examples and textual evidence.

2.5 Write persuasive compositions:
  a. State a clear position on a proposition or proposal.
  b. Support the position with organized and relevant evidence.
  c. Anticipate and address reader concerns and counterarguments.

WRITTEN AND ORAL ENGLISH LANGUAGE CONVENTIONS

The standards for written and oral English language conventions have been placed between those for writing and for listening and speaking because these conventions are essential to both sets of skills.

1.0 Written and Oral English Language Conventions Students write and speak with a command of standard English conventions appropriate to this grade level.

Sentence Structure

1.1 Use simple, compound, and compound-complex sentences; use effective coordination and subordination of ideas to express complete thoughts.

Grammar

1.2 Identify and properly use indefinite pronouns and present perfect, past perfect, and future perfect verb tenses; ensure that verbs agree with compound subjects.

Punctuation

1.3 Use colons after the salutation in business letters, semicolons to connect independent clauses, and commas when linking two clauses with a conjunction in compound sentences.

WRITTEN AND ORAL ENGLISH LANGUAGE CONVENTIONS
(continued)

Capitalization

1.4   Use correct capitalization.

Spelling

1.5   Spell frequently misspelled words correctly (e.g., *their, they're, there*).

LISTENING AND SPEAKING

1.0   Listening and Speaking Strategies Students deliver focused, coherent presentations that convey ideas clearly and relate to the background and interests of the audience. They evaluate the content of oral communication.

Comprehension

1.1   Relate the speaker's verbal communication (e.g., word choice, pitch, feeling, tone) to the nonverbal message (e.g., posture, gesture).

1.2   Identify the tone, mood, and emotion conveyed in the oral communication.

1.3   Restate and execute multiple-step oral instructions and directions.

Organization and Delivery of Oral Communication

1.4   Select a focus, an organizational structure, and a point of view, matching the purpose, message, occasion, and vocal modulation to the audience.

1.5   Emphasize salient points to assist the listener in following the main ideas and concepts.

1.6   Support opinions with detailed evidence and with visual or media displays that use appropriate technology.

1.7   Use effective rate, volume, pitch, and tone and align nonverbal elements to sustain audience interest and attention.

Analysis and Evaluation of Oral and Media Communications

1.8   Analyze the use of rhetorical devices (e.g., cadence, repetitive patterns, use of onomatopoeia) for intent and effect.

1.9   Identify persuasive and propaganda techniques used in television and identify false and misleading information.

2.0   Speaking Applications (Genres and Their Characteristics) Students deliver well-organized formal presentations employing traditional rhetorical strategies (e.g., narration, exposition, persuasion, description). Student speaking demonstrates a command of standard American English and the organizational and delivery strategies outlined in Listening and Speaking Standard 1.0. Using the speaking strategies of grade six outlined in Listening and Speaking Standard 1.0, students:

LISTENING AND SPEAKING (continued)

2.1 Deliver narrative presentations:
  a. Establish a context, plot, and point of view.
  b. Include sensory details and concrete language to develop the plot and character.
  c. Use a range of narrative devices (e.g., dialogue, tension, or suspense).

2.2 Deliver informative presentations:
  a. Pose relevant questions sufficiently limited in scope to be completely and thoroughly answered.
  b. Develop the topic with facts, details, examples, and explanations from multiple authoritative sources (e.g., speakers, periodicals, online information).

2.3 Deliver oral responses to literature:
  a. Develop an interpretation exhibiting careful reading, understanding, and insight.
  b. Organize the selected interpretation around several clear ideas, premises, or images.
  c. Develop and justify the selected interpretation through sustained use of examples and textual evidence.

2.4 Deliver persuasive presentations:
  a. Provide a clear statement of the position.
  b. Include relevant evidence.
  c. Offer a logical sequence of information.
  d. Engage the listener and foster acceptance of the proposition or proposal.

2.5 Deliver presentations on problems and solutions:
  a. Theorize on the causes and effects of each problem and establish connections between the defined problem and at least one solution.
  b. Offer persuasive evidence to validate the definition of the problem and the proposed solutions.